P9-DMG-533

# Political and Social Inquiry

*The concepts of science are the knots in a network of systematic interrelationships in which laws and theoretical principles form the threads ... The more threads converge upon, or issue from, a conceptual knot, the stronger will be its systematizing role, or its systematic import.*

Carl Hempel

*A survey of the state of theories in the social sciences will reveal that there are very few that can be used for explanation and prediction. Often, to speak in terms of Hempel's analogy, one discovers isolated knots with loose threads attached, awaiting systematic effort needed to tighten them and to tie them together. And, most frequently, even knots are not yet available.*

Claire Selltiz

*Theories are nets cast to catch what we call "the world": to rationalize, to explain, and to master it. We endeavour to make the mesh ever finer and finer.*

Karl Popper

*Theories are nets: only he who casts will catch.*

Novalis

# POLITICAL AND SOCIAL INQUIRY

Dickinson McGaw
George Watson
Arizona State University

JOHN WILEY & SONS, INC.
New York   London   Sydney   Toronto

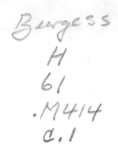

Burgess
H
61
.M414
c.1

Copyright © 1976 by John Wiley & Sons, Inc.

All rights reserved. Published simultaneously in Canada.

Reproduction or translation of any part of this work beyond that
permitted by Sections 107 or 108 of the 1976 United States Copyright Act without the permission of the copyright owner is unlaw-
ful. Requests for permission or further information should be
addressed to the Permissions Department, John Wiley & Sons, Inc.

*Library of Congress Cataloging in Publication Data:*

McGaw, Dickinson, 1941–
   Political and social inquiry.

   Includes index.
   1. Social sciences—Methodology.  I. Watson,
George, 1943–  joint author.  II. Title.

H61.M414    300′.1′8    75-31913
ISBN 0-471-58403-7

Printed in the United States of America

10 9 8 7 6 5

To Beth, Michelle, and Amy and
To Nancy and Matthew

1982 MAR 2 5    IW,

# PREFACE

This book attempts to present an introductory but comprehensive overview of research methods in the social sciences. It is an outgrowth of our many failures and some modest successes in teaching research methods and statistics courses at Arizona State University over the past seven years. In the beginning, we were humbled by the problems involved in trying to present students with a scientifically adequate yet motivating learning experience in research methods. We soon discovered several recurring problems and began to recognize the need for a systematic approach to them.

First of all, we found that, contrary to our desires, students were not particularly interested in learning about methods of empirical inquiry. They were more concerned with the "important" substantive social and political problems of the day. Our students thus could be characterized as concerned but somewhat reluctant, captive learners. Our task, then, was to demonstrate the relevancy of research methods to an understanding of the substantive problems in which the students were interested. In this book we have made a concerted effort to focus on such "relevant" political and social problems and the skills related to an effective analysis of them. The students, for example, learn to identify logical fallacies, engage in deductive and inductive reasoning, formulate hypotheses about their social environment, deduce consequences, and conduct empirical tests. Students soon learn that social scientific method is not only relevant to their substantive concerns, but it also sharpens their everyday thinking and conversation. It helps them to become what C. Wright Mills has termed critical and self-conscious thinkers, people aware of the assumptions and implications of their arguments.

Second, we concluded that many instructional materials available in the field of research methods were not particularly well suited to the needs of our students. These books were either too difficult or too easy, too long or too short, or simply irrelevant to the interests of social science students. A number of books did deal effectively with some of the course topics such as the philosophy of science, research design, data collection, and data analysis; but none, in our opinion, effectively integrated the various phases of empirical inquiry into a comprehensive overview that an introductory student could understand and appreciate.

Finally, we confronted the problem of how we might approach such a task. We turned to the educational research literature to identify the components of an instructionally sound text. Our reading of the literature suggested that most current texts did not take advantage of a number of educational principles. Having adopted some basic learning principles as postulates in our instructional system, we proceeded to develop our courses and this text in accordance with them. In addition, we wanted to design the text so that its underlying instructional principles would not restrict the educator to a particular classroom teaching technique.

The details of our instructional system and the principles underlying the writing of this text are described more thoroughly elsewhere.[1] Here, however, is presented a summary of the most important assumptions and the techniques for their implementation in the present text:

1. *Specification of objectives.* Learning improves if students know precisely what learning outcomes are desired and reinforced by the instructor. At the outset of each unit in this book, students are presented with a set of performance objectives that clarify for them the scope, content, expectations, and goals of the unit.

2. *Evaluation/objectives congruence.* Learning improves if the evaluation of the students' performance is consistent with the specification of objectives presented in the unit. In our courses, we do not test on objectives that are not made explicit to the students.

3. *Active responding.* Learning improves if students are actively engaged with the subject matter. In this book, active responding is achieved by having students identify fallacies, formulate hypotheses and theories, operationalize concepts, analyze data, and so forth. As an intermediate step to learning important definitions and principles, students are also asked to fill in the blanks of certain statements. Students should keep in mind that the process of filling in the blanks is an important halfway step toward learning the entire concept or principle. It helps to get the student to respond and to learn key words and phrases. Our terminal objective is, of course, to have the student explain the concept or principle without any such cues or promptings.

4. *Small (short) units of instruction.* Learning improves if the subject matter is well organized into relatively small segments or units of information. This text is organized into seventeen units of information. Each unit is divided into at least three or four subunits.

5. *Immediate feedback.* Learning improves if students are given immediate knowledge of the results of their performance. At the end of each subunit, students are presented with a "Learning Aid," a set of exercises with answers that test students' mastery of the unit objectives. Students should not skip over the Learning Aids but should work them out before progressing in the text. We accept the principle of mastery before advancement. That is, the student should test himself to know whether he is adequately comprehending the material before he advances to new subject matter. The Learning Aids are an integral part of this principle, and the students should complete them religiously before

---

[1] George Watson and Dickinson McGaw, "Personalizing Instruction in Political Science," *PSI and Political Science,* ed. Ralph Earle, Jr. (Washington, D.C.: The Division of Educational Affairs of the American Political Science Association, 1975), pp. 21–50.

continuing in the book. We also include an appendix at the end of the text. Consisting of several research articles, the appendix illustrates the application of many important research concepts and principles in the professional literature. To assist the students in locating examples of concepts and principles (such as "hypothesis" or "independent variable"), key words are emphasized in the text of the articles. Thus the student has immediate access to an application for many of the concepts he is learning.

6. *Frequent evaluation.* Learning improves as the frequency of evaluation increases. In a course, learning is more effective if it is spaced and frequently tested throughout the semester rather than massed and tested only once or twice. In our courses, we test the students over one unit at a time. Review tests are also given after every four or five units. This text is adaptable to a variety of classroom and testing techniques. We have used it successfully in lecture–discussion, student self-pacing, and instructor pacing formats.

7. *Positive conditions and consequences.* Learning improves if students are in the presence of positive conditions and consequences whenever they are involved with the subject matter. In writing this text, we have tried to make the material interesting, useful, and easy to master. Our experience has been that these techniques are less aversive and more motivating to the student than any that we have yet found.

The division of labor in writing this book is as follows. Both authors contributed to the formulation of the instructional approach. Dick McGaw was the main author of units 1 to 9 and 14 to 17, whereas George Watson was the major author of units 10 to 13. Each author edited and revised the other's work.

We are indebted, of course, to many people for assisting us in the formulation of the content and approach of this book. Dick McGaw is especially thankful to Milton Hobbs for stimulating his interest and providing a foundation in the philosophy of science. Other mentors opening vistas for us in social science, statistics, and research methods include: Ton DeVos, Charles Hyneman, Elton Jackson, Allan Kornberg, Charles McCall, and Leroy Rieselbach. Those colleagues and friends who critically read or provided insight and support are: Morris Axelrod, George Balch, Richard Hofstetter, John Johnson, Bruce Merrill, and Stephen Walker. We express our deep appreciation to Peter Killeen, William Coplin, and David McGaw for stimulating us to formulate and refine our philosophy of education. We are grateful to Adele Broadston, Andrea Field, and Sue Wright for typing assistance in the preparation of the manuscript. Finally, we thank our students who taught us some valuable lessons by shattering our egos, producing honest criticism, and forcing us toward improved techniques of instruction.

# CONTENTS

# 1
# Social Science
# Methodology

## INTRODUCTION

### Rationale

Social scientists are confronted with a variety of problems that are different from those which physical scientists face. Social scientists, for example, are often part of the subject matter they are studying. Social scientists also have values and biases that can interfere with the way they conduct their research. Because of these special problems, social scientists must be particularly aware of and sensitive to the way they go about their work. The procedures by which researchers go about their work of describing, explaining, and predicting phenomena are called *methodology*. Most professions provide special courses in methodology because it is important to be aware of the obstacles in the path of reliable knowledge and the alternative methods of unblocking the path of inquiry. This unit is about the methodology of social science.

The unit begins with a definition of research methodology. We then turn to an inquiry into the alternative sources of knowledge. This involves an examination of the various ways we come to know something. After finding that science is based primarily on sense experience, the characteristics of a scientific approach are presented next, followed by the basic assumptions underlying the scientific approach. Since understanding logic is a fundamental tool of the social scientist, we then undertake a study of logic by examining informal fallacies. Finally, the unit concludes with an effort to list and answer the most prevalent arguments against the possibility of the existence of a social science.

### Learning Objectives

After completing this unit you should be able to:

1. Define and identify the significance of "research methodology."

2. Name and explain the four sources on which a claim to knowledge may be based.

3. Identify the source of knowledge on which a knowledge-claim is based.

4. Define and identify the goals of "science."

5. Name and explain some of the basic assumptions of the scientific approach.

6. Identify and explain the following informal fallacies:

   a. appeal to authority

   b. argument against the man

    c.   appeal to force

    d.   appeal to pity

    e.   appeal to ignorance

    f.   appeal to a straw man

    g.   appeal to popular sentiments

    h.   hasty generalization

    i.   accident

    j.   false cause

    k.   faulty analogy

    l.   begging the question

    m.  complex question

    n.   irrelevant conclusion

    o.   equivocation

7.   Refute any of the anti–social science arguments from a social science perspective.

## RESEARCH METHODOLOGY

*Research methodology* is the description, explanation, and justification of various methods of conducting research.[1] The methods may be either general techniques such as experiments and surveys, which are common to many sciences, or logical procedures such as formulating research problems, constructing theories, deriving hypotheses, forming and measuring concepts, collecting and analyzing data, which are common to any science. The purpose of learning about methodology is to understand the process of social scientific inquiry. This understanding involves describing, analyzing, and evaluating various methods; specifying their assumptions; identifying their strengths and weaknesses; and suggesting new applications. Methodology may be classified as either empirical or normative. *Empirical methodology* describes, analyzes, and explains what researchers actually do. *Normative methodology* prescribes what researchers ought to do. It is concerned with establishing the standards by which research can be judged. In this program we will be concerned with both types of methodology.

    We will approach the study of methodology from a process perspective, conceptualizing social scientific inquiry as a decision-making process involving a number of stages that are analytically distinct. Figure 1–1 shows the major components of our study of methodology. It is convenient to conceptualize the

| STAGE | DESCRIPTION |
|---|---|
| Problem Formulation | What type of problem, how to select it, how to word it. |
| ↓ | |
| Concept Formation | What type, how to formulate it, what use does it have. |
| ↓ | |
| Concept Measurement | What type, how reliable and valid. |
| ↓ | |
| Hypothesis Formation | What type, how to derive it, how to state and confirm it. |
| ↓ | |
| Theory Formation | What type, how to construct and test it, what use does it have. |
| ↓ | |
| Data Collection | What type, what strengths and weaknesses, what applications. |
| ↓ | |
| Data Processing and Analysis | How to record, arrange, compile, and statistically analyze information. |
| ↓ | |
| Report Writing and Analysis | How a research report should be written and analyzed. |

**Figure 1–1.  The Process of Social Scientific Inquiry**

process as a sequence of decisions indicated by the arrows, although in reality the later stages often are taken into account during the early stages and earlier decisions revised at later stages.

Of what use to the student is the study of methodology? Methodological training has both academic and practical value. First, its academic value is that the student is likely to become more competent in the conduct of his own research and more analytical in his review of others' research. Although methodological training is no guarantee that he will formulate good problems, significant concepts and theories, it will help him to identify and correct more quickly ones that are poorly formulated. It will, in other words, help to unblock the road to inquiry. Second, its practical value is that it assists in understanding and evaluating information that affects everyday choices. How is one to judge the adequacy of studies which purport that busing children is helpful, that marijuana is not harmful, that smoking is harmful, that the guaranteed annual income system is effective, that mutual funds are better investments than common stocks, and so forth? People are confronted daily with many such studies that relate directly to their health, happiness, well-being, and role in the political system. Some of these studies may have been conducted with the greatest care and objectivity, whereas others may have been prepared carelessly or influenced by political or commercial considerations. How can a person deal with information of this type? Should he: (1) accept the information he likes and reject the information he dislikes; (2) reject all such information on the grounds that it is biased or that he cannot understand it; (3) accept all such information on the grounds that it probably comes from an authority more competent than himself; or (4) train himself in methodology so he can evaluate what is worth accepting and what is worth rejecting? Well-educated persons should be able to make informed judgments on matters that so directly affect their lives. Training in methodology assists in developing informed judgments. To master methodology is to become what C. Wright Mills calls a "self-conscious thinker, a man at work and aware of the assumptions and implications of whatever he is about."[2]

## LEARNING AID

1.  Research methodology is the _____, _____, and _____ of various methods of conducting research.
2.  Whereas _____ methodology prescribes what researchers ought to do, _____ methodology describes what researchers actually do.
3.  The authors approach the study of methodology from a _____ perspective.
4.  Methodological training has both _____ and _____ value.

. . . . . . . . . . . . . . . . . . . . . . . . . . . . . . . . . . . . . . . . . . . . . . . . . . . . . . . . . . . . . . .

1.  description, explanation, justification
2.  normative, empirical
3.  process
4.  academic, practical

## SOURCES OF KNOWLEDGE

Social scientists attempt to develop bodies of reliable knowledge. Specifically, they aim at reliable descriptions, explanations, and predictions. In this section some alternative paths to knowledge are examined. This will lead to an analysis of scientific knowledge and its assumptions.

There are four basic sources from which a claim to knowledge may be derived: sense experience, reason, authority, and intuition.[3]

### Sense Experience

I know "X is true" because my sense experience (hearing, seeing, touching, and smelling) indicates that it is true. *Empiricism* is the philosophical position which maintains that sensory experience is the most reliable source of knowledge.

Examples: How do I know that I am sitting in a chair? Because I can see the chair and touch it. How do I know that the Peoples' Republic of China is a member of the United Nations? Because I see that this nation is listed on the membership roster and because I see its representatives formally participate in the meetings of the UN.

We all recognize that perceptual errors are common occurrences, but it would be wrong to conclude that sense experience is necessarily a fallible source of knowledge. It would be more accurate to conclude that our "judgment" about the sense experience is fallible. All sense experience requires judgment. It is the judgment about the sense experience that is true or false. Any perceptual mistake, therefore, resides not with the sensation but with the judgment. We see or experience the rising and setting of the sun. We may wrongly conclude that the sun revolves about the earth. It is not, however, our sense experience that is false, but our judgment or interpretation of the sense experience.

## Reason

I know "X is true" because my reasoning indicates it is true. Reasoning involves taking certain statements as the basis for making one or more other statements. The use of one or more statements (called the "premises" of an argument) to infer another statement (called the "conclusion") is reasoning. The philosophical position called *rationalism* accepts human reason as the chief instrument and ultimate authority in man's search for truth.

Examples: How do I know that 500 plus 500 equals 1000? I figure it out using calculation and reasoning. I do not refer to my sense experience for the solution of complicated mathematical problems. How do I know that the Peoples' Republic of China is a member of the UN? Since the UN includes most of the nations of the world and since the Peoples' Republic of China is a nation, I reason that it is likely that the Peoples' Republic of China is a member of the UN.

There are two major types of reasoning processes: deductive and inductive. In *deductive reasoning* the premises lead necessarily to the conclusion; if the premises are true, the conclusion must be true. Example: All men are mortal; Socrates is a man; therefore, Socrates is mortal. In *inductive reasoning* the premises provide evidence only for the conclusion; if the premises are true, the conclusion is likely to be true. Example: President Nixon is a man, President Johnson is a man, President Kennedy is a man; therefore, all American leaders are men. At a later point we shall discuss the types of logical fallacies that may enter into deductive and inductive forms of reasoning.

## Authority

I know "X is true" because Z says so, and Z is an authority on the subject.
• Example: Abuse of power is an impeachable offense, because Professor Berger of the Law College says so. Although authority is often used as a source of knowledge, it is not a primary source. Professor Berger, for example, had to know that abuse of power is an impeachable offense by means of some other source such as reasoning, intuition, or sense experience (evidence). Even if his source is an authority, the chain of authority can be pushed back to one of the other basic sources.

We accept many truth-claims in everyday life on the basis of authority when we do not have the time, energy, interest, or capability of investigating the matter any further. Accepting truth-claims on authority, however, often leads to unreliable knowledge since authorities can be wrong too. Before accepting a claim on authority, we should:

1.  make sure the person is really an expert in this particular field of knowledge;

2.  suspend judgment or investigate the prior sources of knowledge when different authorities are in disagreement; and

3.  accept a statement on authority only when we know how we could test the statement if we had the time, energy, and capability.

## Intuition

I know "X is true" because my intuition tells me. Intuition is a conviction of certainty that sometimes is experienced quite suddenly, such as a "flash of intuition." Examples: "I know God exists. He must." "Capitalism is more efficient and productive than socialism. Why do you think so? I don't know; I'm just sure its true." "Candidate Jones will make a good legislator. Why? I just feel it."

Intuition is sometimes inappropriately identified as a source of knowledge when a judgment is actually based on a rapid and almost subliminal type of observation or reasoning process. Knowledge based on intuition is often unreliable and difficult to test. To reduce the risk of error in accepting claims based on intuition, we should:

1.  make sure the claim is really based on intuition and not on some form of sense experience, reasoning, or authority.

2.  recognize that different persons' intuitions conflict, and yet all of the intuitions cannot be true at the same time. Thus, there is no criterion in intuition that distinguishes between true and false claims.

3. understand that intuition tells us we know something, but it does not explain how we come to know it. Knowing that we have had an intuitive experience does not necessarily mean that what the experience says is true.

## LEARNING AID

1. Name the four sources on which a claim to knowledge may be based.
2. Whereas rationalists hold that _____ is the ultimate source of knowledge, empiricists maintain that _____ is the ultimate source.
3. Identify the sources of knowledge for each of the following statements:
   a) Guaranteed annual income is more effective than the present welfare system because Dr. Moynihan has said so in his latest book.
   b) Guaranteed annual income is more effective than the present welfare system because the president's research commission has demonstrated it.
   c) Guaranteed annual income is more effective than the present welfare system because 60 percent (hypothetical data) of those under the experimental guaranteed income program are able to retrain and return to the work force whereas only 30 percent of those on the present welfare system return to work.
   d) Guaranteed annual income is more likely to satisfy the basic needs of persons than the present system. When persons have their basic needs satisfied, they are more likely to have incentives to work and get off of governmental assistance.
   e) Guaranteed annual income is more effective than the present welfare system because I feel it to be true.
   f) The polls a month before Truman's victory over Dewey in 1948 indicated that Dewey was going to win.
   g) Truman is going to win; I just know it.
   h) Dewey is going to win according to the *Chicago Tribune.*
   i) Sources close to the president say that he will lower the tariffs.
   j) We are going to have another recession because prices and unemployment are increasing.
   k) Medicare is a mistake because many respected doctors have testified to that effect.
   l) National medical insurance will be adopted because I have faith in the American people.
   m) We have the right to free speech because the Constitution says so.

. . . . . . . . . . . . . . . . . . . . . . . . . . . . . . . . . . . . . . . . . . . . . . . . . . . . . . . . . . . . . . . . . . . . . . . . .

1. Sense experience, reasoning, authority, and intuition
2. reason, sense experience

**3.** (a) authority, (b) primarily authority, secondarily sense experience, (c) sense experience, (d) reason, (e) intuition, (f) primarily sense experience, secondarily authority, (g) intuition, (h) authority, (i) authority, (j) reason, (k) authority, (l) intuition, (m) primarily authority, secondarily sense experience

## THE SCIENTIFIC APPROACH

This program takes a scientific approach to the study of political and social phenomena. Although there are many available definitions of the word "science," we will find the following definition useful: *Science* is an objective, logical, and systematic method of analysis devised to describe, explain, and predict observable phenomena.

The following characteristics should be emphasized in the above definition:

1. Science is a *method of analysis,* not a body of knowledge. Science is an activity, a process, distinguishable from the product. There is a common method of analysis in all the sciences, even though the content and technique vary from field to field. The sciences have in common the basic rules of evidence and logic.

2. The ultimate objectives of science are to *describe, explain, and predict.* Political scientists, for example, attempt to describe, explain, and predict such varied phenomena as elections, revolutions, wars, legislative actions, protests, judicial decisions, alliances, governmental performances, and international behavior.

a. *Description* attempts to answer the question of who, what, where, when, or how much. It reports what happens. Political scientists may ask: When do protests occur? Where do they tend to occur? How intense are most protests? Are lower income people more likely to participate in protests than higher income people? Description is an indispensable part of science and usually precedes explanation and prediction.

b. *Explanation* attempts to answer "why" types of questions. Why are higher educated, lower income people more likely to participate in protests than lower educated, lower income people? Explaining questions such as these is the core of scientific activity.

c. *Prediction* attempts to answer questions about what will occur in the future. Political scientists may be interested in predicting the conditions under which protests are likely to occur in the future.

3. *Observable phenomena* are the objects of description, explanation, and prediction. Objects that cannot be directly or indirectly observed are not amenable to scientific analysis. This excludes supernatural and metaphysical topics from the realm of scientific investigation.

4. Science is *objective, logical, and systematic.*

a.  *Objective* means that the claims of science in principle can be publicly tested by any competent person. Another word for "objectivity" is frequently used in scientific discourse, *intersubjective testability,* which means the same thing, namely that different competent people ought to be able to test the proposed claims. The requirement of objectivity or intersubjective testability rules out knowledge claims accessible only to privileged individuals such as mystics or gurus. Only claims open to repeatable, public test qualify as scientific questions.

b.  *Logical* means that science is guided by the accepted rules of reasoning such as the rules of definition, inductive and deductive inference, and theory of probability.

c.  *Systematic* refers to a well-connected, coherent, and logically organized set of regularities that are open to modification or falsification by new evidence.

Thus, we may restate the definition of *science:*

It is an objective
     logical
     systematic method of analysis devised to describe
                                      explain
                                      predict observable
                                      phenomena.

## LEARNING AID

1.  What are the goals of a scientific approach to the study of politics?
2.  How are these goals achieved?
3.  What kinds of phenomena are studied scientifically?
4.  Define *science*.

· · · · · · · · · · · · · · · · · · · · · · · · · · · · · · · · · · · · · · · · · · · · · · · · · · · · · · · · · ·

1.  Description, explanation, and prediction
2.  Objectivity (intersubjective testing), logically, systematically
3.  observable
4.  *Science* is an objective, logical, and systematic method of analysis devised to describe, explain, and predict observable phenomena.

## THE POSTULATES OF SCIENCE

In the previous section we defined "science" as a method of analysis. Underlying any method of acquiring knowledge is a set of postulates, beliefs, or assumptions that are neither true nor false but that are presupposed in order to proceed with communication and inquiry. Although authors differ somewhat on the number of the basic assumptions of scientific method, we shall focus on nine standard postulates.[4]

1. *All behavior is naturally determined.* The principle of determinism is assumed, that is, that every event has a cause. This postulate also asserts that every event has a "natural" cause, referring to things that can be objectively and empirically observed. Thus, spiritual, magical, and supernatural explanations are excluded from scientific investigation because they are not amenable to empirical observation and intersubjective testability.

Students often question whether the principle of determinism is inconsistent with their belief in a deity or free will. These are difficult questions that philosophers have struggled with for centuries and that have no firm answers. Some scientists, however, argue that belief in God and freedom are not necessarily inconsistent with the principle of determinism. Some who believe in God simply assume that God is both the Creator and the Cause of all the natural phenomena they may observe. Those who believe in free will often argue that our actions are caused by our decisions or choices. Although our choices are determined to a large extent by prior circumstances, they are also partially shaped by our desires and wants. When values and desires affect our choices, free will becomes an important component of our behavior, so says the determinist who also believes in free will. Thus, belief in free will or God is not necessarily incompatible with determinism.

2. *Man is part of the natural world.* Man is just as much a part of nature as any other animal, plant, or mineral. Although man possesses distinctive traits, he can be studied by the methods broadly common to all the sciences.

3. *Nature is orderly and regular.* Events do not occur haphazardly or purely by chance. "Chance" occurrences are used in science to refer to unknown and unpredictable events, not uncaused events. Scientists assume that nature operates according to certain patterns of regularity. Although many phenomena appear to be unique and inexplicable (snowflakes, tornadoes, revolutions, and elections), certain patterns of forces do underlie them; and when discovered, they do permit better explanations and prediction than ordinary intuition, authority, and sheer guesswork.

4. *Nature changes slowly.* Although most things change eventually, many things change slowly enough to permit the accumulation of a reliable body of knowledge. Although a piece of coal may change imperceptibly by tomorrow, it will still be similar enough to permit valid generalizations made about it to hold for a given period of time. Without this postulate, it would be impossible to know anything except for the brief moment that an observation is taking place.

Because revolutions consist of rapid changes, we may wonder whether they are amenable to scientific analysis. A description of a phase of a revolution may apply for only a brief period of time, but revolutions recur and scientists have found regularities, patterns of actions, and stages of change in revolutions.

Studying patterned activities is an important part of scientific analysis. It helps scientists not only to explain and predict revolutions but also to determine how long a generalization may validly apply to an event.

5. *All observable phenomena are eventually knowable.* This postulate assumes that human intelligence is capable of unlocking the secrets of the universe. No matter how unpopular or apparently unfruitful his curiosity is, the scientist regards all observable phenomena as potential objects of study.

6. *Nothing is self-evident.* Truth must be intersubjectively demonstrable. Reliance should not be placed on common sense, tradition, folk wisdom, intuition, or authority. The scientist knows from the history of science that assumed truth is quite often different from objective, empirical confirmation.

7. *Truth is relative.* Truth is relative to the existing body of knowledge. Knowledge is not static but dynamic. What is thought to be true at one point in time is often rejected at another point in time by new evidence or reinterpretation.

8. *The world is perceived through our senses.* All reliable knowledge about the world is derived from our sense impressions. This, we recall, is the principle of empiricism.

9. *Our perceptions, memory, and reasoning can be trusted.* Scientists assume that our senses are relatively reliable agencies for acquiring facts. This assumption does not imply that any and all perceptions, memories, and reasons are reliable. Psychology convincingly documents the occurrence of unreliable sensory impressions, recall, and reasoning processes. It does imply that the safeguards such as intersubjective testability built into the scientific method of analysis help to prevent errors from going undetected. It also implies that the ultimate resolution of any empirical dispute should be based on sensorily perceived data and the accepted rules of logic—not on mental notions, intuition, authority, and so on. Although our sense experiences are occasionally faulty, scientists maintain that empirical strategy is a more reliable approach to the acquisition of knowledge about the world than any of the laternatives.

## LEARNING AID

1. Be able to list at least five of the nine postulates of the scientific approach.
2. Be able to explain any of the nine postulates of science.

## LOGIC: INFORMAL FALLACIES

The study of logic contributes to both our scientific and personal development. Logic is the study of the methods and principles used in distinguishing valid from invalid reasoning. Science is not only empirically based on sense experience but also is rationally based on the principles of logic. Because science involves the systematic arrangement of facts, theories, and instruments, science also involves the rules of reasoning. Competence in science, therefore, demands competence in logic. Similarly, in our personal conversations, reading, and television viewing, we are exposed to various kinds of arguments. Arguments are sequences of sentences in which some sentences (premises) are claimed to be the justification or support for another sentence (conclusion). Many of our decisions depend on our ability to distinguish valid from invalid arguments. Thus, competent living also demands competent use of logic. Logic then has a direct bearing both on the development of science and on the conduct of our personal lives.

We begin our study of logic in this section by learning how to identify informal fallacies. This will assist us in studying various kinds of antiscience arguments in the next section. In a later unit, we will learn about formal fallacies.

Arguments may be either sound or unsound (see Figure 1–2). A sound argument is one that is valid and that has only true premises. A valid argument is one that is logically correct; if the premises are true, the conclusion must also be true. An argument may be unsound for three reasons:

1. It may be invalid or formally fallacious, that is, something may be wrong with its logical form or structure.
2. It may contain false premises.
3. It may be irrelevant or circular.

Errors relating to the first reason are called "formal fallacies," whereas errors relating to the second and third reasons are called "informal fallacies." We will now take up some of the more common types of informal fallacies.

## Appeal to Authority

It was noted earlier that authority is one of the four main sources of knowledge.[5] An attempt to support a conclusion by citing some person, institu-

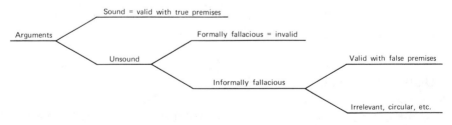

**Figure 1-2. Types of Arguments.**

tion, or piece of writing which asserts that conclusion is an appeal to authority. This type of argument takes the following form:

Form:

X asserts P (a proposition).
Therefore, P is true.

Example:

Einstein says Zionism is in the national interest of the United States.
Therefore, Zionism is in the national interest of the United States.

This form of an appeal-to-authority argument is fallacious. Appeals to authority are often misused in the following ways:

1. The authority (e.g., Einstein) may be misquoted or misinterpreted.

2. An authority may make a judgment about something outside his special field of competence (e.g., Einstein was an expert on mathematics and physics, not foreign policy).

3. Authorities may express opinions about matters concerning which they could not possibly have any evidence (many moral, religious, and political judgments may not be amenable to the collecting of intersubjectively testable evidence).

4. Authorities who are equally competent often may disagree.

Although many arguments based on appeals to authority are fallacious, some are quite legitimate. Authority plays an indispensable role in the accumulation of knowledge in science. By rejecting all appeals to authority, we must become an expert ourselves on everything in which a decision must be made. This is impossible. So, we must learn to distinguish incorrect from correct appeals to authority. Correct appeals to authority are based on reliable authorities. An authority is more likely to be reliable if he is honest, well informed, and bases his judgments on intersubjectively testable evidence in his field of expertise. This argument takes the following form:

Form:

X is a reliable authority concerning P.
X asserts P.
Therefore, P is true.

Example:

George Gallup is a reliable authority concerning public opinion issues.
Gallup says that confidence in the president is at an all-time low.
Therefore, confidence in the president is at an all-time low.

This form is inductively correct. The premises provide evidence for the conclusion. It is not deductively valid because the premises could be true and the conclusion false. Reliable authorities sometimes do make errors.

## Argument Against the Man

Argument against the man concludes that a statement is false because it is made by a certain person. It is similar to the appeal to authority, except that it is negative rather than positive. In the appeal to authority, the fact that a certain person asserts a proposition is taken as evidence that the proposition is true. In the argument against the man, however, the fact that a certain person asserts a proposition is taken as evidence that the proposition is false. The argument against the man takes the following form:

| Form: | Example: |
|---|---|
| $X$ is a reliable anti-authority about $P$.<br>$X$ asserts $P$.<br>Therefore, $P$ is false. | The KKK usually takes bad positions on racial issues.<br>The KKK believes that the schools ought to be segregated.<br>Therefore, the schools ought *not* to be segregated.<br><br>Commies are bad guys.<br>Commies believe national health care systems are effective.<br>Therefore, national health care systems are *not* effective. |

The argument against the man is committed when, instead of trying to disprove the truth of what is asserted, one attacks the man who made the assertion. This argument is fallacious because the personal character or the circumstances of a man are logically irrelevant to the truth or falsehood of what he says.

## Appeal to Force

The fallacy of appeal to force is committed when one appeals to force or the threat of force to cause acceptance of a conclusion. If a certain view is not accepted, some kind of force is threatened to be applied. The appeal to force, however, is logically irrelevant to the merits of the conclusion. Thus, the appeal-to-force argument does not prove the truth or correctness of the conclusion; it merely proves that force is an effective method of getting one's way.

Form:

Either $X$ is true or force will be applied.
Therefore, $X$ is true.

Example:

Either Israel is the aggressor nation or we (Arabs) will stop sending you oil.
Therefore, Israel is the aggressor nation.

## Appeal to Pity

The fallacy of appeal to pity is committed when pity is appealed to for the sake of getting a conclusion accepted.

Form:

If $X$ occurs, then a pitiful consequence will follow.
Therefore, don't allow $X$ to occur.

Example:

If you fail me, then I'll be kicked out of school.
Therefore, don't fail me.

Although an appeal to pity may be persuasive, it is logically irrelevant to the merits of the conclusion. The question in the example is whether or not a student deserves to fail, not what will happen if he fails.

## Appeal to Ignorance

The fallacy of appeal to ignorance is committed when it is argued that a proposition is true simply on the basis that it has not been proved false or that it is false simply because it has not been proved true. However, ignorance of how to prove or disprove a proposition does not establish the truth or falsehood of a proposition. When we make an assertion, we usually must assume the responsibility of defending it. If this responsibility is shifted to the other side, the fallacy of appealing to ignorance is committed.

| Form: | Example |
|---|---|
| $X$ asserts $P$ is true.<br>$Y$ denies $P$ is true.<br>$X$ challenges $Y$ to disprove $P$.<br>$Y$ can't disprove $P$.<br>Therefore, $P$ is true. | $X$: More than one person killed JFK.<br>$Y$: That is not true.<br>$X$: Then prove it is not true.<br>$Y$: I can't. I have no evidence.<br>$X$: Then, more than one person killed JFK. |

## Appeal to a Straw Man

The fallacy of appeal to a straw man is committed when a weak argument for a view or an implausible statement of a view is attacked instead of stronger or more plausible arguments. Straw men are caricatures or cheap imitations of the real arguments. They are usually absurd and easily attacked. A straw man argument is, therefore, logically irrelevant to the genuine argument. Example: "Darwin's theory of evolution boils down to the claim that our relatives are monkeys."

## Appeal to Popular Sentiments

The fallacy of appeal to popular sentiments is committed in directing an emotional appeal "to the people" or to their feelings to win acceptance of a conclusion unsupported by valid argument. Popular acceptance of ideas or polities, however, does not prove them to be true.

| Form: | Example: |
|---|---|
| $P$ is popular.<br>Therefore, $P$ is true. | Most of the voters are supporting me.<br>Therefore, vote for me. |

## LEARNING AID

Identify the names of the informal fallacies in the following examples:
1. City councilman Smith owns a great deal of land in the city, and he favors beautification of the city because it will increase the value of his land. Therefore, beautification may not be such a good thing for the city.

**2.** Since you can't prove that the communists are not trying to dominate the world, I say that It's true that they are trying to dominate the world.

**3.** Senator, if you vote for the Kennedy Health Care Plan, then the American Medical Association will not contribute to your next campaign.

**4.** Most of the good students are supporting Smith. So, vote for him.

**5.** Dr. William Shockley, a Stanford physicist and Nobel Laureate, says that blacks are genetically inferior to whites. Thus, blacks are genetically inferior to whites.

**6.** The president should not be impeached because he would be disgraced.

**7.** Social science is impossible because people are not numbers.

**8.** Since he does not practice what he preaches, what he preaches is false.

**9.** Paul Newman, the movie star, supports George McGovern's candidacy for president in 1972. Vote for McGovern.

. . . . . . . . . . . . . . . . . . . . . . . . . . . . . . . . . . . . . . . . . . . . . . . . . . . .

**1.** Argument against the man.
**2.** Appeal to ignorance.
**3.** Appeal to force.
**4.** Appeal to popular sentiments.
**5.** Appeal to authority.
**6.** Appeal to pity.
**7.** Appeal to a straw man.
**8.** Argument against the man.
**9.** Appeal to authority.

## MORE INFORMAL FALLACIES

### Hasty Generalization

The fallacy of hasty generalization is committed when one improperly infers that a group has a property after observing only a small number of exceptional cases. The theory of statistics and sampling helps scientists to identify the degree of hasty generalization.

Form:

> $X_1$ is a $Z$, $X_2$ is a $Z$, $X_3$ is a $Z$.
> Therefore, $X$'s tend to be $Z$'s.

Example:

This black is wealthy, that black is wealthy
Therefore, blacks tend to be wealthy

## Accident

The fallacy of accident is committed when a generalization is improperly applied to a single instance. Applying a general rule to a particular case with "accidental" or unusual circumstances may render the rule inapplicable. What is true in general may not be true universally and without qualification because circumstances may alter cases.

Form:

Example

> $X$'s tend to be $Z$'s.
> Therefore, $X_1$ is a $Z$.

Blacks tend to be Democrats.
Therefore, Senator Brooke is a Democrat.

## False Cause

The fallacy of false cause is committed when some event is erroneously considered the cause of another event.

Form:

Example:

> $X$ is associated with $Y$.
> Therefore, $X$ causes $Y$.

Ice cream consumption is related to juvenile delinquency.
Therefore, ice cream consumption is a cause of juvenile delinquency.

## Faulty Analogy

Two things are analogous insofar as they are similar. In an argument by analogy one argues that because two things are analogous or similar in some respects, they are likely to be similar in other respects as well. A faulty analogy may be committed if: (1) the conclusion of an analogical argument is considered certain, or (2) the analogous things have important differences.

Form:

Example:

> $X$ has properties $a, b, c, d,$ and $e$.
> $Y$ has properties $a, b, c,$ and $d$.
> Therefore, it is likely that $Y$ also has $e$.

Persons talk, write, read, and feel.
Computers talk, write, read.
Therefore, it is likely that computers can also feel.

## Begging the Question

The fallacy of begging the question is committed when one assumes as a premise for his argument the very conclusion he intends to prove.

Form:

| If $P$, then $P$. |
|---|

Example:

If every man has the freedom of speech, then each individual has the liberty of expressing his thoughts.

## Complex Question

The fallacy of a complex question is committed when a question is phrased so that it cannot be answered without granting a particular answer to some question at issue. A complex question consists of a plurality of questions. Whenever this type of question is undetected and a single answer is demanded or returned to a complex question as if it were a simple one, the fallacy of a complex question is committed. The best procedure for handling complex questions is for the respondent to divide or analyze them into their component parts and to answer the questions one at a time.

Example:

Are you for Republicans and prosperity or not?

Example:

Is the U.S. still the freest country in the world?

The first example contains two questions: Are you for Republicans? and Are you for prosperity? By requiring a yes or no answer, the respondent is likely to answer yes since most people are for prosperity and at the same time grant approval to Republicans, with which he may disagree. The second example also contains two questions: Was the U.S. in the past and is it now the freest nation in the world? To answer that the U.S. is still the freest nation in the world is also to grant that it also was the freest nation in the world in the past, which is a separate question. Do not let a double-barrelled or complex question force you into an unsatisfactory answer. Separate the issues and answer them individually.

## Irrelevant Conclusion

The fallacy of an irrelevant conclusion is committed when an argument supposedly intended to establish a particular conclusion is directed to proving a
different conclusion.

Form:

> $X$ is true (or good).
> Therefore, $Y$ is true (or good).

Example:

Health care is desirable.
Therefore, Bill 04268 should be
passed.

Murder is a horrible crime.
Therefore, the defendent is guilty.

In the first example, the argument that health care is desirable is logically irrelevant to whether this particular bill provides better health care than any
practical alternative. In courts of law, as the second example illustrates,
prosecutors may argue at length that murder is a horrible crime and illogically
but perhaps persuasively infer that the defendant is guilty. In emotional settings arguments such as these may be quite effective. Nevertheless, they are still
fallacies.

## Equivocation

Equivocation is committed when the double meaning of a term is used to mislead someone. Many words have more than one meaning, and when these
meanings are kept separate, we have no difficulty. But when we confuse the
different meanings of a word, we use the word equivocally, and we commit the
fallacy of equivocation.

Example:

When my professor said that
politics makes strange bedfellows, I think he means that
most politicians are homosexuals.

Example

That senator is really loaded.

In the first example the student is confused over the meaning of the phrase, "strange bedfellows." Although the professor was obviously referring to unusual and surprising coalitions, the student picked up on another meaning. In the second example, the reader is left not knowing whether the senator was loaded with money, pot, or alcohol.

## LEARNING AID

Identify the names of the informal fallacies in the exercises below:

**1.** In 1968 Richard Nixon broke a bathroom mirror. Then he had seven years' bad luck.
**2.** If a majority of the senators vote for the health care plan, then it will be supported by more than 50 percent of the legislators in the Senate.
**3.** Since most great leaders are tall men, Napoleon must not have been a great leader.
**4.** The Watergate Hearings demonstrated that all politicians are corrupt.
**5.** Making war is like making love; you feel a whole lot better when it's over. Making love restores the body. Thus, making war restores the nation.
**6.** Are you still a bleeding-heart liberal?
**7.** The end of life is happiness. Since death is the end of life, death is happiness.
**8.** The Japanese are very industrious; the United States should consult them more in the making of defense policy.
**9.** Why is private development of resources so much more efficient than any public control?
**10.** Most democratic governments tend to be English-speaking nations. Therefore, speaking English produces democracy.

. . . . . . . . . . . . . . . . . . . . . . . . . . . . . . . . . . . . . . . . . . . . . . . . . . . . . . . . .

1. False cause
2. Begging the question
3. Accident
4. Hasty generalization
5. Faulty analogy
6. Complex question
7. Equivocation
8. Irrelevant conclusion
9. Complex question
10. False cause

## ANTI-SOCIAL SCIENCE ARGUMENTS

Every student of social science should be familiar with the nature of the arguments against the scientific analysis of social and political phenomena. In this section we will present the core of the arguments against social science and attempt to show various lines of refutation.[6] The arguments are reduced to their fundamental points, and we have tried to present them so that they are not merely straw man characterizations. After studying this material, the student should be able to answer from a scientific perspective the major anti–social science arguments.

1. *Since experimentation is a necessary condition for science and since experimentation is not feasible in social science, social science cannot be scientific.*

a. This argument is unsound first of all because the premise that experimentation is a necessary condition for science is false.

(1) Astronomy and geology are both considered sciences, and yet neither of these employs experimentation.

(2) This premise confuses scientific method with scientific techniques. Although scientific method (i.e., the logic of forming concepts, theory construction, hypothesis testing, and so on) is the same across various fields, scientific techniques (survey research, experimentation, content analysis, and so on) vary. Experimentation is a scientific research technique and is not a necessary condition of scientific method.

(3) Controlled investigation, however, is necessary for science. Controlled investigation involves a deliberate search for two things: contrasting instances in which the phenomenon is present and those in which it is absent, and the factors relating to differences in the phenomenon. Experimentation is only one technique of achieving this requirement of controlling investigation. Social science achieves the effect of controlled investigation through a variety of techniques.

b. This argument is also unsound because the second premise, that experimentation in social science is not feasible, is false.

(1) Experiments such as the following are increasingly conducted in social science: persuasive communication experiments involving the manipulation of propaganda films, speeches, or messages; small group experiments involving changes in the form of leadership, size, and structure of groups; voting experiments in which methods of balloting or methods of campaigning are varied; decision-making experiments in which resources, goals, and information are varied; social program experiments such as the Headstart Program, guaranteed income experiment, or busing programs in which stimuli are introduced on a complex and mass basis; and time series experiments involving the study of the economic effects of a war or the formation of an organization such as the United Nations or the European Economic Community.

2. *Since quantification is a necessary condition for science and since quantification is impossible in social science, social science cannot be scientific.*

a. This argument is unsound because the premise that quantification is a necessary condition of science is false.

(1) Quantification, like experimentation, is a scientific research technique and not a necessary condition of science. Quantification, when possible, is advantageous but not essential.

(2) This premise suggests a specious qualitative–quantitative distinction. The argument is sometimes rephrased: Since human affairs are essentially qualitative and since science is quantitative, social science cannot be specific. We maintain, however, that every descriptive term is science is fundamentally qualitative. There are basically three types of concepts: classificatory, comparative, and quantitative. Classificatory concepts refer to things that either possess or do not possess the *quality* (e.g., religion, in which a person possesses the quality of being a Protestant, Catholic, Jew, or something else). Comparative concepts refer to things that have more or less of a *quality* (e.g., alienation, in which persons possess the quality of being more or less alienated). Quantitative concepts refer to how much of a *quality* things possess (e.g., income, which measures how much of a quality persons possess). Thus, each of the basic terms of science is qualitative in the sense that it refers to some quality. Numbers are applied only as a logical elaboration of "quality." Whereas comparative concepts may use numbers to show that one thing has more of a quality than another thing, quantitative concepts specify how much of a quality a thing has. Therefore, the qualitative–quantitative distinction is largely a false dichotomy, and the first premise remains unsupported.

b. The premise which states that quantification is impossible in social science is also false.

(1) Some social and political variables, such as the following, in fact are quantitative concepts as we defined them above: percentage voting turnout, Gross National Product, degree of voting district inequality, magnitude of political violence, growth rate, assassination rate, and rate of legislative turnover.

3. *Since science is nomothetic* (i.e., deals with generalizations, generalizes) *and since social and political phenomena are ideographic* (i.e., unique, singular), *social science cannot be scientific.*

a. Just as every person and event is unique in a certain sense, so also is every physical object, from every tree and snowflake to every eclipse of the sun. Since this argument would not be taken seriously to question the possibility of a physical or natural science, it also should not be taken seriously to question the possibility of a social science.

b. The fact that social processes vary with their institutional setting may limit the scope of some generalizations in social science, but it does not preclude the possibility that we have not yet discovered underlying similarities that make the differences understandable.

4.  *Social and political phenomena are too complex and have too many variables to study scientifically.*

a.  Social and political phenomena are certainly complex, but we are not at all certain that they are any more complex than physical and biological phenomena.

b.  Phenomena that first appear to be hopelessly complex prior to the formulation of scientific explanations often lose this appearance after the explanation and discovery are made. Political behavior may appear more simple and understandable when the relevant antecedents are discovered.

c.  Just because social and political phenomena are complex, it does not necessarily mean that social science is impossible any more than physical science is impossible because physical phenomena are complex.

5.  *Investigation of social and political behavior may alter that behavior.* This argument takes two forms:

a.  *The subject matter is altered by the means used to investigate it.*

(1)  Interviewing respondents may in fact alter their behavior (such as their turnout in an election), but this also occurs in the physical sciences where measuring the pressure of a tire alters that pressure or measuring the temperature of a liquid by a thermometer slightly alters the temperature of the liquid when the thermometer is of a different temperature. The altering effect, however, does not pose an insurpassable obstacle. If the measurement process has little effect on the behavior, the effect may be ignored. If, however, the effect is significant, then it can be precisely measured and allowances can be estimated on the basis of known laws.

(2)  A great deal of social science data is not of the kind that is likely to influence the subject matter. Much of aggregate data analysis comes from public records such as voting statistics, legislative roll call votes, budgets, judicial records, biographical histories—where subjects are observed indirectly.

b.  *Behavior is altered when the results of research are known.*

(1)  As a matter of fact people do not always alter their behavior on learning of generalizations about it. For years prior to the occurrence of the "energy crisis" scientists forecast what was likely to happen, yet very little behavior was modified until the pinch was felt.

(2)  If the knowledge of predictions or results alters that behavior, then the results are not falsified but their scope is restricted to those people who do not have knowledge of the results. What then is required and what is possible is to develop additional generalizations about the ways in which individuals alter their behavior when they have knowledge of the predictions of the social scientist.

6. *Since relevant social and political data are often inaccessible, a social scientific approach is inappropriate.*

a.   There are many situations where social scientists have difficulty gaining access. Executive sessions in legislative bodies, the marking of ballots in the voting booths, the making of decisions in jury rooms, and the formulation of foreign policy by the president in secret sessions with his advisers. Some of these difficulties may be overcome. The press of the United States is continuously advocating opening up many legislative and administrative committee meetings. The memoirs of participants in high level and secretive positions often provide valuable information to the social scientist.

b.   A large proportion of relevant social and political data are already accessible, and generalizations about them are accumulating.

c.   Arguing from the difficulties of acquiring data in parts of a field to the inappropriateness of a social scientific approach to the field as a whole is a fallacious method of reasoning.

7. *Since social scientists have values and since their values affect their selection of problems, social science cannot be conducted objectively.*

a.   It is true that social scientists do have values and their areas of inquiry are usually determined by their interests, but this is no different from physical scientists who also select areas in which they also have deep interests and commitments (ecology, medicine, and so on).

b.   One value scientists have is that of scientific objectivity. They should make every effort to limit the effect of their values on the collection and analysis of data. Studies may be replicated by many different social scientists (intersubjective testability) having different values to provide checks and balances against bias. Thus, even when problems are selected on the basis of other values, the collection and analysis of the data can still be objective.

8. *Since social scientists have values and since their values affect the collection and analysis of their data, social science cannot be conducted objectively.*

a.   It is true that scientists have values and that their values sometimes interfere with their analysis of social and political phenomena. It is not easy in any area of inquiry to prevent our attitudes and values from coloring our conclusions. Physicists and astronomers were influenced for centuries by the popular religious views about the solar system. Just as it has taken centuries for natural scientists to develop safeguards that are still not infallible, social scientists also must develop techniques that will lead to the accumulation of reliable social science knowledge.

b.   Social scientists have already developed some procedures that help to prevent values from interfering with their analysis. First, they state their value assumptions as explicitly and fully as they can so that they themselves and others will be aware of the values that might interfere. Second, their analyses are expressed in an open forum where their ideas are tested with data and where scholars with different values can criticize and test the data themselves.

9. *Since human affairs continuously change and since science does better under constant conditions, a social science is impossible.*

It is true that society constantly changes, but most of the time this change is evolutionary. When there are revolutionary changes, the previous generalizations are often inapplicable and too limited in scope to deal with the new situation. But the process of change usually has its own regularities and patterns that can be studied scientifically. New generalizations can be formulated and tested to apply to the new conditions.

10. *Social science has yielded trivial results.*

a. One of the assumptions of science is that nothing is self-evident. What is obvious to one person is not at all obvious to another.

b. A famous sociologist frequently provides his class with a list of "common-sensical" social science findings, and the class generally agrees on their obviousness. He then discloses that these were false results and that findings are actually in the opposite direction. So, what often seems to be trivial and obvious may actually be false.

c. Science must obtain a firm foundation before it advances to problems involving greater complexity.

## LEARNING AID

Be able to refute from a social science perspective any of the anti–social science arguments.

## FOOTNOTES

1. Abraham Kaplan, *The Conduct of Inquiry* (San Francisco: Chandler, 1964), p. 23.
2. C. Wright Mills, "On Intellectual Craftsmanship," *Symposium on Sociological Theory,* ed. L. Gross (New York: Harper and Row, 1959), p. 25.
3. John Hospers, *Introduction to Philosophical Analysis,* 2d ed., Englewood Cliffs, N.J.: Prentice-Hall, 1967), pp. 122–41.
4. Carlo Lastrucci, *The Scientific Approach* (Cambridge: Schenkman, 1963), pp. 37–47.
5. For a more thorough treatment of informal fallacies, see A. Michalos, *Improving Your Reasoning* (Englewood Cliffs, N.J.: Prentice-Hall, 1970); W. Salmon, *Logic* (Englewood Cliffs, N.J.: Prentice-Hall, 1963); and I. Copi, *Introduction to Logic* (New York: Macmillan, 1961).

6. The material in this section relies on: Ernest Nagel, *The Structure of Science* (New York: Harcourt, Brace & World, 1961), pp. 447–502, Bernard Phillips, *Social Research* (New York: Macmillan, 1966), pp. 62–65; Herbert Feigl and May Brodbeck, eds., *Readings in the Philosophy of Science* (New York: Appleton-Century-Crofts, 1953), pp. 14–18; and Milton Hobbs, "Logical Positivism and the Methodology of Political Science: Analysis and Program" (Ph.D. dissertation, Northwestern University, 1961).

# 2
# Formal Fallacies and Causation

# INTRODUCTION

## Rationale

Explaining, predicting, and establishing cause–effect relationships are activities essential to the development of a science. Social scientists attempt to explain and predict such events as elections, riots, wars, congressional behavior, and individual attitudes. To explain and predict events such as these also involves, in part, a search for their causes.

This unit covers formal fallacies and the logic of causation. The next unit includes explanation and prediction. Formal logic, that is, the study of deductive and inductive arguments, is fundamental to understanding social science. Causation, explanation, and prediction are special forms of deductive reasoning. Describing empirical generalizations depends on inductive reasoning. Approaches to confirming and disconfirming theories are based on the logic of conditional arguments. Formal logic, then, is closely related to the logic of social inquiry. In addition, knowing formal logic assists the student in detecting fallacies in his own and others' thinking.

## Learning Objectives

After completing this unit the student should be able to:

1. Identify, diagram, and assess the validity of the four types of conditional arguments (affirming the antecedent, affirming the consequent, denying the antecedent, and denying the consequent).

2. Classify categorical statements as types A, E, I, or O.

3. Determine whether a term is distributed or undistributed in a categorical statement.

4. State the three tests for the validity of deductive arguments.

5. Diagram and test the validity of deductive arguments.

6. Construct, diagram, and test an original deductive argument.

7. Identify and define statistical and universal generalizations.

8. Identify and define statistical syllogisms.

9. Identify and define the fallacies of biased statistics, insufficient statistics, and statistical deduction.

10. Construct an original political example of an inductive argument.

11. Summarize the ways in which deductive arguments differ from inductive arguments.

12. Define and identify necessary, sufficient, contingent, contributory, alternative, remote, and proximate conditions.

13. Name and define the criteria required for inferring causality.

14. Name and explain the three methods of reducing the possibility of spuriousness.

## LOGIC: FORMAL FALLACIES

In the previous unit we examined some of the more common types of informal fallacies. This unit emphasizes how to identify formal fallacies, arguments that are unsound because of their logical form or structure.[1] It is important for social scientists to know how to identify formal fallacies because scientific explanations and theories consist of logically connected sets of statements, and social scientists test the validity of explanations and theories in part by their logical structure. Knowing the principles of formal fallacies, as with the principles of informal fallacies, further arms social scientists against arguments that are designed primarily to persuade and propagandize.

Logic is primarily concerned with distinguishing valid from invalid arguments. *Arguments* are sets of sentences divided in such a way that some of them claim to be the reason, justification, or support for some other sentence in the set. The sentences that provide the reason or support are called *premises*. The sentence that is supposed to be supported by the premises is called the *conclusion*.

Our study of formal fallacies begins by distinguishing validity from truth. *Validity* means that the premises of an argument are related to the conclusion in such a way that the conclusion must be true if the premises are true. Validity is a property of arguments. It describes their logical form. It says nothing about the truth or falsity of individual statements. Valid arguments may have true premises and a true conclusion, false premises and a true conclusion, or false premises and a false conclusion. However, if the premises of a valid argument are true, then the conclusion must be true also. In contrast to validity, truth is a property of individual statements, such as individual premises or the conclusion. Just as it is meaningless to call a single statement "valid," it also is meaningless to call an argument "true." Arguments are valid or invalid; individual statements are true or false.

## Conditional Arguments

*Conditional statements* are compound statements joined by "if" and "then." The "if" clause is called the "antecedent" and the "then" clause is called the "consequent." Conditional statements have the following form:

Form:

| If *P*, then *Q*. |
|---|

Example:

*If* the president commits a criminal act, *then* the President can be impeached.

where *P* represents the antecedent and *Q* represents the consequent.

*Conditional arguments* consist of affirming or denying the antecedent or consequent clauses of conditional statements. We shall now examine the form and the validity of the four types of conditional arguments implied by the previous statement.

AFFIRMING THE ANTECEDENT: A VALID ARGUMENT

This type of argument has the following form:

Form:

If *P*, then *Q*.

*P*.
_____

Therefore, *Q*.

Example:

If the president commits a criminal act, then he can be impeached.
The president commits a criminal act.
_____

Therefore, he can be impeached.

This argument has two premises and a conclusion. The first premise is a conditional statement. The second premise affirms p, the antecedent statement. Hence, we obtain the name of this argument, "affirming the antecedent," from the second premise. The conclusion then infers the consequent. This is a valid form of argument. If the premises are true, the conclusion must be true.

## 34 Formal Fallacies and Causation

DENYING THE ANTECEDENT: AN INVALID ARGUMENT

This argument takes the following form:

| Form: | Example: |
|---|---|
| If *P*, then *Q*.<br><br>Not *P*.<br>_____<br>Therefore, not *Q*. | If the president commits a criminal act, then he can be impeached.<br>The president does not commit a criminal act.<br>_____<br>Therefore, he cannot be impeached. |

The first premise is a conditional statement. By stating the opposite of the condition in the antecedent clause, the second premise "denies the antecedent" of the conditional statement. The conclusion then infers the denial of the consequent in the conditional statement.

In a valid argument the conclusion must be true if the premises are true. To argue by denying the antecedent is invalid because the premises can be true, yet the conclusion may still be false. In the above example, the president might still be impeached for other reasons such as abuse of public trust, even though he may not have committed a criminal act.

AFFIRMING THE CONSEQUENT: AN INVALID ARGUMENT

| Form: | Example: |
|---|---|
| If *p*, then *q*.<br><br>*q*.<br>_____<br>Therefore, *p*. | If the president commits a criminal act, then the president can be impeached.<br>The president can be impeached.<br>_____<br>Therefore, the president commits a criminal act. |

The first premise is a conditional statement. The second premise affirms the consequent, and the conclusion infers the antecedent. This argument is invalid because the premises may be true and the conclusion may still be false. The president, in the above example, may be impeached for causes other than committing criminal acts.

DENYING THE CONSEQUENT: A VALID ARGUMENT

| Form: | | Example |
|---|---|---|
| If $p$, then $q$. | | If the president commits a criminal act, then he can be impeached. |
| not $q$. | | The president cannot be impeached. |
| Therefore, not $p$. | | Therefore, the president has not committed a criminal act. |

The first premise is a conditional statement. The second premise denies the consequent of the conditional statement, and the conclusion infers the denial of the antecedent. This form of argument is valid. If the premises are true, the conclusion must be true.

Sometimes it is difficult to remember the validity status of each of the four types of conditional arguments. Table 1 can serve as a memory aid. The table is set up with the "AA's" (*A*ffirming the *A*ntecedent) in the upper left hand cell. The arguments along the major diagonal (upper left and lower right cells) are valid. The arguments along the minor diagonal (upper right and lower left cells) are invalid.

## LEARNING AID

1. Affirming the consequent is a (valid, invalid) form of argument.
2. Denying the antecedent is a (valid, invalid) form of argument.
3. Denying the consequent is a (valid, invalid) form of argument.
4. Affirming the antecedent is a (valid, invalid) form of argument.
5. Diagram the standard form of affirming the antecedent.
6. Diagram the standard form of denying the consequent.

**Table 2-1**  THE VALIDITY STATUS OF CONDITIONAL ARGUMENTS

| | The Second Premise: | |
|---|---|---|
| | Affirms | Denies |
| Antecedent | $V$ | $-V$ |
| Consequent | $-V$ | $V$ |

**7.** Diagram the standard form of affirming the consequent.

**8.** Diagram the standard form of denying the antecedent.

**9.** Whereas validity is a property of (arguments, statements), truth is a property of (arguments, statements).

**10.** It (is, is not) possible for a valid argument to have false premises.

**11.** The conclusion (must, may not) be true if the premises are true in a valid argument.

**12.** Identify the type of conditional argument and its validity status for each of the following:

    a.   If people are hungry, then they will riot. People are rioting. So, they must be hungry.

    b.   If it is raining, the streets are wet. It is not raining. So, the streets are not wet.

    c.   If the people want higher taxes, then the people will vote for my opponent. The people do not vote for my opponent. Thus, the people do not want higher taxes.

    d.   If people are frustrated, then they tend to exhibit aggressive behavior. People are frustrated; they exhibit aggressive behavior.

    e.   If Chicago is in California, then Chicago is in the United States. Chicago is in the United States. Thus, Chicago is in California.

    f.   If the communists win in South Vietnam, they will win all of Southeast Asia. The communists are winning in South Vietnam. Therefore, they will win in Southeast Asia.

    g.   If wage increase, then prices increase. Wages do not increase. Therefore, prices do not increase.

    h.   If people feel like they are deprived relative to other people in their society, then they are likely to rebel. They are not likely to rebel. So, they do not feel like they are deprived relative to other people in their society.

    i.   If Dwight Eisenhower was assassinated, then he is dead. Eisenhower is dead. Therefore, Eisenhower, was assassinated.

. . . . . . . . . . . . . . . . . . . . . . . . . . . . . . . . . . . . . . . . . . . . . . . . . . . .

**1.** invalid

**2.** invalid

**3.** valid

**4.** valid

**5.** if $p$, then $q$.

    $p$.

    ——————

    Thus, $q$.

**6.** If $p$, then $q$.

    not $q$.

    ——————

    Thus, not $p$.

7. If $p$, then $q$.

   $q$.
   _____
   Thus, $p$.

8. If $p$, then $q$.

   not $p$.
   _____
   Thus, not $q$.

9. arguments, statements

10. is

11. must

12. a.  Affirming the consequent; invalid; people may be rioting for reasons other than hunger, such as oppression.

    b.  Denying the antecedent; invalid; the streets may be wet for other reasons such as a broken fire hydrant, sprinklers, street cleaners, or rain earlier in the day.

    c.  Denying the consequent; valid.

    d.  Affirming the antecedent; valid.

    e.  Affirming the consequent; invalid; in addition to being invalid, the conditional statement is false.

    f.  Affirming the antecedent; valid; although the argument is valid, the truth of the first premise may be doubtful.

    g.  Denying the antecedent; invalid; prices may increase because profits increase even though wages stay the same.

    h.  Denying the consequent; valid.

    i.  Affirming the consequent; invalid; the first premise is also false.

## Deductive Arguments

A *deductive argument* is one whose premises provide conclusive evidence for the conclusion. If all the premises are true, the conclusion must be true. Deductive arguments proceed from general premises to more specific conclusions. All other information contained in the conclusion is contained at least implicitly in the premises. The function of the deductive argument is to make explicit the information contained in the premises.

CATEGORICAL STATEMENTS

The premises and conclusions of deductive arguments consist of different kinds of categorical statements. Before we can assess the validity of a deductive argument, we must learn how categorical statements are diagramed and distributed.

Categorical statements take the following form:

| Quantifier | (Subject) | verb | (Predicate) |
|---|---|---|---|

Examples:

| All | politicians | are | statesmen. |
| No | politicians | are | statesmen. |
| Some | politicians | are | statesmen. |
| Some | politicians | are not | statesmen. |

To ascertain the validity of deductive arguments, we must learn to diagram them. The subject and predicate of a categorical statement are represented by $S$ and $P$, respectively. There are four forms of categorical statements: universal affirmative ($A$), particular affirmative ($I$), universal negative ($E$), and particular negative ($O$). Two of the forms are universal ($A$, $E$), and two are particular ($I$, $O$). Two are affirmative ($A$, $I$), and two are negative ($E$, $O$).

1. *Universal affirmative = A*
   Example: All politicians are statesmen.
   Form:

   | $S$ | $A$ | $P$ |

   Meaning: Every member of $S$ is a member of $P$.

2. *Particular affirmative = I*
   Example: Some politicians are statesmen.
   Form:

   | $S$ | $I$ | $P$ |

   Meaning: Some members of $S$ are members of $P$.

3. *Universal negative = E*
   Example: No politicians are statesmen.
   Form:

   | $S$ | $E$ | $P$ |

   Meaning: No member of $S$ is a member of $P$.

4. *Particular negative = O*
   Example: Some politicians are not statesmen.
   Form:

   | $S$ | $O$ | $P$ |

   Meaning: At least one member of $S$ is not a member of $P$.

CATEGORICAL ARGUMENTS

*Categorical arguments* are arguments that consist of categorical statements, which we defined earlier. Every categorical argument has two premises and one conclusion. Each argument contains three terms: the subject of the conclusion ($S$); the predicate of the conclusion ($P$); and the middle term, which is contained only in the premises ($M$). The subject and predicate of the conclusion also are called "end" terms, in contrast to the "middle" term appearing in the premises. There are fifteen different forms of valid deductive arguments and many other forms of invalid arguments. Here is an example of a deductive argument and its form:

|  | Example: | | Form: | |
|---|---|---|---|---|
| All politicians are courageous people. | $S$ | $A$ | $M$ |
| All courageous people are statesmen. | $M$ | $A$ | $P$ |
| Therefore, all politicians are statesmen. | $S$ | $A$ | $P$ |

The middle term in this argument is "courageous people" because it is a term that is contained in the premises but not in the conclusion. $A$ refers to the fact that each statement is of the universal affirmative type. $S$ and $P$ refer to the terms in the conclusion of the argument.

DISTRIBUTION

Before we can test the validity of categorical arguments, we still must learn whether the subjects and predicates of categorical arguments are distributed or undistributed. A term is *distributed* in a categorical statement if it refers to all the members of the class designated by the term. A distributed term refers to each and every member of a class, individually. An undistributed term does not refer to each and every member of a class, individually. When a term is distributed, the subscript $d$ is assigned to it; and when a term is undistributed, the subscript $u$ is assigned to it. Now we can provide a complete diagram of each of the four types of categorical statements:

1. *Universal affirmative*
   Example: All politicians are statesmen.
   Meaning: Each and every member of $S$ is a member of $P$.
   *Form:*  $\boxed{S_d \qquad A \qquad P_u}$

2. *Particular affirmative*
   Example: Some politicans are statesmen.
   Meaning: Some members of $S$ are members of $P$.
   Form:  $\boxed{S_u \qquad I \qquad P_u}$

3. *Universal negative*
   Example: No politicians are statesmen.
   Meaning: Each and every member of $S$ is not a member of $P$.
   Form:  $\boxed{S_d \qquad E \qquad P_d}$

4. *Particular negative*
   Example: Some politicians are not statesmen.
   Meaning: Some members of S are not members of P.
   Form:  $\boxed{S_u \qquad O \qquad P_d}$

Fortunately, the distribution of terms follows a specific pattern: *The subject of a universal statement is distributed; the predicate of a negative statement is distributed; and all other terms are undistributed.* To help you remember this rule, we suggest the memory cue: "USNP" (Uncle Sam Never Panics), which stands for *u*niversal–*s*ubject, *n*egative–*p*redicate. In the identification of terms as "distributed" or "undistributed," the middle term is evaluated as if it were a subject or predicate term, depending upon its use as the subject of the verb or the predicate of the verb.

### DEDUCTIVE VALIDITY

At last we are ready to assess the validity of deductive arguments. A valid deductive argument must pass three tests or rules:

M    I.    The *m*iddle term must be distributed exactly one time.
E    II.    No *e*nd term (S or P) may be distributed only one time.
N    III.    The number of *n*egative premises must equal the number of negative conclusions.

These rules should be memorized. (Use "MEN" as a cue, if that helps).

The evaluation of the validity of a deductive argument can proceed in the following manner. First, $S$ and $P$ are assigned to the terms appearing in the conclusion. S and P should be assigned to the same terms appearing in the premises. Notice that the $P$ appearing in the conclusion may actually be the subject of one of the premises (see Example 3 below). Second, each statement is classified as *A, E, I,* or *0*. Third, each of the terms is designated as distributed or undistributed, according to the "USNP" rule. Finally, we apply the three tests to determine if the argument is valid or invalid.

|  | Example 1: | | Form: | |
|---|---|---|---|---|
| All politicians are courageous persons. | $S_d$ | $A$ | $M_u$ |
| All courageous persons are statesmen. | $M_d$ | $A$ | $P_u$ |
| Therefore, all politicians are statesmen. | $S_d$ | $A$ | $P_u$ |

Let's analyze the above example:

   I.    Satisfied; the middle term ($M$) is distributed exactly one time.
   II.    Satisfied; no end term is distributed only one time; $S$ is distributed twice and $P$ is not distributed at all.
   III.    Satisfied; the number of negative premises (zero) equals the number of negative conclusions (zero).

Since this argument passes all three tests, it is a valid argument.

| Example 2: | | Form: | | |
|---|---|---|---|---|

All Quakers are pacifists.      $M_d$   $A$   $P_u$
No generals are Quakers.      $S_d$   $E$   $M_d$
_____
Therefore, no generals are pacifists.    $S_d$   $E$   $P_d$

    I.   Violated; the middle term is not distributed only one time. It is distributed twice.
   II.   Violated; $P$ is distributed only one time.
  III.   Satisfied; there is one negative premise and one negative conclusion.

Since two of the rules are violated, this argument is invalid.

| Example 3: | | Form: | | |
|---|---|---|---|---|

Some generals are warmongers.      $P_u$   $I$   $M_u$
All warmongers are frightening people.    $M_d$   $A$   $S_u$
_____
Therefore, some frightening people are generals.   $S_u$   $I$   $P_u$

    I.   Satisfied; the middle term is distributed exactly once.
   II.   Satisfied; no end term is distributed exactly once.
  III.   Satisfied; the number of negative premises (zero) equals the number of negative conclusions (zero).

Since all three tests are passed, this argument is valid.

| Example 4: | | Form: | | |
|---|---|---|---|---|

Some politicians are not well adjusted.      $S_u$   $O$   $M_d$
Some well-adjusted people are not ambitious.    $M_u$   $O$   $P_d$
_____
Therefore, some politicians are not ambitious.    $S_u$   $O$   $P_d$

    I.   Satisfied; the middle term is distributed exactly once.
   II.   Satisfied; neither S nor P is distributed exactly once.
  III.   Violated; there are more negative premises than negative conclusions.

Since one test is violated, the argument is invalid.

## LEARNING AID

1.   Classify each of the following categorical statements as A, E, I, or O:
    a.   Some high income people are not Republicans.
    b.   Some wars are justified extensions of diplomacy.
    c.   No Arabs are Jewish.
    d.   All TV stations are members of the F.C.C.

    e.   Some judges are not lawyers.

    f.   No American presidents are women.

    g.   All Texans are Americans.

    h.   Some Americans are not Texans.

    i.   Some politicians are corrupt people.

    j.   No John Birchers are communists.

**2.** The subject of a _____ statement is distributed; the predicate of a _____ is distributed; and all other terms are _____.

**3.** Diagram each of the statements listed in the first question.

**4.** In a valid deductive argument, the _____ term must be distributed exactly one time.

**5.** In a valid deductive argument, no _____ term may be distributed only one time.

**6.** The number of _____ premises must equal the number of _____ conclusions in a valid deductive argument.

**7.** Diagram, test·each validity rule, and determine the validity of the following arguments:

    a.   No men are women.

         All American presidents are men.

         Thus, no American presidents are women.

    b.   All patriots are Americans.

         Some Texans are patriots.

         Thus, all Texans are Americans.

    c.   No Republicans are Democrats.

         Some Democrats are high income people.

         Thus, some high income people are not Republicans.

    d.   Some conservatives are John Birchers.

         No conservatives are communists.

         Thus, no John Birchers are communists.

    e.   Some lawbreakers are not corrupt people.

         No corrupt people are civil disobedients.

         Thus, some civil disobedients are lawbreakers.

**8.** Construct, diagram, and test an original political deductive argument.

. . . . . . . . . . . . . . . . . . . . . . . . . . . . . . . . . . . . . . . . . . . . . . . . . . . . . . . .

**1.**  a.      O          f.   E

      b.      I          g.   A

      c.      E          h.   O

      d.      A          i.   I

      e.      O          j.   E

**2.**  universal, negative, undistributed

**3.**  a.      $S_u$   O    $P_d$

      b.      $S_u$   I     $P_u$

      c.      $S_d$   E    $P_d$

|     |     |     |     |
|-----|-----|-----|-----|
| d.  | $S_d$ | A | $P_u$ |
| e.  | $S_u$ | O | $P_d$ |
| f.  | $S_d$ | E | $P_d$ |
| g.  | $S_d$ | A | $P_u$ |
| h.  | $S_u$ | O | $P_d$ |
| i.  | $S_u$ | I | $P_u$ |
| j.  | $S_d$ | E | $P_d$ |

4. middle
5. end
6. negative, negative
7.

| a. | $M_d$ | E | $P_d$ | I. | Satisfied |
|----|-------|---|-------|-----|-----------|
|    | $S_d$ | A | $M_u$ | II. | Satisfied |
|    | $S_d$ | E | $P_d$ | III. | Satisfied; therefore (a) is valid. |
| b. | $M_d$ | A | $P_u$ | I. | Satisfied |
|    | $S_u$ | I | $M_u$ | II. | Violated |
|    | $S_d$ | A | $P_u$ | III. | Satisfied; therefore (b) is invalid. |
| c. | $P_d$ | E | $M_d$ | I. | Satisfied |
|    | $M_u$ | I | $S_u$ | II. | Satisfied |
|    | $S_u$ | O | $P_d$ | III. | Satisfied; therefore, (c) is valid. |
| d. | $M_u$ | I | $S_u$ | I. | Satisfied |
|    | $M_d$ | E | $P_d$ | II. | Violated |
|    | $S_d$ | E | $P_d$ | III. | Satisfied; therefore, (d) is invalid. |
| e. | $P_u$ | O | $M_d$ | I. | Violated |
|    | $M_d$ | E | $S_d$ | II. | Violated |
|    | $S_u$ | I | $P_u$ | III. | Violated; therefore, (e) is invalid. |

8. Check your originally constructed argument with the rules, a classmate, or your instructor.

## Inductive Arguments

Unlike deduction, which derives particular conclusions from general premises, inductive argument derives a generalized conclusion on the basis of particular, often empirically derived, premises or observations. An *inductive argument* is one whose premises make the conclusion probable, but not certain. The reliance of scientific discovery and confirmation on the inductive approach attests to the importance of induction in social scientific inquiry.

Inductive argument contains statements very much like the categorical statements in deductive argument. A quantifier, subject, verb, and predicate are all identifiable, as well as the universal/particular and affirmative/negative classifications. The inductive argument itself contains a conclusion and one or more premises that establish the probability of the truth of the conclusion. An inductive argument takes the following form:

Form:                                                    Example:

| |
|---|
| $N\%$ of the $S$'s in a sample are $P$. |
| |
| Therefore, $N\%$ of the $S$'s in a population are $P$. |

85% of the Republicans in a sample favor the candidate.

Therefore, 85% of the Republicans in the nation favor the candidate.

The English language offers some versatility in stating inductive arguments. Sometimes the "if–then" form of expression is used in place of the "$S$ are $P$" form:

Alternate Form:                                          Example:

| |
|---|
| If $S$ in a sample, (then the probability of $P$ is $N\%$). |
| |
| Therefore, if $S$ in a population, (then the probability of $P$ is $N\%$). |

If a person is a Republican in a sample, then there is an 85% chance that he favors the candidate.

Therefore, if a person is a Republican in the population, there is an 85% chance that he favors the candidate.

STATISTICAL AND UNIVERSAL GENERALIZATIONS

Inductive arguments may be distinguished by the types of statements that appear in their conclusions. If the conclusion of an inductive argument contains a particular (*I, O*) type of statement, then the conclusion is called a *statistical generalization*. It can also be classified as affirmative or negative.

Particular Affirmative (*I*)

Form:  | $N\%$ (some) $S$ are $P$. |

Example:   85% of the Republicans favor the candidate.

Particular Negative (*O*)

Form:  | $N\%$ (some) $S$ are not $P$. |

Example:   15% of the Republicans do not favor the candidate.

If the conclusion of an inductive argument contains a universal (*A, E*) type of statement, then it is called a *universal generalization*. It also may be classified as affirmative or negative.

### Universal Affirmative (*A*)

Form:  | 100% (all) *S* are *P*. |

Example:  All Republicans favor the candidate.

### Universal Negative (*E*)

Form:  | 0% (no) *S* are *P*. |

Example:  No Republicans favor the candidate.

One characteristic of an inductive argument is that it establishes a conclusion whose content goes beyond its premises. From an observation of a sample, an inference is made about a population. A pollster, for example, draws an inference about the attitudes of a nation from a sample of voters. This is called the "inductive leap," jumping from the premises, which concern an observed sample, to the conclusion, which concerns the entire population. The greater the number of representative units observed in the sample, the smaller is the inductive leap. The smaller the number of representative units observed in the sample, the greater is the inductive leap.

The premises of an inductive argument, then, establish the probability of the truth of the conclusion. Unlike deductive argument, the premises of inductive argument do not establish the conclusion conclusively. Thus, the premises of a valid inductive argument may be true, and the conclusion can still be false. It is possible, for example, that some social system not yet observed is not socially stratified or that the majority of Republicans in the population do not favor the candidate, even though the majority of Republicans in the sample do favor the candidate. The premises of an inductive argument only support or lend weight to the conclusion. They do not make the conclusion certain.

STATISTICAL SYLLOGISMS

Some inductive arguments are formulated so that they resemble deductive arguments. These are called "statistical syllogisms." A *statistical syllogism* is an inductive argument consisting of statistical generalizations that take the form of a deductive argument. A statistical syllogism is not a valid deductive argument because the conclusion can be false even though the premises are true. Without at least one universal generalization, a deductive argument cannot be valid. It is impossible to satisfy the three validity requirements without the presence of a universal categorical statement. An argument consisting of two "*I*" premises is invalid because the middle term is not distributed. An argument consisting of two "O" premises is invalid because the number of negative premises does not equal the number of negative conclusions. An argument consisting of an "*O*" and an "*I*" premises is invalid because either the end term or middle term rule is violated.

Since statistical syllogisms do not contain any universal generalizations (by definition), they cannot be valid deductive arguments. Statistical syllogisms, like valid deductive arguments, can assume a variety of forms. Here is a representative form of a statistical syllogism:

| e.g., Form: | Example: |
|---|---|
| $N\%$ of $S$ are $M$.<br>$N\%$ of $M$ are $P$.<br><br>Therefore, $N\%$ of $S$ are $P$ where $N$ does not equal 100 and where the double lines mean the conclusion is probable but not certain. | $N\%$ of Catholics are Democrats.<br>$N\%$ of Democrats are liberal.<br><br>Therefore, $N\%$ of Catholics are liberal. |

If one of the premises is a universal generalization (i.e., $N = 100\%$ or $0\%$), the syllogism by definition is no longer statistical but deductive. If the premises are true, the conclusion would have to be true. Whereas valid deductive arguments require at least one universal generalization in the premises, inductive arguments do not require universal generalizations in the premises in order to be valid.

The strength of statistical syllogisms depends on the strength of $N\%$. If $N\%$ is very close to 100, there is strong support for the conclusion that $S$ is $P$. If $N\%$ is close to zero, there is strong support for the conclusion that $S$ is not $P$. If $N\%$ is 50, then the support is just as strong for the conclusion that $S$ is $P$ as it is for the conclusion that S is not P. From this discussion it is clear that the closer $N\%$ is to 100 or to 0, the more the premises of an inductive argument support the conclusion.

INDUCTIVE FALLACIES

The fact that the conclusion of an inductive argument can be false even though the premises are true poses special problems for social scientists. Every effort must be made to prevent drawing false conclusions during the course of inductive argument. The error of deducing a false conclusion from premises involving only statistical generalizations is called the *fallacy of statistical deduction*. Social scientists attempt to minimize the occurrence of this error by minimizing two other types of inductive fallacies: insufficient statistics and biased statistics.

The *fallacy of insufficient statistics* is the error of making an inductive generalization before enough data have been accumulated to warrant the generalization. Suppose, for example, that the pollster concludes that 85% of the Republicans in the nation favor the Republican candidate after observing only 10 Republicans instead of 1500. The smaller the sample of observations, the less support the premises provide for the conclusion. The conclusion is more likely to be false when an "insufficient" number of observations or statistics have been accumulated. Social scientists make use of probability and statistics to determine how likely it is that fallacy of insufficient statistics has been committed.

The *fallacy of biased statistics* is the error of making an inductive generalization on the basis of unrepresentative observations. Suppose, for example, that the pollster concludes that 85% of the Republicans in the nation favor the candidate after interviewing only those Republicans who live in Orange County, California, or only those Republicans who make more than $25,000 a year. The generalization would be false because it would be based on biased or unrepresentative observations. If inductive generalizations are to be reliable, they must rest on samples that are representative of the populations toward which the generalizations are directed. Unrepresentative and biased samples, even if large, can still prejudice the outcome and render a false conclusion.

To minimize the probability of jumping to a false inductive conclusion, the fallacy of statistical deduction, social scientists try to make sure that the number of observations they take are sufficient and that the observations are not biased but representative.

THE DEDUCTIVE–INDUCTIVE DISTINCTION

The student by now should have clearly in mind the distinction between deductive and inductive forms of argument. We may summarize the major differences:

|  | *Deduction:* |  | *Induction:* |
|---|---|---|---|
| 1. | Form: $S \quad A \quad M$<br>$\dfrac{M \quad A \quad P}{S \quad A \quad P}$ | 1. | *Form:*<br>$N\%$ of $S$ in a sample are $P$.<br>Therefore, $N\%$ of $S$ in the population are $P$. |
| 2. | If the premises are true, the conclusion must be true. | 2. | If the premises are true, the conclusion is probably, but not necessarily, true. |
| 3. | A universal generalization is required in the premises for a valid argument. | 3. | A universal generalization is not required in the premises for a valid argument. |
| 4. | The conclusion does not contain information that is not contained at least implicitly in the premises. | 4. | The conclusion does contain information not present in the premises. |

**LEARNING AID**

1.  "Two percent of all whites have a Ph.D. degree." This is a generalization.
2.  An argument that takes the form below is called _____.

$N\%$ of $S$ are $M$.
$N\%$ of $M$ are $P$.

─────────────

$N\%$ of $S$ are $P$.

3.  Give an original political example of an inductive argument.
4.  When social scientists deduce a false conclusion from statistical premises, they are guilty of the fallacy of _____.
5.  The fallacy of _____ is the error of making an inductive generalization on the basis of unrepresentative observations.
6.  When a social scientist errs by making an inductive generalization before enough data have been accumulated, he has committed the fallacy of _____.
7.  If the premises are true, the conclusion must be true in valid (inductive, deductive) arguments.
8.  A universal generalization is required in the premises of valid (inductive, deductive) arguments.
9.  The conclusion does contain information not present in the premises of (inductive, deductive) arguments.

· · · · · · · · · · · · · · · · · · · · · · · · · · · · · · · · · · · · · · · · · · · · · · · · · · · · · · · · ·

1.  statistical
2.  statistical syllogism
3.  Check with your classmates or instructor.
4.  statistical deduction
5.  biased statistics
6.  insufficient statistics
7.  deductive
8.  deductive
9.  inductive

## CAUSATION

When we hear that poverty causes crime, or that frustration causes aggression, or that nationalism causes war, what is meant by the word "cause?" What precisely is the relationship of the cause, $C$, to the effect, $E$, when it is said that $C$ causes $E$? Causal assertions are central to social science, but they are frequently imprecise, ambiguous, and difficult to establish.

This section deals with the logic of political and social causation by specifying the role of causation in scientific inquiry, by clarifying the terms associated with the different meanings of "cause," and by delineating the criteria necessary for inferring statements that assert that $C$ causes $E$.[2]

Causation has an important role in social scientific inquiry. One of the primary assumptions of science is the principle of determinism, which states that every event has a cause. Events are assumed not to be random occurrences but to be determined naturally. Causation, then, is one of the fundamental postulates of science. It is closely related to explanation and prediction, two of the basic goals of science.

## The Language of Causation

We have pointed out that references to causes in the social science literature are often vague and ambiguous. To facilitate systematic thinking, social scientists have adopted a set of terms that help them to sort out the various uses of the word "cause." The purpose of this section is to identify these terms and to apply them to various social and political contexts.

NECESSARY CONDITION

A necessary condition for the occurrence of an event is a circumstance, $C$, in the absence of which the event, $E$, cannot occur. Oxygen, for example, is a necessary condition for the occurrence of fire, since fire cannot occur if oxygen is absent.

| Form: | Example |
|---|---|
| If not $C$, then not $E$. | If a person is not older than 18 years of age, then he cannot vote. Thus, a necessary condition for voting is being 18 years of age or older. |

SUFFICIENT CONDITION

A sufficient condition for the occurrence of an event is a circumstance in whose presence the event must occur. Oxygen is not a sufficient condition for the occurrence of fire because oxygen can be present without fire occurring. Oxygen, combined with combustible material and a high enough temperature, however, is a sufficient condition for fire to occur. When they are present, fire occurs.

| Form: | Example: |
|---|---|
| If $C$, then $E$. | If a person is 18 years or older ($C_1$), a citizen of the United States ($C_2$), and a resident of a community for 30 days ($C_3$), then he is eligible to vote in the election. Thus, age, citizenship, and residence are a sufficient condition for voting eligibility. |

In the above, example, the sufficient condition consists of three necessary conditions. Whenever there are necessary conditions, they also must be listed as part of the sufficient condition. However, not all sufficient conditions contain necessary conditions. For example, take the statement, "If it rains, then the street gets wet." Rain is sufficient to get the streets wet, but it is not necessary. The streets could be wet because of other circumstances, such as a broken fire hydrant or overflowing lawn sprinkling system, or city street cleaning.

CONTRIBUTORY CONDITION

A contributory condition for the occurrence of an event is a circumstance that increases the probability that an event will occur. A contributory condition makes an event more likely, but it does not make it certain. Smoking, for example, increases the probability that a person will get cancer, but it does not make it certain. A contributory condition, therefore, is not a sufficient condition. It is only one among a number of factors that make an event more likely to occur.

| Form: | Example: |
|---|---|
| If $C$, then $E$ is more likely. | If a child comes from a broken home ($C$), then he is more likely to be delinquent ($E$). Coming from a broken home is neither a sufficient nor a necessary condition of delinquency. It contributes to a sufficient condition. |

ALTERNATIVE CONDITION

An alternative condition for the occurrence of an event is one of a number of circumstances in whose presence the event is likely to occur. The broken fire hydrants, overflowing sprinkling systems, and city street cleaning are alternative conditions to rain. Alternative conditions may be either contributing or sufficient.

<table>
<tr><td align="center">Form:</td><td align="center">Example:</td></tr>
</table>

| Form: | Example: |
|---|---|
| If $C_1$, or $C_2$, or $C_n$, then $E$. | If a nation is attacked $(C_1)$, or is threatened to be attacked $(C_2)$, or is severely deprived by another nation $(C_3)$, then it declares war on the other nation $(E)$. Each condition is an alternative but sufficient condition for the declaration of war. |

### CONTINGENT CONDITION

A contingent condition for the occurrence of an event is a circumstance that modifies the effect of a contributory condition. When contributory conditions are influenced by or are dependent on other circumstances, they are dependent on contingent conditions. A factor that is a contributory condition of an event under one set of circumstances may not be so under another. The factor may be contingent on another set of circumstances. Minority group status, for example, is a contributory condition of political participation; minority members are generally less likely to participate in politics. Education, however, modifies the effect of minority status so that the relationship is reversed; highly educated minority members are more likely to participate in politics than highly educated nonminority members. Thus, the effect of minority status is "contingent" (dependent) on education. Education is the contingent condition because it modifies the effect of a contributory condition.

| Form: | Example: |
|---|---|
| If $CC$, then<br>  if $C$, then $E$. | If a person perceives an election to be close, then if he also identifies strongly with a party, he is likely to turnout to vote. |
| If not $CC$, then<br>  if $C$, then not $E$. | If a person perceives an election to be one-sided, then if he also identifies strongly with a party, he is not more likely to vote. |

PROXIMATE AND REMOTE CONDITIONS

Where there is a causal sequence or a chain of events such as $A$ causing $B$, $B$ causing $C$, $C$ causing $D$, and $D$ causing $E$, we can regard E as the effect of the preceding causes or conditions. The nearest, $D$, is the "proximate" cause of $E$, and the other events are more "remote" conditions. $A$ is the most remote condition of all.

Form:

| |
|---|
| If $A$, then $B$, then $C$, then $D$, then $E$ where the closer the event to $E$ the more proximate the condition and the farther the event from $E$ the more remote the condition. |

Example:

"For want of a nail a shoe was lost; for want of a shoe, a horse was lost; for want of a horse a rider was lost; for want of a rider a battalion was lost; for want of a battalion a battle was lost; for want of a victory a kingdom was lost— all for want of a nail." The most proximate condition for losing the kingdom is "for want of a victory" whereas the most remote condition is "for want of a nail."

PLURAL CAUSATION

Plural causation is a principle which asserts that most political and social events are complex phenomena and are not usually the result of a single condition. In social and political analysis, the student will discover that there are normally a number of circumstances that contribute to an effect and that frequently there are a number of alternative sets of sufficient conditions. Social scientists tend to be quite skeptical of one-factor causal theories. The political analyst should learn to search for alternative sufficient and contributory conditions.

## Criteria for Inferring Causality

The word "cause" is commonly used in a number of different senses. Sometimes it refers to some sort of physical force compelling something to move. Sometimes it applies to something in the sense of logical necessity, such as a necessary condition or the idea of a necessary relation between two propositions. Scientists attempt to remove such ambiguity and confusion from this concept by specifying three defining characteristics of the concept, "cause." These are: (1) temporal precedence, (2) constant conjunction, and (3) nonspurious-ness. The word "cause" as used in scientific discourse means nothing more than these three defining characteristics. To assert that "*C* is a cause of *E*" is to assert that: (1) C precedes E in time, (2) *C* is regularly associated or paired with *E*, and (3) variables other than *C* are not the cause of *E*.

## TEMPORAL PRECEDENCE

To infer that *C* is a cause of *E*, we first must determine that *C* occurs before or at the same time as *E*. A cause, by definition, cannot occur after the effect has taken place.

To infer that party identification is a cause of candidate preference, we must establish that party identification precedes candidate preference in time. Temporal precedence is established by observation. One method of observation is survey research. Current behavioral surveys indicate that people usually identify with a party at an early age and develop orientations to specific candidates at a later time. So, a social scientist might be willing to accept the assumption of temporal precedence on these grounds alone. However, a researcher who is studying changes in party identification among adults may hypothesize that a strong attachment to a particular candidate may cause the acquisition of a new party identification. In either case, the researcher is guided in his selection of the cause on the basis of temporal precedence. A second method of observation is experimental. Although it is not practical for this particular problem, it is applicable to many social science problems. Experiments provide strong evidence for temporal precedence, because the experimenter controls when the treatment (*C*) is introduced. He can be quite sure that *C* precedes *E* in time.

## CONSTANT CONJUNCTION

To say that *C* causes *E*, we must establish in addition to temporal precedence constant conjunction, that *C* and *E* are regularly associated (paired, conjoined, connected, or related). Constant conjunction is present in a relationship if whenever *C* occurs, *E* also occurs.

To infer that frustrated hopes cause civil disorders, social scientists must empirically demonstrate constant conjunction. Whenever frustrated hopes occur, civil disorders should also occur. Constant conjunction is established by empirical observation. One method of observing and measuring constant conjunction is to apply statistical measures of association such as correlation coefficients. These measures tell us how often two events are related or associated with each other. Another method of observing constant conjunction is by means of experiments. The design of an experiment enables us to infer how frequently the introduction of a treatment (*c*) is regularly followed by a particular change (*E*). Social scientists, for example, may observe with a quasiexperiment whether the introduction of wage and price controls (*c*) is regularly followed by a lower rate of inflation (*E*). If the two events are regularly paired, then there is evidence for accepting the assumption of constant conjunction.

NONSPURIOUSNESS

To infer that *C* is a cause of *E*, we must first determine whether *C* precedes *E* in time. Then we test whether *C* is regularly associated with *E*. Finally, we must determine whether factors other than *C* could possibly be the cause of *E*. If other factors are eliminated as the cause of *E*, then the assumption of "nonspuriousness" can be accepted. If other factors are found to cause *E*, then the association between *C* and *E* is declared "spurious" (false). Whenever the association is spurious (i.e., when some event is erroneously considered to be the cause of another event), then the fallacy of the false cause has been committed. Just because *X* regularly occurs (constant conjunction) before (temporal precedence) *Y* does not establish that *X* causes *Y*. For example, ice cream consumption is highest in July, and in August occur the highest rates of juvenile delinquency. Yet few would suggest that ice cream consumption is a cause of juvenile delinquency, even though temporal precedence and constant conjunction can be established. It is more reasonable to infer that the association is coincidental and spurious. Likely, the two are associated because they have a common cause. Both ice cream consumption and juvenile delinquency are higher because both occur in the summer when it is hotter and when juveniles are not in school. Thus, the association is probably spurious.

Nonspuriousness, like temporal precedence and constant conjunction, is demonstrated by observation. Nonspuriousness is the most difficult of the three criteria to fulfill because of the uncertainty concerning whether or not all the possible alternative causes have been exhausted or eliminated. Nevertheless, there are several methods that assist in evaluating the prospects of nonspuriousness.

One method is to *hold constant* (control) alternative causes. In many experiments in physics, temperature is held constant so that it can be ruled out as affecting the relationship between two other variables. Social scientists similarly control alternative causes by holding some variables constant. If sex is likely to be an alternative cause, then it can be held constant by conducting the research on only one sex or by conducting the analysis separately on both sexes.

*Randomization* is a second method that reduces the possibility of spuriousness. By randomly selecting and assigning subjects in experiments and surveys, social scientists reduce the probability that any variable extraneous to the situation will unduly influence the relationship between the presumed cause and effect.

*Statistical analysis* is a third means of identifying spuriousness. At the analysis stage, alternative causes can be controlled or held constant by use of partial correlation coefficients and various techniques of standardization.

## LEARNING AID

1. Specify the form of:
   a. necessary condition
   b. sufficient condition
   c. contingent condition
   d. contributory condition

2. Determine whether the causal references in the following statements refer to necessary, sufficient, alternative, contributory, contingent, proximate, or remote conditions:
   a. White racism is essentially responsible for the explosive mixture that has been accumulating in our cities since the end of World War II.
   b. Pervasive discrimination and segregation result in the continuing exclusion of great numbers of minorities from the benefits of economic progress.
   c. Frustrated hopes, a climate encouraging violence, and the frustrations of powerlessness are the ingredients of the explosive mixture producing the 1967 civil disorders.
   d. Frustrated hopes, a climate encouraging violence, or the frustrations of powerlessness caused the riots to occur.
   e. Frustrated hopes, a climate encouraging violence, or the frustrations of powerlessness encourages riots to occur.
   f. The police brutality against Johnny Doe touched off the Watts Riot.
   g. The cause of the Watts riot was the introduction of slavery into the United States.
   h. The level of violence is generally a function of the level of frustration; but if the police react quickly with overwhelming force, the level of violence is not affected by the level of frustration.

3. Name and define the criteria required for inferring causality.

4. Explain how you might test the three criteria for inferring causality in the following statement: "White racism is a cause of riots."

. . . . . . . . . . . . . . . . . . . . . . . . . . . . . . . . . . . . . . . . . . . . . . . . . . . . . . . . . . .

1. a. If not $C$, then not $E$.       c. If $CC$, then.
   b. If $C$, then $E$.                   If $C$, then $E$.
                                          If not $CC$, then.
                                          If $C$, then not $E$.
                                       d. If $C$, then $E$ is more likely.

2. a. The causal reference is very vague. The answer depends on the interpretation of the phrase "essentially responsible." If it is interpreted as meansing "primarily" but not totally responsible, then it is a contributory condition. If it is interpreted to mean that without white racism the explosive mixture would not occur, then the reference is a

        necessary condition. Many causal references in ordinary language are unclear as to the precise sense in which they are being used.

  b.   sufficient condition

  c.   contributory conditions

  d.   alternative conditions that are also sufficient

  e.   alternative conditions that are also contributory

  f.   proximate condition that is also a contributory condition

  g.   remote condition that is also a contributory condition

  h.   contingent condition; police reaction modifies the outcome of the hypothesis

**3.**  a.   temporal precedence = C precedes E in time

     b.   constant conjunction = C and E are regularly associated

     c.   nonspuriousness = factors other than C are not the causes of E.

**4.**  a.   temporal precedence: surveys of racial attitudes or observation of behavioral indicators of white racism (e.g., membership size of KKK, number of lynchings, rate of interracial marriages, and so on) would test whether white racism preceded the occurrence of riots.

     b.   constant conjunction: statistical measures of association such as correlation coefficients can be used to measure the extent to which attitudes or indicators of white racism correlate with the occurrence of riots.

     c.   nonspuriousness. This is the most difficult criterion to test because you have to control for every possible alternative cause. We cannot be sure that we have specified all the alternatives. We can control for a number of alternative causes through various techniques of partial correlation and standardization. Some of the variables that can be controlled for are: size of minority population, average level of income of minorities, average level of minority education, and the like.

## FOOTNOTES

1.  This treatment of logic relies on W. Salmon, *Logic* (Englewood Cliffs, N.J.: Prentice-Hall, 1963), pp. 14–63; A. Michalos, *Improving Your Reasoning* (Englewood Cliffs, N.J.: Prentice-Hall, 1970), pp. 18–23; and I. Copi, *Introduction to Logic,* 2d ed. (New York: Macmillan, 1961), pp. 187–94.

2.  The following serve as major sources for this treatment of causation: J. Hospers, *Introduction to Philosophical Analysis,* (2d ed., Englewood Cliffs, N.J.: Prentice-Hall, 1967) pp. 279–319; I. Copi, *Introduction to Logic,* (2d ed., New York: Macmillan Co., 1961) 355–363; C. Selltiz et al., *Research Methods in Social Relations,* rev. ed. (New York: Holt, Rinehart, and Winston, 1959), pp. 80–94; and A. Stinchcombe, *Constructing Social Theories* (New York: Harcourt, Brace & World, 1968), pp. 31–38.

# 3
# Explanation and Prediction

# INTRODUCTION

## Rationale

Two of the basic goals of scientific inquiry are explanation and prediction. Political scientists in particular seek to explain and predict the political behavior of individuals and groups of individuals. Explanation takes practically the same logical form as prediction. Both are based on a form of deductive argument, about which the student has already learned. Since explaining and predicting are the ultimate goals of science, learning the logic of explanation and prediction is fundamental to understanding and doing scientific research.

## Learning Objectives

After completing this unit the student should be able to:

1. Explain, diagram, and formulate deductive and inductive covering-law explanations.

2. Explain and apply the various degrees of explanatory completeness to formulated explanations.

3. Define, diagram, and identify: genetic, rational, dispositional, and functional explanations.

4. Explain and diagram the form of scientific predictions.

5. Explain the circumstances of explanation without prediction and prediction without explanation.

## COVERING-LAW EXPLANATIONS

Explanations are answers to "why" questions. Why do nations rise and fall? Why does power tend to gravitate toward the few and not the many? Why have third parties not been viable in American politics? Why are democracies usually industrialized nations? Why did the United States intervene in South Vietnam? Why do wars occur? Why do people participate in politics? Why do people rebel against illegitimate authority? These are examples of some of the many types of "why" questions that social scientists ask and attempt to answer by means of scientific explanation. We shall examine the logic, potentiality, and limitation of various forms of explanation.

There are many styles of explanation: genetic, rational, dispositional, functional, and so on. However, these types of explanation derive from a more basic mode of explanation. We maintain that all adequate scientific explanation includes a set of laws or generalizations in the premises of the explanation. These laws or generalizations are called "covering laws" because they cover the situation to be explained. Accordingly, explanations that use covering laws are called "covering-law explanations," or sometimes "nomological explanations" ("nomos" is a Greek word meaning "law"). There are two types of covering-law explanations: deductive and inductive.[1]

## Deductive Explanations

Deductive explanations take the form of valid deductive arguments. They are the most powerful type of explanation because their conclusions must be true if their premises are true and because they explain individual as well as general events. Deductive explanations consist of two parts: the explanandum and the explanans.

The *explanandum* is the thing to be explained and is the conclusion of a deductive argument. The explanandum may be an individual event, such as the Japanese attack on Pearl Harbor, or a more general class of events, such as aggressive acts by nations toward other nations.

The *explanans* explains the explanandum. The explanandum is deduced from the explanans. The explanans are the premises, and the explanandum is the conclusion of a deductive argument. The explanans includes two types of statements: (1) a set of universal generalizations (the covering laws), and (2) a set of initial conditions (the particular facts of the situation). We diagram the deductive argument in standard form below:

| Form: Why does $E$ occur? | | |
|---|---|---|
| Explanans: | $uG_1, uG_2......uG_n$ | Universal Generalizations |
| | $C_1, C_2.............C_n$ | Initial Conditions |
| Explanandum: | $E$ | Event to be explained |

Universal generalizations are represented by the symbol $uG$ in the diagram. We will recall that they may take any of the following forms:

> "If $p$, then always $q$."
> "100% of $S$ are $P$."
> "If $p$, then never $q$."
> "0% of $S$ are $P$."

The initial conditions are represented by the symbol, $C$. They specify the circumstances or the facts of the immediate situation. They have the effect of affirming the antecedent condition of the covering law; therefore, they allow the explanandum to be deduced from the explanans. The deductive explanation is a valid argument because it takes the form of the conditional argument, affirming the antecedent, which is a valid form of inference:

|  | Deductive Argument: | Affirming the Antecedent: |
|---|---|---|
| Universal Generalization: | If $C$, then always $E$. | If $p$, then $q$. |
| Initial Conditions: | $C$ | $p$ |
| Explanandum: | $E$ | $q$ |

The structure of a deductive explanation may be illustrated by an example from the natural sciences:

Example: *Why* is this water boiling?

| uG: | If water is heated at sea level to 212 degrees F, then it always boils. |
|---|---|
| $C_1$: | This is water. |
| $C_2$: | The altitude is sea level. |
| $C_3$: | The water temperature is $212°F$. |
| $E$: | This water is boiling. |

The explanandum in this example is the occurrence of a particular event, the boiling of some water. This event is explained by deducing it from a covering law taking the form of a universal generalization and a set of initial conditions, which affirms the antecedent condition of the covering law.

Deductive explanation is very powerful. Since it is a valid form of deductive argumentation, the explanandum must be true if the explanans are true. Thus, we may explain with certainty both individual and general events if the covering laws and initial conditions are true.

Although they are a powerful form of explanation, deductive explanations have limited applicability to the social sciences at this time. Notice that even our example comes from the natural sciences. The reason for its limited utility is that it requires a universal generalization in the explanans, and the social sciences have few, if any, interesting universal generalizations at this time. Nevertheless, there are several reasons for studying deductive explanations. It is the ideal form of explanation. Our understanding of deductive explanations helps us to understand inductive explanations because the forms are similar in a number of respects. Furthermore, social scientists should not give up the search for universal generalizations. Some day deductive explanations may be feasible in some areas of the social sciences. Finally, deductive arguments and explanations are employed frequently by proponents of various causes and observers of social phenomena. Students should be able to challenge the validity as well as the truth of such arguments and explanations.

## LEARNING  AID

1.  The statement to be explained in a scientific explanation is called the _____.

2.  The statements doing the explaining in scientific explanations are called the _____.

3.  The explanans of deductive explanations consist of two types of statements: _____ and _____.

4.  Deductive explanation is a valid form of deductive reasoning taking the form of the conditional argument, _____.

5.  If the _____ of a deductive explanation are true, the _____ must be true.

6.  Diagram the standard form of the deductive explanation.

7.  Formulate a deductive explanation in standard form explaining, "Why did the Watergate participants adopt extralegal tactics against their opposition?" Use the following generalization in the explanans and assume that it is a universal generalization: "If political office holders fear and distrust their opposition, they always adopt extralegal tactics against their opposition."

8.  Formulate at least two other generalizations that are relevant to the explanation in the previous question and that we may assume are universal in form.

· · · · · · · · · · · · · · · · · · · · · · · · · · · · · · · · · · · · · · · · · · · · · · · · · · · · · ·

1.  Explanandum
2.  Explanans
3.  Universal generalizations (covering laws), initial conditions
4.  Affirming the antecedent
5.  Explanans, explanandum
6.  See standard form diagram of deductive explanations.
7.  Why do political office holders adopt extralegal tactics against their opposition?

> $uG_1$:  If political office holders fear and distrust their opposition, then they always adopt extralegal tactics against their opposition.
>
> $C_1$:  The Watergate participants were political office holders.

$C_2$:    The Watergate participants feared and distrusted their opposition.

E:     The Watergate participants adopted extralegal tactics against their opposition.

**8.** For example, recall Lord Acton's statement: "Absolute power corrupts absolutely." We might use this as the basis for a universal generalization: "If a party in office possesses an inordinate amount of resources and power relative to its opposition, then it always tends to adopt extralegal tactics against its opposition." Check your original generalizations with your classmates or your instructor.

## Inductive Explanations

Most explanations in the social sciences are inductive rather than deductive. Many of the explanations in the natural sciences are also inductive. Like deductive explanations, inductive explanations have an explanandum and explanans. Inductive explanations, however, contain statistical rather than universal generalizations in the explanans. The explanandum, therefore, cannot be deduced from the explanans with certainty. The explanandum is implied by the explanans as being probable. The explanans confers support or evidence for the explanandum but does not make the explanandum certain. The explanans could be true and the explanandum could still be false in inductive explanation.

Inductive explanations can explain either the probability of individual events or statistical generalizations. An inductive generalization explaining the probability of an individual event takes the following form:

| | Form: Why does $E$ occur? | |
|---|---|---|
| Explanans: | $sG_1, sG_2, \ldots sG_n$ | Statistical Generalizations |
| | $C_1, C_2, \ldots C_n$ | Initial Conditions |
| Explanandum: | $E$ (pr.) | Event |

where the double line indicates that $E$ is probable but not certain and "pr." indicates the probability of $E$.

The explanans contains at least one statistical generalization. A statistical generalization, we recall, asserts that if each member of a class has a certain characteristic, then a certain fraction or percentage of them will have another characteristic. Statistical generalizations take the following forms:

"If $p$, then the probability of $q$ is $N\%$."
"$N\%$ of $S$ are $P$."

Since the explanandum is derived from a statistical generalization, we cannot infer that a specific event will or will not occur. All we can infer is the probability of an event occurring. Here is an example of an inductive explanation that explains the probability of an individual event occurring:

Example: Why does John vote Democratic?

$sG_1$: If a person is black, then there is 90% probability of his voting Democratic.

$C_1$: John is black.

E: John votes Democratic (90% probable)

The inductive explanation provides good grounds for believing that John votes Democratic. Since 90% of blacks vote Democratic and since John is a black, we have strong grounds for believing John votes Democratic. But 10% of the blacks do not vote Democratic, so we cannot be certain that John votes Democratic. If John in fact does not vote Democratic, we commit the fallacy of statistical deduction, which is the error of deducing a false conclusion from statistical premises.

Inductive explanations can also explain statistical generalizations. When they explain statistical generalizations, they take the form of statistical syllogisms. From a set of statistical generalizations in the explanans, a statistical generalization is deduced in the explanandum. The deduction of the probability in the explanandum is derived by means of the mathematical theory of statistical probability and is too complex to be treated here. The statistical generalizations in the explanans imply the probability level of the statistical explanandum.

Form:

Why are $N\%$ of $S$'s also $P$'s?

$N\%$ of $S$ are $M$.
$N\%$ of $M$ are $P$.

$N\%$ of $S$ are $P$.

Example:

Why are $N\%$ of Catholics also liberals?

$N\%$ of Catholics are Democrats.
$N\%$ of Democrats are liberals.

$N\%$ of Catholics are liberals.

Whereas one negative event can falsify a deductive explanation, one negative event cannot falsify an inductive generalization. Deductive explanations employ universal generalizations, but inductive explanations employ statistical generalizations. To falsify an inductive explanation, a negative mass event, a high relative frequency of negative events (such as a high percentage of Catholics who are not liberals, not just one Catholic who is not liberal, is required).

We may now summarize the major differences between deductive and inductive explanations:

| *Deductive:* | *Inductive:* |
|---|---|
| 1. The explanans must contain at least one universal generalization. | 1. The explanans must contain at least one statistical generalization. |
| 2. The explanans make the explanandum certain. | 2. The explanans make the explanandum probable but not certain. |
| 3. One negative event can falsify the explanation. | 3. One negative event cannot falsify the explanation. A mass event with a high negative relative frequency is required to falsify it. |
| 4. It can explain the occurrence of individual and general events. | 4. It can explain the probability of the occurrence individual and general events. |

## LEARNING AID

**1.** Inductive explanations must contain at least one _____ generalization.

**2.** Diagram the standard form of an inductive explanation of an individual event.

**3.** In inductive explanations, the explanans make the explanandum _____ but not _____.

**4.** Inductive explanations may be falsified by (one, a relative frequency of) negative event(s).

**5.** Whereas deductive explanations explain individual and general events, inductive explanations explain the _____ of individual and general events.

**6.** Formulate an inductive explanation in standard form to explain why "Nation $X$ declared war on Nation $Y$." Use the following generalization in the explanation: "If nations possessing high military capability are attacked but not destroyed, they declare war 95% of the time."

**7.** Formulate an original explanation explaining why the American revolution occurred.

**8.** Summarize the differences between deductive and inductive explanations.

. . . . . . . . . . . . . . . . . . . . . . . . . . . . . . . . . . . . . . . . . . . . . . . . . . . . . .

**1.** Statistical

**2.** See the form in the text.

**3.** probable, certain

**4.** a relative frequency of

**5.** probability (relative frequency of)

**6.** $sG_1$:  If nations possessing high military capability are attacked but not destroyed, then they declare war 95% of the time.

$C_1$:  Nation $X$ possesses high military capability.

$C_2$:  Nation $X$ is attacked by Nation $Y$.

$C_3$:  Nation $X$ is not destroyed.

Nation $X$ declared war. (95% probable)

**7.** Check the form of the explanation with your classmates or instructor.

**8.** Check the text.

## Explanatory Completeness

Scientific explanations appearing in the social and natural science periodicals seldom are diagramed in standard form with the generalizations and initial conditions explicitly specified. They normally appear in paragraph form. This method of presentation is thought to contribute to the "readability" of the material. So long as the explanations in paragraph form can be reconstructed into standard form and the explanans logically implies the explanandum, there is no harm done. Many explanations expressed in paragraph style, however, conceal unspecified and untested generalizations or initial conditions. By reconstructing explanations in standard form, students learn to think more systematically about the content and form of the explanation.

Here is an explanation found in a social science journal explaining why blacks actually participate more actively than whites:

*If it is true, as suggested by Orum's work, that blacks actually tend to participate more actively than whites in a wide range of social and political activities, once the limiting effects of socioeconomic status (and possibly also age) have been removed, what theoretical interpretation can be given to this empirical generalization?*

*One line of reasoning is that . . . blacks attempts to compensate for the racial discrimination they encounter in many realms of social life by forming relationships and organizations among themselves, in which they can at least partially escape white racism. In Orum's words: "Since Negroes are deprived of the usual social and psychological satisfactions of everyday life, they are compelled to seek such satisfactions collectively through other means. Opportunities for association are restricted by explicit or tacit observance of segregation in public places of entertainment. The oppressive atmosphere of slum dwellings also does not offer a congenial environment for social activity. Quite naturally, then, clubs and associations become focuses for Negroes' social life."*[2]

The above explanation may be diagramed in the following standard form:

Example:  Why do blacks tend to participate more actively than whites when socioeconomic status and age are controlled?

$sG_1$:  If persons are deprived of social and psychological satisfactions of everyday life, then they tend to compensate by seeking satisfactions collectively through other means.

$sG_2$:  If opportunities for public association are restricted by discriminatory practices, then ethnic clubs and associations tend to be the center of social activity.

$C_1$:  Blacks are more deprived of social and psychological satisfactions than whites.

$C_2$:  Discriminatory practices have historically restricted blacks from opportunities for public association.

_____

$E$:  Blacks tend to participate more actively than whites when socioeconomic status and age are controlled.

Diagraming the above explanation shows the analyst that the statistical generalizations are quite clearly specified but that the initial conditions must be filled in. The analyst should ask if it is in fact true that blacks are more deprived of social and psychological satisfactions than whites and if discriminatory practices have historically restricted blacks from opportunities for public association. Diagraming also clarifies the logical relationship of the explanans to the explanandum. There are two statistical generalizations in the explanans and one in the explanandum. The analyst should ask if the generalizations in fact are true, if they are all necessary for the inference to the explanandum, if some generalizations are omitted but required for the inference, or if alternative

**Table 3-1 DEGREES OF EXPLANATORY COMPLETENESS**

| | Generalizations and Initial Conditions are: | |
| | *Totally Specified* | *Partially Specified* |
| --- | --- | --- |
| *Totally Known* | Complete Explanation | Elliptic Explanation |
| *Partially Known* | Partial Explanation | Explanation Sketch |

generalizations may yield the same inference. Thus, diagraming explanations stimulates further analysis of the phenomena to be explained.

Since explanations tend to vary in terms of their completeness it is useful to characterize the thoroughness with which an explanation is expressed.[3] Explanatory completeness is a function of two factors: (1) the extent to which all the relevant generalizations and initial conditions are known, and (2) the extent to which all the relevant generalizations and initial conditions are specified. For purposes of analyzing explanations, we may distinguish four degrees of explanatory completeness: (1) complete explanation, (2) elliptic explanation, (3) partial explanation, and (4) explanation sketch (See Table 3-1).

COMPLETE EXPLANATIONS

In complete explanations, all the relevant generalizations and initial conditions are known and all of them are specified. Complete explanations, in the strict sense, are virtually unattainable because it is normally impossible to determine whether all the relevant laws and facts are known. Complete explanations are scientific ideals.

ELLIPTIC EXPLANATIONS

In elliptic explanations, all the generalizations and initial conditions are known, but not all of them are specified. The writer assumes that the reader already knows them and does not mention them. This type of explanation is incomplete in a rather harmless sense because the explanation can easily be reconstructed with all the information specified. In explaining an automobile accident, for example, an elliptic explanation is usually provided. It is an abbreviated and simplified account omitting reference to many of the laws of physics, which are relevant to a complete explanation but which are assumed to be known by the person to whom the explanation is directed. If someone wants a more complete explanation, it is easy to supply him with the necessary generalizations and facts.

PARTIAL EXPLANATIONS

In partial explanations, not all the relevant generalizations and initial conditions are known, but the ones that are known are specified. The explanandum in a partial explanation usually appears to claim more than what appears in the explanans. Strictly speaking, the explanandum cannot be deduced from the explanans because relevant generalizations and facts are missing. Many social science explanations may be characterized as partial explanations.

EXPLANATION SKETCHES

Explanations sketches are the least complete form of explanation. All the relevant generalizations and conditions are not known. Some are hypothesized as being relevant and are specified in a rather crude sense. However, explanation sketches can be the beginnings of a more complete explanation. They postulate the general outlines of what might be gradually elaborated into a partial, elliptic, or complete explanation.

An analyst must use judgment in deciding which of the four types of explanatory completeness applies to a particular explanation. He must judge what is the intent of the account and what is left unstated because it is assumed rather than unknown. These categories, however, are useful for comparing the development of various explanations and thinking systematically about things to be explained.

## LEARNING AID

1. The following explanation attempts to explain why blacks participate more actively than whites. Construct it in standard form:

*"An alternative explanation, which might be termed the 'ethnic community thesis' . . . suggests that members of ethnic minorities—whether based on race, religion, or nationality—may become active in social and political affairs because of social pressures exerted upon them within their ethnic community to conform to the norms of that community. Members of such an ethnic community are often more aware of their common bonds, and hence are more socially cohesive, than are white Anglo-Saxon Protestants—largely because of discrimination by WASPs. As a consequence, their ethnic community serves as a salient reference group for them. If the norms of this community stress social and political activism, these people will tend to exert pressures (both informal and formal) upon one another to conform to these norms by taking part in a variety of activities aimed at improving their common conditions."[4]*

**2.**  Explanations in which all the relevant generalizations and initial conditions are known but are not specified are called _____.

**3.**  Explanations in which all the relevant generalizations and conditions are known and are specified are called _____.

**4.**  Explanations in which not all the relevant generalizations and initial conditions are known but in which all that are known are specified are called _____.

**5.**  It (is, is not) necessary for a complete explanation to be diagramed in standard form.

**6.**  Explanations in which relevant generalizations and initial conditions are unknown and those that are known are specified in a very crude and general manner are called _____.

. . . . . . . . . . . . . . . . . . . . . . . . . . . . . . . . . . . . . . . . . . . . . . . . . . .

**1.**  Why do blacks tend to participate more actively than whites?

$sG_1$:  If persons are members of an ethnic minority, they tend to conform to the norms of that reference group.

$sG_2$:  If the norms of an ethnic community stress social and political activism, then the members of the ethnic minority tend to exert pressures on one another to participate.

$C_1$:  Blacks are members of an ethnic minority.

$C_2$:  The norms of the black community stress social and political activism.

$E$:  Blacks are more likely to participate more actively than whites.

Notice that this explanation does not contain a generalization that states that the black community stresses participation norms more than the white community. The inference to E cannot be made unless this generalization is assumed. Again, this demonstrates the value of diagraming explanations by pointing out missing premises and facts.

**2.**  elliptic explanations

**3.**  complete explanations

**4.**  partial explanations

**5.**  is not

**6.**  explanation sketches

## COROLLARY EXPLANATIONS

Covering-law explanations account for events by subsuming them under generalizations and statements of initial conditions. Not all social science explanations, however, explicitly follow the covering-law model. Frequently mentioned alternative forms of explanations are genetic, rational, dispositional, and functional explanations. We shall examine the logic of each of these in their pure form. In reality social science explanations often contain elements of different types of explanation.

We shall maintain in this section that these four types of explanations either contain implicit reference to generalizations and initial conditions, which make them compatible with covering law explanations, or they are inadequately formulated accounts. Their explanatory power is, thus, a function of their correspondence to the requirements of covering-law explanations. Since their explanatory power derives from satisfying covering-law requirements, they are called corollary explanations.

## Genetic Explanations

Explanations that give the history of an event by presenting the phenomenon as the final stage of a developmental sequence are called *genetic explanations.*[5] They begin at the "genesis" with the most remote cause and proceed through the history of the event to the most proximate cause. They take the following form:

Form:

$e_1, e_2, e_3, e_4, e_5, \ldots \ldots E$

where $E$ is the event to be
explained and $e_1$ are events
preceeding $E$ in a time
sequence.

Genetic explanations usually, though not always, contain many more singular statements with proper names than general statements with common names. Although many historical aspects of an event are described, a complete description of the historical sequence is just as impossible as a complete covering-law explanation. Here is a genetic account of the making of a president in 1968:

*In 1968, it was as if the future waited on the first of each month to deliver events completely unforeseen the month before. Thus, on January 1st of 1968, no one could foresee the impact of the Tet offensive at the end of the month. On February 1st, no one could forecast the student invasion of New Hampshire or the withdrawal of George Romney. On March 1st, no one could forecast the entry of Robert Kennedy into the race, or Lyndon Johnson's withdrawal on March 31st. On April 1st, no one could foresee the assassination of Martin Luther King, or the riots that followed, or Rockefeller's entry into the race. On May 1st, no one could foresee Robert Kennedy's stunning victories in the primaries of Indiana and Nebraska, or his defeat in Oregon—or foretell the course of negotiations in Paris. On June 1st, no one could foresee the assassination of Robert Kennedy in Los Angeles. . . .* [6]

A description of the historical development of an event such as the one above undoubtedly improves our understanding, but it does not systematically explain the final event. A sequence of events by themselves no more explains why a candidate wins an election than a sequence of descriptions of your turning and reading of the pages explains why you are reading this book. A description of preceding events is a statement of particular facts. These are useful, but they must be supplemented with generalizations or laws to provide an adequate account of the final event. Genetic explanations, however, frequently do not make explicit the relevant generalizations. The events that form the historical sequence in genetic explanations are often selected on the basis of what the author assumes to cause the final event. Assumptions such as these are tacit generalizations.

A specification of these generalizations together with a description of the sequence of specific events provides an explanans that qualifies as a covering-law explanation. So, genetic explanations need not be fundamentally different from covering-law explanations. Adequate genetic explanations account for events by subsuming them under generalizations and statements of specific facts. Each of the events in Theodore White's account of the 1968 election, for example, may be an instance of some generalization. The Tet offensive may be an instance of the proposition that when parties in office lose decisive military battles they tend to lose votes in the next election. Kennedy's assassination or LBJ's withdrawal may constitute the generalization that when front-running candidates withdraw from the campaign their opponents tend to benefit. If genetic explanations are able to be formulated in a covering-law form, they constitute a proper and valid form of explanation.

## Rational Explanations

Explanations of the actions of persons or groups by taking into account the agent's calculation of the means available in a situation for the attainment of his objectives are called *rational explanations*. They explain actions by listing the reasons that motivate an agent to act. Mathematical theories of decision making and other models of rational choice are often rational explanations of behavior. These theories explain an agent's behavior by calculating the utilities or payoffs under different conditions. Rational explanation is also prevalent in foreign policy analysis where the actions of a state or a decision maker are explained by reasons or motives assumed to act on the agent in certain circumstances. Here is an example of a rational explanation of America's Cold War containment policy:

*. . . the rationale for a containment strategy identified through application of the key variables indicated above illustrates analysis from a strategic perspective. The breakdown of the wartime alliance between the United States and the Soviet Union and the transformation of the relationship from partnership to conflict are interpreted primarily as the logical pursuit of self-interest of each party, which, after the defeat of Germany, made continued partnership more costly than desirable. A growing belief on the part of American policy makers that the Soviets would not, in any event, adhere to the pacts of postwar cooperation that had been signed in the waning months of the war contributed to the feeling that the United States must pursue a vigorous policy of containment of Communist expansion. The strategy of the Soviets seems to most American policy makers to be based upon the assumption that conflict between the two systems was inevitable and that continual probing and exploitation of weak spots in the West was a fruitful means of expanding the domain of communism. The appropriate response to such a strategy seemed to meet pressure with counter-pressure—to yield nowhere, thereby convincing the Soviets that they must adopt a more moderate position.[7]*

Rational explanations, like genetic explanations, contain tacit generalizations and can be reconstructed in the form of a covering-law explanation:

---

Form: Why did $A$ do $X$?

$sG_1$:    If any rational agent is in a situation of type $C$, he tends to do $X$.

$C_1$:    $A$ was in a situation of type $C$.

$C_2$:    $A$ is a rational agent.

$E$:    Therefore, $A$ did $X$.

---

The example that explains America's containment policy may be reconstructed in the following covering law form:

Example: Why did the United States adopt the policy of Soviet containment?

$sG_1$: If a nation perceives its self-interest is pursued by breaking up a partnership with another nation, it will break up the partnership.

$sG_2$: If the decision makers of a nation perceive that an expansionist nation will not adhere to its agreements, they tend to adopt a policy of expansionist containment.

$sG_3$: If the decision makers of a nation perceive the strategy of an expansionist nation to be to continue expanding at the expense of the nonexpansionist nation, the decision makers tend to respond with counterpressure in the form of adopting a containment policy.

$sG_4$: If rational decision makers are in the above situation ($sG_1$, $sG_2$, $sG_3$), they tend to adopt a containment policy.

$C_1$: The Soviet Union perceived its self-interest was pursued by breaking its partnership with the United States.

$C_2$: American decision makers perceived that the Soviets would not adhere to their agreements.

$C_3$: American decision makers perceived that the Soviets would continue their expansion at American cost.

$C_4$: American decision makers were rational.

$E$: Therefore, American decision makers adopted the policy of Soviet containment.

The reconstructed form of this rational explanation illustrates its covering-law character. An event is explained by subsuming it under a set of generalizations and a set of specific facts. The weaknesses of many rational explanations are twofold. First, the generalizations are often hypothesized rather than confirmed regularities. To the extent that the generalizations are untested, rational explanations are conjectures. Second, they often assume that the required initial conditions obtain without independent evidence. By reconstructing rational explanations in covering-law form, we can see which premises are missing and which are weakened by lack of corroborating evidence.

## Dispositional Explanations

Dispositions are tendencies to behave in certain ways. Some people tend to be authoritarian, civic-minded, Machiavellian, conservative, isolationist, extroverted, or violent. Other persons may display the opposite tendencies. Social scientists frequently use such orientations to explain why people behave as they do. Explanations of behavior that take into account the ways (e.g., personality traits, attitudes, beliefs) persons tend to behave are called *dispositional explanations*.[8]

Dispositional explanations can be reconstructed in covering-law form:

---

Form:  Why did this object behave in manner $B$?

$sG_1$:  If an object has the disposition $D$ and is in the situation $S$, then it tends to behave in manner $B$.

$C_1$:  This object has the disposition $D$.

$C_2$:  This object is in the situation $S$.

$E$:  This object behaved in manner $B$.

---

The U.S. Riot Commission Report on civil disorders provides an illustration of a dispositional explanation.[9] It attempts to explain why riots occurred in the ghettos during 1967. The account is too long to portray here, but we may see how it can be interpreted within the covering-law framework:

Example:  Why did blacks riot in 1967?

$sG_1$:  If people have the feelings of frustrated hopes, powerlessness, and the legitimacy of violence and are in the situation of pervasive discrimination, minority migration and majority exodus, and racial ghettos, then they tend to riot.

$C_1$:  In 1967 blacks in the urban ghettos had feelings of frustrated hopes $(D_1)$, powerlessness $(D_2)$, and the legitimacy of violence $(D_3)$.

$C_2$:  In 1967 blacks were in the situation of pervasive discrimination $(S_1)$, black migration and white exodus $(S_2)$, and the formation of black ghettos $(S_3)$.

$E$:  Blacks rioted in 1967.

By translating dispositional explanation into the covering law form, we can see what generalizations in fact are being invoked and whether the dispositions and situations ascribed to the objects of the explanation actually hold.

## Functional Explanations

Explanations of recurrent activities or behavior patterns that take into account their role in maintaining a system or bringing about a goal are called *functional explanations.*[10] Functional explanations attempt to account for some recurrent behavior $B$ in a system $S$. Functional analysis shows that $S$ requires certain conditions $C$ to remain in adequate working order and that behavior $B$ has effects that satisfy $C$. Behavior $B$, therefore, satisfies a need or a functional requirement of system $S$. Adequately formulated functional explanations may be translated in the following form:

Form: Why is behavior $B$ present in system S?

| | |
|---|---|
| $G_1$: | If behavior $B$ is present in system $S$, then condition $C$ is satisfied. |
| $G_2$: | If $C$ is satisfied, then $S$ functions adequately. |
| $C_1$: | $S$ functions adequately. |
| | |
| $E$: | Behavior $B$ is present in system $S$. |

Example 1: Why is there a heartbeat present in this body?

$G_1$: If heartbeats are present in bodies, then blood circulates and other necessary conditions are satisfied.

$G_2$: If blood circulates and other necessary conditions are satisfied, then a body functions adequately.

$C_1$: This body functions adequately.

$E$: A heartbeat is present in this body.

We may now turn to a functional analysis of political opinion holding:

*An adolescent develops a violent hatred for Fascism, the Nazis, and for Hitler, particularly during the 1930s. Although he is not accepted because of his age, he is aroused to the point of volunteering for the Abraham Lincoln Brigade during the Spanish Civil War. Upon entry of the United States into the War, he volunteers, is rejected, but flings himself into a lather of civilian war activity from which he derives a deep satisfaction.*

*Whence the tremendous intensity of this attitude? Leaving aside the realities of the situation, the grave threat with which Fascism did in fact confront the world and which our subject sensed, why was there such an extraordinarily intense compulsion to do something about his feelings? Analysis reveals in this man a strong and unresolved fear of rejection by powerful figures who can be reached neither through their sympathies nor through their intellect: the figure of an inchoate, powerful, cruel, but basically unreachable force. We need not examine the genesis of this deeply repressed fear. It suffices that it existed. The emergence of Hitler and the Nazis served for the adolescent as a concretization or "binding" for this fearsome and rejecting figure. Hitler in a unique way*

*could serve as the apotheosis of that figure which could be reached neither by
sympathy nor by reason. Energies previously directed at coping with the inner
problem could now be liberated and focused on an external object. If anxiety
could thereby be reduced, so much the better.*[11]

We can try to construct the preceeding explanation in standard form:

Example 2:    Why are antifascist attitudes and behaviors
present in this adolescent?

$G_1$:    If antifascist attitudes and behaviors ($B$) are present in this adolescent
($S$), then he can attack powerful figures.

$G_2$:    If he ($S$) attacks powerful figures, his anxiety over fear of rejection by
powerful leaders is reduced ($C$).

$G_3$:    If his anxiety ($C$) is reduced, he ($S$) functions adequately.

$C_1$:    He now functions adequately.

_____

$E$:    Antifascist attitudes and behaviors are present in this adolescent. (S)

The student should notice that a functional explanation takes a different
logical form from the covering-law explanation. Whereas covering-law explanations take the form of affirming the antecedent conditional arguments, functional explanations take the form of extended affirming the consequent conditional arguments. We recall that the latter form is potentially a fallacy. In a
functional argument, the last premise affirms the consequent of the previous
premise, and the antecedent of the first premise is ultimately inferred. (If $B$,
then $C$; if $C$, then $S$; $S$, therefore, $B$.) The problem with affirming the consequent is that there may be alternative events that may cause $B$. Recall the
example: If it rains, the streets get wet; the streets are wet; therefore, it rained.
There are what functionalists call, "functional equivalents" to rain or to the
antifascist behavior. The adolescent may have been able to reduce his anxiety
by means other than be exhibiting antifascist opinions and behavior. This need
may have been satisfied through other religious, political, social, or business in-
volvements. Thus, inferring $B$ in a functional explanation can be risky. All we
can infer legitimately is $B$ *or* some functional equivalent.

Functional explanations occur frequently in political science, and many are
poorly constructed. Often the generalizations that "$B$ satisfies $C$" and that "$C$
is necessary for $S$" are not clearly specified and are not based on firm empirical
findings. Also, many functional terms are not defined specifically enough so
that they can be employed in testable statements. For example, what is meant
by the statement, "$S$ functions adequately"? Finally, many functional explanations neglect mention of the alternative behaviors or functional equivalents that

could satisfy condition $C$ and go ahead to infer $B$ and only $B$. When functional explanations are formed in such a manner, they claim more in the conclusion than what can be justified logically in the premises.

## LEARNING AID

**1.** Explanations that give the history of an event by presenting the phenomenon as the final stage of a developmental sequence are called _____ explanations.

**2.** Explanations of recurrent activities or behavior patterns by taking into account the role they play in maintaining a system or bringing about a goal are called _____ explanations.

**3.** Explanations of the actions of persons or groups by taking into account the agent's calculation of the means available in a situation for the attainment of his objectives are called _____ explanations.

**4.** Explanations of behavior that take into account the ways persons tend to behave are called _____ explanations.

**5.–8.** Diagram the forms of genetic, rational, dispositional, and functional explanations.

**9.** Adequate genetic explanations account for events by subsuming them under _____ and statements of _____.

**10.** Adequate rational explanations can be translated into the form of _____ explanations.

**11.** Functional explanations take the form of the conditional argument called _____, a form of (valid, invalid) argument.

**12.** Inferring the behavior pattern $B$ in a functional explanation can be risky. All that can be legitimately inferred is $B$ or some functional _____.

. . . . . . . . . . . . . . . . . . . . . . . . . . . . . . . . . . . . . . . . . . . . . . . . . . . . . . . . . . . .

**1.** genetic
**2.** functional
**3.** rational
**4.** dispositional
**5.** See the diagrams in the text.
**9.** generalizations (laws), initial conditions (specific facts)
**10.** covering law
**11.** affirming the consequent, invalid
**12.** equivalent

## SCIENTIFIC PREDICTIONS

### Definition

Predictions are answers to questions that ask about what will occur in the future. Along with explanation, prediction is a basic goal of science. Prediction is one rough measure of the scientific development of a discipline. Predicting the empirical consequences of a theory is a strong test of the theory's adequacy. Prediction enables us to apply the knowledge of social science to the solving of practical social and political problems. It enables us to anticipate and perhaps avert negative events that might occur in the future. It gives us some lead time to change social processes that may lead to catastrophic consequences. For these reasons, social scientists seek more reliable predictions of social and political phenomena.

### Form

Predictions are structurally identical with explanations.[12] Predictions have covering laws and initial conditions as do explanations. The only difference is that in explanations the conclusion has already occurred and the explanans are sought, but in predictions the explanans are given and the conclusion is sought. Thus, every adequate explanation is potentially a prediction, and every adequate prediction is potentially an explanation. Later we will try to understand the practical effects of being able to explain but not predict or being able to predict but not explain. Now, however, we shall examine the form that predictions take:

| | Form: Will $E$ occur? | |
|---|---|---|
| Explanans: | $G_1, G_2, G_3, \ldots \ldots G_n$ | Generalizations |
| | $C_1, C_2, C_3, \ldots \ldots C_n$ | Initial Conditions |
| Explanandum: | $E$ | Event to be Predicted |

When the covering-law generalizations are universal, predictions about individual events can be made:

Example: Will this water boil?

$uG_1$: If water is heated at sea level to 212 degrees F, then it will boil.

$C_1$:     This is water.
$C_2$:     The altitude is sea level.
$C_3$:     The water is heated to 212 degrees F.

$E$:       The water will boil.

In universal law prediction, the event to be predicted is deduced from the universal generalization and a set of particular facts called the initial conditions. Since universal generalizations are rarely found in the social sciences, few predictions take the universal covering-law form. Predictions in the social sciences are usually inferred from statistical generalizations and sets of initial conditions. Statistical predictions do not predict individual events; they predict the probability of an individual event occurring, the relative frequency of an event occurring in a class of events. Just as one negative event does not falsify an inductive explanation, one negative event does not falsify a statistical law prediction. It is not an individual event that can falsify a prediction; it is a relative frequency of an event occurring in a class of events that falsifies a statistical prediction.

Example:   Will John Doe vote Democratic?

$sG_1$:    If a person is black, then there is a 90% probability that he will vote Democratic.
$C_1$:     John Doe is black.

$E$:     John Doe will vote Democratic (90% probable)

Notice that predictions are potential explanations. If we want to explain why John Doe voted Democratic, we already have the relevant set of generalizations and initial conditions to infer the event to be explained.

## Predictions and Explanations

If predictions are structurally identical with explanations, then we might ask why we can sometimes explain something without being able to predict it or predict something without being able to explain it. The answer is that relevant information in the explanans is missing. An example of explanation without prediction is the present ability to explain but not predict the occurrence of earthquakes. The relevant laws and initial conditions that explain the occurrence of earthquakes are known, but current technology cannot detect when the initial conditions are present. Until instruments are developed that can accurately measure conditions far below the surface of the earth, it is impossible to know when the initial conditions obtain and, therefore, when to expect the occurrence of the event. If this information were available, the occurrence of earthquakes could be predicted.

The opposite situation of prediction without explanation also occurs. This is also a result of a lack of relevant information in the explanans. The statistical prediction of election results is far better than the explanation of them. We can predict the probability of pregnancy for women using IUDs (intrauterine devices), but scientists are not certain why they work. The prediction of the probability of the occurrence of cancer is far better than any explanation of why cancer occurs. Prediction without explanation occurs when only some of the initial conditions are known but none of the relevant laws are known. If some of the initial conditions are related to the occurrence of an event, then a correlation between some of the initial conditions and an event can be observed. For example, scientists have noted a correlation between smoking and lung cancer. This correlation enables the statistical prediction of lung cancer on the basis of knowledge of some of the initial conditions, which are used as indicators of the remaining unknown initial conditions and laws. But this prediction is not an informed or complete scientific prediction. Still unknown are what laws and initial conditions are necessary to infer the explanandum. When these laws and the remaining initial conditions are discovered, the event can be explained as well as predicted.

## LEARNING AID

1. Predictions are structurally (different from, identical with) explanations.
2. Diagram the standard form of a prediction.
3. Predictions based on statistical laws can be falsified only by (one negative event, a high relative frequency of negative events).
4. Formulate a sketch of a prediction in standard form of whether the next presidential election will be won by the Democrats or the Republicans.
5. When we are able to explain but not predict, we frequently lack information about the (relevant laws, presence of the initial conditions, explanandum).
6. When we can predict but not explain, we frequently lack information about (all the laws, all the initial conditions, some of the initial conditions and all the laws, all the initial conditions and some of the laws).

. . . . . . . . . . . . . . . . . . . . . . . . . . . . . . . . . . . . . . . . . . . . . . . . . . . . . . . .

1. identical with
2. See text.
3. a high relative frequency of negative events

4. Check with your classmates or instructor. Here is an example:

Will the Democrats or the Republicans win in 1976?

$sG_1$: If a party is in office for eight years, the opposition party tends to win the next election.

$sG_2$: If a party in office suffers a major scandal, it tends to lose at the next election.

$sG_3$: If a party has more registered voters than another party, it tends to win the election.

$C_1$: The Republican party has been in office for eight years.

$C_2$: The Republican party suffered the Watergate scandal.

$C_3$: The Democratic party has more registered voters than the Republican party.

$E$: The Democratic party will win the election in 1976 (probably)

5. presence of the initial conditions.
6. some of the initial conditions and all of the laws.

## FOOTNOTES

1. See Carl Hempel, *Aspects of Scientific Explanation* (New York: Free Press, 1965), pp. 333–411; and Carl Hempel, *Philosophy of Natural Science* (Englewood Cliffs, N.J.: Prentice-Hall, 1966), pp. 47–69.
2. Marvin Olsen, "Social and Political Participation of Blacks," *American Sociological Review* 35 (August, 1970): 683–84.
3. Carl Hempel, *Aspects of Scientific Explanation*, pp. 415–24.
4. Olsen, "Social and Political Participation of Blacks," p. 684.
5. Hempel, *Aspects of Scientific Explanation*, pp. 447–53; Ernest Nagel, *The Structure of Science* (New York: Harcourt, Brace & World, 1961), pp. 25–26; and Robert Brown, *Explanation in Social Science* (Chicago: Aldine, 1963), pp. 47–57.
6. Theodore H. White, *The Making of the President: 1968* (New York: Pocket Books, 1970), back cover page.
7. John Lovell, *Foreign Policy in Perspective* (New York: Holt, Rinehart & Winston, 1970), p. 98.
8. Hempel, *Aspects of Scientific Explanation*, pp. 457–63; Brown, *Explanation in Social Science*, pp. 75–98.
9. U.S. Riot Commission, *Report of the National Advisory Commission on Civil Disorders* (New York: Bantam Books, 1968), pp. 203–4.
10. Hempel, *Aspects of Scientific Explanation*, pp. 297–330; Nagel, *Structure of Science*, pp. 23–25; and Brown, *Explanation in Social Science*, pp. 109–32.
11. Smith, J. Bruner, and R. White, *Opinions and Personality* (New York: John Wiley & Sons, 1964), pp. 43–44.
12. Carl Hempel, *Aspects of Scientific Explanation*, pp. 364–76; A. Kaplan, *The Conduct of Inquiry* (San Francisco: Chandler, 1964), pp. 346–51.

# 4
# Problem Formulation

# INTRODUCTION

## Rationale

All scientific investigation begins with asking a question. It proceeds from one answer to the asking of more fundamental questions. Question posing challenges us to learn, to explain, to predict, to experiment, to observe, and to advance the limits of our knowledge.

The formulation of a question is perhaps the most critical and difficult decision an investigator makes in the course of his inquiry. The selection and the formulation of the research problem affects all subsequent research activities. It is the foundation for the house of inquiry. If the inquiry is based on a weak foundation, it surely will not stand for long. Discovering a significant question to ask is both an exciting and taxing intellectual activity. The precise phrasing of the question also requires careful consideration. This unit focuses on basic principles of problem formulation and analysis.

## Learning Objectives

After completing this unit, the student should be able to:

1. Name the conditions affecting the discovery of scientific problems.

2. Define and identify empirical, analytic, and normative problems.

3. Reformulate normative problems into empirical problems by changing the frame of reference and by changing to the if–then form.

4. Define and identify the concepts of ethical naturalism, ethical nonnaturalism, and the naturalistic fallacy.

5. Name, define, and identify the types of empirical problems.

6. Name and explain the criteria for adequate problem formulation.

7. Distinguish adequate/inadequate problem formulations.

8. Reformulate inadequate problems.

9. Formulate an original political research problem.

## THE PROBLEMATIC BASIS OF SCIENCE

Systematic investigation begins with the formulation of a problem. Sometimes posing significant questions can be a very difficult task. Although the process of finding significant problems is not altogether known, it appears to be related to perceiving inconsistencies within a theory, between theories, or between theories and observations.[1]

## Inconsistencies Within Theories

Just as inconsistencies within the testimony of a witness raise new questions in the mind of a lawyer, inconsistencies in the Ptolemaic system of astronomy, which was based on the assumption that the sun revolves around the earth, raised new questions in the mind of Copernicus, who developed a theory that replaced the Ptolemaic system. Thus, inconsistencies within a theory may suggest problems involving the reformulation of theories.

## Inconsistencies Between Theories

Learning theory and cognitive dissonance theory provide inconsistent predictions with respect to behavior change. Whereas learning theory suggests that the more a discrepant response is reinforced the more likely it is to recur, cognitive dissonance theory predicts that the less a discrepant response is reinforced the more dissonance is created and the more likely it will recur. This contradictory expectation implies conducting crucial tests to determine which theory is false or reformulating a theory. So, inconsistences between theories often are the problems scientists select for study.

## Inconsistencies Between Theories and Observations

Classical democratic theory was built on the assumption of an interested, informed, and active citizenry. With the development of scientific public opinion polls, social scientists have observed that most citizens' involvement in politics is more peripheral, uninformed, and passive than what the theory assumed. The inconsistencies between the theory and the observations have caused some social scientists to reformulate democratic theory.

Marxist theory predicted that capitalism would destroy itself in a short period of time. Lenin, however, observed that capitalism continued to grow. The inconsistency between the theory and the observation led Lenin to formulate his theory of imperialism to explain why capitalism had not consumed itself.

Scientific revolutions are made out of such problems, anomalies, and puzzles that we have been considering.[2] Emerson once said, "A foolish inconsistency is the hobgoblin of little minds." We may rephrase this thought to state that, "An important inconsistency is the concern of great minds."

Science not only starts with problems, but it proceeds from such problems to new problems, problems of ever-increasing depth. A problem that is solved only raises a newer, deeper problem. The solution of this problem in turn raises even more fundamental questions.

The spirit of this process may be reflected to some extent in David Mc-Clelland's inquiry into achievement motivation.[3] McClelland initially asks why nations rise and fall. He theorizes that the rise and fall of nations are directly related to their economic development and that differences between nations in economic development may be explained by differences in achievement motivation. What causes differences in achievement motivation? He finds differences in child-rearing practices affect differences in achievement motivation. What causes differences in child-rearing practices? Differences in self-reliance values. What produced differences in self-reliance values? The Protestant Reformation caused a separation from the Church and the emphasis on self-reliance rather than dependency. McClelland traces the relationship of self-reliance values (working hard, saving money, reinvesting, and so on) to socialization practices emphasizing early independence training in children to the development of high achievement motivation, which directly affects the productive capability of nations. The establishment of each link in the chain suggests for McClelland a new and deeper problem requiring resolution. Thus, science proceeds from problems to new problems, problems of ever-increasing depth.

## LEARNING AID

1. Systematic investigation begins with (theories, hypotheses, problems, concepts).
2. Name the three conditions affecting the discovery of scientific problems.
3. Science proceeds from problems to newer, more fundamental

——————.

. . . . . . . . . . . . . . . . . . . . . . . . . . . . . . . . . . . . . . . . . . . . . . . . . . . . . . . . . . . . . . . . . . . .

1. problems
2. inconsistencies within theories, inconsistencies between theories, and inconsistencies between theories and observations.
3. problems.

## TYPES OF PROBLEMS

Social scientists distinguish three types of problems: empirical, analytic, and normative.[4] They differ in content, form, and method of verification.

### Empirical Problems

*Empirical problems* are questions whose answers depend on sense experience.

Examples:   1.   Are all bachelors young men?
2.   Are all democracies industrialized nations?
3.   Is political instability related to political inequality?

The answers to questions such as these are true or false according to their correspondence to the way the world is, to sense experience. To determine, for example, whether all bachelors are young men, investigators observe the correlation of instances of being a bachelor and instances of being young. Similarly, instances of democracies are observed with instances of industrialization to determine whether all democracies are industrialized nations. Social scientists as "scientists" are concerned with empirical problems, questions whose answers depend on sense experience for their verification.

### Analytic Problems

*Analytic problems* are questions whose answers depend on the meaning of the words in the sentences expressing them. In analytic statements, the predicate merely repeats the subject of the sentence. Analytic statements are definitional, not empirical. Thus, analytical problems are essentially language and conceptual problems, not factual and scientific problems. The answers to analytic questions do not depend on the way the world is; they depend on the definition of the words in the sentences that express them. A statement may be identified as analytic by negating it. If negating the statement results in a self-contradiction, then the statement is analytic and definitional.

Examples:   1.   Are all bachelors unmarried men?
2.   Are all democracies democratic governments?
3.   Is political instability related to political change?

To state that bachelors are unmarried men is to make an analytic statement. Bachelors are by definition unmarried men. The predicate merely restates the subject of the sentence. By negating the sentence, "Bachelors are not unmarried men," we arrive at a self-contradiction and thus an analytic statement. To confirm that bachelors are unmarried men, we do not need to refer to sense experience. The confirmation resides in the use of words. The problem is definitional and analytic, not empirical.

Scientists must be careful to distinguish analytic from empirical statements. Asking whether democracies are democratic governments is obviously asking an analytic question. It would be silly to look for confirmation for such a statement by referring to sense experience. Our language, however, makes some distinctions difficult to make. Asking whether political instability is related to political change may pose such an ambiguity. If "political change" merely repeats the concept of "political instability," then the statement is clearly analytic. It would be foolish to try to verify it by observing the correlation of political instability with political change; they would be perfectly correlated, not because one causes the other, but because they are one and the same thing. If "political change" means something like policy change and if "political instability" refers to change in officeholders, then the subject refers to something quite different from the predicate, and the negation of the statement would not be self-contradictory. Thus, the statement is empirical and not analytic. The appropriate method of verification is sense experience, not semantics.

## Normative Problems

*Normative problems* are questions whose answers depend primarily on value judgments. Value judgments are statements of what is desirable, preferred, moral, imperative, or obligatory. Normative problems may take either an evaluative or prescriptive form. The distinction is presented more clearly in statement rather than question form.

*Evaluative statements* are personal assertions of whether things are preferred, moral, or good.

Examples:   1.   All bachelors are evil.
2.   Democracies are better than dictatorships.
3.   Justice is more important than law and order.

The meaning of evaluative statements is not derived from sense experience. Evil is not a characteristic of common sense experience; it is an expression of an attitude on the part of a perceiver. Similarly, the words "better" and "more important" in the second and third examples are not something that everybody can experience. Evaluations such as these are mentalistic assessments of objects. They are not verifiable by sense experience.

The meaning of evaluative statements is also not derivable from the use of words. These sentences are not analytic, because "evil" is not part of the meaning of "bachelor". Evaluative statements depend primarily on value judgments for their meaning.

*Prescriptive statements* are expressions of imperatives, actions that "should" or "ought" to be taken.

Examples:   1.   All bachelors ought to get married.
2.   Adopt a national health care plan!
3.   All governments should be democratic.

Claims such as these are not verifiable by appealing solely to sense experience. Although experience may indicate what tends to happen if people do or do not get married, the prescription to get married is not derivable from sense experience. This simply is an expression of an attitude that marriage is good and that bachelors ought to get married.

Prescriptive statements are also distinguishable from analytic statements. Each of the above statements can be negated without having a self-contradiction. So, prescriptive statements do not depend primarily on the definition of their words for their meaning. Prescriptive statements are justified by appealing to value judgments about what is desirable, moral, or obligatory.

## LEARNING AID

1. Analytic problems are questions whose answers depend on _____.
2. Normative problems are questions whose answers depend primarily on

_____.

3. Empirical problems are questions whose answers depend on

_____.

4. Prescriptive statements are expressions of _____, actions that "should" or "ought" to be taken.
5. Evaluative statements are personal assertions of whether things are _____, _____, or _____.
6. If the negation of a statement results in a self-contradiction, then the statement is _____.
7. To say that a triangle is not a three-sided enclosed figure is to state a _____ and, therefore, a _____ statement.
8. Identify whether the following problems are empirical, analytic, or normative:

    a. Is it the duty of citizens to participate in civic affairs?
    b. Is participation in civic affairs a norm of the American political culture?
    c. Is political efficacy the feeling of having an impact on the political process?
    d. What is the impact of education on voting turnout?
    e. Is ethnic solidarity ethnic power?
    f. What effect does ethnic solidarity have on ethnic power?
    g. Should might make right?
    h. Is it obligatory to disobey illegitimate authority?
    i. Does the American Declaration of Independence specify the rights to life, liberty, and the pursuit of happiness?

j.  Ought all Americans have the right of life, liberty, and the pursuit of happiness?
k.  Are liberals more favorable to social change than conservatives?
l.  Is it better for things to change or to stay the same?
m.  Is authority a hierarchical relationship?

. . . . . . . . . . . . . . . . . . . . . . . . . . . . . . . . . . . . . . . . . . . . . . . . . . . . . . . . . . . . . . . .

1.  the meaning of words in the sentences expressing them
2.  value judgments
3.  sense experience
4.  imperatives
5.  preferred, moral, or good
6.  analytic
7.  self-contradiction, analytic
8.  (a) N, (b) E, (c) A, (d) *E,* (e) A, (f) E, (g) N, (h) N, (i) E, (j) N, (k) E, (l) N, (m) A


# THE EMPIRICAL REFORMULAIION OF NORMATIVE PROBLEMS

Normative analysis has always played an important role in social and political thinking. From the time when Plato, St. Augustine, Hobbes, and Rousseau conceived alternative plans for the moral and good body politic to the present attempts among policy scientists to create alternative futures, social and political thinkers have expressed their value judgments about what is politically desirable, moral, and obligatory. Important aspects of such theories are descriptive statements about the nature of man and about societal relationships. These parts are amenable to empirical analysis. The application of sense experience to these descriptive statements tests the validity of assumptions on which normative judgments are based.

By reformulating normative problems, the normative analyst can often gain further empirical information that will be relevant to the value judgment he must ultimately make. For example, a normative problem may ask whether democracies are better than dictatorships. A philosopher may simply say "yes" and justify it on the grounds of his preference for popular control of government. The problem, however, has an empirical side to it. The philosopher might have asked: What are the empirical consequences of the two types of political systems. Is press censorship greater under one form or the other? Is party competition more lively under one than the other? Do dictatorships experience more political crimes than democracies? Answers to such questions can be determined empirically. By reformulating normative problems, a broader range of relevant information can often be generated. The analyst may then value one set of consequences more highly than the other and determine which form is "better." Problem reformulation does not take the value judgment out of normative analysis; it merely broadens the scope of relevant information on which an evaluative or prescriptive statement is partially based. The two basic ways of reformulating normative problems are to change the frame of reference or to change the form of the problem.

## Reformulation by Changing the Frame of Reference

Some normative statements can be reformulated to provide relevant information by identifying the source of the value judgment. By changing the frame of reference of a normative statement, an argument from authority can often provide support for a statement. The frame of reference can be changed to what some people, most people, or particular authorities believe about the statement. Examples:

|  | Original form: | Reformulated form: |
|---|---|---|
| a. | Evaluative: "Totalitarian dictatorships are bad." | "Most people (or the philosopher, Rousseau) think(s) totalitarian dictatorships are bad." |
| b. | Prescriptive: "Adopt a national health care plan." | "Most citizens favor a national health care plan." |

Although reformulation does not solve the problem of making value judgments, it does provide relevant information. For example, knowing the popular support for a national health care plan may affect the extent to which it is imperative that one be adopted.

## Reformulation by the If–Then Form

A second method of reformulating normative problems is to translate them into an if–then sentence form. The connection between the "if" and the "then" clauses can be empirically tested, similar to the testing of a means–end relationship. Examples:

|  | Original form: | Reformulated form: |
|---|---|---|
| a. | Evaluative: "Totalitarian dictatorships are bad." | "If governments are totalitarian dictatorships, then a higher proportion of the people are arrested for political crimes." |

b.  Prescriptive: "Adopt a national health care plan."

"If a country adopts a national health care plan, then the health condition of its citizens improves."

If–then reformulation involves translating a value term such as "bad" into a set of factual approximations. One such approximation of "bad" perhaps may be a high proportion of political crimes. This is something that can be observed and correlated with instances of totalitarian dictatorships. The reformulation thus provides some specific information that may help the normative analyst in making a value judgment.

To prescribe the adoption of a health care plan is equivalent to saying that "if" one is adopted "then" something good will result. When the consequence is translated into an empirical approximation, it can be observed and correlated with instances of national health care plans. Then the normative analyst can determine if the prescription is an effective means to another end, the improvement of the health condition of the citizens of the country.

## Ethical Naturalism and the Naturalistic Fallacy

We have seen that science can contribute a great deal to normative problem solving. Empirical knowledge may help to predict the consequences of alternative actions, evaluations, and prescriptions. Normative analysis, on the other hand, assists the scientist in clarifying the value assumptions and implications of his research activities. We shall now examine some assumptions and pitfalls of normative problem reformulation.

We must be careful not to overstate the value of reformulating normative problems in terms of factual approximations. Sometimes the reformulation errs by going astray from the original normative problem. Sometimes the reformulation errs by suggesting that value judgments can be made and justified solely in terms of empirical evidence. These are clearly errors that should be avoided by political analysts. Normative problem reformulation, as we previously emphasized, does not allow the analyst to escape from making value judgments. It merely provides more empirical evidence on which he can make an informed judgment.

Philosophers call the practice of reformulating normative problems in terms of factual approximations "ethical naturalism." Stated in its extreme form, *ethical naturalism* maintains that all ethical sentences (statements that contain "should," "ought," "good," "right," and other such ethical terms) are translatable without loss of meaning into nonethical ones. Naturalistic theories, in other words, maintain that ethical and value judgments can be justified simply as ordinary factual statements. They claim that "values" can be defined in terms of "facts" and that "oughts" can be defined in terms of "is's."

Some philosophers rightfully reacted against some of the errors and excesses that many normative problem reformulators fell into. Opponents of ethical naturalism accused them of committing the *naturalistic fallacy,* which involves identifying ethical or value judgments with factual judgments. Ethical nonnaturalists, as they call themselves, explain why this is a fallacy. A naturalist may say that the normative statement "$X$ is good" may be reformulated and justified either in the if–then form, "If $X$, then $Y$," ($X$ is good because it can be shown that $X$ leads to $Y$, which is good), or frame of reference form, "Most people like $X$." A nonnaturalist argues that the naturalistic fallacy has been committed, that ethical sentences are claimed to be identical with factual sentences. The nonnaturalist suggests that the normative problem has not been solved. It may be true that $X$ may bring about $Y$; but how do we know that $Y$ is good? How can it be claimed that because many people or some authority likes $X$, $X$ is good? The nonnaturalist concludes by saying that "ought" statements cannot be derived from "is" statements because terms cannot be deduced in a conclusion of a deductive argument that are not contained in the premises.

The nonnaturalists, we think, properly attack the extreme form of ethical naturalism. Certainly difficult normative problems cannot be settled by simply translating them into factual equivalents. Regardless of how much a value problem is reformulated, normative problems ultimately depend on value judgments. On the other hand, naturalists rightfully stress the crucial role empirical evidence plays in normative decision making. Reformulating normative problems in terms of factual approximations often yields important information relevant to the making of a value judgment.

Both naturalists and nonnaturalists are wrong in suggesting that empirical evidence either totally determines or is totally irrelevant to the making of value judgments. A modified approach to normative decision making is perhaps most judicious. Normative problem reformulation does involve some loss of meaning. It does not preclude the necessity of making value judgments. It should be used with caution to generate more empirical evidence on which an informed value judgment can be made.

## LEARNING AID

**1.** Reformulating normative problems into empirical problems helps to produce more empirical information relevant to the _____ that normative analysts must ultimately make.

**2.** Name the two methods of reformulating normative problems into empirical problems.

3. Reformulate the following statements by changing the frame of reference:
   a. Smoking is bad.
   b. Don't become involved in a guerrilla war!
   c. The executive branch of government should not become more powerful than it already is.
4. Reformulate the statements listed in the previous question by changing to the if–then form.
5. Philosophers call the practice of reformulating normative problems into empirical problems _____.
6. Ethical naturalism maintains that all ethical sentences are translatable without loss of meaning into _____ sentences.
7. The naturalistic fallacy is a concept particularly emphasized by ethical (naturalists, nonnaturalists).
8. The naturalistic fallacy involves identifying ethical or value judgments with _____ judgments.

. . . . . . . . . . . . . . . . . . . . . . . . . . . . . . . . . . . . . . . . . . . . . . . .

1. value judgments
2. changing the frame of reference, changing to if–then form
3. Here is one way to do it:
   a. Doctors say smoking is bad.
   b. Military experts say not to become involved in a guerrilla war.
   c. Most people feel that the executive branch of government should not become more powerful than it already is.
4. Here are some examples:
   a. If people smoke, then they are likely to get lung cancer.
   b. If countries become involved in guerrilla wars, then expenditures for domestic social welfare programs and civilian support for the war effort decrease.
   c. If the executive branch of the government becomes more powerful than it is today, then more incidents of governmental corruption will occur.
5. ethical naturalism
6. nonethical
7. nonnaturalists
8. factual (empirical)

## EMPIRICAL PROBLEMS

The problems social scientists select for study are empirical and may be classified according to goals and complexity of analysis. Since the goals of social science are to describe, explain, and predict, we may classify empirical problems as *descriptions, explanations,* or *predictions.* Empirical problems may further be distinguished by their complexity. Those problems involving only one variable are called *univariate,* whereas those involving two or more variables may be called *multivariate.*

In a later unit variables will be defined more completely. For now we can think of *variables* as labels for properties that take on different values. For example, "party registration" can be thought of as a variable because it is a property or characteristic that takes on different values (Democrat, Republican, Independent, and the like). "Social class" is also a variable because it names a property that takes on different values (upper, middle, working). "Age" names a property taking on different values (23, 45, 65, and so on). "Male" is not a variable. It is one of the values of the variable, "sex," which names a property taking on different values (male, female). If "maleness" as opposed to "male" is referred to, however, it may be thought of as a variable taking on different values (very masculine, masculine, not very masculine).

By cross-classifying goals of analysis with complexity of analysis (Table 4–1), we can identify six basic types of problems: (a) univariate descriptions, (b) multivariate descriptions, (c) univariate explanations, (d) multivariate explanations, (e) univariate predictions, and (f) multivariate predictions. The student should be able to identify each of these problem types when problems are posed in empirical studies. Since the type of question asked determines the kinds of methods that are appropriate to use, identifying problem types is a crucial phase of problem formulation and analysis.

## Univariate Descriptive Problems (A)

*Univariate descriptive problems* ask about the present or past status of a property (variable). Examples:

1.  What is the proportion of first term legislators in state assemblies?
2.  What happened in the March 1969 Sino–Soviet border dispute?
3.  What is the incidence of political protest in the United States?

**Table 4–1.  TYPES OF PROBLEMS**

|                     | Complexity of Analysis | |
| ------------------- | ---------- | ------------ |
| Goals of Analysis   | Univariate | Multivariate |
| Description         | a          | b            |
| Explanation         | c          | d            |
| Prediction          | e          | f            |

## Multivariate Descriptive Problems (B)

*Multivariate descriptive problems* ask about the present or past status of a relationship among two or more properties (variables). Examples:

1. Is the proportion of first-term legislators related to the effectiveness of legislative bodies?
2. Is the incidence of political protest related to the openness of political systems?
3. Is the occurrence of the 1969 Sino–Soviet border dispute related to the occurrence of the Cultural Revolution?

## Univariate Explanatory Problems (C)

*Univariate explanatory problems* ask why a property (variable) has a particular status. Univariate explanatory problems assume the descriptive status of the property has already been determined (described) and ask why it is that way. Examples:

1. Why has the proportion of first-term legislators in state assemblies declined from 75 percent in 1893 to 25 percent in 1965?
2. Why did cities from 100,000 to one million in population average about three protest incidents in 1968?
3. Why did the March 1969 Sino–Soviet border dispute occur?

## Multivariate Explanatory Problems (D)

*Multivariate explanatory problems* ask why two or more properties (variables) are associated. Examples:

1. Why is the proportion of first-term legislators related to the effectiveness of legislative bodies?
2. Why is the incidence of political protest related to the openness of political systems?
3. Why is the occurrence of the 1969 Sino–Soviet border dispute related to the occurrence of the Cultural Revolution?

## Univariate Predictive Problems (E)

*Univariate predictive problems* ask about the future status of a property (variable). Examples:

1. Will the proportion of first-term legislators continue to decrease in state assemblies?
2. Will the incidence of political protest continue to increase?
3. Will more Sino–Soviet border disputes occur?

## Multivariate Predictive Problems (F)

*Multivariate predictive problems* ask about the future status of a relationship among two or more properties (variables). Examples:

1. Will the proportion of first-term legislators continue to be related to the effectiveness of legislative bodies?
2. Will the incidence of political protest continue to be related to the openness of political systems?
3. Will the occurrence of Sino–Soviet border disputes continue to be related to the Cultural Revolution?

Knowledge about a field usually proceeds from description to explanation and prediction. Exploratory studies often provide the facts that must be known before adequate explanation and prediction can occur. Although explanation and prediction are higher order scientific goals, descriptive studies still play an important role in the accumulation of knowledge. If an exploratory study provides the groundwork for eventual explanation and prediction, it should not be referred to in a negative sense as being "merely descriptive" but should be recognized as a contribution to a developing field of inquiry. At the same time, social scientists should not remain content being photographers, describing the social and political terrain. They should constantly strive for reliable explanation and prediction, the ultimate objectives of scientific inquiry.

### LEARNING AID

1. Name the six basic types of empirical problems.
2. Variables are labels for _____ which take on different values.
3. _____ problems ask about the future status of a property.
4. _____ problems ask about the present or past status of a relationship among two or more properties.
5. _____ problems ask why a property has a particular status.
6. _____ problems ask why two or more properties are associated.
7. _____ problems ask about the present or past status of a property.
8. _____ problems ask about the future status of a relationship among two or more properties.

9. Knowledge about a field often proceeds from _____ to _____ to _____.

10. Identify the type of empirical problem posed in each of the following questions:

    a. Is the proportion of malapportioned legislative districts related to the proportion of seats held by the majority party in the state legislature?

    b. Why is frustration related to aggression?

    c. What is the current level of unemployment?

    d. At the current rate of population growth, when will the United States reach a population of 700 million?

    e. Why are there more incidents of violence in the United States than in any other country?

    f. Will the relationship between race and voting turnout decrease as blacks obtain more education?

. . . . . . . . . . . . . . . . . . . . . . . . . . . . . . . . . . . . . . . . . . . . . . . . . . . . .

1. univariate descriptive, multivariate descriptive, univariate explanatory, multivariate explanatory, univariate predictive, multivariate predictive

2. properties

3. univariate predictive

4. multivariate descriptive

5. univariate explanatory

6. multivariate explanatory

7. univariate descriptive

8. multivariate predictive

9. description, explanation, prediction

10. (a) multivariate descriptive, (b) multivariate explanatory, (c) univariate descriptive, (d) univariate predictive, (e) univariate explanatory, (f) multivariate predictive

## DIMENSIONS OF PROBLEM FORMULATION

The formulation of an empirical problem is the first, the most difficult, and perhaps the most fundamental decision an investigator makes during the course of his inquiry. Every subsequent decision is affected by the initial formulation of the research problem. In this section, the student will learn what constitutes an adequately formulated research problem. The student should be able to identify the six criteria of adequate problem formulation, to distinguish good problems from poor ones, to reformulate inadequate problems, and to formulate inadequate problems, and to formulate an adequate political research problem.[5] We shall first examine the six criteria of problem formulation. Research problems should be explicit, clear, original, testable, theoretical, and relevant.

## Explicitness

An experienced researcher learns to formulate explicit statements of his problems early in his inquiry. Failure to do so usually creates many inconveniences and problems later on. One such difficulty is that he tends to waste time wandering aimlessly from one intellectual dilemma to another if he has not explicitly stated the question for himself.

Explicit problem formulation sets an objective for the investigator. He knows where he is and where he wants to go. He is able to separate central from peripheral issues. He knows when he is beginning to get sidetracked and what he has to do to get back on the right course to answer the question. He knows when he has achieved his objective and when he can stop or go on to a more fundamental question.

Problems should also be explicitly formulated when research studies are reported in papers, articles, and books. The research problem should be stated explicitly near the beginning of the paper. The reader should not have to search for the problem statement, nor should he have doubts about what the problem is. Research that lacks a problem focus often is executed poorly and should be scrutinized carefully before its results are accepted. Implicit problem statements should indicate to the reader to be aware of what follows. It may be intellectual confusion.

The most effective way to state a problem explicitly is simply to formulate it in question form. Asking a question clearly indicates to the reader the focus of the inquiry. It also puts the question directly to the one who is responsible for answering it, the investigator.

|  Implicit:  |  Explicit:  |
| --- | --- |
| It has been established with varying degrees of certainty that many human traits that unquestionably matter to their possessors and to society are genetically conditioned. Intelligence, personality, and special abilities are all susceptible to modification by genetic as well as environmental influences. Recent sensational and inflammatory pronouncements about the genetic basis for racial and socioeconomic differences in IQ make mandatory a critical consideration of the subject. | To what extent is IQ inherited? |

The first example has somewhat of a problem focus, which is better than none at all, but it presents a variety of subjects without indicating specifically what is to be asked. The second example asks the question directly and simply. It is explicit and leaves little room for confusion in the reader's mind.

## Clarity

To have a clear answer, we first must have a clear question. Writing clear questions is a difficult but learnable skill. The research problem should not be stated in ambiguous or vague language. It should mean the same thing to different well-informed and intelligent persons. In other words, it should be intersubjectively understandable. A question that is clear is usually a question that is also simple, precise, and limited. Complex questions should be subdivided into specific and clear subquestions.

Unclear:

Does decentralization help minorities?

Clearer:

Under what conditions does decentralization of health, educational, and welfare decisions increase opportunities for disadvantaged American minorities?

a. What is the effect of changing decision making from federal to state, state to local, and local to neighborhood communities on the participation of disadvantaged minorities in decision making?

b. What is the effect of decentralizing decision making on the expenditure of funds for health, education, and welfare programs?

c. Does decentralized decision making result in a larger number of programs specifically directed toward disadvantaged minorities?

d. What economic, political, and racial characteristics of various levels of government are associated with increased expenditures for health, education, and welfare programs?

The first example is deceptively simple. It omits reference to many points that must be known before the question can be empirically answered. It does not indicate what decentralization refers to. Does it refer to decentralization of policies? If so, which policies? Does it refer to governmental or nongovernmental policies? What levels of government does it refer to? Which kind of minorities are considered? What is meant by the term "help"? The second illustration shows that this question is complex and can be divided into a number of subsidiary questions. Although this question itself is not totally clear, it is more precise and limited than the first. It is one that at least admits of some type of empirical testing.

## Originality

Formulated problems vary in terms of their originality. Many problems endure, having been asked many times by different researchers. New approaches to old questions and replications of old approaches often contribute to the accumulating body of knowledge. Examining the classic questions can often be very valuable. Original problems, however, are likely to receive more attention and credit than replication studies.

To assess the originality of a problem, a student should examine the author's bibliography and his introduction to the problem. Relevant research should be summarized in these places. If the researcher has done a thorough literature review, properly noting related studies, the student should have an idea as to the originality of the author's problem.

In addition students can consult literature summaries on topics in a number of standard handbooks, references, and encyclopedias such as: *The International Encyclopaedia of the Social Sciences, The ABC Guide to Recent Publications in the Social and Behavioral Sciences, International Bibliography of Political Science, International Political Science Abstracts, Psychological Abstracts, Sociological Abstracts,* and *The Universal Reference System.*

## Testability

Posing a scientific problem implies that it is possible to test and to answer empirically the research question. Problems that do not contain testing implications are not truly scientific questions. There are, of course, many important problems that are not scientific questions because they are not testable. Many theological, ethical, and philosophical questions are of this sort. For example, to ask what form of government is best is to ask essentially a nonscientific question. It is primarily an ethical and moral problem involving value judgments, which are not capable of being empirically justified. Although evidence may be relevant to the judgment, the answer to a value question depends at least to some extent on one's values.

Speculative empirical questions may also be untestable. To ask when world government will occur or when war will occur is to ask an empirical question that is untestable at this time. The data, theory, and techniques are not available to answer questions such as these. Although they may be significant questions, they also are not factually answerable; therefore, they are not scientific questions. The only questions that scientists ask as scientists are questions that are empirically testable. But this does not mean that these are the only questions worth asking, perhaps from other perspectives.

All adequate research questions can be answered with the resources available to the investigator. Students often pose interesting empirical questions that assume the availability of resources, methods, or techniques not at their disposal. Questions such as these are not adequate scientific questions. Good research questions imply the feasibility of answering the question.

| Untestable: | More testable: |
| --- | --- |
| What is the best form of government? | Do democratic governments have higher median incomes, median years of education, and higher health conditions than nondemocratic countries? |

The first question is a value question, as it is stated. Therefore, it is not a scientific question. The second question illustrates how the first question can be reformulated so that relevant empirical information may be acquired. The value question is still not answered with the reformulation. It is still a value question as to whether it is better to have higher income, education, and health. This judgment will still have to be faced. If these conditions are better, however, then it is possible to determine factually whether democratic or nondemocratic governments maximize these values the most.

## Theoretical Significance

Problems that are formulated adequately should also contribute to the development of a body of knowledge. When a problem relates to a set of interrelated empirical generalizations, which we call a "theory," we say the problem is theoretically significant. If a problem is totally detached from the development of a theory, then we say it is theoretically insignificant or atheoretical.

| Atheoretical: | Theoretical: |
|---|---|
| Is the length of the feet of politicians related to the number of times they put their feet into their mouths? | Is sense of relative deprivation related to the occurrence of rebellions? |

Whereas the first example illustrates a problem that bears no relation to a known set of political empirical generalizations, the second one relates to a number of generalizations and theories about the causes of revolutions.

## Relevance

The ultimate objectives of problem posing are to explain and predict sociopolitical phenomena. Explanation and prediction, however, are not simply "academic" activities. They also provide the possibility of being able to shape the environment in which we live. If we know why events occur, the laws and the facts relevant to their explanation, we might also be able to modify these factors so as to bring about desirable outcomes. An adequate economic theory, for example, would indicate why such events as recessions, depressions, and periods of high inflation and unemployment occur. It should also indicate what steps can be taken to alleviate such problems.

Many problems confront us in the social and political sphere—problems of war, race, poverty, education, crime, environment, and health. Social science is merely beginning to address itself to such issues. When empirical research problems potentially contribute to the solution or to the understanding of such issues, we say the problems are practically relevant.

| Less relevant: | More relevant: |
|---|---|
| Are elective office holders taller than appointive office holders? | Is a sense of relative deprivation related to the occurrence of rebellion? |

The first example illustrates a problem that conceivably may relate to some theory of leadership (that leaders are taller than average population); but it does not relate to the solution of an immediate, pressing problem such as the second example.

## LEARNING AID

1.  When a problem relates to a set of interrelated _____, which is a theory, we say the problem is theoretical.
2.  A problem that is theoretical (can, cannot) be relevant to the solution of social and political problems.
3.  Name the six criteria for formulating problems adequately.
4.  Compare problems *A* and *B* in terms of the six criteria for formulating problems, using the table below.

| | *A* | | *B* | |
|---|---|---|---|---|
| | What is the relationship between income and party identification? | | The concern of this study is to examine the incidence of protest as a function of the opportunity structure of cities. | |
| | | More: | Less: | |
| Explicit | | _____ | _____ | |
| Clear | | _____ | _____ | |
| Original | | _____ | _____ | |
| Testable | | _____ | _____ | |
| Theoretical | | _____ | _____ | |
| Relevant | | _____ | _____ | |

5.  Now compare problems A and B using the "extent scale." Assign one of the following numbers to each of the cells of the table below:
    (5) to a very great extent, (4) to a great extent, (3) to some extent, (2) to a little extent, and (1) to a very little extent.
Complete your evaluation of the six criteria for problem A before turning to B.

| | *A* | *B* |
|---|---|---|
| Explicit | _____ | _____ |
| Clear | _____ | _____ |
| Testable | _____ | _____ |
| Theoretical | _____ | _____ |
| Relevant | _____ | _____ |
| Sum | _____ | _____ |

Now sum the scores for each problem. This method of problem analysis provides a more specific judgment, according to which a number of different problems can be evaluated.

**6.**  Which of the six types of empirical problems (e.g., univariate descriptive) discussed in the previous section are problems A and B?

**7.**  Reformulate the following problem by making it more explicit, clear, and testable: "The purpose of this project is to explore the ethnic concept of being militant and its translation into forms of political redress so as to bring about a better environment in which all races can live in harmony."

**8.**  Formulate two multivariate explanatory problems and analyze them in terms of the six problem formulation criteria.

. . . . . . . . . . . . . . . . . . . . . . . . . . . . . . . . . . . . . . . . . . . . . . . . . . . . . . . . . . . . .

**1.**  generalizations

**2.**  can. Don't fall into the trap of thinking that what is theoretical cannot be practical. We are defining theoretical in terms of a set of empirical generalizations or relationships. A theory of voting or a theory of revolution can be very practical for those who want to win elections or overturn governments.

**3.**  An adequately formulated problem should be explicit, clear, original, testable, theoretical, and relevant.

**4.**  The answer to this question is a matter of judgment, of course. This is how we would classify the problems:

|             | *More* | *Less* |
|-------------|--------|--------|
| Explicit    | A      | B      |
| Clear       | A      | B      |
| Original    | B      | A      |
| Testable    | A      | B      |
| Theoretical | B*     | A*     |
| Relevant    | B      | A      |

* Judging the theoretical significance of a problem assumes a certain knowledge about the literature in both the fields of *A* and *B*. The voting literature is highly developed, and income is frequently related to other important variables. The literature on protest is still relatively new. The concept of opportunity structure so far has not been systematically related to many other variables.

**5.**  Again, this is a matter of judgment. Here are our results:

|             | *A* | *B* |
|-------------|-----|-----|
| Explicit    | 5   | 3   |
| Clear       | 4   | 3   |
| Original    | 1   | 5   |
| Testable    | 5   | 3   |
| Theoretical | 2   | 4   |
| Relevant    | 2   | 5   |
| Sum         | 19  | 23  |

It appears that $B$ is a slightly more adequate formulation of a problem than $A$. Notice that this refined measuring scale differentiates the two problems, but the cruder comparison scale used in question 4 does not.

**6.** A is multivariate descriptive because it asks what the relationship is between two variables. $B$ is multivariate explanatory because it asks whether protest is caused by another variable. Causal questions are explanation problems.

**7.** The question can be reformulated in a number of different ways. This formulation is more clear, explicit, and testable than the original: "What is the effect of attitudes of ethnic militancy on the political participation of ethnic minority members?"

**8.** Check with your classmates or instructor.

## FOOTNOTES

1. Karl Popper, *Conjectures and Refutations: The Growth of Scientific Knowledge* (New York: Harper and Row, 1963), p. 222.
2. Thomas Kuhn, *The Structure of Scientific Revolutions* (Chicago: University of Chicago Press, 1962), pp. 52–76.
3. David McClelland, *The Achieving Society* (New York: Free Press, 1961).
4. John Hospers, *Introduction to Philosophical Analysis,* (2d ed., Englewood Cliffs, N.J.: Prentice Hall, 1967) pp. 568–79; William Frankena, *Ethics* (Englewood Cliffs, N.J.: Prentice-Hall, 1963), pp. 80–92; Fred Frohock, *Normative Political Theory* (Englewood Cliffs, N.J.: Prentice-Hall, 1974), pp. 1–7; Herbert Jacob and Robert Weissberg, *Elementary Political Analysis,* 2nd ed. (New York: McGraw-Hill, 1975), pp. 91–112.
5. See Carlo Lastrucci, *The Scientific Approach* (Cambridge: Schenkman, 1967), pp. 52–74; Fred Kerlinger, *Foundations of Behavioral Research* (New York: Holt, Rinehart, & Winston, 1964), pp. 18–20; and E. Terrence Jones, *Conducting Political Research* (New York: Harper & Row, 1971), pp. 12–15.

# 5
# Concept Formation

## INTRODUCTION

### Rationale

In your social science education, you have probably come across a number of technical terms such as polyarchy, political efficacy, system equilibrium, interest aggregation, and anomie. Terms such as these occur infrequently in common language. Undoubtedly, you have wondered why such complex terms are invented for things that could be explained more simply. You may have even called such words "verbose" or "jargon."

Social scientists, on the other hand, vigorously defend their use of technical terms. They argue that everyday language often contains words that are too vague to use in the precise manner desired. They claim that common language frequently lacks words that succinctly express a complex thought. Social scientists, therefore, say they introduce technical terms to clarify the meaning of words, to specify precisely the objects to which words apply, and to reduce the number of words needed for communicating an idea.

In this unit we shall examine the need for technical terms in social science, the various types of technical terms, and the principles of scientific concept formation.

### Learning Objectives

After completing this unit, the student should be able to:

1. Reconstruct the terminology tree.

2. Define and identify examples of the following terms:
   a. Logical and descriptive words
   b. Proper and common names
   c. Unit, character, and relational terms
   d. Concepts and constructs
   e. Words and definitions
   f. Defining and accompanying characteristics
   g. Designation, denotation, and connotation
   h. Reportive and stipulative definitions
   i. Theoretical and pretheoretical terms
   j. Conceptual and operational definitions

3.  Explain the following principles:

    a.  Freedom of stipulation

    b.  Operationism

    c.  Reconstructed operationism

    d.  Empirical import

    e.  Systematic import

4.  State and explain the two principles of proper concept formation.

5.  Identify the conditions under which stipulation should occur.

6.  Formulate and identify operational definitions.

## SOCIAL SCIENCE TERMINOLOGY

### Descriptive and Logical Words

Social scientists talk about the world and its events using declarative sentences. The words that make up such statements are either "descriptive" or "logical."[1] *Descriptive words* give sentences their meaning by referring to things (or events), properties of things (or events), or relations among these. "The United States of America is the most powerful nation in the world" is an example of a declarative statement that contains four descriptive terms: "United States of America," "most powerful," "nation," and "world." "United States of America" refers to a particular nation. "Most powerful" refers to a certain kind of relation of the United States to other nations. "Nation" and "world" refer to things or objects. Descriptive words, then, refer to things (or events), properties of things (or events), and relations among these.

We have seen that descriptive terms are connected with each other to form statements such as: "Industrialized nations tend to be democratic." The statements of a theory in turn are connected to form compound sentences such as: "Industrialized nations tend to be democratic, *and* the United States is an industrialized nation." Compound sentences express connections. The words that do the connecting are called "logical words."

*Logical words* give sentences their form and do not refer to anything. They give sentences their form or structure by connecting descriptive terms. Words such as "and," "or," and "if . . . then . . ." are logical words. They do not point to anything; an "and" or an "or" does not exist out there like a "nation" or a "political party."

Compound sentences vary in terms of both their content and form. Two compound sentences may have the same content (descriptive terms) but have a different form (logical terms):

> "He is a politician *and* he is a statesman."
> "He is a politician *or* he is a statesman."

Also, two compound sentences may have different content (descriptive terms) but the same form (logical terms):

> "The judge is elected *or* the judge is appointed."
> "He is a politician *or* he is a statesman."

Lest you get lost in the maze of distinctions, let us provide you with a roadmap. Figure 5–1, the terminology tree, is a diagram of the relationships which obtain among the various kinds of technical terms considered in this section.

## Proper and Common Names

Descriptive terms consist of two types: proper names or common names. Common names are also called *concepts*. *Proper names* are descriptive terms that refer to individual objects or events. "United States of America," "Richard Nixon," "Watergate," "United Nations," and "War of 1812" are proper names because they are terms describing individual objects, persons, or events. *Common names* are descriptive terms that refer to objects or events in general. "Nation," "man," "corruption," "organization," and "war" are common names because they are terms describing objects, persons, or events in general.

Common names tend to appear more frequently in social scientific statements and journals than proper names. This is because social scientists focus more on repeatable, general phenomena than unique, individual phenomena. One of the objectives of social science is to develop generalizations that help to

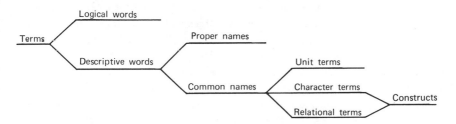

Figure 5-1. The Terminology Tree. (We thank Milton Hobbs for suggesting the general notion of this diagram.)

explain and predict phenomena. Generalizations are based on repeated observation of similar phenomena, such as certain types of wars. Although the set of phenomena social scientists observe consists of individual cases with proper names, such as the War of 1812, social scientists usually are concerned more with making statements about wars in general than about wars in particular. Therefore, they are more likely to use common names than proper names in any statement of hypotheses and theories.

## Unit Terms and Constructs

Three kinds of common names can be distinguished: unit terms, character terms, and relational terms.

*Unit terms* are common descriptive terms that refer to objects or things. Objects are simply systematic combinations of properties that form a unit or a thing. Hence, we call them "unit" terms. "Book" is a unit term; it refers to an object that systematically combines certain properties of size, weight, width, color, texture, and so on to make it a "book." "Political party" is also a unit term referring to an object that combines the properties of a group of persons, being organized, and seeking political power through elective office. "Nation" refers to another general object that combines the properties of a stable community of people who share territory, history, culture, and language.

*Character terms* are common descriptive terms that refer to properties of objects or events. "Weight" is a character term; it refers to a characteristic of something, such as a book or a person. "Wealth" refers to a characteristic of a person, group, or nation. "Self-esteem," "conservatism," "IQ," "social class," and "political awareness" are also character terms because they describe properties of persons. "Magnitude" or "duration" are properties that may describe events such as protests, wars, or revolutions.

*Relational terms* are common descriptive terms that refer to relations between properties or things. "Being outside of" in the statement, "The United States is outside of the Common Market" is a relational term. It refers to the relationship (being outside) between two objects (United States and Common Market). In the statement, "Japan is allied with the United States," a relation (being allied) is expressed between two objects (Japan and the United States). This is similar to the statement, "John is married to Jane," which expresses a relation (being married) between two persons. The statement, "Party identification is associated with social class," also specifies a relational term (being associated with) between two terms. "Income varies with education" expresses a relation (varying with) between two terms. Each of the above sentences asserts relational terms since they express relations between properties or things.

*Constructs* are labels for indirectly observed properties of things. This definition rules out proper names such as "reformation" and unit terms such as "nation," since these terms refer to things and not "properties" of things. It also eliminates character or relational terms that are directly observable such as "green" and "larger." The word "construct" is reserved for character or relational terms that express properties not directly observable. "IQ," "conservatism," and "influence" are properties of things and are not directly observable. We cannot directly observe a person's IQ, but we can indirectly observe it by means of setting up a testing situation (an IQ test) and observing results (IQ scores).

The difference between unit and character terms should by now be clear. Characteristics or properties do not exist by themselves but occur as aspects of things that we call units. Nor do units exist by themselves, but rather as special combinations or properties. The distinction between unit and character terms is important because hypotheses specify relationships among character terms, not unit terms. We can measure and relate properties of units to each other, but we cannot measure and relate units per se. A book cannot be measured, but the properties (weight, length, width, and the like) of the book can be measured. Similarly individuals, political parties, nations, and culture are immeasurable by their very nature; but each of these units possesses properties that can be measured and related to other properties. Since science consists largely of relating properties to other properties and since character terms and relational terms refer to properties, concepts tend to play a more prominent role in social science than unit terms.

## LEARNING AID

1.  Reconstruct the "terminology tree."
2.  Descriptive words give sentences their _____ by _____ to things (or events), or _____ among these.
3.  Logical words give sentences their _____ and do not _____ to anything.
4.  Descriptive terms referring to individual objects or events are _____ names.
5.  Descriptive terms referring to general objects or events are _____ names.
6.  Unit terms are common descriptive terms that refer to _____ or things.
7.  Character terms are common _____ terms that refer to _____ or objects or events.

**8.** Relational terms are common descriptive terms that refer to _____ between _____ or _____.

**9.** Constructs are _____ for _____ observed _____ of things.

**10.** Constructs _____ (do, do not) refer to unit terms.

**11.** Hypotheses _____ (do, do not) specify relations between unit terms.

**12.** Proper names are _____ (more, less) likely to appear in scientific statements than common names.

**13.** Identify the major kinds of terms employed in the following hypotheses:
   a. If integration decreases, then instability increases in African nations.
   b. Age is associated with conservatism.
   c. Foreign policy opinion is a function of social position.
   d. If organizations increase in growth, then internal conflicts decrease.
   e. Blacks tend to participate more than whites when age and socioeconomic status are held constant.

. . . . . . . . . . . . . . . . . . . . . . . . . . . . . . . . . . . . . . . . . . . . . . . . . . . . . . . . . . . . . . . . . .

1. See Figure 5–1.
2. meaning, referring, relations
3. form, refer
4. proper
5. common
6. objects
7. descriptive, properties
8. relations, properties, things (objects)
9. labels, indirectly, properties
10. do not
11. do not
12. less
13. a.  If, then = logical terms; integration, instability = character terms or constructs; decreases, increases = relational terms; African nations = unit term;
    b.  Age, conservatism = character terms or constructs; is associated with = relational term;
    c.  Foreign policy opinion, social position = character terms or constructs; is function of = relational term;
    d.  If, then = logical terms; organizations = unit term; growth, internal conflicts = character terms or constructs; increases, decreases = relational terms;
    e.  (This statement may confuse you somewhat. The hypothesis asserts a relationship between two constructs, race and participation, holding

two other constructs constant. Since blacks and whites are persons, you may have classified them as unit terms. But being white or black is a racial characteristic; therefore, white and black (or race) is a character term.) Black, white (race), participation, age, socio-economic status = character terms or constructs; more than, is held constant = relational terms; when = logical term.

## THE DEFINITION OF SCIENTIFIC CONCEPTS

In this section we will examine the relationship of descriptive words to the world, various methods of defining the technical terms of social science, and the principles of proper concept formation.

### Words, Meanings, and Things

*Words* are arbitrary signs or symbols that refer or point to things. Words are not the things themselves. Words simply stand for *things* (or qualities, behaviors, events, relations, and so on). The word "dog" is an arbitrary sign, a special noise that is used to refer to a special kind of thing. Another noise could have been used instead. The *meaning* of a word is determined by a convention, agreement, or rule that assigns words to things. Meanings, then, are originally assigned to words; they are not discovered. The meaning of a word may be established either informally through customary usage or formally through definition. A *definition* specifies meaning because it is a rule that assigns words to objects (things). The word "dog" is assigned to a certain object if the object corresponds to the rule, "a domesticated quadruped of the Canis family." (See Figure 5–2) The word "protest" is applied to an event (thing) if the event corresponds to the rule, "a formal statement of objection." Words, then, are arbitrary symbols that stand for things and have meaning when rules assign them to things.

| Word/Term/ Concept | Meaning/Rule/Definition | Thing/Object/ Referent |
|---|---|---|
| "dog" | "domesticated quadruped of Canis family" | |
| "protest" | "a formal statement of objection" | |
| "violence" | "physical force used so as to injure" | |

**Figure 5-2.  Relationship of Words, Meanings, and Things.**

## LEARNING AID

1. Words are _____ (absolute, arbitrary) signs or symbols.
2. Signs or symbols point to or _____ to things.
3. The meaning of a word is determined by a _____.
4. The meanings of words are originally _____ (discovered, assigned).
5. A definition is a _____ that assigns words to _____.

. . . . . . . . . . . . . . . . . . . . . . . . . . . . . . . . . . . . . . . . . . . . . . . . . . . . . . .

1. arbitrary
2. refer
3. convention (agreement, rule)
4. assigned
5. rule, objects (things)

## Defining and Accompanying Characteristics

A *definition,* we have learned, is a rule that assigns a word to a thing. The rule enumerates a list of defining characteristics of a term. A *defining characteristic* is a characteristic whose presence is necessary for a word properly to apply to a thing (or quality, behavior, relation, event).[2] If an absent characteristic renders the word inapplicable to an object, the characteristic is defining. If, on the other hand, a characteristic is absent, but the word still applies appropriately to an object, the characteristic is said to be accompanying. An *accompanying characteristic* is one whose presence is common but not necessary for a word to apply to an object or thing. Statements that assert defining characteristics are called definitions or analytic statements. Analytic statements are those whose predicate merely repeats the subject of the sentence and whose negation is self-contradictory. Statements that assert accompanying characteristics, however, are called factual or empirical statements. Whereas defining characteristics are an essential part of the meaning or definition of words, accompanying characteristics are only facts about the thing being named by the term.

Several examples may clarify the distinction between defining and accompanying characteristics. The rule or definition we are using for the term "dog" is "domesticated quadruped of Canis family." The rule enumerates three defining characteristics: quadruped, domestication, and membership in the Canis family. The rule specifies that if any of these characteristics is lacking in a thing the word "dog" should not be assigned to it. Other characterics, of course, are usually associated with being a dog, such as barking and having a wet nose; but these are not defining characteristics. They are accompanying characteristics since things can lack these characteristics and we still apply the label "dog" to them. For a second example, "protest" is defined as "a formal statement of objection." The rule clearly specifies the defining characteristics. The characteristics of violence or change may accompany protest but are not included as part of its meaning.

Social science publications occasionally contain statements that are ambiguous as to whether they assert defining or accompanying characteristics. The distinction is important. If a defining characteristic is asserted, then refuting the statement is a verbal dispute and depends on how words are defined, but if an accompanying characteristic is asserted then refuting the statement is a factual dispute and depends on how the world really is. A writer may claim, "Political equality is a requisite of democracy." We should ask ourselves, "Is this a definitional or factual assertion?" To test whether the characteristic being asserted is definitional or factual, we can ask whether we would still call a country "democratic" if it lacked "political equality." If the answer is no, the characteristic is defining; if the answer is yes, it is accompanying. If we interpret the characteristic as defining and we want to take issue with the assertion, we dispute the definition. If we interpret the characteristic as accompanying and we still desire to disagree, then we put forth contrary evidence to dispute the factual claim.

Several words of caution should be noted about the defining/accompanying characteristic distinction. Occasionally an accompanying characteristic, in time, can become regarded legitimately as a defining characteristic. When a characteristic almost universally accompanies an object, there is a tendency for it to be drawn into the list of defining characteristics. For example, before the causes of diseases were known, diseases were defined by their symptoms. So it was with syphilis. When a bacteria called "spirochete" was discovered with a microscope, scientists observed that whenever spirochete was present the symptoms of syphilis also occurred. Eventually syphilis came to be defined in terms of spirochete: if the spirochete was present, the patient had syphilis; if it wasn't, he didn't have it. Thus, at one point in time a characteristic was regarded as accompanying and at another, defining. Sometimes, however, the shift from accompanying to defining characteristic is made illegitimately by debaters, propagandists, politicians, or fuzzy-headed thinkers. A debater, for example, may state, "Communist countries have classless social structures." It is not clear whether he intends this as a factual or definitional statement. Interpreting the statement as factual, his opponent argues that sociological evidence shows that communist countries like the Soviet Union and the Peoples Republic of China in fact have class structures. The debater responds that these countries then are not really communist since a communist country by definition must have a classless social structure. Alternatively, interpreting the statement as a definition, his opponent disagrees with defining communist countries as classless social structures. The debater responds saying this is not a definition but a factual statement that classlessness tends to accompany the fact of being a communist country. Thus, when challenged, the debater can shift either way to suit his argument and to avoid careful testing of his statements. With the defining/accompanying characteristic distinction, we can identify and cut through such ambiguous and illusory claims.

## LEARNING AID

**1.** A *defining characteristic* is one whose _____ is _____ for a _____ to apply to a thing.

**2.** An *accompanying characteristic* is one whose _____ is common but not _____ for a _____ to apply to a thing.

**3.** Indicate whether the underlined words in the following statements are defining or accompanying characteristics:

    a. *Political equality* is a requisite of democratic government.
    b. Bureaucracies have *office hierarchies*.
    c. *Economic development* is necessary for democracies.
    d. Mass societies have a high degree of *alienation.'*
    e. *Political instability* leads to political change.
    f. Revolutions occur *when attempts to change the regimes of states are violent, and sudden, and illegal.*
    g. Justice is related to *fairness.*

. . . . . . . . . . . . . . . . . . . . . . . . . . . . . . . . . . . . . . . . . . . . . . . . . . . . . .

**1.** presence, necessary, word
**2.** presence, necessary, word
**3.** The answers to these questions depend, of course, on how a concept is defined. These answers suggest an approach to each problem.

    a. Defining characteristic. Many political theorists include political equality among the defining characteristics of democracy. See Robert Dahl, *A Preface to Democratic Theory* (Chicago: University of Chicago Press, 1956) and Deane Neubauer, "Some Conditions of Democracy," *American Political Science Review* 61 (December, 1967): 1002–9.
    b. Defining characteristic. Max Weber, a noted sociologist, lists office hierarchy among the defining characteristics of bureaucracies. See H. Gerth and C. W. Mills, eds., *From Max Weber* (New York: Oxford University Press, 1958), pp. 196–98.
    c. Accompanying characteristic. It is likely but not necessary that a democracy be economically developed. See S. M. Lipset, "Some Social Requisites of Democracy," *American Political Science Review* 53 (March, 1959): 69–105.

d. Accompanying characteristics. Kornhauser defines "mass society" as a social system in which elites are readily accessible to influence by nonelites and nonelites are readily available for mobilization by elites. Alienation may then be empirically associated with but not part of the meaning of mass society. See William Kornhauser, *The Politics of Mass Society* (New York: The Free Press of Glencoe, 1959), p. 39.

e. It depends on how broadly the concept "political instability" is defined. If "instability" is defined as a condition in which conflict in social systems is no longer adequately regulated in a rapid and relatively extreme change in the structure of the system, then "political change" is a defining characteristic. If "instability" is defined in terms of incumbent or regime turnover and "change" is defined in terms of policy or program differences, then "political change" is an accompanying characteristic. See D. Morrison and H. Stevenson, "Integration and Instability," *American Political Science Review* 66 (September, 1972): 903–4.

f. Defining characteristic.

g. Defining characteristic. Don't be fooled by connectors ("is related to", "varies with", and so on) implying empirical relationships.

## Designation, Denotation, and Connotation

Three words are commonly used and confused in the context of specifying the meaning of a concept. *"Designation"* refers to the defining characteristics of a concept. The word "revolution" "designates" a sudden, violent, and illegal change of regimes. These are the characteristics that must be present for the word "revolution" to apply to a situation or event. *"Denotation"* refers to the things (qualities, events, relations, and so on) to which the word is applicable. Revolution "denotes" the American Revolution, French Revolution, Russian Revolution, Mexican Revolution, and so forth until all the cases to which the word can be applied are listed. *"Connotation"* refers to the mental associations a word suggests by persons who use it. For most people, "revolution" creates an unfavorable mental image. For some persons, however, it suggests a favorable meaning.

## LEARNING AID

1. "Designation" refers to the _____ characteristics of a concept.
2. "Connotation" refers to the _____ _____ a word suggests by those who use it.
3. "Denotation" refers to the _____ to which a word can apply.

**4.** "Communism" _____ (connotes, denotes, designates) an economic system involving state ownership of all property.

**5.** "Communism" _____ (connotes, denotes, designates) a negative meaning to most Americans.

**6.** "Communism" _____ (connotes, denotes, designates) all the instances of economic systems that involve state ownership of property.

**7.** Although "protest" _____ a formal statement of objection, it _____ for many people something that is violent.

. . . . . . . . . . . . . . . . . . . . . . . . . . . . . . . . . . . . . . . . . . . . . . . . . . . . . . . . . .

**1.** defining
**2.** mental associations
**3.** things
**4.** designates
**5.** connotes
**6.** denotes
**7.** designates, connotes

## Reportive and Stipulative Definitions

Concepts are provided with meaning either in the form of a reportive or a stipulative definition. A *reportive definition* states the accepted meaning of a term already in use. Reportive definitions are similar to dictionary definitions since they state the conventional meaning of a term. They take the following form:

"*X*" *has* the same meaning as "_____.

"Protest" has the same meaning as "a formal statement of objection."

"Integration" has the same meaning as "to bring together into a whole."

The term on the left is the word to be defined, whereas the term on the right is the defining expression. Since reportive definitions state the accepted usage of terms, they can be more or less accurate in reporting correct usage and, therefore, are either true or false as correct reporting.

Whereas reportive definitions state the conventional meanings of terms, *stipulative definitions,* on the other hand, assign new and special meanings to terms already in use. Stipulative definitions take the following form:

"*X*" *will* have the same meaning as "_____."

"Protest" will have the same meaning as "a host of collective manifestations, disruptive in nature, designed to provide relatively powerless people with bargaining leverage in the political process."

"Integration" will have the same meaning as "the degree of cohesion that binds members of social systems together and is generally thought of in terms of values, institutions and communication that facilitate escalating sequences of social contact, cooperation, and consensus."

Again the term on the left is the word to be defined, and the word on the right is the defining expression. The connecting expression, "will have the same meaning as," indicates that the term is to be used in a special sense. Since stipulative definitions are proposals for word usage, they are either accepted or rejected by other users of the language. Stipulative definitions, unlike reportive definitions, are neither true nor false but are more or less useful and, accordingly, are accepted or rejected. Stipulative definitions are based on the *principle of freedom of stipulation*. It states that any sign can be used to refer to anything so long as it is made clear what the sign refers to. The purpose of this principle is to prevent common language usage from impeding original conceptualization and scientific discovery.

The principle of freedom of stipulation, however, can lead to semantic chaos if carried to the extreme. To reduce the confusion and inconvenience that would come about if everybody coined their own symbols for anything they wanted to refer to, scientists agree to follow common usage wherever possible. Stipulation, in fact, should be applied only under any of the following conditions:

1.  *Absent terminology:* a word does not exist for what we want to refer to, so we invent a new word.
2.  *Vagueness:* a word exists for what we want to refer to, but it is indefinite and hazy, so we stipulate a more precise meaning.
3.  *Ambiguity:* A word exists for what we want to refer to, but it has multiple meanings, so we stipulate which one of the meanings we are using.

When a student attempts to formulate his own definition or to criticize someone else's definition of a scientific concept, he may benefit from reviewing some commonly accepted guidelines for judging the form of definitions. Five rules are frequently stated:

1.  A definition should state the essential attributes of the thing (object, item, and so on).
2.  A definition should not be circular, using the word to be defined in the defining expression.
3.  A definition should be neither too broad nor too narrow.
4.  A definition should not be expressed in ambiguous, obscure, or figurative language.
5.  A definition should not be negative if it can be affirmative.

## LEARNING AID

1. Whereas _____ (reportive, stipulative) definitions assign new meanings to terms, _____ (reportive, stipulative) definitions state accepted meanings of terms.

2. The idea that we can use any sign to refer to anything we want as long as we make clear what we are using the sign to refer to is called the principle of

_____ .

3. The three conditions under which a new concept or meaning may be stipulated are:

    a.  _____

    b.  _____

    c.  _____

4. If a "stipulative definition" is defined as a "definition that stipulates a new meaning," it violates the guideline for forming definitions which states that a definition should _____ .

5. If "democracy" is defined as a "nontotalitarian form of government," it violates the guideline that a definition should _____ .

6. If a "legislator" is defined as a "public official," the definition violates the rule that a definition should _____ .

. . . . . . . . . . . . . . . . . . . . . . . . . . . . . . . . . . . . . . . . . . . . . . . . . . . . . . . . . . . . . . . .

1. stipulative, reportive
2. freedom of stipulation
3. absent terminology, vagueness, ambiguity
4. not be circular
5. not be negative where it can be affirmative
6. not be too broad

## Theoretical and Pretheoretical Terms

Political theories consist of logically related statements of empirical regularity. All the terms that appear in a theory may be classified as either theoretical or pretheoretical. *Theoretical terms* refer to those characteristics, entities, or processes that are not directly observable. *Pretheoretical terms* refer to those characteristics, entities, or processes that are more or less directly observable and available independent of the theory. In other words, pretheoretical terms refer to those things and occurrences that we already know how to observe, measure, and describe.

For theoretical terms to be useful in science, they have to relate to empirical phenomena with which we are already acquainted. To put it another way, "theoretical unobservables" must connect in some way with "pretheoretical observables." The assumptions made in bridging the unobservable with the observable are called *bridge principles*. Bridge principles make the theory capable of being tested. Some bridge principles connect the unobservable with the observable by defining theoretical terms directly by means of pretheoretical terms. Other bridge principles connect unobservables with observables by defining theoretical terms by means of other theoretical terms, which in turn are defined by means of pretheoretical terms. Regardless of whether theoretical terms are defined directly or indirectly by means of pretheoretical terms, the unobservable must connect with the observable if the theory is to be tested.

Figure 5-3 illustrates the relationships among theoretical terms, pre-

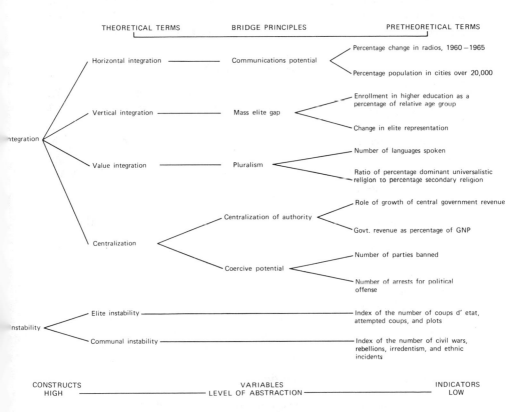

**Figure 5-3.** Relationship of Theoretical terms, Pretheoretical terms and Bridge Principles. (Adopted from Donald Morrison and Hugh Stevenson, "Intergration and Instability: Patterns of African Political Development," *American Political Science Review, 66,* 907 (1972). Copyright © 1972 by the American Political Science Association. Reprinted by the permission of the publisher.

theoretical terms, and bridge principles. In their study of African political development, Morrison and Stevenson hypothesize that as integration increases instability decreases.[3] The hypothesis specifies a relationship between two theoretical terms—integration and instability. These terms are defined by means of other less abstract theoretical terms, which in turn are defined by means of pretheoretical terms. Accordingly, "integration" is defined by means of four theoretical terms (horizontal integration, vertical integration, and so on). Each of these is defined by means of another theoretical term (e.g., communications potential). Each of these in turn is defined by means of several pretheoretical terms (e.g., percentage change in radios from 1960–1965). The assumptions made to connect such theoretical terms as "integration" to such pretheoretical terms as "percentage change in radios" are called bridge principles. If the theoretical terms are not bridged by observable characteristics, then the integration–instability hypothesis is untestable.

## LEARNING AID

**1.** Those characteristics, entities, or processes that are more or less directly observable and available independent of the theory are called _____ terms.

**2.** Theoretical terms refer to those characteristics, entities, or processes that are not directly _____.

**3.** The assumption that must be made to connect the _____ terms to the _____ are called _____ principles.

**4.** Without _____ _____ theories cannot be tested.

**5.** Figure 5–3 shows that a variable is a concept of _____ (low, medium, high) level of abstraction.

. . . . . . . . . . . . . . . . . . . . . . . . . . . . . . . . . . . . . . . . . . . . . . . . . . . . . . . . . . . . . . . . . .

**1.** pretheoretical
**2.** observable
**3.** theoretical, pretheoretical, bridge
**4.** bridge principles
**5.** medium

## Conceptual and Operational Definitions

Concepts are defined at two levels of abstraction, the theoretical and the observational. Definitions at the theoretical level are called "conceptual definitions," and definitions at the observational level are called "operational definitions."

*Conceptual definitions* define concepts by means of other abstract concepts. Conceptual definitions are theoretical and convey the general meaning of a term.

| | |
|---|---|
| Example: "Integration" | Example: "Political Efficacy" |
| "the degree of cohesion that binds members of social systems together and is generally thought of in terms of values, social contact, cooperation, and concensus." | "the feeling that individual political action does have or can have an impact on the political process." |

Conceptual definitions such as these are abstract and theoretical. They indicate what the term means in a general sense, and they suggest how the concept relates to other concepts. Conceptual definitions, however, do not specify unequivocal instructions for observing and measuring instances of a concept.

*Operational definitions* define concepts by specifying the operations (instructions) for observing and measuring their instances. Operational definitions connect theoretical unobservables with pretheoretical observables.

| | |
|---|---|
| Example: "Integration" | Example: "Political Efficacy" |
| Go to the reference book, *Black Africa: A Comparative Handbook* and determine for each country the percentage of the population in cities over 20,000. | Ask respondents whether they agree or disagree with the following statements: |
| Go to the reference book, *Black Africa: A Comparative Handbook* and determine for each country the number of languages spoken. | 1. "I don't think that public officials care much what people like me think." |
| Go to the reference book, *Black Africa: A Comparative Handbook* and determine for each country the governmental revenue as a percentage of GNP. | 2. "Voting is the only way that people like me can have a say about how the government runs things." |
| Example: "Sex" | If the respondents disagree with both statements, then they have "high political efficacy"; if the respondents disagree with one statement and agree with the other, then they have "medium political efficacy"; and if the respondents agree with both statements, then they have "low political efficacy." |
| The interviewer observes the physical characteristics of respondents and classifies them as "male" or "female." | |

The above operational definitions connect theoretical concepts with sense experience, with something that is observable. Without operational definitions theories would remain abstractions and could not be tested. Operational definitions facilitate the intersubjective testing of theories by specifying instructions any competent researcher can follow to arrive at unequivocal measurements and observations of the phenomena under study.

In 1927 the physicist P. W. Bridgman first formulated the *principle of operationism*. It states that every scientific term must be specifiable by indicating a definite testing operation that provides a criterion for its application. The purpose of operationally defining concepts is to ensure the objective testability of all statements in which the concepts appear. Objective testability means that the test can be unambiguously carried out by any competent observer and that the results are not dependent on who performs the test.

*Original operationism* postulates that the operational definition fully and exclusively determines or interprets the meaning of a term. Our concept of "integration" would mean nothing more than the set of test conditions and consequences. Bridgman argues that the concept is in fact synonymous with the corresponding set of test operations. Thus, he maintains that different operational criteria should be regarded as characterizing different concepts. Accordingly, Bridgman would argue that each of Morrison and Stevenson's operational criteria for "integration" really measures different concepts and that it would not be cautious to regard two or more operational criteria as defining the same concept.

Original operationism today is regarded as an unnecessarily extreme position and is rejected in favor of a modified version called "reconstructed operationism." *Reconstructed operationism* holds that the operational definition only partially interprets or determines the meaning of a term. To understand the meaning of a term and to use it properly, we must know not only its empirical foundation (i.e., its operational definition) but also its systematic role (i.e., its relationship to other terms in the theory). In addition, several alternative criteria for the application for a term usually exist; since any one set of test operations provides criteria of application for a concept only within a limited range of conditions, a scientific term is not fully determined by one and only one set of test operations. The operational criteria only partially interpret the meaning of social science terms.

## LEARNING AID

1. Conceptual definitions are _____ (concrete, abstract) rules that define concepts by means of other _____ and that convey the general _____ of terms.

2. Operational definitions define concepts by specifying the operations (_____) for _____ or _____ their instances.

**3.** Whereas _____ (conceptual, operational) definitions provide objective criteria for the testing of statements in which concepts occur, _____ (conceptual, operational) definitions specify the general meaning of terms.

**4.** If "degree democratization" is defined as "the extent to which nations institute and maintain over time multiple political party systems and open elections," this type of definition is _____ (conceptual, operational).

**5.** If "electoral competition" is defined as "the percentage of the time period in which the dominant party held office," the definition is _____ (conceptual, operational).

**6.** Operational definitions connect theoretical _____ with pretheoretical _____.

**7.** Formulate a conceptual definition for the concept, "party identification."

_____

_____

**8.** Formulate an operational definition for the concept, "party identification."

_____

_____

_____

_____

**9.** The principle of operationism holds that every scientific term must be _____ by indicating a definite testing operation that provides a _____ for its _____.

**10.** Whereas _____ (original, reconstructed) operationism holds that operational definitions only partially interpret the meaning of a term, _____ (original, reconstructed) operationism holds that operational definitions fully and exclusively interpret the meaning of terms.

. . . . . . . . . . . . . . . . . . . . . . . . . . . . . . . . . . . . . . . . . . . . . . . . . . .

1.   abstract, concepts, sense (meaning)
2.   instructions, observing, measuring
3.   operational, conceptual
4.   conceptual
5.   operational
6.   unobservables, observables
7.   e.g., the individual's subjective attachment to a political party.
8.   e.g., Ask respondents: "Do you think of yourself as a Republican, Democrat, Independent, or what?" Their response will be their party identification.
9.   specifiable (definable), criterion, application
10.   reconstructed, original

## Empirical and Systematic Import

Social scientists evaluate the adequacy of concepts by their fulfillment of two requirements: empirical and systematic import.[4] *The Principle of Empirical Import* states that all scientific concepts ultimately must be definable in terms of observable characters. In other words, all concepts must be operationally definable; they must have clear criteria of application. Theoretical terms must be defined in terms of pretheoretical observables.

The rule of empirical import ensures the objective testability of all scientific statements. If every concept is defined by indicating a definite observational or testing operation that provides a criterion for its application, then any competent observer can carry out the procedure and determine whether a sentence containing the term is true or false. The results are not affected by who carries out the procedure. This is what makes statements intersubjectively testable: Different persons applying the same procedure can obtain the same results.

The *Principle of Systematic Import* states that all scientific concepts must be usable in generalizations, laws, or theories. Significant scientific concepts are systematically connected to many other concepts. The more the connections, the greater the systematic import of the concept. Carl Hempel depicts systematic import metaphorically:

*Scientific systematization requires the establishment of diverse connections by laws or theoretical principles, between different aspects of the empirical world, which are characterized by scientific concepts. Thus, the concepts of science are the knots in a network of systematic interrelationships in which laws and theoretical principles form the threads. . . . The more threads converge upon, or issue from, a conceptual knot, the stronger will be its systematizing role, or its systematic import.*[5]

Concepts must satisfy both principles to be useful to social scientists. A concept may have empirical import but still may not be useful. The concept "cephalic index," for example, can be empirically defined as the ratio of the width of a person's head to its length. Thus it has empirical import. But the concept is still not useful because a person's cephalic index has no known connection with his behavior. Since there are no known laws connecting it with other concepts, cephalic index cannot be used in predicting or explaining behavior. Lacking systematic import, it is a trivial concept. The concept of "party identification," on the other hand, is useful to social scientists. It can be empirically defined, and it fits in a number of generalizations that help us to predict and explain voting behavior. It is systematically connected to a number of concepts. "Party identification" is a significant concept for political scientists because it has both empirical and systematic import.

## LEARNING AID

1. The Principle of Empirical Import states that all scientific concepts ultimately must be _____ in terms of _____ characters.
2. The Principle of Empirical Import helps to ensure that all scientific statements can be _____ tested.
3. "Objectivity" means the same thing as _____, that different
persons applying the same procedure can obtain the same results.
4. The Principle of Systematic Import states that all scientific concepts must
be _____ in generalizations, _____ or _____.
5. A concept that has been operationally defined has _____ import.
6. A scientific concept is useful if it satisfies _____ (either, both)
principles of concept formation.
7. A concept that is theoretically connected to a number of other concepts has
_____ import.

. . . . . . . . . . . . . . . . . . . . . . . . . . . . . . . . . . . . . . . . . . . . . . . . . . . . . . . . . . . . . . . . .

1. definable, observable
2. objectively (intersubjectively)
3. intersubjectivity
4. usable, laws, theories
5. empirical
6. both
7. systematic

## FOOTNOTES

1. May Brodbeck, ed., *Readings in the Philosophy of the Social Sciences* (New York: Macmillan, 1968), pp. 580–81; Gustav Bergmann, *The Philosophy of Science* (Madison: University of Wisconsin Press, 1958), pp. 12–24.

2. John Hospers, *An Introduction to Philosophical Analysis,* 2nd ed. (Englewood Cliffs, N.J.: Prentice-Hall, 1967), pp. 1–66.

3. Donald Morrison and Hugh Stevenson, "Integration and Instability: Patterns of African Political Development," *American Political Science Review* 66 (1972): 902–27.

4. Brodbeck, *Readings in the Philosophy of the Social Sciences,* 6–8; Hempel, *The Philosophy of Natural Science,* pp. 91–98.

5. Hempel, *The Philosophy of Natural Science,* p. 94.

# 6
# Concept Analysis

# INTRODUCTION

## Rationale

Since concepts refer to properties of things, concepts may be analyzed by the types of properties being characterized. By recognizing the logical status of conceptual properties, social scientists are more likely to take advantage of the theoretical potential of their concepts and to avoid logical problems in "unmixable" properties in hypotheses. Figure 6–1 shows that concepts may be analyzed in terms of four properties: (1) level of analysis, (2) level of measurement, (3) level of abstraction, and (4) theoretical role. We shall discuss each of these in turn.

## Learning Objectives

After completing this unit, the student should be able to:

1. Analyze the conceptual properties of each of the terms appearing in scientific hypotheses.

2. Define and identify examples of the following terms:

    a. Individual concepts

    b. Group concepts

    c. Fallacy of division

    d. Ecological fallacy

    e. Fallacy of composition

    f. Methodological collectivism

    g. Methodological individualism

    h. Classificatory concepts

    i. Comparative concepts

    j. Quantitative concepts

    k. Concepts

    l. Variables

    m. Indicators

    n. Compound concepts

    o. Dependent variables

    p. Independent variables

    q. Extraneous variables

| LEVEL OF ANALYSIS | LEVEL OF MEASUREMENT | LEVEL OF ABSTRACTION | THEORETICAL ROLE |
|---|---|---|---|
| Individual | Classificatory | Indicator | Independent |
| Group | Comparative | Variable | Dependent |
| | Quantitative | Construct | Extraneous |
| | | Compound Concept | |

**Figure 6–1   Properties of Concepts**

## LEVELS OF ANALYSIS

### Individual Concepts

Political concepts refer to characteristics of individuals or characteristics of groups. Concepts referring to properties of individuals are called *individual concepts*. A term is an individual concept if: (1) a property is attributed to an individual, or (2) each and every member of a group individually could be the subject of the proposition.

"Richard Nixon is conservative" is an example of the first case, where a property ("conservative") is attributed to an individual ("Richard Nixon"), a proper name. This statement asserts a singular fact, that a particular person is conservative. It asserts an instance of a concept. Since the property is attributed to an individual, the term "conservative" is an individual concept.

"Republicans tend to be conservative" is an example of the second case, where each and every Republican could be the subject of the proposition. This hypothesis associates one property ("being Republican") with another property ("conservative"). Both properties express characteristics of individuals. The hypothesis, therefore, relates two individual concepts and asserts a general fact, that Republicans tend to be conservative. "Sex is related to political participation" contains individual concepts since "sex" (being male or female) is a characteristic attributed to individuals and not a group.

The two previous examples of individual concepts illustrate properties that focus exclusively on the individual. No other information is taken into account. Some individual concepts, however, do take other information into account. Individuals, for example, may be characterized by their relative position in a group. "Persons with high socioeconomic status tend to be conservative" specifies a relationship between two concepts (socioeconomic status and conservatism). Both concepts refer to properties of persons. So, both concepts are individual concepts. "Socioeconomic status" refers to the property of an individual's relative position in a group. It is a relational property because it describes an individual's relation to a group. "First born children are more likely to have higher achievement motivation than later born children" is a similar example, where "first born" is a relational property of an individual; hence, it is an individual concept.

Individuals also may be characterized by the context or environment in which they live. "Persons living in suburban areas tend to be conservative" is a hypothesis that asserts a relationship between two properties of individuals ("living in suburban areas" and "being conservative"). What is interesting about the concept, "living in suburban areas," is that it takes into account information about the individual's context or environment. It expresses a contextual property. A similar type of hypothesis states: "Students from small colleges tend to be more conservative than students from large universities."

## Group Concepts

Concepts referring to properties of groups are called *group concepts*. A "group" may be defined as a set of elements that are systematically related. A term is a group concept if: (1) a property is attributed to a group collectively, or (2) the group itself could be the subject of the proposition.

"The Republican Party is cohesive" satisfies both cases. A property (cohesiveness) is attributed to a group (Republican Party), which is a proper name; and the group (Republican Party), is the subject of the proposition. This statement asserts that the concept "cohesiveness" has an instance (the Republican Party). It asserts a singular fact, that the Republican Party is cohesive, not a general fact, that political parties in general are cohesive. Being a property of a group, "cohesiveness" is a group concept.

"Integration is inversely related to stability" is a hypothesis specifying a relationship between two properties of a group. In their article, Morrison and Stevenson conceptualize "integration" and "stability" as characteristics of nations, which are groups. The group could be the subject of the proposition: "Nations with integration are likely to be unstable." "Nation" is a group-level unit term. The properties "integration" and "instability" are group concepts. The hypothesis specifies a relationship between two group concepts.

As with individual concepts, group concepts can focus on different kinds of group properties. Some group concepts characterize groups by performing a statistical calculation on each member of the group (e.g., a city's average income, group size, a precinct's percentage of voting turnout). Other group concepts characterize groups by describing their structural properties, that is, how subunits of the group relate to each other (e.g., cohesiveness, integration, consensus). Finally, group concepts may characterize groups by describing the relationship of a group to its context or environment (e.g., a nation's type of government, a nation's membership or nonmembership in NATO).[1]

Several important consequences result from distinguishing individual from group levels of analysis. First, individual concepts are generally not related to group concepts in the same proposition. This is a case of mixing oranges and apples; individual and group concepts do not go together. It does not make sense to say, "Richard Nixon is cohesive," since we generally construe the word to be a property of groups and not of individuals. We would have to change the conceptual definition to refer to some kind of psychological property (such as a person who has got it all together?) to employ it with another concept at the individual level of analysis. Similarly it makes neither theoretical nor logical sense to say, "bipolarity in the international system is related to the age of individuals." This combines a group property, bipolarity, with an individual property, age of individuals. This proposition could be reformulated to at least be at a consistent level of analysis if "age of individuals" is changed to "average age," which then is a group property characterizing the international system.

## Fallacy of Division and Ecological Fallacy

Second, properties that are established for a group cannot validly be inferred to hold for each individual in the group. Commission of this logical error is called the *fallacy of division*. For example it is fallacious to infer that since a football team is good every member on the team is good or that since a book is heavy every page of the book is heavy. A sociologist by the name of William Robinson pointed out an example of the fallacy of division which he called the "ecological fallacy."[2] The *ecological fallacy* can occur when we make inferences from units of observation at a higher level to units of observation at a lower level. Using census area data, which is group level analysis, he found a strong correlation (0.95) between the percentage of Negro population and the percentage of illiteracy. From these group level observations, one would be tempted to infer a strong correlation between race and illiteracy at the individual level, that is, if race and illiteracy were correlated for each individual instead of for each census area. When Robinson measured the relationship at the individual level, however, he found a low correlation (0.20). Thus we would commit the fallacy of division or the ecological fallacy if we argued from "census areas with higher percentages of blacks had higher percentages of illiteracy" to "black individuals were more likely to be illiterate than whites."

## Fallacy of Composition

Third, the converse of the fallacy of division is to infer that a property that is true of parts of a whole is also true of the whole. This logical error is called the *fallacy of composition.*[3] It is fallacious to infer that since people are made of cells and since cells are small, people must also be small; or that since every player on a team is a good athlete, the team also must be good. Since atomic bombs dropped during World War II individually did more damage than ordinary bombs, one falsely infers that atomic bombs did more total damage than ordinary bombs. This is false because there were many more bombs of the conventional type dropped than atomic ones. To proceed from what is true about members of a class to what is true of the class is an example of the fallacy of composition.

## Methodological Collectivism

Fourth, distinguishing between individual and group concepts raises the question that has become a point of controversy among social scientists—how to define group concepts.[4] One view, which is called *methodological collectivism* or *holism,* maintains that group concepts are group entities or wholes that have group properties of their own and are not definable in terms of individual behavior. Some political theorists, for example, have argued that a people possesses a "general will" that is distinct from the wills of its individual members. Sociologists have used the concept "group minds" to account for decision-making behavior. Social scientists have also used the concept "national character" to explain differences in international behavior. And sociologists have ascribed a "psyche" to mobs to explain mass hysteria. Unfortunately many group terms have been formulated far too loosely to be used in testable hypotheses. Consequently methodological holism fell into disrepute in some quarters of the scientific community.

## Methodological Individualism

To correct many such abuses that occurred in the formulation of group concepts, a contrary view called "methodological individualism" was proposed as a program for group concept formation. *Methodological individualism* asserts that all group concepts in principle should be definable in terms of individual concepts or behavior. This is usually expressed as an ideal that is to be approximated as closely as possible in practice. It assumes that statements in which group terms are used are more testable if group terms are explicitly defined by way of individual terms than if the group terms remain undefined, unobservable, and mysterious group forces. The "cohesiveness," a group concept, of a bloc of Democratic Senators may for example be defined as the "ratio of the number of times they voted in agreement with the Democratic leadership on roll call vote issues to the total number of times they voted on roll call votes." In formulating the group concept "value integration," Morrison and Stevenson explicitly relate the concept to individuals, for example, the percentage of the population speaking the major language. Although the debate between the methodological collectivists and the individualists still divides social scientists and is a complex argument, we believe that the principle of methodological individualism offers a more cuatious approach in formulating concepts that ultimately fit into testable theories. No longer should we waste time with impersonal and unobservable group forces. We should try to define group forces. We should try to define group concepts in terms of individual behavior.

## LEARNING AID

**1.** Whereas group concepts refer to properties of _____, individual concepts refer to properties of _____.

**2.** As a general rule, individual concepts _____ (should, should not) be related to group concepts in the same proposition.

**3.** Inferring that a property that is true of parts of a whole is also true of the whole is called the fallacy of _____.

**4.** Inferring that properties that are established for a group also hold for each individual in the group is called the fallacy of _____.

**5.** Another name for the fallacy of _____ is the _____ fallacy.

**6.** The position that maintains that group concepts are group entities or wholes which have _____ properties of their own and are not definable in terms of _____ behavior is called methodological _____ or _____.

**7.** The position that maintains that all group concepts in principle should be _____ in terms of individual concepts or behavior is called _____.

**8.** An investigator who finds a correlation in the percentage of the vote for the Democratic candidate for governor and the percentage Democratic registration at the precinct level _____ (is, is not) guilty of the ecological fallacy.

**9.** If he infers from this information that Democrats were more likely to vote for the Democratic candidate for governor, he _____ (could, could not) be guilty of the _____ fallacy.

**10.** If an investigator counts the types of political values in the platforms of both political parties and infers that these are the values of the American people, he is likely to have committed the fallacy of _____.

**11.** An investigator finds that intensely discontented people who believe in violence are likely to rebel. The concepts are measured in terms of aggregate data, at the national level, and he finds a strong correlation among the variables. He then infers that there is an equally strong correlation between individuals being discontented, holding violent attitudes, and rebelling. What kind of fallacy is this?

**12.** Distinguish whether the following concepts are likely to be group (G) or individual (I) terms:

|   |   |   |   |
|---|---|---|---|
| a. | party identification | f. | Gross National Product |
| b. | party realignment | g. | number of protests |
| c. | partisan attitude | h. | ethnic identification |
| d. | segregation | i. | crime rate |
| e. | legislative norms | j. | religious affiliation |

**13.** "Public opinion" is a group concept that has occasionally been used in the holistic sense to refer to a group mind. Suggest how a methodological individualist might define the concept.

**14.** The United States Senate is a distinguished institution; therefore, every senator is a distinguished man. What kind of fallacy is this?

. . . . . . . . . . . . . . . . . . . . . . . . . . . . . . . . . . . . . . . . . . . . . . . . . . . . . . . .

1. groups, individuals
2. should not
3. composition
4. division
5. division, ecological
6. group, individual, collectivism, holism
7. definable, methodological individualism
8. is not
9. could, ecological
10. composition
11. ecological
12. (a) I, (b) G, (c) I, (d) G, (e) G, (f) G, (g) G, (h) I, (i) G, (j) I
13. "Public opinion" may be defined as a collection of individual attitudes.
14. fallacy of division

# LEVELS OF MEASUREMENT

The properties named by the concepts are more or less measurable. Consequently, we can distinguish concepts from each other by the extent to which they name properties of things which are measurable. The three levels of concept measurement are classificatory, comparative, and quantitative.[5]

## Classificatory Concepts

*Classificatory concepts* name properties that are either present or absent in objects. Classificatory concepts divide a domain into classes, categories, or types. "Sex" is a classificatory concept; it divides people into two categories, males or females, and a person is classified depending on whether certain properties are present or absent. Classificatory concepts have an "either . . . or" character. People are either males or females. "Party registration" is also a classificatory concept; it divides persons into Democrats, Republicans, Independents, other, or unregistered. "Region" classifies persons according to a property, living in the north, south, east, or west.

## Comparative Concepts

*Comparative concepts* name properties which are more or less present in objects. "Influence" may be considered a comparative concept since some people are more influential or less influential than others. "Alienation" also names a property by which persons can be compared. Some persons are more alientated than others.

## Quantitative Concepts

*Quantitative concepts* name the degree to which properties are present in objects. "Total family income" names how much money the family earned. "Number of years schooling" names how much education is acquired. "Gross National Product" names the degree of national wealth. "Voting turnout" indicates the degree to which people turn out to vote.

Distinguishing concepts by their levels of measurement has several implications. First, the level of measurement for a concept may vary depending on the user's need and the state of knowledge. Generally, the more we know about a field, the more refined the distinctions we make. Sometimes concepts initially formulated as classificatory at a later time are reconceptualized and reformulated as comparative or quantitative. Depending on how much information we want to give, we may say the weather is "hot" or "cold" (classificatory), "hotter" or "colder" (comparative), or "40 degrees C" (quantitative). A political scientist may initially categorize nations as "democratic" or conceptualize and rank order countries and say that one country is "more democratic" (comparative) than another. As knowledge improves, he may reformulate the concept and talk about the "degree of democratization" (quantitative). As we learn more about a field, we are likely to want more refined distinctions. During the initial stages of inquiry, however, we may not have the capability for quantitative measurement. We may have to remain content with cruder types of distinctions.

Second, the distinction between qualitative and quantitative becomes somewhat specious, since all concepts are based on qualities or what we call properties. The difference is that in classificatory concepts we look for whether a quality is present or absent; in comparative concepts we look for whether an object has more or less of a quality than another object; and in quantitative concepts, we look for exactly how much of a quality is present in objects. In this sense all research is qualitative. And third, distinguishing levels of measurement influences the way in which the investigator approaches the problem of analyzing the data. We shall elaborate on this at a later time.


## LEARNING AID

1. Classificatory concepts name properties that are either _____ or _____ in objects.
2. Comparative concepts name properties that are _____ or _____ present in objects.
3. Quantitative concepts name the _____ to which properties are present in objects.
4. All concepts are qualitative since they all are based on _____.
5. Determine the most likely level of measurement for the following concepts:

|     |     |     |     |
| --- | --- | --- | --- |
| a. | Gross National Product | f. | Strength of partisanship |
| b. | Socioeconomic status | g. | Number of alliances |
| c. | Voting turnout | h. | Protest intensity |
| d. | Type of government | i. | Number of protests |
| e. | Ethnicity | j. | Type of protest |

. . . . . . . . . . . . . . . . . . . . . . . . . . . . . . . . . . . . . . . . . . . . . . . . . . . . . . . . . . . . . . . . . . . .

1. present, absent
2. more, less
3. degree (extent)
4. qualities (properties)
5. (a) quantitative, (b) comparative, (c) quantitative, (d) classificatory, (e) classificatory, (f) comparative, (g) quantitative, (h) comparative, (i) quantitative, (j) classificatory


## LEVELS OF ABSTRACTION

Scientific terms vary according to their level of abstraction, that is, their proximity to observable data or sense experience. Terms close to sense experience have a low level of abstraction; terms remote from sense experience have a high level of abstraction. Terms with the highest level of abstraction are called "constructs"; terms with intermediate abstraction, "variables"; and terms with low level abstraction, "indicators." In addition to these terms, we shall discuss in this section "compound concepts," terms that have popular but little scientific value.

Figure 6–2 illustrates the logical relationship among constructs, variables, and indicators. Notice that the hypothesis specifies a relationship between two constructs, which are highly abstract terms observed only indirectly. To test the hypothesis, constructs must connect with observable phenomena. Constructs frequently subdivide into several more specific properties or dimensions, which

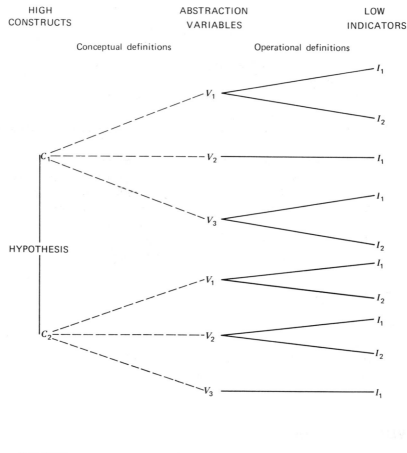

Figure 6-2. Levels of Abstraction.

CONSTRUCTS                    VARIABLES                    INDICATORS

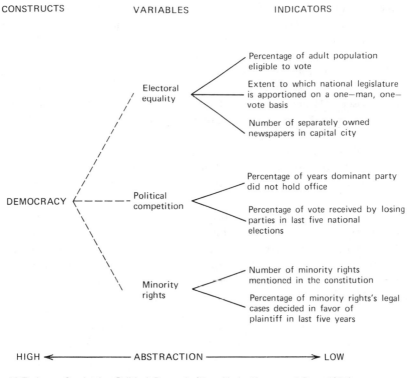

Figure 6-3.   Specification of the Levels of Abstractions for the Concept "Democracy."

we call "variables." Variables are constructs that are more or less directly observable and that take on different values. Variables connect with constructs through conceptual definitions. Variables in turn connect with directly observable phenomena, indicators, by operational definition.

We may now define each term somewhat more precisely:

1. *Constructs* are labels for properties that are indirectly observable.

2. *Variables* are labels for properties that are more or less directly observable and that take on different values.

3. *Indicators* are labels for properties that are directly observable and that take on different values.

Figure 6–3 shows the various levels of abstraction for the construct "democracy."[6] "Democracy" qualifies as a construct since it refers to a property, a type of government, that we cannot directly observe. We can, however, break the construct down into several variables—electoral equality, political competition, and minority rights—terms standing for phenomena more directly observable than "democracy." Variables in turn must be operationalized so as to fully relate abstract constructs to observable reality. Indicators, pointing at observable phenomena, serve this purpose. Indicators are directly observable and take on different values. When we say that variables and indicators "take on different values," we mean they can vary. Electoral equality, for example, is operationally defined by the indicator, percentage adult population eligible to vote, which takes on many different values ranging from complete equality to varying degrees of inequality. The indicator also can take on many different values: varying percentages of the adult population eligible to vote. For a second example of specifying and subdividing constructs into variables and variables into indicators, turn to Figure 5–3, which illustrates the relationship of integration and instability.

4. *Compound concepts* are labels for unsystematic combinations of different kinds of properties.[7] The label tends to highlight one of the more important properties. Compound concepts are usually vague abstractions that characterize a bundle of properties. "Mass society" is a compound concept that refers to a society that is massive, heterogeneous, pluralistic, diffuse in goals, urbanized, industrialized, centralized, and so on. "Under-developed nation" refers to a broad set of properties that are also unsystematically combined. "Other-directed personality" is another example summarizing a large set of characteristics used to describe personalities. "Communist country" refers to an assorted mixture of properties. Concepts such as these are usually too vague to be of much scientific value. They require reformulation before they can be used in the statement of hypotheses.

The social science literature is replete with concepts such as these. Appearing in the early stages of inquiry in new fields when investigators are grasping for labels to describe what they think are significant patterns and regularities in nature, compound concepts tend to remain in vogue for a period of time. When properties and relationships are unsystematically bundled together, conceptual confusion tends to result. When a term's meaning is not fully specified, it is not usable in hypotheses. Although perhaps useful in introducing some aspects of a discipline to introductory students, compound concepts must be carefully reformulated (e.g., "democracy") with properties fully specified and systematically combined before they can be used in the statement of scientific hypotheses.

Social scientists select, utilize, and analyze concepts in their search for knowledge. Concepts are explicated when initially vague and imprecise concepts are provided more exact meanings. As concepts are explicated, intersubjective understanding increases. Concepts are explicated both analytically and empirically.[8] The analytical analysis of a concept involves searching for the implicit and explicit assumptions inherent in the various meanings attributed to the concept and analyzing its conceptual properties (level of analysis, level of measurement, level of abstraction, theoretical role, and so on). The empirical analysis of a concept involves testing the assumptions exposed by the analysis of meanings. Through the explication of important concepts, social scientists advance the formation and testing of theories.

## LEARNING AID

**1.** Labels for properties that are more or less directly observable and that take on different values are called _____.

**2.** Labels for properties that are directly observable and that take on different values are called _____.

**3.** Labels for properties that are indirectly observable are called _____.

**4.** Labels for unsystematic combinations of different kinds of properties are called _____.

**5.** Although sometimes a matter of judgment, try to identify the level of abstraction for the following terms:

| | | | |
|---|---|---|---|
| a. | Bureaucracy | f. | Index of number of civil wars and rebellions |
| b. | Party identification | | |
| c. | Integration | g. | Communal instability |
| d. | Mass–elite gap | h. | Instability |
| e. | Number of languages spoken | i. | Political modernization |
| | | j. | Sex |

. . . . . . . . . . . . . . . . . . . . . . . . . . . . . . . . . . . . . . . . . . . . . . . . . . . . . .

**1.** variables
**2.** indicators
**3.** constructs
**4.** compound concepts
**5.** (a) compound concept, (b) construct or variable, (c) construct, (d) variable, (e) indicator, (f) indicator, (g) variable, (h) construct, (i) compound concept, (j) variable.

## THEORETICAL ROLE

Finally, concepts may vary according to whether they operate as dependent, independent, or extraneous variables. Concepts that are to be explained or predicted are called "dependent variables." They are consequences of other forces, influences, or variables. They "depend" on the values of other variables. We may loosely think of them as effect variables.

Concepts used as bases for predicting or explaining other concepts are called "independent variables." They precede in time or are antecedent to the dependent variable. They are presumed to influence the dependent variable. We may loosely think of them as causal variables.

Concepts other than independent variables that may influence the dependent variables are "extraneous variables." These are variables outside the relationship between the independent and dependent variables that may influence the relationship. Before an investigator can discern the precise relationship between the independent and dependent variables, he must achieve some measure of control over extraneous variables. It is for this reason that extraneous variables are often called "control" variables and are held constant while the investigator examines the relationship between the independent and dependent variables.

Concepts, then, may operate in hypotheses or theories primarily as:

1.  *Dependent variables*—concepts that are to be explained and predicted and that occur as a consequence of other variables.

2.  *Independent variables*—concepts used to explain and predict other concepts and that occur antecedent to the dependent variable.

3.  *Extraneous variables*—concepts other than the independent variables that may influence the relationship and that occur antecedent to the dependent variable.

The same concept may occupy different theoretical roles in different theories and sometimes even in the same theory. For example, "alienation" can be an independent variable in some relationships, dependent in others, and extraneous in others still.

Let's examine several hypotheses. "Older persons tend to be more conservative than younger persons." In this hypothesis "age" is the independent variable and "conservatism" is the dependent variable. It is hypothesized that age affects attitude toward conservatism. Conservatism occurs as a consequence of age, and age is antecedent to conservatism. Age is an explanatory or predictor variable; conservatism is the variable to be explained or predicted. We can often identify the theoretical role of a concept by asking ourselves two questions: Which variable is more likely to come first in time, and which variable makes more theoretical sense as being the cause? In this case it makes theoretical sense that age influences a person to become more conservative, but not that conservatism influences a person to become older (chronologically).

"Political knowledge is associated with party identification, controlling for socioeconomic status." First of all, socioeconomic status is clearly indicated as an extraneous variable since it is the one being held constant. Now, which variable is the independent variable and which is the dependent variable? We ask ourselves which variable makes more theoretical sense as being the cause. Does it make more sense that as people become more knowledgeable about politics they are likely to identify more with a political party or does it make more sense that as people identify with a party they are likely to have more political knowledge? Both lines of reasoning make at least some theoretical sense. Since this does not solve our problem, we should turn to the second question: Which variable is more likely to occur antecedent to the other variable? We know (research shows) that people generally acquire identification with a political party at an early age, between five and eight years of age. Political knowledge, on the other hand, is learned later on. Since independent variables are antecedent to dependent variables and since party identification is antecedent to political knowledge, we may conclude that party identification is the independent variable and political knowledge is the dependent variable.

## LEARNING AID

1. Independent variables are concepts that are used to _____ and _____ other concepts and that occur _____ to the dependent variable.

2. Extraneous variables are concepts other than _____ variables that may influence the relationship and that occur _____ to the _____ variable.

3. Dependent variables are the concepts that are to be _____ and _____ and that occur as a _____ of other variables.

4. Identify the theoretical role of each of the variables in the following hypotheses:

   a. The incidence of protest will vary negatively with open structure of political opportunities.
   b. Foreign policy opinion is a function of social position.
   c. The potential for collective violence varies strongly with the intensity and scope of relative deprivation among members of a collectivity.
   d. The likelihood of internal war varies with the degree of foreign support of dissidents.
   e. The more frequent the occurrence of a particular form of political violence in a collectivity, the greater the expectation that it will recur.
   f. Growth tends to reduce internal conflicts in an organization.
   g. Organizations tend to become more conservative as they get older, unless they experience periods of rapid growth or internal turnover.
   h. The more a solitary group is affected by an issue, the higher the probability it will attempt to influence decisions relating to it.

i. Blacks tend to participate more than whites when age and socioeconomic status are held constant.

j. *Ceteris paribus* (everything else being equal), the probability of communist voting among workers in Western Europe will increase with lower socioeconomic status and increasing economic insecurity.

. . . . . . . . . . . . . . . . . . . . . . . . . . . . . . . . . . . . . . . . . . . . . . . . . . . . . . . . . . .

1. explain, predict, antecedent (prior to)
2. independent, antecedent, dependent
3. explained, predicted, consequence (result)
4. a. DV (dependent variable) = incidence of protest, IV (independent variable) = open structure of political opportunities;
   b. DV = foreign policy opinion, IV = social position;
   c. DV = potential for collective violence, $IV_1$ = intensity of relative deprivation, $IV_2$ = scope of relative deprivation;
   d. DV = likelihood of internal war, IV = degree of foreign support of dissidents;
   e. DV = expectation of recurrence, IV = frequency of occurrence of a particular form of political violence;
   f. DV = internal conflicts, IV = growth;
   g. DV = conservatism, IV = age, $EV_1$ = rapid growth, $EV_2$ = internal turnover;
   h. DV = influence attempts, IV = issue effect on group;
   i. DV = participation, IV = race, $EV_1$ = age, $EV_2$ = socio-economic status;
   j. DV = Communist voting, $IV_1$ = socio-economic status, $IV_2$ = economic insecurity, EV = all other variables

## SUMMARY FEEDBACK

(IDENTIFY THE PROPERTIES OF EACH OF THE CONCEPTS UNDERLINED IN THE FOLLOWING HYPOTHESES:)

1. Blacks tend to participate more than whites when age and socioeconomic status are held constant.

|  | Black/White | Age | Socioeconomic Status |
|---|---|---|---|
| ANALYSIS | | | |
| MEASUREMENT | | | |
| ABSTRACTION | | | |
| ROLE | | | |

2.  Growth tends to reduce the <u>number of internal conflicts</u> in organizations.

|  | Growth | No. Internal Conflicts |
|---|---|---|
| ANALYSIS | | |
| MEASUREMENT | | |
| ABSTRACTION | | |
| ROLE | | |

3.  The incidence of <u>protest</u> will vary negatively with <u>open structure of political opportunities</u>.

|  | Incidence of Protest | Open Structure of Pol. Opp. |
|---|---|---|
| ANALYSIS | | |
| MEASUREMENT | | |
| ABSTRACTION | | |
| ROLE | | |

. . . . . . . . . . . . . . . . . . . . . . . . . . . . . . . . . . . . . . . . . . .

SINCE OPERATIONAL DEFINITIONS ARE NOT PROVIDED, SOME CLASSIFICATIONS ARE SOMEWHAT JUDGMENTAL. IN THESE CASES ALTERNATIVE ANSWERS ARE PROVIDED.

1.

|  | Black/White | Age | Socioeconomic Status |
|---|---|---|---|
| ANALYSIS | individual | individual | individual |
| MEASUREMENT | classificatory | quantitative | comparative |
| ABSTRACTION | variable | variable | variable |
| ROLE | independent | extraneous | extraneous |

2.

|  | Growth | No. Internal Conflicts |
|---|---|---|
| ANALYSIS | group | group |
| MEASUREMENT | quantitative | quantitative |
| ABSTRACTION | construct (variable) | variable |
| ROLE | independent | dependent |

3.

|  | Incidence of Protest | Open Structure of Pol. Opp. |
|---|---|---|
| ANALYSIS | group | group |
| MEASUREMENT | quantitative | classificatory (or comparative) |
| ABSTRACTION | construct | construct |
| ROLE | dependent | independent |

## FOOTNOTES

1. Paul Lazarsfeld, "Evidence and Inference in Social Research," *Daedalus* 87 (1958): 111–17.
2. William Robinson, "Ecological Correlations and the Behavior of Individuals," *American Sociological Review* 15 (June, 1950): 351–57. Also see T. R. Gurr, *Politimetrics* (Englewood Cliffs, N.J.: Prentice-Hall, 1972), pp. 33–35.
3. Irving Copi, *Introduction to Logic,* 2nd ed. (New York: Macmillan, 1961), pp. 79–81.
4. May Brodbeck, "Methodological Individualisms: Definition and Reduction," in *Readings in the Philosophy of Social Science,* ed. May Brodbeck (New York: Macmillan, 1968), pp. 280–303; Ernest Nagel, *The Structure of Science* (New York: Harcourt, Brace, and World, 1961), pp. 535–46.
5. Carl Hempel, *Fundamentals of Concept Formation in Empirical Science* (Chicago: University of Chicago Press, 1952), pp. 54–62.
6. E. Terrence Jones, *Conducting Political Research* (New York: Harper and Row, 1971), pp. 16–19.
7. This term is similar to Dubin's "summative unit." See Robert Dubin, *Theory Building* (New York: The Free Press, 1969), pp. 60–63.
8. See Richard Dumont and William Wilson, "Aspect of Concept Formation, Explication, and Theory Construction in Sociology," *American Sociological Review* 32 (December, 1967): 985–95.

# 7
# Hypothesis Formulation

# INTRODUCTION

## Rationale

Scientific knowledge is not arrived at simply by observing phenomena and collecting facts. Rather, it is achieved by the method of hypothesis, by inventing hypotheses as tentative answers to problems and subjecting them to empirical test.[1] Conjecture, bold ideas, speculations—hypotheses—are our primary means for interpreting nature. Hypotheses provide an important link between abstract theories and sense experience. Furthermore, formulating and testing hypotheses are important and exciting parts of the scientific game.

Hypotheses may be likened to fishing nets: Only he who casts will catch.[2] In this unit the student learns to cast hypotheses. The unit begins with an examination of the definition, function, and form of hypotheses. Next are considered the criteria for formulating scientifically adequate hypotheses. The unit concludes with an inquiry into various techniques social scientists use to stimulate their scientific imagination and to encourage scientific discovery.

## Learning Objectives

After completing this unit the student should be able to:

1. Define and identify: scientific hypotheses, laws, univariate and multivariate hypotheses, associational and nonassociational hypotheses, directional and nondirectional hypotheses, universal and statisical hypotheses, deducibility, testability, ordinary and theoretical propositions, generalizations, temporal and cross-sectional hypotheses.

2. Explain the function of hypotheses.

3. Name the three factors affecting testability.

4. Identify violations in the testability of hypotheses.

5. Formulate an adequate original political hypothesis.

6. Name and explain the five techniques of social scientific discovery.

7. Formulate hypotheses through the method of constructing cross-classification tables.

8. Formulate theoretical and ordinary propositions.

## HYPOTHESES

### Definition

*Scientific hypotheses* are empirically testable statements derived from a theory. "John is strong" is not a scientific hypothesis if it is not derived from a theory. If it is derived from a theory (e.g., Lumberjacks are strong. John is a lumberjack. Therefore, John is strong.), then the statement qualifies as a hypothesis, albeit a very low level and uninteresting one. "World government will bring everlasting peace" is not a scientific hypothesis either. It is possible to imagine how it might be deduced from a theory, but it is still not a hypothesis because it is not empirically testable. There is no way of telling whether world government will end wars forever. Thus, for statements to qualify as scientific hypotheses, they must be both empirically testable and derivable from a theory.

It may be helpful to distinguish hypotheses from several other closely associated terms, namely, propositions, generalizations, and laws. The word *proposition* occurs in two different scientific contexts. It is sometimes used to refer to any type of declarative statement, e.g., "This proposition is vague and ambiguous." It also is used to refer to the confirmation status of a statement. Before a statement has been tested and confirmed, it is referred to as a "hypothesis." After it has been tested and confirmed, it is often referred to as a "proposition." Usually the context in which "proposition" appears makes clear which sense of the term is being used.

*Generalizations* are general statements that include common names or concepts. The term "generalization" is usually interchangeable with the term "hypothesis," although "hypothesis" tends to emphasize the conjectural status of the concept.

*Laws* are confirmed hypotheses with broad scope. They are hypotheses that have been tested and confirmed. Many scientists argue that laws must take the form of a universal generalization, that is, "If $X$, then $Y$ always." Being deduced from higher level generalizations and being used to deduce lower level generalizations, laws also occupy strategic locations in scientific theory.

### Function

Hypotheses are significant for two reasons. *First, hypotheses help to provide systematic import.* They do so by connecting concepts systematically. By organizing concepts into statements, hypotheses help us to make sense out of what we observe. We previously quoted Carl Hempel's analogy between concepts and knots, on the one hand, and hypotheses and threads, on the other.[3] The more that threads converge on or emerge from a conceptual knot, the stronger will be its systematizing role. Thus, hypotheses play the important role of providing systematic import.

*Second, hypotheses facilitate the testing of scientific theories.* Theories are simply sets of generalizations connected deductively. Theories usually are tested indirectly by deducing and testing hypotheses. When hypotheses are tested, they advance scientific knowledge by indicating the confirmation status of a theory. Hypotheses link abstract theories to the empirical world.

## Form

Hypotheses may be classified according to whether they are univariate or multivariate, associational or nonassociational, universal or statistical and temporal or cross-sectional.

### UNIVARIATE AND MULTIVARIATE HYPOTHESES

*Univariate hypotheses* assign a value (category) of a variable to a unit (individual, group, event, or object) of observation. "Voting turnout in the United States is 60%" is a univariate hypothesis because it assigns the value "60%" of the variable "voting turnout" to a unit of observation, "United States" "Nixon is an active–negative" is also univariate because it assigns a value or category (active–negative) of a variable (type of personality) to a unit (Nixon, an individual). Sometimes, as in the latter example, a category but not the variable is specified; the variable is implicit and must be inferred. Thus, both the statements are univariate because they assign a value of a variable to a unit of observation. They are both hypotheses because they are derivable from some theory and are capable of empirical test. Statements lacking theoretical import are simply descriptive sentences and should not be labeled "hypotheses." Since univariate hypotheses have only one variable, they are not classifiable as associational or nonassociational, directional or nondirectional, universal or statistical, and temporal or cross-sectional.

Many statements in political science are univariate hypotheses because they involve the description, explanation, or prediction of individual persons or nations. Some scientists maintain that such statements are of such a low level that they are simply descriptive and do not deserve to be called scientific hypotheses.[4] We disagree. So long as they meet the tests of being derivable from a theory and are empirically testable, they should qualify as hypotheses just as other satements do. In addition, the natural sciences abound with significant singular statement hypotheses. For example, in the field of astronomy, Adams and Leverrier deduced from Newton's theory and from certain facts about the orbit of Uranus that an undiscovered planet (Neptune) exists.[5] This was an important discovery contributing to the testing of a significant theory and advancing scientific knowledge. It should not be relegated to a minor status simply because of the form of the statement in which it appears. Since citing individual facts about individual planets does not appear to be logically different from citing individual facts about individual nations or persons, univariate hypotheses can be legitimate and significant tools in social science just as they are in physical science.

*Multivariate hypotheses* are statements that relate two or more variables. "National health varies with national wealth," "If income increases, then alienation decreases," and "Education is associated with political participation, controlling for income and ethnicity" are all examples of multivariate hypotheses, which relate two or more variables. Multivariate hypotheses are the type that is found most often in the academic journals.

### ASSOCIATIONAL AND NONASSOCIATIONAL HYPOTHESES

*Associational hypotheses* specify that two or more variables are related. Associational hypotheses may be directional or nondirectional. *Directional hypotheses* specify that two or more variables are related positively or negatively. Examples include: "If wages increase, then prices increase," "Education is positively associated with political participation," "Poverty is inversely related to education," and "If inflation increases, then real personal income decreases." *Nondirectional hypotheses* specify that two or more variables are related but the direction is not indicated. Examples of nondirectional associational hypotheses include: "Wages are related to prices," "Education is associated with political participation," and "Foreign policy opinion is a function of social position."

*Nonassociational hypotheses* specify that two or more variables are not related. Such hypotheses are also called *null hypotheses* ("null" means "no," referring to no relationship between the variables). A typical example of a null hypothesis is "There is no association between sex and voting turnout."

### UNIVERSAL AND STATISTICAL HYPOTHESES

*Universal hypotheses* take the form: If $X$, then always $Y$. Universal hypotheses are seldom, if ever, found in the social sciences, and they are usually indicated by such words as "always" and "never." *Statistical hypotheses* take the form: If X, then probably Y. An example of a universal hypothesis is, "If water is heated to 212 degrees F at sea level, then it always boils." An example of a statistical hypothesis is, "If a candidate for the United States Senate is an incumbent senator, then it is 90% probable that he will win."

### TEMPORAL AND CROSS-SECTIONAL HYPOTHESES

*Temporal hypotheses* state that one variable precedes the other in time. "If wages increase, then prices increase at a later time" is a temporal hypothesis.

*Cross-sectional hypotheses* state that the variables occur at the same point or section in time. They do not imply causality as do temporal hypotheses. "The greater the alienation, the less the participation in politics" is a cross-sectional hypothesis since it does not specifically mention a time component.

## LEARNING AID

**1.** Scientific hypotheses are empirically _____ statements derived from a _____.

**2.** Laws are _____ hypotheses with _____ scope.

**3.** Hypotheses have two functions:

    a. _____

    b. _____

**4.** Whereas _____ hypotheses relate two or more variables, _____ hypotheses assign a value (category) of a variable to a unit of observation.

**5.** Whereas _____ hypotheses specify that two or more variables are related, _____ hypotheses, also called _____ hypotheses, state that two or more variables are not related.

**6.** Hypotheses that take the form, "If $X$, then probably $Y$" are called _____ hypotheses, whereas those that take the form, "If $X$, then always $Y$" are called _____ hypotheses.

**7.** Hypotheses that state that the variables occur at the same time are called _____ hypotheses, whereas those that state that one precedes the other are _____ hypotheses.

**8.** Identify whether the following hypotheses are univariate $(U)$ or multivariate $(M)$, associational $(A)$ or nonassociational $(NA)$, directional $(D)$ or nondirectional $(ND)$, universal $(U)$ or statistical $(S)$, and temporal $(T)$ or cross-sectional $(CS)$. If the adjective pair is not appropriate, leave the line blank.

|  |  | U/M | A/NA | D/ND | U/S | T/CS |
|---|---|---|---|---|---|---|
| a. | If nations are frustrated in achieving their foreign policy goals, then they later tend to be aggressive. | ____ | ____ | ____ | ____ | ____ |
| b. | IQ is not a function of race. | ____ | ____ | ____ | ____ | ____ |
| c. | The United States will probably sign a non-aggression pact with China. | ____ | ____ | ____ | ____ | ____ |

    d.   If presidents are assassinated, then the vice-presidents always become president.   ——  ——  ——  ——  ——

    e.   The occurrence of revolution is a function of sense of relative deprivation.   ——  ——  ——  ——  ——

    f.   Arizona is conservative.   ——  ——  ——  ——  ——

    g.   Catholics are more likely to be liberal than Protestants.   ——  ——  ——  ——  ——

    h.   If nations are democratic, then they are probably industrialized.   ——  ——  ——  ——  ——

. . . . . . . . . . . . . . . . . . . . . . . . . . . . . . . . . . . . . . . . . . . . . . . . . . . . . . . . . . . . . .

**1.** testable, theory
**2.** confirmed, broad
**3.** They help to provide systematic import, they facilitate the testing of scientific theories.
**4.** multivariate, univariate
**5.** associational, nonassociational, null
**6.** statistical, universal
**7.** cross-sectional, temporal
**8.**  a.  multivariate, associational, directional, statistical, temporal
      b.  multivariate, nonassociational, leave blank, statistical (inferred by the nature of the variables and not from the form), cross-sectional
      c.  univariate, leave blank, leave blank, leave blank, leave blank
      d.  multivariate, associational, directional, universal, temporal
      e.  multivariate, associational, nondirectional, statistical (inferred from the nature of the variables), cross-sectional
      f.  univariate, leave blank, leave blank, leave blank, leave blank
      g.  multivariate, associational, directional, statistical, cross-sectional
      h.  multivariate, associational, directional, statistical, cross-sectional

## HYPOTHESIS ANALYSIS

In the previous section hypotheses were examined in terms of their definition, function, and form. We shall now investigate two principles underlying the formulation of adequate hypotheses, the principle of deducibility and the principle of testability.

## Deducibility

Hypotheses are defined as empirically testable statements derived from a theory. By definition hypotheses must be related to a theory. Moreover, hypotheses must have "systematic" or "theoretical" import. Hypotheses have systematic import when they connect deductively with other statements in a theory. They are derived from a theory when they satisfy the *principle of deducibility, which states that all hypotheses should be deducible from or be used to deduce other statements contained in a theory.* Hypotheses that lack deducibility do not permit scientific explanation and prediction, two of the primary goals of social science. Thus, everything else being equal, hypotheses with the greatest deducibility are the most highly preferred. For the rules of deduction refer back to the unit on formal fallacies.

## Testability

The definition of hypotheses stipulates not only that hypotheses should be deducible but that they also should be testable. Statements that cannot be tested and falsified do not qualify as scientific hypotheses. Thus, hypotheses should satisfy the *principle of testability, which states that all hypotheses should be capable of being confirmed or disconfirmed with observational evidence.* This requirement ensures that scientific statements have what is termed "empirical import." The criterion of testability separates scientific knowledge, which rests on sense experience, from metaphysical knowledge, which is based on intuition, reason, and authority.

Testability is a complex concept. Several factors affect the testability of hypotheses.[6]

### CONCEPT CLARITY

Hypotheses should be conceptually clear. They should be stated so that they can be easily understood by different competent persons. Hypotheses should mean the same thing to different researchers. In other words, hypotheses should be intersubjectively meaningful.

### CONCEPT MEASUREMENT

Hypotheses should contain operationally definable concepts. That is, concepts must be definable in terms of observational characters. Hypotheses containing concepts that cannot be defined operationally are not testable, and therefore, are not adequate scientific hypotheses.

RESOURCE AVAILABILITY

Hypotheses should be related to available research techniques. A common error among beginning students is to formulate hypotheses that cannot be tested for lack of resources (e.g., time, energy, money, interviewers, coders, and the like) or the inavailability of certain kinds of data collection devices. This does not mean that hypotheses should not be formulated that are presently too complex to be handled by contemporary techniques. Obviously, many great scientific theories were proposed before they could actually be tested. However, many of these theories were scorned and unproductive until they could be tested objectively. It is especially prudent that beginning social scientists consider constraints on resources and data collection devices as they formulate hypotheses for research papers, theses, and dissertations.

## LEARNING AID

**1.** Two principles underlie the formulation of adequate hypotheses: the principle of _____ and the principle of _____.

**2.** The principle of deducibility states that all hypotheses should be deducible _____ a theory or be used to _____ other statements contained in a theory.

**3.** Hypotheses that have deducibility also have _____ or _____ import.

**4.** The principle of testability states that all hypotheses should be capable of being _____ or _____ with _____ evidence.

**5.** Hypotheses that are testable also have _____ import.

**6.** Name three factors affecting the testability of hypotheses:

    a. _____

    b. _____

    c. _____

**7.** Discuss which factor of testability is most seriously violated in each of the following hypotheses:

    a. The average intelligence of the Founding Fathers was higher than the average intelligence of current United Stated Senators.

    b. Community integration is inversely related to violence.

    c. The larger the membership size of a pressure group, the greater its potential power.

**8.** Formulate an adequate, original, political hypothesis that is also multivariate, associational, and statistical.

. . . . . . . . . . . . . . . . . . . . . . . . . . . . . . . . . . . . . . . . . . . . . . . . . . . . . . . . . .

**1.** deducibility, testability

**2.** from, deduce

3. systematic, theoretical
4. confirmed, disconfirmed, observational
5. empirical
6. concept clarity, concept measurement, resource availability
7. a. Resource availability. We can easily identify and measure such concepts as "intelligence" (I.Q.), "Founding Fathers" (signers of the Declaration of Independence and the Constitution), "average" (arithmetic mean), "current United States Senators" (roster), but it is practically impossible to arrive at an I.Q. score for the Founding Fathers and very unlikely that senators will submit to such a test. This hypothesis is not testable because of resource constraints.
   b. Concept clarity. The hypothesis is unclear as to which level of community is being referred to: city, neighborhood, national, international, and so on. It also is not clear whether "integration" refers to the narrow concept of racial integration or the broader concept meaning "cohesion," such as the social, cultural, or economic cohesion of a community. The concept of "violence" is also unclear. Violence may refer to political violence, property violence, personal injury violence, violence to achieve ends, violence to express rage, and so forth. This hypothesis is loaded with concepts that must be more clearly and specifically defined before it can be tested.
   c. Concept measurement. Membership size is both conceptually clear and operationally definable. "Potential power," however, defies current measurement techniques. How is power observed? Political scientists are very concerned with measuring power and yet have not produced a reliable and valid operational definition for it. Also, how does one measure "potential," a futuristic concept describing something that has not yet occurred. This hypothesis is, therefore, not testable on the ground of lacking concepts that can be operationally measured and observed.
8. Check with your classmates or instructor.

## TECHNIQUES OF SCIENTIFIC DISCOVERY

The discovery of ideas, theories, and hypotheses is one of the most important but perhaps least understood aspects of science. Whereas the context of scientific confirmation has a particular logic, the context of scientific discovery is a creative enterprise that, so far, defies a logical basis. By observing great scientists at work and by reading their memoirs, we can, however, formulate some generalizations about the way they approach their problems. Specifically, five techniques that have assisted social scientists in generating new ideas, hypotheses, and theories can be identified: (1) insight, (2) record maintenance, (3) cross-classification, (4) alternative hypotheses, and (5) deduction.

## Insight

Some social scientists develop new ideas by reading as much material on the subject under consideration as possible, by talking to other people about the problem, by living in the subculture or environment they are studying, by immersing themselves totally in their topic. Gradually and subconsciously their mental processes seem to put some order to the mass of information they are processing. Sometimes a flash of insight—an intuition—springs forth, and an idea is born. These scientists do not simply wait for flashes of insight to hit them. They carefully prepare themselves by absorbing a great deal of particular and general information. They work hard and keep an alert mind with the problem constantly in focus. From specific pieces of information, they leap, deductively and inductively (they don't actually intuit), to a conclusion, a bold hypothesis, or a theory.

## Record Maintenance

Some social scientists recommend the utility of keeping a notebook or diary of one's mental processes. The notebook helps to retain many ideas that otherwise would be forgotten or lost. The process of writing one's ideas often clarifies and crystallizes a thought. It may stimulate other thoughts. The notebook can contain any thought of interest to the scientist: isolated ideas, summaries of articles and books, critiques of articles and books, proposed research designs, and the like.

One can begin to observe patterns in the development of ideas after keeping a journal for some time. Generalizations about the conditions (subject matter, time of day, environment, and so forth) that elicit creativity and professional productivity can be proposed. Rereading older entries often stimulates the imagination. Rearranging, resorting, and relabeling entries also may help to generate new perspectives on old subjects. By keeping a notebook, the scientist takes one more step toward becoming a self-aware and self-conscious intellectual craftsman.[7]

## Cross-Classification

Scientists sort phenomena into like and unlike categories. They formulate and apply labels called concepts to these categories. They frequently cross-classify

concepts to generate new types or categories. James David Barber, for example, formulated four types of legislative roles by cross-classifying two variables.[8] He hypothesized that freshmen legislators' activity in the legislature and their willingness to return to future sessions are important factors in their behavior. By cross-classifying activity and willingness to return, Barber identifies four types of legislators: lawmakers, spectators, advertisers, and reluctants (Table 1).
This typology of legislative behavior can be used to generate hypotheses relating legislative role and background, personality, career history, and attitudes.

Cross-classification is a popular technique in the social sciences for generating hypotheses and clarifying the factors underlying a concept. C. Wright Mills depicts its utility:

> *For a working sociologist, cross-classification is what making the sign of the cross is for a good Catholic, or diagramming a sentence is for the diligent grammarian. In many ways, cross-classification is the very grammar of the sociological imagination.*[9]

## Alternative Hypotheses

Scientists sometimes become wedded to a favorite hypothesis. This is not particularly desirable, since they may be more interested in protecting the hypothesis than objectively testing it. Strong objective tests compare a hypothesis with its most likely alternative. Thus, conceptualizing alternative hypotheses becomes an important scientific task, as Arthur Stinchcombe points out:

> *Because the advance of science is more economical when we can explicitly eliminate the most likely alternative theories, and because formulating the alternative theories, and deriving their consequences is pre-eminently a theoretical task, the central gift of the great methodologist is his facility at formulating and deriving the consequences of alternative theories in such a way that the observations can actually be made to decide the question.*[10]

**Table 7-1.  FOUR PATTERNS OF ADAPTATION**

| | | Activity | |
| --- | --- | --- | --- |
| | | High | Low |
| Willingness to Return | High | Lawmakers | Spectators |
| | Low | Advertisers | Reluctants |

Rapid advances in some scientific fields, in fact, may be due largely to the systematic creation of alternative hypotheses and crucial experiments. John Platt advises that whenever a hypothesis is proposed the scientist should begin to ask what evidence or experiment could disprove it. Also, whenever an experiment or piece of evidence is cited, the scientist should ask what hypotheses can it disprove. For Platt, strong tests of hypotheses involve conceptualizing alternative hypotheses and crucial experiments and evidence, focusing on the falsification of a hypothesis. He predicts:

*The man to watch, the man to put your money on, is not the man who wants to make a survey or a "more detailed study," but the man with the notebook, the man with alternative hypotheses and crucial experiments; the man who knows how to answer your questions of disproof, and is already working on it.*[11]

## Deduction

Deduction or some informal variation thereof also plays an important role in the context of scientific discovery. In the next unit will be examined the role of deduction in the context of verification. Previously unconceptualized hypotheses occasionally are discovered in the process of formally deducing theorems from a set of axioms. Hypotheses can also be discovered through less formal methods of deduction, which we shall now examine.

One of the primary goals of science is explanation. Scientists seek deeper, more fundamental explanations of the regularities they observe. Karl Popper reminds us to, "leave nothing unexplained. . . . always try to deduce statements from others of higher universality."[12] One way of discovering new hypotheses, then, is to search for higher level hypotheses that can serve to explain lower level hypotheses.

Hans Zetterberg emphasizes this approach to discovery by teaching his students to derive theoretical propositions from ordinary ones and ordinary ones from theoretical ones.[13] He defines *theoretical propositions* as hypotheses containing concepts that are both abstract and general. Because their concepts are general and abstract, they imply a number of different consequences that can prove them incorrect. *Ordinary propositions,* on the other hand, are hypotheses that contain concepts that are concrete and specific. Accordingly, they imply fewer falsifying consequences. Ordinary propositions are lower level generalizations. Theoretical propositions are to ordinary propositions as axioms are to theorems. Suppose we try to derive an ordinary proposition from the following theoretical proposition:

*Persons with fewer and weaker social attachments are more likely to commit suicide.*

The subject of this proposition, "persons with fewer and weaker social attachments," is very general. From it, one may derive a number of ordinary propositions that can be used to test the more abstract, general, and theoretical one. Bachelors, for example, probably have fewer and weaker social attachments than married persons. If this is true, then we may derive the ordinary propositions:

*Bachelors are more likely to commit suicide than married men.*

We may also deduce other statements:

*Married persons without children are more likely to commit suicide than married persons with children.*

*Divorced persons are more likely to commit suicide than married persons.*

The subject of each of these ordinary propositions is a subset of the subject of the theoretical proposition. The ordinary propositions are specific consequences of the theoretical propositions. The ordinary propositions are also easier to test than the theoretical propositions, although theoretical propositions imply more situations that can potentially falsify them than do ordinary propositions.

Social science presently contains many low level, ordinary propositions. As scientists press for deeper, more fundamental explanations, taking Popper's prescription seriously—to always try to deduce statements from others of high levels of universality—they in effect are deriving theoretical propositions from ordinary ones. This is done by taking the subject or predicate of an ordinary proposition and imagining what concept it is a subset of. The ordinary proposition may be regarded as the conclusion of a deductive syllogism. The scientist has to conceptualize from which alternative, higher level propositions it can be deduced.

We may now try to derive a theoretical proposition from an ordinary one:

*Strength of partisanship correlates with voting turnout.*

We know, of course, that theorems can be deduced from an unlimited number of alternative axions. The student should ask himself why partisanship correlates with turnout, what concept contains partisanship as a subset, what concept contains turnout as a subset. Although a variety of answers is possible, for the purposes of this exercise we may think of strength of partisanship as a kind of political attitude and voting turnout as a kind of political behavior. Thus, from the ordinary proposition we may derive a more universal, theoretical proposition,

*Political attitudes tend to be consistent with political behavior.*

We may derive an even more universal theoretical proposition:

*Attitudes tend to be consistent with behavior.*

Creative and productive scientists almost reflexively think in terms of deriving propositions from higher or lower levels of generality. The student should also try to acquire this habit. We do not yet know a great deal about what makes great scientists or great discoveries. The techniques and conditions of scientific discovery are just beginning to be recognized by scholars. We do know that the techniques of insight, record maintenance, cross-classification, alternative hypotheses, and deduction do not exhaust the routes to discovery; but they do provide some useful leads for the beginning social scientist.

## LEARNING AID

1. Name five techniques of social scientific discovery:

   a. _____

   b. _____

   c. _____

   d. _____

   e. _____

2. Monica Blumenthal developed a typology on social violence by cross-_____ two dimensions, violence for social control and violence for social change.[14]

3. Construct a table by cross-classifying violence for social control and violence for social change, with both factors having the values of high and low.

4. Monica Blumenthal formulated four roles from the cross-classification typology:

   a. *Pacifists,* who believe that violent means should never be used to achieve either social control or social violence.

   b. *Anarchists,* who justify violence when used for producing social change but not for achieving social control.

   c. *Vigilantes,* who justify forceful police methods but feel violence should not be used to bring about social change.

   d. *Warriors,* who support violence for both social control and social change.

In each cell of the cross-classification table write the appropriate role.

5. Blumenthal also used this typology to generate new _____. For example, she hypothesized that with respect to age warriors and pacifists would not differ from the general population, but she hypothesized that anarchists would tend to be younger than average and that vigilantes would tend to be older than average.

6. One explanation offered for the confirmation of the above hypothesis is that younger people have less of a stake in society and are more ready to change things whereas older people have a greater commitment in the status quo because of family, property, business, and the like and are more likely to justify methods to resist change. As younger people mature their interests will change and so will their violence perspective. An alternative _____ to the finding is that the younger persons come from a generation completely different from the other and that they will continue to remain more anarchistic even as they grow older.

7. Formulate one theoretical and one ordinary proposition from the following proposition: "Age is associated with attitudes toward violence."

· · · · · · · · · · · · · · · · · · · · · · · · · · · · · · · · · · · · · · · · · · · · · · · · · · · · · · · · · · · ·

1. Insight, record maintenance, cross-classification, alternative hypotheses, deduction.
2. classifying
3.

|  | | *Violence Roles* *Violence for Social Change* | |
|  | | *High* | *Low* |
| Violence for Social Control | High | | |
|  | Low | | |

4.

|  | | *Violence for Social Change* | |
|  | | *High* | *Low* |
| Violence for Social Control | High | Warriors | Vigilantes |
|  | Low | Anarchists | Pacifists |

5. hypotheses
6. hypothesis (explanation)
7. Theoretical proposition: e.g., Personal characteristics are associated with social attitudes.
   Ordinary proposition: e.g., Persons between 20 and 29 are more likely to support violence for social change.


## FOOTNOTES

1. Carl Hempel, *The Philosophy of Natural Science,* (Englewood Cliffs, N.J.: Prentice-Hall, 1966) p. 17.
2. Karl Popper, *The Logic of Scientific Discovery,* (New York: Harper and Row, 1959) pp. 11, 280.

3.  Carl Hempel, *The Philosophy of Natural Science*, p. 94.

4.  Fred Kerlinger, *Foundations of Behavioral Research*, 2nd ed., (New York: Holt, Rinehart, and Winston, 1973) pp. 20–21.

5.  Wesley Salmon, *Logic*, (Englewood Cliffs, N.J.: Prentice-Hall, 1963) pp. 80–81.

6.  William Goode and Paul Hatt, *Methods in Social Research* (New York: McGraw-Hill, 1952), pp. 67–73.

7.  C. Wright Mills, "On Intellectual Craftsmanship," *Symposium on Sociological Theory*, ed. L. Gross (New York: Harper and Row, 1959), p. 29, 41.

8.  James David Barber, *The Lawmakers* (New Haven: Yale University Press, 1965), pp. 18–21.

9.  C. Wright Mills, "On Intellectual Craftsmanship," p. 42.

10.  Arthur Stinchcombe, *Constructing Social Theories* (New York: Harcourt, Brace, & World, 1968), p. 28.

11.  John Platt, *The Step To Man* (New York: John Wiley & Sons, 1966), p. 36.

12.  Karl Popper, *The Logic of Scientific Discovery*, p. 123.

13.  Hans Zetterberg, *On Theory and Verification in Sociology* (Totowa, New Jersey: Bedminster Press, 1963), pp. 79–86.

14.  Monica Blumenthal, et al. *Justifying Violence* (Ann Arbor: Institute for Social Research, 1972), pp. 179–90.

# 8
# Theory Formation

# INTRODUCTION

## Rationale

Theories are sets of empirical generalizations that are deductively connected. Social scientists are interested in formulating and testing theories because theories are necessary conditions for scientific explanation and prediction, two of the primary goals of social science. Thus, an understanding of the nature and role of theory is essential for any social scientist.

Understanding the logic of theory formation also has practical benefits. In public affairs, "theories" and "hypotheses" are frequently proposed. They relate to our personal lives, values, public issues, governmental action, foreign policy, and many other such topics. There is no sharp dividing line between scientific and common-sense hypotheses. Thus, the principles presented in this unit are applicable to many practical situations in our daily lives. A prudent application of scientific knowledge may facilitate more informed personal decisions.

This unit begins with a discussion of the meaning and function of theory. It concludes with the logic underlying the testing of theories and hypotheses. The next unit refines the somewhat simplified account in the present unit and discusses a set of dimensions by which theories can be analyzed and evaluated.

## Learning Objectives

After completing this unit the student should be able to:

1. Define, identify, and construct a theory and axiomatic system.

2. Name and explain the four functions of a theory.

3. Name the ways in which the formulation of a theory raises new problems.

4. Explain how an axiomatized theory can be used to test indirectly one of its axioms.

5. Explain the relationship of a theory to explanation and prediction.

6. Name and diagram the steps and form of the hypothetico-deductive method.

7. Deduce in syllogistic form an original test implication from a hypothesis.

8. Explain the relationship between conditional arguments and the confirmation and disconfirmation of hypotheses.

9. Represent Durkheim's theory of suicide in hypothetico-deductive form.

169

## THEORIES AS DEDUCTIVE SYSTEMS

### The Definition of "Theory"

"Theory" is used in a number of different senses in everyday language. Sometimes it refers to anything not relevant to one's immediate practical concerns ("Philosophy is just theoretical; it's not practical."). Sometimes it refers to a conjecture that is not well established, such as a hypothesis ("My theory is that the butler did it."). Sometimes it refers to a guess about what variables occur in the laws of a certain area ("Current theory of voting suggests that political identification, candidate image, and issue orientation are important factors explaining peoples' voting behavior.").

We will not use the word "theory" in any of the above senses. We will use it as it commonly is used in the literature of science and philosophy of science.[1] We define *theory* as a set of empirical generalizations (or hypotheses or laws) that are connected deductively.

The definition of "theory" implies that "deducibility" is a defining characteristic of a theory. For a set of statements to be labeled appropriately as a "theory," it must satisfy the requirement of being arranged deductively. Theories, in other words, must take the form of an axiomatic system. You may remember from geometry that *axiomatic systems* consist of axioms, definitions, and theorems. The *axioms* are statements serving as the premises of a deductive argument. The *theorems* are statements that follow logically from the axioms and that serve as the conclusion of a deductive argument.

To identify a statement as an axiom or theorem is to locate its level of universality in an axiomatic system. The statements on the highest level of universality are axioms; statements on lower levels of universality are theorems. Since theorems are deducible from axioms, theorems are lower level empirical statements relative to axioms.

Hans Zetterberg's version of Durkheim's theory of division of labor will help to understand what an axiomatic system looks like and how it can be applied to social science. From a set of four axioms, Zetterberg deduced five theorems.[2] We will show the axioms theorems and the form of the deductive argument with S and P in the syllogism replaced by key letters in the sentence. Remember the cues USNP and MEN.

### Axioms

AI.   The greater the division of labor, the greater the solidarity.

AII.   The greater the solidarity, the greater the consensus.

AIII.   The greater the number of associates per member, the greater the division of labor.

AIV.   The greater the solidarity, the smaller the number of the rejection of deviants.

## Theorems

*Theorem T1:*                                                                                        *Form:*

AI.   The greater the **d**ivision of labor, the greater the solidarity.                             $D_d \ A \ S_u$

AII.   The greater the solidarity, the greater the consensus.                                        $S_d \ A \ C_u$

T1:   The greater the **d**ivision of labor, the greater the consensus.                              $D_d \ A \ C_u$

*Theorem T2:*                                                                                        *Form:*

AI.   The greater the **d**ivision of labor, the greater the solidarity.                             $D_d \ A \ S_u$

AIII.   The greater the number of **a**ssociates per member, the greater the **d**ivision of labor.  $A_d \ A \ D_u$

T2:   The greater the number of **a**ssociates per member, the greater the solidarity.               $A_d \ A \ S_u$

*Theorem T3:*                                                                                        *Form:*

AII.   The greater the solidarity, the greater the consensus.                                        $S_d \ A \ C_u$

T2.   The greater the number of **a**ssociates per member, the greater the solidarity.               $A_d \ A \ S_u$

T3:   The greater the number of associates per member, the greater the consensus.                    $A_d \ A \ C_u$

*Theorem T4:*                                                                                        *Form*

AI.   The greater the **d**ivision of labor, the greater the solidarity.                             $D_d \ A \ S_u$

AIV.   The greater the solidarity, the smaller number of the **re**jection of deviants.              $S_d \ A \ R_u$

T4: The greater the division of labor, the smaller the number of rejections of deviants.                     $D_d\ A\ R_u$

*Theorem T5:*                                                                *Form:*

AIII. The greater the number of associates per member, the greater the division of labor.              $A_d\ A\ D_u$

T4: The greater the division of labor, the smaller the number of rejection or deviants.                     $D_d\ A\ R_u$

---

T5: The greater the number of associates per member, the smaller the number of rejections of deviants.              $A_d\ A\ R_u$

## LEARNING AID

**1.** A theory is a set of empirical _____ that are connected deductively.

**2.** Theories take the form of _____ systems.

**3.** Thus, theories are sets of empirical generalizations that are connected _____.

**4.** Axiomatic systems consist of: (1) _____, (2) _____, and (3) _____.

**5.** The statements that serve as the premises of a deductive argument are called _____.

**6.** The statements that follow logically from the axioms and that serve as the conclusion of a deductive argument are called _____.

**7.** The relation between axioms and definitions, on the one hand, and theorems, on the other is one of (conclusion, premise) to (conclusion, premise).

**8.** Since theorems are deducible from axioms, theorems are (higher, lower) level empirical statements relative to axioms.

**9.** Referring back to Zetterberg's use of axioms (p. 171), we see that Zetterberg deduces Theorem 2 from _____ and _____.

**10.** Referring back to the axioms (p. 171), we see that Zetterberg deduces Theorem T3 from _____ and _____.

**11.** Our account shows that from four axioms Zetterberg deduces _____ theorems.

**12.** A theory is a set of _____ generalizations that are connected _____.

**13.** Treat the following four axioms as universal–affirmative (A) type statements.

AI. Higher income (HI) persons are more active participators (AP).

AII.  Whites (W) are higher income persons (HI).

AIII.  Higher educated (HE) persons are higher income (HI) persons.

AIV.  Upper class (UC) persons are higher educated (HE) persons.

From these axioms validly deduce as many theorems as you can, diagraming the deductive argument in standard form.

14.  A theory is a set of_____

_____.

. . . . . . . . . . . . . . . . . . . . . . . . . . . . . . . . . . . . . . . . . . . . . . . . . . . . . . . . .

1.  generalizations (laws, hypotheses)
2.  axiomatic (deductive)
3.  deductively
4.  axioms, definitions, theorems
5.  axioms
6.  theorems
7.  premise, conclusion
8.  lower
9.  AI, AIII
10.  AII, T2
11.  five
12.  empirical, deductively
13.

| $T1:$ | | $T2:$ | |
|---|---|---|---|
| AI. | $HI_d \ A \ AP_u$ | AI. | $HI_d \ A \ AP_u$ |
| AII. | $W_d \ A \ HI_u$ | AIII. | $HE_d \ A \ HI_u$ |
| T1: | $W_d \ A \ AP_u$ | T2: | $HE_d \ A \ AP_u$ |

| $T3:$ | | $T4:$ | |
|---|---|---|---|
| T2: | $HE_d \ A \ AP_u$ | AIII. | $HE_d \ A \ HI_u$ |
| AIV. | $UC_d \ A \ HE_u$ | AIV. | $UC_d \ A \ HE_u$ |
| T3: | $UC_d \ A \ AP_u$ | T4: | $UC_d \ A \ HI_u$ |

14.  empirical generalizations that are connected deductively.

## THE FUNCTION OF THEORY

A theory is very useful to the social scientist. It enables him to (1) explain and predict social and political events, (2) raise new problems for research, (3) organize knowledge in a systematic and efficient manner, and (4) suggest the limits of its own application. Each of these functions of theory will be discussed in turn.[3]

## Explanation and Prediction of Phenomena

In an earlier unit we stated that individual facts are explained and predicted by subsuming them under generalizations and statements of initial conditions. For example, to explain (or predict) why "John votes Democratic," the explanandum is deduced from covering-law generalizations and statements of particular fact:

| | |
|---|---|
| If a person is black, then he tends to vote Democratic. | Generalization |
| John is black. | Initial Conditions |
| John tends to vote Democratic. | Explanandum |

The covering-law generalization (If a person is black, then he tends to vote Democratic) may in turn be explained by deducing it from other laws:

| | |
|---|---|
| Lower income persons tend to vote Democratic. | Law 1 |
| Blacks tend to be lower income persons. | Law 2 |
| Blacks tend to vote Democratic. | Explanandum |

Laws 1 and 2 in turn may be explained by deducing them from even higher level laws. This process of deductive subsumption of laws under more comprehensive and fundamental laws continues, since there is no logically ultimate explanation. Explanation stops simply when we do not know any more.

Covering-law explanations such as the ones above are deductive in character. All three generalizations may, of course, be false. If, however, the first two laws are true, then the generalization contained in the explanandum must also be true (by definition of a deductive argument). Inductive arguments similarly imply a conclusion, but they imply a specified probability of the truth of the explanandum statement, not the necessity for its truth.

A theory has a logical form similar to that of an explanation or prediction. A theory is a set of generalizations connected deductively. Explanations of laws, we have just observed, also contain generalizations deductively arranged. Explanations of individual facts are deduced from generalizations and initial conditions. Both theory and explanations involve the deduction of generalizations from other generalizations. Thus, theories and explanations (or predictions) have similar logical forms.

The laws that do the explaining in an explanation are called the explanans. In a theory these are called the axioms. The laws (or facts) that are explained in an explanation are called the explanandum. In a theory these are called theorems.

The axioms indicate the relative position of a law in a theory. An axiom in one theory may be a theorem in another. Axioms are empirical generalizations whose truth is temporarily taken for granted to see what other empirical assertions, the theorems, must also be true. By testing the theorems, we indirectly test the credibility of the axioms.

If a theory enables the social scientist to explain and predict phenomena, then formulating a theory is instrumental in achieving two primary goals of science. That is why theory is prized so highly by social scientists.

## Raising New Problems

The formulation of a theory is not the end of scientific inquiry. It always raises new questions to answer. The first way in which a theory raises a new problem is *by generating new propositions to test.* When a theory is axiomatized, new theorems are deduced that otherwise may not have been conceived. The derivation of a new theorem implies the problem of its consistency with other theorems or its consistency with observational evidence.

Theory formation also raises new problems *by identifying inconsistencies within a theory.* Axiomatizing a theory forces the social scientist to make his assumptions and deduction explicit. It helps him to locate what premises or definitions were overlooked and assumed. It allows him to explore the implications of the deductions and to determine whether they are inconsistent with other deductions.

Third, a theory raises new problems *by identifying inconsistencies between theories.* Axiomatizing alternative theories assists the theorist in locating differences in their form and in their descriptive terms. If two theories are alternative explanations for the same phenomenon and if both are found to be internally consistent, then the theorist looks for inconsistencies between the theorems of the two theories for a crucial test of the theories.

Fourth, theories raise problems *by identifying inconsistencies between theories and observations.* When a theory is axiomatized, its theorems can be subjected to empirical testing. When a theorem is falsified by observational evidence, then the theorist reasons that one or both of the axioms from which it is deduced is also false. He locates the false axiom(s) by deducing backward, from the confirmed theorems to the axioms. He may find that there is more support for one of the axioms than the other. He may locate the axiom that has the least empirical support and eliminate it along with the theorems that are derived from it.

Finally, theories raise problems *by identifying strategic and manageable propositions for test.* Suppose that we want to test the proposition that sense of relative deprivation leads to the occurrence of rebellion. Suppose also that we cannot directly test this proposition, because of some practical limitation, such as not having indicators for the two concepts for the same collectivity. Assume further that we have evidence that income inequality is related to a sense of relative deprivation. We can then use axiomatized theory to test indirectly the original proposition:

| | | |
|---|---|---|
| AI. | A sense of relative deprivation leads to rebellion. | $RD_d \ A \ R_u$ |
| AII. | Income inequality leads to relative deprivation. | $II_d \ A \ RD_u$ |
| T1: | Income inequality leads to rebellion. | $II_d \ A \ R_u$ |

Axiom AI is the proposition we want to test. We cannot do so for some practical reason. If we have evidence for AII, we may assume it to be true and use it along with AI to deduce T1. T1 then may be a more manageable proposition to test. By testing T1, we indirectly test AI by logical implication. Thus, an axiomatic theory permits the scientist to locate the most strategic and manageable propositions for test.

## Organizing Knowledge

A theory organizes knowledge in a very systematic and efficient manner. An axiomatized theory shows how each concept and proposition logically inter-relates with other concepts and propositions. It vividly shows what is connected with what.

At the same time, a theory is the most efficient ("parsimonious") summary of its propositions. Our treatment of the theory of division of labor entails nine propositions (four axioms and five theorems). Yet only the axioms need to be remembered or retained, because the theorems can be derived from them. We can reduce the nine propositions to four. Thus, an axiomatized system permits a very efficient and effective summary of propositions.

## Suggesting the Limits of its Application

A good theory is applicable to a number of diverse phenomena. It explains and predicts things that were not known previously. It indicates the range of application of a previous theory, that is, under what conditions a previous theory yields accurate explanations and predictions.

A theory also should indicate the range of its own application. A properly axiomatized theory increases the scientist's confidence in any one proposition. A proposition may be confirmed in isolation from other propositions, but confidence increases in it if it is corroborated by being connected deductively to other confirmed propositions.

In summary, a theory is useful to the social scientist because it:

1. *E*xplains and predicts phenomena.
2. *R*aises new problems.
3. *O*rganizes knowledge.
4. *S*uggests the limits of its application.

We might say a theory is so valued that it is an object of love for the scientist. Accordingly, we may remember the four functions of a theory by the cue, "EROS," the Greek god of love.

## LEARNING AID

1. State the four functions of a theory:

    a. _____

    b. _____

    c. _____

    d. _____

2. Theory has a logical form that is (similar to, different from) an explanation or prediction.

3. The explanandum is to the explanans as (axioms, theorems) are to (axioms, theorems).

4. Just as theorems are deduced from _____, the (explanans, explanandum) is deduced from the (explanans, explanandum).

5. An axiom in one theory (may, may not) be an axiom in another theory.

6. Theories raise new problems by:

    a. _____

    b. _____

    c. _____

    d. _____

    e. _____

7. A theory organizes knowledge in a very _____ and _____ manner.

**8.** Suppose you have a theory containing the following two axioms:

AI.   Higher income persons are more active participators.

AII.  Whites are higher income persons.

Suppose also that you have data that indicate AI is true, but you do not have any data with which to test AII. Explain how you can use an axiomatized theory to test AII indirectly.

**9.** Again, name the four functions of a theory.

. . . . . . . . . . . . . . . . . . . . . . . . . . . . . . . . . . . . . . . . . . . . . . . . . . . . . . . . .

**1.** (a) explanation and prediction of phenomena, (b) raising new problems, (c) organizing knowledge, and (d) suggesting the limits of its application.

**2.** similar to

**3.** theorems, axioms

**4.** axioms, explanandum, explanans

**5.** may

**6.** (a) generating new propositions to test, (b) identifying inconsistencies within a theory, (c) identifying inconsistencies between theories, (d) identifying inconsistencies between theories and observations, and (e) identifying strategic and manageable propositions for test.

**7.** systematic, efficient

**8.** Using AI and AII, I would deduce a theorem to the effect that whites are active participators. It is hoped that this theorem would be more manageable to test than AII. If the theorem is false, then AII is probably also false (denying the consequent).

**9.** See question 1.

## THE LOGIC OF THEORY TESTING: A SIMPLIFIED ACCOUNT

We have defined theory as a set of hypotheses or laws that are connected deductively. The axioms of a comprehensive theory are abstract, higher level hypotheses. Usually remote from the level of observation, axioms are seldom tested directly. Instead, they are tested indirectly by deriving and testing theorems, or what we shall call test implications, which are lower level hypotheses close to observable phenomena. In this section, a simplified version of the logic of hypothesis testing will be examined. In later sections, complicating factors will be added to the discussion.

### Hypothetico-Deductive Method

The method by which theories are tested is usually identified as the *hypothetico-deductive method*.[4] It consists of four steps:

1.  Setting up a hypothesis (axiom).
2.  Deducing empirical consequences from the hypothesis (theorems or what we shall call *test implications*).
3.  Checking by observation to see whether these consequences are true or false.
4.  Concluding whether the hypothesis is confirmed or disconfirmed. (When a test implication is true, it is a confirmatory instance of the hypothesis.)

The steps of the hypothetico-deductive method may be represented in standard form with H standing for a hypothesis and I symbolizing a test implication.

Form:

| | |
|---|---|
| 1) | *H*. |
| 2) | If *H*, then *I*. |
| 3) | *I* is true or false. |
| 4) | *H* is confirmed or disconfirmed. |

The hypothetico-deductive method of theory testing employs both deductive and inductive modes of reasoning. Step 2 (If *H*, then *I*) is deductive since a test implication (theorem) is deduced from a hypothesis (axiom). Step 3 (*I* is true or false) is inductive since it is determined by observation. Step 4 (*H* is confirmed or disconfirmed) is deductive since it is the conclusion of a deductive argument. Thus, theory testing is based on both deductive and inductive logic. Consequently, the name "hypothetico-deductive method" derives from the idea that theory testing involves the deduction of test implications from hypotheses.

Durkheim's theory of suicide is a classic example of the application of the hypothetico-deductive method to social science theory.[5] Durkheim begins with the abstract hypothesis: "A higher degree of individualism (IND) in a social group causes higher suicide rates (SR) in that group." By individualism, Durkheim means the extent to which morality is dictated by the individual rather than by other people in the environment. A person is in an individualistic situation when fewer demands are made on him by others. From his hypothesis, Durkheim derives a test implication: "Protestants (*P*) will have higher suicide rates (*SR*) than Catholics (*C*)." He deduces the test implication by means of another premise, which states that Protestants are more individualistic than Catholics. We will call this added premise an *auxiliary hypothesis* (*A*), and we will have more to say about its role in the next unit. The deduction of the test implication may now be represented in syllogistic form.

Durkheim's Deduction of a Test Implication:

| | |
|---|---|
| Hypothesis: | *IND* leads to greater *SR*. |
| Auxiliary Hypothesis: | *P* are more *IND*. |
| | |
| Test Implication: | *P* will have greater *SR*. |

Having derived the test implication, Durkheim's theory may be represented in hypothetico-deductive (H–D) form.

| H–D Form: | Example: |
|---|---|
| 1) *H*. | 1) *IND* causes greater *SR*. |
| 2) If *H*, then *I*. | 2) If (*IND* causes *SR*) and if (*P* more *IND*), then (*P* have greater *SR*). |
| 3) Is *I* true or false? | 3) Is (*P* have greater *SR*) true or false? |
| 4) Is *H* confirmed or disconfirmed? | 4) Is (*IND* causes greater *SR*) confirmed or disconfirmed? |

Observing the suicide rates for Protestants and Catholics in France (step 3) permits Durkheim to confirm or disconfirm the hypothesis (step 4).

## Disconfirmation and Falsification

The reader should notice that the hypothetico-deductive method resembles a type of argument that he has already learned, namely, the conditional arguments of affirming or denying the consequent. The student will remember that denying the consequent is a valid form of argument.

| Denying the Consequent: | A Negative H–D Argument: |
|---|---|
| If $p$, then $q$. | If *H*, then *I*. |
| $q$ is false. | *I* is false. |
| | |
| $p$ is false. | *H* is false. |

The hypothesis implies a test implication, $I$. The test implication is observed to be false. Therefore, the hypothesis is rejected. And this is a valid form of inference.

When the hypothesis is rejected, it is said to be disconfirmed or falsified. There is a difference in the meaning of the two terms. To *disconfirm* a hypothesis is to make such observations that would permit the conclusion that it is "probably" false, but to *falsify* a hypothesis is to make such observations that would permit the conclusion that it is "definitely" false. Regardless of whether disconfirmation or falsification is imputed, false test implications logically imply the rejection of the hypothesis. Accordingly, if Protestants in France in fact do not have higher suicide rates than Catholics, then the hypothesis is disconfirmed or falsified.

## Confirmation and Verification

When the test implication is observed to be true, then the argument takes the form of affirming the consequent, which is an invalid form of argument.

| Affirming the Consequent: | A Positive H–D Argument: |
|---|---|
| If $p$, then $q$. | If $H$, then $I$. |
| $q$ is true. | $I$ is true. |
| $p$ is true. | $H$ is true. |

In the affirming mode of argument, the hypothesis implies a test implication, and the test implication is observed to be true. Durkheim's hypothesis implies the test implication that Protestants should have higher suicide rates than Catholics, and the observations demonstrate the test implication to be true. It is sorely tempting to conclude that the hypothesis must also be definitely true; but alas, affirming the consequent is weak at best and invalid at worst. One cannot validly infer the truth of the antecedent from the truth of the consequent. It is important to remember that the most serious problem with this form of argument is that the consequent, the test implications, could be true for a number of reasons other than the one specified in the antecedent, the hypothesis. There are in fact an unlimited number of alternative hypotheses that could explain why the test implication is true. Just as a theorem can be deduced from any number of conceivable axioms, test implications also can be deduced from an unlimited number of hypotheses. For example, to explain why Protestants have higher suicide rates than Catholics (I), we may deduce I from the alternative hypothesis ($H_2$): "Protestants place less emphasis on the immorality of suicide then Catholics." The test implications serve as the observed initial conditions of an explanation. They may be deduced from any number of alternative covering laws, as we have pointed out previously.

Since an unlimited number of alternative hypotheses can explain why I is true, scientists should be cautious in accepting H as true. Because affirming the consequent is an invalid form of inference, philosophers maintain that hypotheses can never be verified. Because denying the consequent is a valid form of argument, they claim that hypotheses can be falsified or disconfirmed.

We now need to distinguish confirmation from verification. To *confirm* a hypothesis means that such observations have been made so as to conclude that the hypothesis is "probably" true; to *verify* a hypothesis means that such observations have been made so as to conclude that the hypothesis is "definitely" true.

Because of the logical status of affirming the consequent, we will maintain that theories and hypotheses can never be verified. Under appropriate conditions that we will begin to specify, there can be strong reasons for accepting theories and hypotheses as being confirmed. Also, because of the logical status of denying the consequent, we shall maintain that theories and hypotheses can be disconfirmed or falsified. Complete falsification, however, is much rarer than disconfirmation of a hypothesis or theory.

## LEARNING AID

**1.** Name and diagram the steps and form of the hypothetico-deductive method.

**2.** The hypothetico-deductive method is based on (deductive, inductive, deductive and inductive) logic.

**3.** Reproduce the content and form of Durkheim's deduction of a test implication.

**4.** Represent Durkheim's theory of suicide in hypothetico-deductive form.

**5.** Take the following hypothesis and deduce in syllogistic form an original test implication from it. H: "A higher sense of relative deprivation (RD) leads to a greater incidence of rebellion (IR)."

**6.** Represent your theory of rebellion in hypothetico-deductive form.

**7.** Whereas affirming the consequent is a (valid, invalid) form of argument, denying the consequent is a (valid, invalid) form of argument.

**8.** When a hypothesis is said to be falsified, it means that the hypothesis is (probably, definitely) false.

**9.** There is an unlimited number of alternative _____ that could explain why the test implication is true.

**10.** To confirm a hypothesis means that it is (probably, definitely) true.

**11.** Because of the logical status of _____ the consequent, we will maintain that theories and hypotheses can never be _____.

**12.** Because of the logical status of _____ the consequent, we will maintain that theories and hypotheses can be _____ or _____.

**13.** Under certain conditions, there are strong reasons for accepting theories and hypotheses as _____.

**14.** Explain the relationship between conditional arguments and the confirmation and disconfirmation of hypotheses.

. . . . . . . . . . . . . . . . . . . . . . . . . . . . . . . . . . . . . . . . . . . . . . . . . . . . . . . . .

**1.** see text

**2.** deductive and inductive

**3.** see text

**4.** see text

**5.** H: *RD* leads to greater *IR*

    A: South American countries have greater *RD* than North American countries.

---

    I: South American countries have greater *IR* than North American countries.

**6.**

| *H.* | *RD* leads to *IR*. |
|------|---------------------|
| If *H*, then *I*. | If (*RD* leads to *IR*) and if (South America more RD), then (South America more IR). |
| Is *I* true or false? | Is (South America more *IR* than North America) true or false? |
| Is *H* confirmed or disconfirmed? | Is (*RD* leads to *IR*) confirmed or disconfirmed? |

**7.** invalid, valid

**8.** definitely

**9.** hypotheses (axioms, generalizations)

**10.** probably

**11.** affirming, verified

**12.** denying, falsified, disconfirmed

**13.** confirmed

**14.** Affirming and denying the consequent are conditional arguments. Since affirming the consequent is an invalid form of argument, theories can never be verified, but they can be confirmed. Since denying the consequent is a valid form of argument, theories can be falsified or disconfirmed.

## FOOTNOTES

1. See Gustav Bergmann, *Philosophy of Science* (Madison: University of Wisconsin Press, 1958), pp. 34–35; May Brodbeck, *Readings in the Philosophy of the Social Science* (New York: Macmillan Co., 1968), pp. 457–458; Johan Galtung, *Theory and Methods of Social Research* (New York: Columbia University Press, 1967), pp. 451–53; Karl Popper, *The Logic of Scientific Discovery* (New York: Harper & Row, 1959), pp. 71–72; and Carl Hempel, *Philosophy of Science* (Englewood Cliffs, N.J.: Prentice-Hall, 1966), pp. 47–59.

2. Hans Zetterberg, *On Theory and Verification in Sociology*, 3rd ed. (New York: Bedminster Press, 1963), pp. 159–61. Zetterberg actually deduces six theorems from four axioms. Theorems 2–4, however, are invalidly deduced. Theorems 2 and 3 can be salvaged by rearranging the sequence of the concepts in the premises and conclusions. Theorem 4 can not be validly deduced. We have renumbered his theorems, omitting his original Theorem 4.

3. The sources that were particularly helpful in writing this section are: May Brodbeck, ed., *Readings in the Philosophy of the Social Sciences* (New York: Macmillan Co., 1968), pp. 9–11, 457; and Hans Zetterberg, *On Theory and Verification in Sociology* 3rd ed. (New York: Bedminster Press, 1963), pp. 96–100, 161–66. Also see Gustav Bergmann, *The Philosophy of Science,* pp. 35–36; Carl Hempel, *Philosophy of Natural Science,* pp. 70, 75–77; and Karl Popper, *Conjectures and Refutations* (New York: Harper and Row, 1963), p. 222.

4. Wesley Salmon, *Logic,* (Englewood Cliffs, N.J.: Prentice-Hall, 1963) pp. 78–79.

5. An excellent treatment of Durkheim's theory and of the logic of scientific inference may be found in Arthur Stinchcombe, *Constructing Social Theories* (New York: Harcourt, Brace, and World, 1968), pp. 15–28. Much of the discussion which follows is influenced by Stinchcombe's analysis.

# 9
# Theory Analysis

# INTRODUCTION

## Rationale

This unit is a continuation of the previous unit on theory formation. It begins by refining the simplified account of the logic of theory testing, examines various dimensions by which theories can be analyzed, and concludes by examining the developmental stages of a theory.

## Learning Objectives

After completing this unit the student should be able to:

1. Name and explain the three procedures that strengthen the confirmation of a hypothesis.

2. Diagram and explain the logic of multiple test, varied test, crucial test, and auxiliary test situations.

3. Define and identify auxiliary and ad hoc hypotheses.

4. Construct and diagram the deduction of test implications of two conflicting theories.

5. Diagram the crucial test of the two rival hypotheses formulated in the previous objective.

6. Name and define the eight dimensions of theory analysis.

7. Name, define, and explain the six stages of theory formation.

## THE LOGIC OF THEORY TESTING

### A Refined Account

In the last section it was pointed out that although hypotheses can never be completely verified they can be strongly confirmed under certain conditions. In this section these conditions will be specified. A strong confirmation of a hypothesis involves building into the hypothetico-deductive method safeguards that lessen the probability of drawing false inferences due to the logic of affirming the consequent. Specifically, the confirmation of a hypothesis is enhanced when (1) multiple and varied test implications are deduced and tested, (2) measures are taken to avoid the fallacies of insufficient and biased statistics, and (3) all plausible rival hypotheses are proposed and disconfirmed. Each of these precautions will be discussed in turn.

187

DEDUCING AND TESTING MULTIPLE AND VARIED TEST IMPLICATIONS

The greater the *number* of test implications deduced from a hypothesis, the more credible the hypothesis becomes. When a hypothesis has been subjected to many severe tests and has withstood them, we have good reason to have confidence in the confirmation. In other words, multiple tests of hypotheses are more desirable and convincing than single tests. For these reasons, situation A represented below is a stronger test of a hypothesis than situation B:

| A: Multiple Test | B: Single Test |
|---|---|
| If $H$, then $I_1, I_2, I_3, \ldots I_n$.<br>$I_1, I_2, I_3, \ldots I_n$ are true.<br>―――――――<br>$H$ is true. | If $H$, then $I$.<br>$I$ is true.<br>―――――――<br>$H$ is true. |

Durkheim employs the tactic of developing multiple test implications. $I_1$ is, of course, the test implication that Protestants should have higher suicide rates than Catholics. In addition, he deduces and tests $I_2$: bachelors should have higher suicide rates than married men with children. $I_3$ is also deduced and tested: Protestant countries should have higher suicide rates than Catholic countries. Multiple tests give more of an opportunity for the hypothesis to be falsified than single tests. They are, therefore, more severe tests.

In addition to the number of test implications, the *variety* of the test implications influences the severity of the test. The more varied the test implications, the stronger the test becomes. If all the test implications are very similar, then a large number of tests does not increase the credibility of the hypothesis much. If the test implications are quite different from each other, then there is greater opportunity for the hypothesis to be falsified. Therefore, the test is even stronger. When a hypothesis withstands many different tests, we are willing to place a great deal more confidence in it than when it withstands only one test or many similar tests. Situation C, depicted below, is therefore a stronger test of a hypothesis than situation D:

| C: Varied Test | D: Similar Test |
|---|---|
| If $H$, then $I_1, I_2, I_3 \ldots I_n$.<br>$I_1, I_2, I_3 \ldots I_n$ are different<br>and true.<br>―――――――<br>$H$ is true. | If $H$, then $I_1, I_2, I_3 \ldots I_n$.<br>$I_1, I_2, I_3 \ldots I_n$ are similar<br>and true.<br>―――――――<br>$H$ is true. |

Durkheim deduces and tests varied test implications. Although $I_1$ and $I_3$ are quite similar, since both deal with religious attachments, they are quite different from $I_2$, which concerns a totally different context—marital and family attachments. By deducing multiple and varied test implications, Durkheim reduces the probability of drawing false inferences.

AVOIDING THE FALLACIES OF INSUFFICIENT AND BIASED STATISTICS

In step 3 of the hypothetico-deductive method, the test implications of the hypothesis are checked by observation to determine whether they are true or false. This step is inductive; from a sample of observed instances, a generalization about a population of instances is formed. The premises make the conclusion probable but not certain. The investigator can prevent some false inferences by reducing the probability of an inductive fallacy occurring in step 3 of the hypothetico-deductive method.

The two major inductive fallacies are ones we have already discussed—the fallacies of insufficient and biased statistics. The *fallacy of insufficient statistics* is the error of making an inductive generalization before enough data have been accumulated to warrant the generalization. This fallacy can be avoided by taking sufficiently large samples of observations. The theory of probability and sampling is highly developed and specifies the relationship between sample size and probability of false inference.

The *fallacy of biased statistics* is the error of making deductive generalizations on the basis of unrepresentative observations. This fallacy can be avoided by selecting representative samples. Again, sampling theory provides clear guidelines for representative and random selection of observations.

PROPOSING AND DISCONFIRMING ALL PLAUSIBLE RIVAL HYPOTHESES: THE CRUCIAL TEST

As was pointed out previously, a test implication can be deduced from or explained by an unlimited number of alternative hypotheses. The observation that I is true does not prove that H is necessarily true, for the alternative hypotheses $H_2$, $H_3$, . . . $H_n$ also may be confirmed by the observation that I is true. If the most plausible alternative hypotheses are proposed and if test implications can be deduced on which the hypotheses differ, then some of the hypotheses can be falsified. This increases the credibility of the surviving hypotheses. Thus, situation E produces a stronger test than situation B.

|  E:   The Crucial Test  |  B.  |
| --- | --- |
| $H_1$ and $H_2$ are plausible rival hypotheses. <br> If $H_1$, then $I_1$. <br> If $H_2$, then not-$I_1$. <br> $I_1$ is true. | If $H$, then $I$. <br><br><br> $I$ is true. |
| $H_2$ is false, and <br> $H_1$ is confirmed. | $H$ is true. |

The test shown in situation E is called a *crucial test*. It is a conclusive test between two or more rival hypotheses. If rival hypotheses are supported equally well by available evidence and if they predict conflicting test implications, then one can be refuted and the other can be supported.

Durkheim's research on suicide provides a classic illustration of situation E, the crucial test. At that time the most plausible rival hypothesis was that mental illness rather than individualism was the cause of high suicide rates. Durkheim, therefore, proposed the two rival hypotheses:

$H_1$:    The higher the degree of individualism ($IND$) in a social group, the higher the suicide rate ($SR$) for that group.

$H_2$:    The higher the mental illness rate ($MI$), the higher the suicide rate ($SR$).

Durkheim was then able to deduce test implications from the rival hypotheses, where conflicting outcomes were predicted:

$I_1$:    There should not be a correlation between rates of mental illness and rates of suicide.

$I_2$:    There should be a correlation between rates of mental illness and rates of suicide.

Using census type of aggregate data, Durkheim observed that the correlation between mental illness rates and suicide rates in various districts was statistically insignificant. Thus, the mental illness theory, the leading rival theory, was disconfirmed. Durkheim's individualistic theory of suicide became even more credible, having survived a crucial test. Here is the logical form of Durkheim's crucial test:

E:    Durkheim's Crucial Test

---

Individualistic theory and mental illness theory are rival hypotheses.
If *IND* is true, then there should be no correlation between *MI* and *SR*.
If *MI* is true, then there should be a positive correlation between *MI* and *SR*.
There is no significant correlation between MI and SR.

Mental illness theory is disconfirmed, and
individualistic theory is confirmed.

---

In summary, the logical status of affirming the consequent implies that false inferences can occur in any confirmation of a hypothesis. When the confirmation is based only on a single test implication, the probability of an incorrect inference is particularly high. There are procedures that can be employed to mitigate the problem of inferring false conclusions. When testing a hypothesis, scientists should attempt to:

1. Deduce and test multiple and varied test implications.
2. Avoid the inductive fallacies of insufficient and biased statistics.
3. Propose and disconfirm all plausible rival hypotheses.

## Some Further Qualifications

The account of the logic of theory testing so far has been somewhat oversimplified to make clear its general thrust. Several qualifications should now be introduced.

### FALSE TEST IMPLICATIONS

The *first qualification* concerns whether a false test implication falsifies an entire theory.[1] The conditional argument of denying the consequent is a powerful inferential tool, indeed. False test implications imply the disconfirmation of a hypothesis because true premises cannot validly imply false conclusions. It would be an overstatement, however, to claim that false test implications can falsify entire theories (systems of hypotheses). A false test implication falsifies only the hypothesis from which it is deduced; it does not, strictly speaking, falsify the whole theory of which the hypothesis is only a part. Falsified hypotheses, however, may indicate the theory to be seriously inadequate. Nevertheless, it is logically impossible to falsify completely a theory without independently falsifying each of the hypotheses of the theory. Even theories that contain falsified hypotheses may be modified or reformulated and subsequently be confirmed. The logic of confirmation may be similarly qualified. Hypothesis confirmation is, of course, based on the weaker form of conditional argument called affirming the consequent. If the previously mentioned three recommendations for confirmation are followed, then a hypothesis can be subjected to a strong test. When a hypothesis is confirmed, however, the theory of which it is a part is not completely confirmed. Complete confirmation of a theory, just as complete disconfirmation, requires independent confirmation of each of its hypotheses.

When a confirmed hypothesis is connected deductively to other hypotheses, its total confirmatory probability is greater than if it were confirmed as an isolated hypothesis. Since it can be deduced from and explained by other confirmed generalizations, we have a better reason for believing it to be true than if it were not deducible from other propositions.

Confirmation should be thought of as only temporary support for a hypothesis or theory. Subsequent negative results can always overthrow it. So long as it survives the most severe tests we can subject it to and so long as it is not superseded by another theory, we say that it is confirmed or corroborated.

AUXILIARY HYPOTHESES

A *second qualification* concerns the difficulty of conducting a definitive crucial test. When $H$ implies $I$ and $I$ is false, $H$ may be falsified. Similarly, when $H_1$ implies $I$ and $H_2$ implies not-$I$ and when $I$ is true, $H_2$ may be falsified. Very few tests, however, are so simple. Most tests contain premises that are tacitly taken for granted in deriving the test implications. These implicit assumptions are called *auxiliary hypotheses*. They are usually well established by prior, independent evidence, but they do complicate a definite crucial test. Auxiliary hypotheses add a new variable to the inference. The argument with auxiliary hypotheses may be represented as follows:

Auxiliary Test

| |
|---|
| If both $H$ and $A$ are true, then so is $I$. $I$ is false. |
| $H$ and $A$ are not both true. |

The problem is obvious; a false test implication only implies that either the hypothesis or the auxiliary hypothesis is false. It does not say which one is false. Thus, the test does not provide conclusive grounds for rejecting H. If the auxiliary hypothesis is established solidly, then the hypothesis is probably false and should be disconfirmed. There is still the possibility, however, that the auxiliary hypothesis is in error.

Recall the auxiliary hypothesis contained in Durkheim's deduction of a test implication. The deduction took the following form:

| | |
|---|---|
| Hypothesis: | *IND* leads to greater *SR*. |
| Auxiliary hypothesis: | *P* are more IND. |
| Test Implication: | *P* will have greater *SR*. |

The auxiliary hypothesis states that Protestants have a higher degree of individualism than Catholics. This is an empirical assumption. If the test implication is falsified (*P* do not have higher *SR*), then one has to decide whether the hypothesis or the auxiliary hypothesis is false. Thus, crucial tests may not provide solutions.

Conclusive resolutions are seldom obtained in science. This does not prevent, however, the accumulation of reliable and valid knowledge. Science has a remarkable record for continuous growth of knowledge. The goal of proposing and eliminating alternative hypotheses is still valuable, even though it may fall somewhat short of complete verification. It can show which of two conflicting theories may be seriously inadequate and thereby lend confirmatory support to its rival. Thus, it provides important assistance in the testing of theories.

## AD HOC HYPOTHESES

A *third qualification* concerns ad hoc hypotheses.[2] *Ad hoc hypotheses* are hypotheses that are introduced for the sole purpose of saving a hypothesis from an adverse test implication. It is almost always possible to save a hypothesis from a negative test result by sufficiently modifying the hypothesis or one of the auxiliary hypotheses. Such special ad hoc revisions should be avoided as much as possible. Mental illness theory, for example, might be saved by introducing after the test the ad hoc hypothesis that the census meanurement of mental illness was neither reliable nor valid.

The interests of science are not well served by protecting our hypotheses and theories. The interests of science are better served by bending over backward trying to overthrow our pet theories and hypotheses. As Karl Popper has observed, the proper scientific attitude is:

*Once put forward, none of our "anticipations" are dogmatically upheld. Our method of research is not to defend them, in order to prove how right we were. On the contrary, we try to overthrow them.*[3]

## LEARNING AID

1.  Name the three procedures that strengthen the confirmation of a hypothesis.
2.  Diagram the logic of multiple test, varied test, crucial test, and auxiliary test situations.
3.  The greater the _____ of test implications, the more credible the hypothesis becomes.
4.  The more _____ the test implications, the more credible the hypothesis becomes.
5.  Step 3 of the hypothetico-deductive method is open to the inductive fallacies called _____ and _____.
6.  A conclusive test between two rival hypotheses is called a _____.
7.  The observation that I is true does not prove that $H$ is necessarily true, for the _____ hypotheses $H_2$, $H_3$, ... $H_n$ may also be confirmed by the observation that I is true.
8.  What was the name of the alternative theory to Durkheim's individualistic theory of suicide?

9.   What test implication would falsify the alternative to Durkheim's theory?

10.   A false test implication falsifies (the entire theory, only the hypotheses from which it is deduced).

11.   Complete confirmation of a theory requires independent confirmation of each of its _____.

12.   When a confirmed hypothesis is connected deductively to other hypotheses, its total confirmatory probability is greater than if it were confirmed as an _____ hypothesis.

13.   Strictly speaking, crucial tests are seldom _____.

14.   The premises taken for granted in deriving test implications are called _____.

15.   The hypotheses that are introduced for the sole purpose of saving a hypothesis from an adverse test implication are called _____.

16.   Our method of research is not to defend our pet theories and hypotheses; on the contrary, we try to _____ them.

17.   In the previous "Learning Aid," the student developed a theory of rebellion $(H_1)$. Now the student should construct an alternative theory $(H_2)$ with test implications that conflict with the test implications of $H_1$. Diagram the deduction of the conflicting test implications of each theory.

18.   Diagram the form and content of this crucial test of two "plausible, rival" hypotheses.

. . . . . . . . . . . . . . . . . . . . . . . . . . . . . . . . . . . . . . . . . . . . . . . . . . .

1.   see text
2.   see text
3.   number
4.   varied
5.   insufficient and biased statistics
6.   crucial test
7.   alternative
8.   mental illness theory
9.   a nonsignificant correlation between rates of mental illness and suicide rates.
10.   only the hypothesis from which it is deduced
11.   hypotheses (parts)
12.   isolated (independent)
13.   conclusive (definitive)
14.   auxiliary hypotheses
15.   ad hoc hypotheses
16.   overthrow (falsify)
17.   An example: "Participation theory" may be formulated as an alternative to relative deprivation theory. It hypothesizes that high political participation $(PAR)$ leads to a high incidence of rebellion $(IR)$. High participation $(PAR)$ is

indicated by high voting turnout ($VTO$). It is assumed that high voting turnout occurs when there is intense concern about unsatisfied demands. When political participation ($PAR$) correlates with incidence of rebellion ($IR$) and when voting turnout ($VTO$) is correlated with political participation, we would expect voting turnout ($VTO$) to be correlated with incidence of rebellion ($IR$). The deduction of the test implication may be diagramed as follows:

$H_2$:    $PAR$ is positively correlated with $IR$.
$A$:    $VTO$ is positively correlated with $PAR$.

$I$:    $VTO$ is positively correlated with $IR$.

Relative deprivation theory alternatively hypothesizes that relative deprivation leads to a high incidence of rebellion ($IR$). Voting turnout ($VTO$) is negatively correlated with relative deprivation ($RD$), because low turnout results in greater political control for the ruling class, which distributes more of the resources to fewer people, thereby increasing the sense of relative deprivation. The theory implies that the way to reduce the incidence of rebellion is to increase voting turnout so that power can be distributed to more people. If power is redistributed, then the sense of relative deprivation ($RD$) can be expected to decrease and the likelihood of rebellion ($IR$) decreases. The deduction of the test implication may be diagramed as follows:

$H_1$:    $RD$ is positively correlated with IR.
$A$:    $VTO$ is negatively correlated with RD.

$I$:    $VTO$ is negatively correlated with IR.

18.    Now the crucial test may be diagramed as follows:

$RD$ theory and $PAR$ theory are plausible rival hypotheses.
If ($RD$ is positively correlated with $IR$), then ($VTO$ is negatively correlated with $IR$).
If ($PAR$ is positively correlated with $IR$), then ($VTO$ is positively correlated with $IR$).
VTO is positively correlated with $IR$.

$RD$ theory is false, and
$PAR$ theory is confirmed.

The student should notice that the auxiliary hypotheses in both of these theories are not well-established propositions. The falsification of the test implication then calls into question the auxiliary assumptions as much as the original hypothesis. Also, the student should know that the test outcome was assumed for the purpose of this exercise and was not based on any empirical evidence. Furthermore, other auxiliary hypotheses were actually involved in the verbal argument but were not included in the formal deduction of the test implications.

## DIMENSIONS OF ANALYSIS

In this section, we will examine eight dimensions along which theories may be analyzed and evaluated, namely: (1) deducibility, (2) explanatory power, (3) predictive power, (4) scope, (5) precision, (6) confirmation, (7) simplicity, and (8) fruitfulness.[4]

### Deducibility

The theory is most preferable that has the most internal and external deducibility. If the propositions within a theory are connected deductively (axiomatized), then the theory has high *internal deducibility*. Since the explanandum is deduced from the explanans, scientific explanation and prediction assume some degree of internal deducibility. If the theory is deducible from another theory (i.e., the axioms appear as deductions in other theories), then the theory has high *external deducibility*. External deducibility provides theoretical support for a theory by subsuming it under more comprehensive laws. Theories with high internal and external deducibility are preferable to theories with lower internal and external deducibility.

### Explanatory Power

The theory is most preferable that explains the most facts not known before the theory was formulated.

### Predictive Power

The theory is most preferable that predicts the most facts not known before the theory was formulated.

### Scope

The theory is most preferable that covers the widest range of phenomena. When it explains and predicts quite diverse phenomena, a theory is broad in scope. If theory 1 is deducible from theory 2, then theory 2 is broader in scope and is preferable.

## Precision

The theory is most preferable that explains or predicts facts in the greatest detail. The more precise the statements deduced from a theory, the stronger the test and the greater the credibility of the confirmation.

## Confirmation

The theory is most preferable that passes the greatest number of strong tests. A theory is also preferable if it confirms the highest level (closest to the axioms) hypotheses. When a theory is tested in competition with other theories and passes more strong tests, then by natural selection it proves itself the fittest to survive.

## Simplicity

The theory is most preferable that is the simplest.

## Fruitfulness

The theory is most preferable that suggests the greatest number and highest quality of additional hypotheses and test implications. The fruits of a theory are its hypotheses and test implications.

## PRETHEORETICAL FORMATIONS

Developing an axiomatized theory is very difficult. Only a few social science efforts legitimately qualify as scientific theories.[5] Because of the dearth of social scientific theory, some social scientists are inclined to call lesser achievements theories. The frustration is certainly understandable, but we believe that it is conceptually confusing and misleading to call so many different developments theories. Rather, we conceive of them as *pretheoretical formations*. These are valuable contributions in themselves, perhaps contributing to the formation of a theory, but they should not be mistaken as theory.

Of the six stages of theory formation, we identify the first five as pretheoretical formations: (1) singular statements, (2) concepts, (3) conceptual approaches, (4) hypotheses, (5) propositional inventories, and (6) theories. The interrelationship of these stages may be seen more clearly in Table 9–1, where form and content are cross-classified to provide the six stages of theory formation, each of which shall now be examined.

## Singular Statements

*Singular statements* are sentences connecting proper names and specifying individual facts. An example is: "Japan attacked Pearl Harbor on December 7, 1941." Singular statements play a dual role in scientific inquiry. First, laws, hypotheses, and generalizations are usually formed after observing many such similar singular statements. Second, explanations and predictions require the use of singular statements in specifying the set of initial conditions. Although

**Table 9–1.  PRETHEORETICAL FORMATIONS**

| | Form | | |
|---|---|---|---|
| Content | Unrelated | Related Nonsystematically | Related Systematically |
| Proper Names | | | 1.  *Singular Statement:* a sentence connecting proper names and specifying individual facts. |
| Common Names | 2.  *Concept:* a label for properties of things. | 3.  *Conceptual Approach:* a set of concepts nonsystematically related but focusing on the same subject matter | 4.  *Generalization:* a sentence connecting common names (concepts) and specifying general facts. |
| General Statements | 4.  *Generalization:* a statement connecting concepts and which is unrelated to other statements. | 5.  *Propositional Inventory:* a set of generalizations nonsystematically related but focusing on the same subject matter. | 6.  *Theory:* a set of empirical generalizations which are connected deductively. |

singular statements are not theories, they do contribute importantly to the scientific enterprise.

## Concepts

*Concepts* are labels for properties of things. Concepts or common names are formed from observation of a number of particular instances. For example, the concept "aggressor nation" may be formed after observing the behavior of Japan, Germany, and Italy during World War II. By developing common names for individual instances, concepts can be interrelated with other concepts, and analysis can be carried on at a higher level of abstraction. Concepts are the building blocks of hypotheses, and hypotheses are the structure of a theory. Although concepts contribute directly to the formation of a theory, they should not be labeled theories.

### CONCEPTUAL APPROACHES

*Conceptual approaches* are sets of concepts that are nonsystematically related but focusing on the same subject matter. Prominent conceptual approaches in political science includes systems, structural–functional, communications, decision–making, and developmental approaches. Such approaches offer a set of key concepts that assist in talking about and classifying important kinds of observations. Conceptual approaches usually assume that their concepts will lead to the formulation of significant hypotheses, and therefore, to the formation of a theory. Few conceptual approaches contain testable hypotheses; none contain a deductively connected set of empirical hypotheses. Although conceptual approaches may be useful, they should not be confused with what they aim to realize, namely, theory.

## Generalizations

*Generalizations* are sentences connecting concepts and specifying general facts. The formation of theory often begins with a bold generalization, conjecture, or hypothesis. Generalizations standing unrelated, however, do not constitute theories.

## Propositional Inventories

*Propositional inventories* are sets of generalizations nonsystematically related but focusing on the same subject matter. The propositions, for example, may concern the antecedents of war, or perhaps the consequents of war. They are interrelated loosely and nonsystematically. Scientists often find propositional inventories useful in providing succinct summaries of generalizations. Scientists sometimes develop axiomatic systems of hypotheses from propositional inventories. Although they approach the theory status, they lack the deductive interrelationship of the hypotheses that would qualify them as theories.

## Theories

*Theories,* of course, are sets of empirical generalizations that are connected deductively (systematically). The systematic relationship of generalizations is the ideal objective of a theory. Sometimes the descriptive terms of a theory are replaced by letters, so that deductions can be checked more easily. The result is the formalization of a theory. When the descriptive terms of a theory are replaced by letters, the theory is *formalized.* Theories are formalized when they are put into syllogistic form to check the validity of their deductions.

Sometimes the generalizations of a theory are not only formalized but they are put into a mathematical form.[6] When the generalizations of a theory take the form of a set of mathematical equations, we say that the theory is *mathematized.* Lewis Fry Richardson has developed a theory of arms races that is both formalized and mathematized.[7] He regards the preparation for war by two nations as the rectangular coordinates of a particle in an international plane. The motion of a particle in this international plane is represented by a set of differential equations:

$$dx/dt = ky - ax + g$$
$$dy/dt = lx - by + h$$

Where $x$ represents one nation's defenses, $y$ represents another nation's defenses, $k$ and $l$ are positive constraints representing a nation's sensitivity toward the opposite nation's defenses, $a$ and $b$ are positive constraints representing the fatigue and expenses of keeping up defenses and, finally, $g$ and $h$ represent grievances. In simple terms, the equations specify three factors that affect the rate of accumulation of arms: (1) the positive effect of the strength of the opponent (represented by $-ky$ or $-lx$), (2) the negative effect of one's own strength (represented by $-ax$ or $-by$), and (3) grievances (represented by $g$ or $h$). From these equations, Richardson mathematically deduces and tests a number of implications. Some of the implications concern the likelihood of war and the likelihood of mutual or unilateral disarmament.

A theory need not be formalized or mathematized. These procedures merely facilitate generating test implications and testing the validity of the deductions.

These tasks can be done in ordinary language, although not as efficiently or effectively.

In this section, we examined five pretheoretical stages of theory formation. We do not mean to imply that theories are formed following strictly the sequence of stages one through six. This sequence may sometimes occur. More frequently, however, different routes to the formation of a theory may appear. A theory, for example, may receive its initial inspiration for the formation of a set of concepts or the posing of a bold hypothesis. What is important is not the route by which a theory is formed but that progress toward theory formation does take place and that pretheoretical formations are not confused with theory itself.

## LEARNING AID

**1.** Name the eight dimensions along which theories may be analyzed and evaluated.

**2.** If the propositions within a theory are deductively connected, then the theory has high _____.

**3.** If the theory is deducible from another theory, then it has high

_____.

**4.** When a theory explains and predicts quite diverse phenomena, it is broad in _____.

**5.** Name the six stages of theory formation.

**6.** Sets of concepts related nonsystematically but focusing on the same subject matter are called _____.

**7.** Sets of generalizations nonsystematically related but focusing on the same subject matter are called _____.

**8.** When the generalizations of a theory take the form of a set of mathematical equations, the theory is _____.

**9.** When the descriptive terms of a theory are replaced by letters, the theory is

_____.

. . . . . . . . . . . . . . . . . . . . . . . . . . . . . . . . . . . . . . . . . . . . . . . . . . . . . . . . . . . .

**1.** (a) deducibility, (b) explanatory power, (c) predictive power, (d) scope, (e) precision, (f) confirmation, (g) simplicity, (h) fruitfulness
**2.** internal deducibility
**3.** external deducibility
**4.** scope
**5.** (a) singular statements, (b) concepts, (c) conceptual approaches, (d) generalizations, (e) propositional inventories, and (f) theories

6. conceptual approaches
7. propositional inventories
8. mathematized
9. formalized


## FOOTNOTES

1. Karl Popper, *The Logic of Discovery* (New York: Harper and Row, 1959), p. 72.
2. Carl Hempel, *The Philosophy of Natural Science,* (Englewood Cliffs, N.J.: Prentice-Hall, 1966) pp. 28–30.
3. Karl Popper, *Logic of Discovery,* p. 279.
4. The eight dimensions were derived from the following sources: Karl Popper, *Conjectures and Refutations,* (New York: Harper and Row, 1963) p. 232; Popper, *Logic of Discovery,* p. 108; Carl Hempel, *Philosophy of Natural Science,* pp. 33–46; Johan Galtung, *Theory and Methods of Social Research,* (New York: Columbia University Press, 1967) pp. 458–67; and Gustav Bergmann, *Philosophy of Science,* (Madison, Wisconsin: University of Wisconsin Press, 1958) p. 32.
5. We have already noted Hans Zetterberg's contributions in this regard. For a discussion of four axiomatic theories in international relations, see Warren Phillips, "Where Have All the Theories Gone?," *World Politics* 26 (January, 1974): 155–88. Also see John Kunkel and Richard Nagasawa, "A Behavioral Model of Man," *American Sociological Review* 38 (October, 1973): 530–42; S. Movahedi and R. Ogles, "Axiomatic Theory, Informative Value of Propositions, and 'Derivation Rules of Ordinary Language,'" *American Sociological Review* 38 (August, 1973): 416–23; Herbert Cosner and Robert Leik, "Duductions from 'Axiomatic Theory,'" *American Sociological Review* 29 (1964): 819–35; and Hubert Blalock, *Theory Construction* (Englewood Cliffs, N.J.: Prentice-Hall, 1969), pp. 10–26.
6. For an excellent discussion of formalization, arithmetic representations, and models, see May Brodbeck, ed., *Readings in the Philosophy of the Social Sciences,* (New York: The Macmillan Co., 1968) pp. 579–600.
7. Warren Phillips, "Where Have All the Theories Gone?," *World Politics* 26 (January, 1974): 777–80.

# 10
# Measurement

# INTRODUCTION

## Rationale

Measurement is the process that permits the social scientist to move from the realm of abstract, indirectly observable concepts and theories into the world of sense experience. Carl Hempel compares the process of measurement to that of building a bridge.[1] A bridge across a river is like a theoretical structure. A bridge is built by first supporting its structure on pontoons or on temporary supports driven into the river bottom. Similarly, the concepts of a theory are first measured by crude and tentative indicators. Just as the bridge is then used as a platform for improving and perhaps even shifting the foundations, the theory also is used to shift and improve its measures. Simultaneously, measurements are adjusted and the superstructure becomes increasingly well grounded and structurally sound. Social scientists are like bridge builders. Both are interested in the reliability and validity of their foundations. Both seek firmer supports. Just as the bridge builder relies on multiple supports for his bridge, the social scientist depends on multiple indicators and methods for inferential safety. In this unit the student will learn how the social scientist bridges theory with sense experience by the process of observation and measurement.

Measurement is probably the most controversial but least understood phase of social science inquiry. Some persons, for example, oppose quantification because they feel that by being numbered they become more like numbers. Yet, people no more become numbers by being numbered than they become snakes by being called snakes. In addition, this argument fails to recognize that units per se (e.g., people, groups, or nations) are not measured; only their properties are measured. Thus, people are not measured; only certain properties of people are measured. This antiquantification line of reasoning advances the specious qualitative–quantitative dichotomy that human affairs tend to be qualitative rather than quantitative in nature. We noted earlier, however, that every descriptive term is essentially qualitative; and any *observable* quality can, in principle, yield to some process of measurement, even if only to the determination of the presence or absence of a particular quality or property. Measurement in the social sciences is still in its early stages of development. We are just beginning to set out the pontoons and drive the temporary supports into the river bottom, so to speak. In this unit the student learns some of the basic principles of measurement. The unit focuses first on the principles of measuring political and social phenomena. It turns next to evaluating the accuracy of measurements and then concludes with a discussion of various measurement techniques.

## Learning Objectives

After completing this unit, the student should be able to:

1. Define measurement, validity, reliability, multiple operationism, and response set.

2. Formulate operational definitions.

3. Identify, distinguish among, and give examples of the different levels of measurement.

4. Name, identify, and distinguish among the four types of validity.

5. Name and explain the three sources of unreliability in measurements.

6. Explain the differences between intersubjective and intrasubjective reliability, between reliability measures for consistency and stability, between obtrusive and unobtrusive measurement, between free and structured response, and between single-item and multiple-item indicators.

7. Explain the value of multiple operationism.

8. Describe and identify different response set biases.

9. Recognize, describe, and give examples of the Likert response format, the semantic differential, and the forced choice format.

10. Construct an index.

11. Distinguish between an index and a scale.

## LEVELS OF MEASUREMENT

*Measurement* is the assignment of numerals to properties of objects according to rules. In essence, these rules are nothing more than operational definitions. The student will recall that *operational definitions* define concepts by specifying the instructions (operations) for observing and measuring their instances. Their function is to provide empirical import by connecting theoretical unobservables with pretheoretical observables. "Political efficacy" was operationally defined in Unit 5 by asking respondents to agree or disagree with two statements. If respondents disagree with both statements, they are assigned a 2 and are classified as persons with high political efficacy. If they disagree with one and agree with the other, they are assigned a 1 and are classified as persons with medium political efficacy. If they disagree with neither statement (i.e., they agree with both statements), then they are assigned a 0 and are classified as persons with low political efficacy. "Sex" was operationally defined by having the interviewer observe the respondents' physical characteristics. If the interviewer observes the presence of certain characteristics, then the respondent is assigned the numeral 1 and is classified as a male. If the interviewer observes the presence of other characteristics, then the respondent is assigned the numeral 2 and is classified as female. Both of the above examples illustrate that complete operationalization of concepts results in measurement, the assignment of numerals to properties of objects according to some rules.

In Unit 6 on Concept Analysis, concepts were distinguished according to the extent to which they named properties of things that are measurable. Classificatory concepts name properties that are either present or absent in objects. Comparative concepts name properties that are more or less present in objects. Quantitative concepts name the degree to which properties are present in objects. We return now to these notions to treat them more from a measurement perspective and less from a theoretical or conceptual perspective.

### Nominal Measurement

In the measurement literature somewhat different terminology is used to refer to classificatory, comparative, and quantitative concepts. For example, the term "nominal level of measurement" is equivalent to our earlier designation of classificatory measurement. *Nominal measurement* classifies observed phenomena into mutually exclusive categories, classes, or types. Assignment to a particular category is determined by the perceived presence of that particular trait designated by the category. In addition to mutually exclusive categories, the list of categories must be exhaustive; all observations must be placed in one, but only one, category. This requirement often prompts the use of a "residual" category, into which unclassifiable and undetermined observations are placed.

The assignment of numerals to categories or values of an indicator is a fairly simple task. With classificatory concepts, numerals can be assigned somewhat arbitrarily since they do not acquire a quantitative interpretation. For example, it matters little whether males are assigned a numeral of 1 and females a 2, or vice versa. Males could be assigned a 0 and females a 5; it normally does not matter. It is customary, however, to assign single digit, positive whole numbers whenever possible.

### Ordinal Measurement

The ordinal level of measurement is equivalent to our earlier designation of comparative measurement. *Ordinal measurement* designates the relative extent to which a property is more or less present in an object. In ordinal measurement, numeral assignment acquires some quantitative interpretation. The categories or scores of a comparative indicator possess an ordered relationship to each other. The assignment of numerals reflects this order. For example, assume that a particular comparative indicator contains three categories, labeled "High," "Medium," and "Low." Normally it is preferable to assign single digit, ordered, contiguous numerals to those categories. The first two columns in Table 10–1 demonstrate this preferred technique. The third column uses ordered single digits, but the numbers are not sequential, a less desirable feature under most circumstances. The fourth column is completely unacceptable since the numerical order does not correspond with the order of the indicator categories.

**Table 10–1.** METHODS OF ASSIGNING NUMERALS TO A COMPARATIVE CONCEPT

|        | Preferred |    | Acceptable | Unacceptable |
|--------|:---------:|:--:|:----------:|:------------:|
| High   | 3         | 1  | 2          | 2            |
| Medium | 2 OR      | 2  | 4          | 1            |
| Low    | 1         | 3  | 7          | 3            |

Although the categories of an ordered measure are arranged along an ordered continuum, they form unequal intervals, the magnitude of which is indeterminant. The numerals can indicate only the relative degree to which the property is present, whether more or less of the property is present. For example, if five individuals are rank ordered along a particular continuum and assigned the numerals 1 through 5, we cannot know whether the magnitude of the difference between ranks 1 and 3 is equal to, greater than, or less than that between ranks 2 and 4. Visually, we may depict the situation in the following manner:

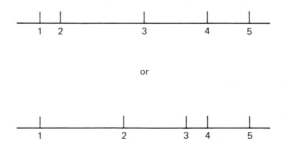

## Interval and Ratio Measurement

Our earlier designation of quantitative measurement actually encompasses two different levels of measurement: interval and ratio. Both *interval and ratio measurement* designate the numeric degree to which properties are present in objects. Both contain equal intervals. The requirement of equal intervals is an important distinction between ordinal measurement and the two levels of quantitative measurement. The presence of equal intervals permits comparisons concerning the magnitude of difference between two sets of observations. For example, if individuals were assigned scores denoting how many letters they had written congressmen in the past year, we can know that the difference between scores 1 and 3 is equivalent to the difference between scores 2 and 4, namely, a difference of two letters in each case.

With quantitative indicators, numerals are used not merely as a symbol to represent the classifications of a concept. The numerals represent scores on the indicators. Moreover, these numerals are numbers, possessing a quantitative interpretation. They indicate the numeric degree to which the property is present in the object. The numeral assignment, then, is normally fixed by the nature of the operational definition. For example,

*"Precinct voter turnout" has the operational definition of the percentage obtained by dividing the number of registered voters in the precinct who vote in a given election by the total number of registered voters in the precinct at the time of that election, and then multiplying the resulting quotient by 100.*

The *difference between interval and ratio measurement* is that the ratio level contains an absolute zero point that denotes the complete absence of the property. Interval measurement has no such absolute zero, although an artificial zero point may be assigned. Whereas interval measurement measures the degree to which a property is present in an object, ratio measurement truly measures the amount of the property present in an object.

## LEARNING AID

1.  Measurement may be defined as _____
_____.

2.  Formulate two different operational definitions for the variable "political participation."

**3.** Specify a numeric assignment for the two indicators created in question number 2.

**4.** A category of an indicator that contains all unclassified or undetermined observations is called a _____ category.

**5.** Nominal measurement classifies phenomena into _____ _____ categories, classes, or types.

**6.** The intervals of an ordinal measure _____ (are/are not) equal.

**7.** The intervals of interval and ratio measures _____ (are/are not) equal.

**8.** The difference between the interval and the ratio level of measurement is that the _____ (interval/ratio) contains an absolute zero point.

**9.** Complete operationalization of concepts results in _____, the assignment of numerals to properties of objects according to _____.

**10.** Define operational definitions.

. . . . . . . . . . . . . . . . . . . . . . . . . . . . . . . . . . . . . . . . . . . . . . . . . . . . . . . .

**1.** the assignment of numerals to properties according to rules.

**2.** Certainly more than two are possible. Two that come to mind are:

Political participation shall be defined in terms of responses to the question, "With respect to your own participation in political matters, would you say that you are quite actively involved in political activities, somewhat active in political matters, slightly involved in political matters, or not involved or active in political matters at all?"

Political participation is defined in terms of the responses to the question, "Would you please indicate to me, by placing a check in the place provided, which of the following political activities you have engaged in during the past year?

_____  publicly displayed a sticker, button, or other device in support of or in opposition to a candidate for public office

_____  contributed money to the campaign of a candidate for public office or to a fund that redistributed money to such candidates

_____  attended a political rally or forum held in behalf of candidates for public office

_____  worked in a campaign on behalf of a candidate for public office

**3.**   1—actively involved
         2—somewhat involved
         3—slightly involved
         4—not involved at all

         ----------

Assign a numeral equal to the number of the activities that are checked. For example, assign a value of 4 if all four items are checked, a 3 if any three items are checked, and so on.

Assign a 0 if no items are checked.
4. residual
5. mutually exclusive
6. are not
7. are
8. ratio
9. measurement, rules
10. Operational definitions are definitions of concepts by specifying the instructions (operations) for observing and measuring their instances.


## ACCURACY OF MEASUREMENTS

Assuming that any observable property can be measured, even if only by its presence or absence, a major concern confronting the analyst is the accuracy of the measurement. In general, two major criteria are used to evaluate the accuracy of measurements: validity and reliability.

Measurement *validity* involves the determination that an indicator actually measures what it purports to measure. Validity concerns questions of definition, meaning, explanation, and prediction. It involves an analysis of whether the operational definition produces an accurate indicator of a somewhat more abstract variable or a considerably more abstract concept or compound concept. Whenever an indicator is not valid, systematic error is present in the measurement process. This biases the accuracy of the measurement. The determination of validity involves questions such as whether the IQ test actually measures intelligence, whether the ten-question F–scale truly measures authoritarianism, whether the test over this unit adequately measures mastery of the unit objectives, whether asking a person if he or she voted in an election really measures voting turnout.

The second accuracy criterion is measurement reliability. Accurate measurement requires the dependable and precise observation and recording of the sense experience specified by the rules of the operational definition. Measurement *reliability* concerns whether the application of the measurement rules produces consistent and stable results. Unreliable measurement tends to produce unsystematic, random error, which reduces the precision of the measurement. The determination of reliability involves questions such as whether the measurement rules for indicators can be interpreted unambiguously both by those who are measuring and, in some instances, by the objects of the measurement, whether the properties observed by different observers will be interpreted in the same way, whether the same indicator will produce the same results over a period of time when other relevant factors remain unchanged.

## Validity

The determination of the validity of a measure is to some extent a function of the purpose or intent of the measurement. Consequently, there are different types of validity.[2] Four types of validity are commonly identified. We will examine, in turn, face validity, content validity, predictive validity, and construct validity.

### FACE VALIDITY

*Face validity* consists of little more than the subjective determination by the researcher that the indicator actually measures what it purports to measure. It is, perhaps, the crudest technique of establishing validity. One merely examines the measurement rules and the property to be measured and ventures a judgment that the indicator does or does not measure the property in question. Face validity is not especially reliable, but in some instances it may be all there is. Especially in the initial stages of measurement development, indicators commonly are adopted on the basis of whether they appear to measure the property under consideration. The use of multiple judges provides a variety of opinions and enhances the probability of developing valid measures. Nevertheless, the subsequent use of additional techniques is strongly recommended.

### CONTENT VALIDITY

*Content validity* involves the determination that the content of the measure is an adequate and representative sample of the content universe of the property being measured. This requires, first of all, that the content universe be known. The content universe refers to the components that constitute the property being measured. (If the content universe is not actually known, it may be hypothesized—with the understanding that this jeopardizes the determination of the "true" content validity.) After identifying the content universe, an attempt should be made to derive an adequate and representative sample of the components that constitute the property. For example, a test over this unit should be designed to measure one's achievement of the unit objectives. The content validity of the test is determined by how well the test covers the objectives listed. The validity of such a test could be impaired in several ways: (1) the test could include questions from outside the scope of the objectives listed; (2) the test could fail to include questions that encompass certain of the objectives listed; and (3) a question could ask for information that is unrepresentative of the material contained within the scope of a particular objective.

### PREDICTIVE VALIDITY

*Predictive validity* involves the determination that one indicator can be used to predict accurately a particular value, criterion, or position on some other indicator. Predictive validity requires, first of all, a criterion indicator of what is to be predicted. Once such an indicator is developed, then various predictor indicators can be developed. The purpose of some predictor indicators may be to forecast some future position on the criterion indicator. For example, law schools may wish to predict an applicant's performance in their law program. The score on the Law School Admissions Test is used by some schools for this purpose. Another use of predictor indicators is as a substitute for some current property more difficult to measure than the predictor indicator. The most common use of such "concurrent" indicators in the social sciences is the development of "short form" tests, which are designed to provide the same discrimination between subjects as longer, more complicated forms of the test.

In addition to the creation of criterion and predictor indicators, the statistical relationship between these two sets of indicators must be determined. Obviously, this procedure requires some initial experience or information concerning the relationship between the predictor and the criterion to be predicted. Thus, a law school cannot accurately use the LSAT score as a predictor for its students until it examines the LSAT scores of students who succeeded and failed in their law school program. Once some initial relationship is established, and assuming the LSAT discriminated sufficiently well between successes and failures in the law program, then the LSAT may be used as a predictor. However, the law school must continue to monitor the performance of students in the program in relationship to their LSAT performances in order to keep the prediction criteria as current as possible.

Predictive validity is distinctly different from face, content, or construct validity. An indicator is valid simply by virtue of its predictive power, regardless of any apparent deficiencies in the perceived relevancy of the content of the indicator. However, the various types of validity are not necessarily unrelated. Face validity is a frequent forerunner of other validity checks. Improving the content validity of a predictor indicator may enhance its predictive discrimination. Moreover, the predictive power of an indicator is also a concern in the establishment of construct validity.

CONSTRUCT VALIDITY

*Construct validity* involves the determination that the indicator relates to other indicators consistent with theoretically derived hypotheses concerning the concepts (constructs) that are being measured. The analysis of construct validity involves an effort to explain the variation in the indicator under question, to determine what factors are related and unrelated to the indicator. In this manner, it is assumed that a more thorough understanding of the indicator will evolve. Achievement of this understanding involves to some extent testing for content and predictive validity. However, the use of theory to derive testable hypotheses to determine if the indicator measures what it purports to measure distinguishes construct validity from the other three forms.

Three steps are followed in the normal procedure to determine construct validity. First, the concept under analysis is hypothesized to relate (or not relate) to other concepts or groups of observations in specific ways. These hypothesized relationships stem from theories and other research concerning the concepts involved. Next, data are gathered and the hypotheses are tested. This hypothesis testing follows the logic of the hypothetico-deductive form of theory testing presented in the Theory Formation unit (Unit 8). Finally, the results of the analysis are interpreted and explanations are sought for the observed relationships, especially explanations that relate to the meaning of the indicators and what it measures.

Milton Rokeach, for example, provided construct validity for his Dogmatism Scale by administering it to individuals judged through observational and interpersonal techniques to possess closed belief systems and also to individuals similarly identified as having open belief systems.[3] His test thus involved administering the measurement device to at least two different groups "known" to differ with respect to the property under scrutiny. In the hypothetico-deductive form, the test appears this way:

| | |
|---|---|
| *Hypothesis:* | Dogmatic individuals will score high on the Dogmatism Scale; nondogmatic individuals will score low on the Dogmatism Scale. |
| *Auxiliary Hypothesis* | Closed system individuals are dogmatic; open system individuals are not dogmatic. |
| *Test Implication* | If the main and auxiliary hypotheses are true, then closed system individuals will score high on the Dogmatism Scale and open system individuals will score low on the Dogmatism Scale. |
| *Test Result* | Closed system individuals score high on the Dogmatism Scale; open system individuals score low on the Dogmatism Scale. The test implication is affirmed. |
| *Conclusion* | The hypothesis is confirmed. |

Bear in mind that affirming the test implication is a matter of affirming the consequent in a conditional argument. Thus, the hypotheses are not verified. However, the evidence does tend toward confirmation of the hypotheses. To the extent that Rokeach is able to test other varied hypotheses that add confirming evidence to the main hypothesis, the validity of his scale becomes more certain.

Construct validity is achieved by testing hypotheses that derive from a theory and that predict relationships between variables or indicators. The confirmation of a construct validity test implication provides either "convergent" or "discriminant" validity for the indicator. *Convergent construct validity* is obtained when an indicator is somewhat strongly related to other indicators as hypothesized. The different indicators agree or "converge" on the same concept. Rokeach, for example, gains convergent validity when the Dogmatism Scale strongly correlates with his indicator of closed-mindedness, as theory predicts. Similarly, convergent validity for political efficacy is evidenced if the political efficacy scale correlates strongly with the self-esteem scale, as political efficacy theory would predict. On the other hand, *discriminant construct validity* is obtained when an indicator relates somewhat weakly or not at all to other indicators as hypothesized. The new indicator under consideration discriminates the concept being measured from other concept indicators. Discriminant validity for political efficacy, for example, is achieved if the political efficacy scale correlates weakly with the social desirability response scale, as anticipated.

One sophisticated approach to an evaluation of measurement reliability and validity is the multitrait–multimethod matrix developed by Donald Campbell and Donald Fisk.[4] Our summary of this technique is contained in Appendix A.

## LEARNING AID

1. Two major criteria are used to evaluate the accuracy of measurements: _____ and _____.
2. Validity involves the determination that an indicator measures what it _____ to measure.
3. Reliability tests whether an indicator is _____ and _____ in the application of the measurement rules and in the results obtained.
4. Four major types of validity are: (a) _____, (b) _____, (c) _____, (d) _____.
5. Face validity consists of the _____ (subjective/objective) determination by the researcher that the indicator actually measures what it purports to measure.
6. Content validity involves the determination that the content of the measure is an adequate and representative _____ of the content universe of the property being measured.
7. Predictive validity involves the determination that one indicator can be used to _____ accurately a particular value, criterion, or position on some other indicator.
8. Construct validity involves the determination that the indicator relates to other indicators consistent with theoretically _____ hypotheses concerning the concepts (constructs) being measured.
9. Convergent construct validity is obtained when an indicator _____.
10. Discriminant construct validity is obtained when an indicator _____.

**11.** What type of validity test is most likely to be employed with the following tests or measures?
   a.   a criminal tendencies test for adolescents
   b.   a foreign language proficiency exam
   c.   a comprehensive exam over this textbook

. . . . . . . . . . . . . . . . . . . . . . . . . . . . . . . . . . . . . . . . . . . . . . . . . . . . . . . . . .

1.   validity, reliability
2.   purports (intends)
3.   consistent, stable
4.   face validity, content validity, predictive validity, construct validity
5.   subjective
6.   sample
7.   predict
8.   derived
9.   is related somewhat strongly to other indicators as hypothesized.
10.   is related weakly or not at all to other indicators as hypothesized.
11.   a.   Either a predictive validity test that is used to predict later criminal violations or a construct validity test that is used to compare the scores of a known group of juvenile delinquents with the scores of a known group of nondelinquents.
      b.   The major functions of such an exam are to place students at a particular level of language instruction or to predict certain perform-ances. Both functions come closest to predictive validity.
      c.   Content validity should be the major concern with any effort to test comprehension over a specified body of information.

## Reliability

*Reliability* is the second criterion used to evaluate the accuracy of measure-ments. Reliability means that the application of the measurement rules provides consistent and stable results.[5] Consistency of measurement includes the uniform application of the measurement rules and the uniform recording and coding of the observations at one particular measurement time. Stability of measurement refers to the uniformity of measurement results over time, assum-ing that nothing else has changed. Sources of unreliability can originate from (1) within the measuring instrument itself, (2) the phenomenon or person being measured, and (3) the observer who is performing the measurement.

INSTRUMENT RELIABILITY

Unreliability in the measuring instrument concerns difficulties with the content of the indicator. Whenever several indicators are used to measure the same property, either within the same measurement device or in separate but equivalent devices, then identical measurement should result on these various indicators. To the extent that identical measurement is achieved, reliability is attained. This is consistent with the definition of reliability by Donald Campbell and Donald Fiske, namely, ". . . the agreement between two efforts to measure the same trait through maximally similar methods."[6] In psychological and attitudinal tests involving the use of multiple indicators to measure the same concept, reliability is enhanced by arranging the test items in some order of difficulty rather than by random assignment, by reducing the interdependence of items in the test, by eliminating items "loaded" with subtle or emotional content, and by increasing the length of a test.

### PHENOMENON RELIABILITY

A second source of unreliability stems from the responses of the individuals or the phenomena being observed. An obvious hazard of psychological testing is the particular mood, feelings, and experiences that a subject brings into the test environment. Differences in fatigue and the conscientiousness with which individuals respond to items are two other potential sources of unreliability. To the extent that individuals are given flexibility in interpreting the test items and in formulating the responses, inconsistencies and instability are fostered.

### OBSERVER RELIABILITY

A third source of unreliability is the observer who performs the measurement. Indicators should be both intersubjectively and intrasubjectively consistent and stable. *Intersubjective reliability* means that two different researchers measuring the same phenomenon according to the same rules obtain the same results. *Intrasubjective reliability* means that the same individual applies the measurement rules uniformly from case to case.

Intrasubjective reliability is somewhat easier to obtain than the intersubjective variety, although anyone who has graded a number of papers or exams is aware of the difficulties of maintaining reliable judgment paper after paper or test after test. Intersubjective reliability becomes a problem whenever there is an increasing number of persons performing the measurement on different cases. In survey research designs that utilize numerous interviewers to administer a questionnaire, inconsistencies and biases among the interviewers are virtually certain. Steps can be taken to minimize such unreliability. Two such steps are the standardization of training techniques for interviewers and the careful recruitment of interviewers possessing shared characteristics.

### MEASUREMENT OF RELIABILITY

*Consistency of measurement* refers to uniform recording, coding, and application of measurement rules at one particular time. Consistency measures are based on the assumption that indicators designed to measure the same thing should correlate highly with each other. For example, equivalent or parallel forms of the same test should correlate highly with each other when administered to the same individual. In instances where several indicators are used to measure a single property, then one-half of the indicators can be correlated with the other half. If they correlate highly, it is an indication that the items consistently measure the property, that the subject's responses were internally consistent, and that the test was administered in a consistent fashion.[7] Intersubjective consistency can be measured in instances where different observers can measure the same phenomenon. To the extent that the observers derive the same results, intersubjective consistency can be established.

*Stability of measurement* refers to uniform measurement over time. It is more difficult to confirm than is consistency because it is difficult to know whether changes in measurement are a result of instability or of actual changes in the phenomenon being measured. A standard technique for measuring stability is the test–retest approach, in which the same test is administered at a later time period. There are obvious problems concerning the effect of the first test measurement on the second measurement. It is preferable to establish the consistency of equivalent forms first and then to administer these separate, but equivalent, forms in the test–retest sequence. Although this does not overcome the fact that the initial measurement may have lingering effects on the second measurement, it at least is less likely than if the same form is used.

## LEARNING AID

1. Define the term reliability.
2. Unreliability in measurements derives from three sources: (a) _____, (b) _____, (c) _____.
3. The variability in the moods and feelings of respondents can contribute to _____ (instrument/phenomenon/observer) unreliability.
4. The variability in the skill of the persons who do the measuring contributes to _____ (instrument/phenomenon/observer) unreliability.
5. The variability in the measuring instrument itself contributes to _____ (instrument/phenomenon/observer) unreliability.
6. Distinguish between intersubjective and intrasubjective reliability.
7. Consistency of measurement refers to uniform _____ _____.
8. Stability of measurement refers to uniform _____ _____.
9. Whereas a test–retest approach is used to determine _____ (consistency/stability), equivalent or parallel forms approach is used to determine _____ (consistency/stability).

**1.** Reliability means that the application of the measurement rules provides consistent and stable results.

**2.** (a) instrument, (b) phenomenon, (c) observer

**3.** phenomenon

**4.** observer

**5.** instrument

**6.** Whereas "intersubjective" reliability means that two different researchers measuring the same phenomenon according to the same rules obtain the same results, "intrasubjective" reliability means that the same individual applies the measurement rules uniformly from case to case.

**7.** recording, coding, and application of measurement rules at one particular time.

**8.** measurement over time.

**9.** stability, consistency

## MEASUREMENT TECHNIQUES

### Variety in Measurement

The variety of measurement techniques used in social science research is considerable. Nevertheless, in specific research areas and on specific topics, measurement of particular concepts tends to lack variation in techniques and approaches. There are some advantages and disadvantages to this situation. Use of the same indicators for a concept, measured in the same fashion, produces the necessary replication of research. This replication provides reliability checks for the measures and validity checks through the confirmation or disconfirmation of certain hypotheses. Furthermore, the use of the same measures in different settings and situations provides additional evidence to support or contradict other research.

MULTIPLE OPERATIONISM

There are, however, distinct disadvantages to reliance on one type of measurement for a concept. In the first place, any operational definition of a concept will contain certain validity and reliability deficiencies. Second, no single measurement *technique* is completely valid or reliable. This second point is especially important because it is often overlooked even by professional researchers. Thus, a researcher may provide a couple of different operational definitions for a concept that differ in substance, but reliance on the same measurement technique (e.g., a face-to-face interview with open-ended objective questions) still produces measurement error. Moreover, this type of method error is not randomly distributed. Instead, it biases the results and confounds the establishment of valid findings. The major remedy for such error is the use of multiple measurement techniques, designed to measure the same property, but with different method error components. The use of multiple measurement techniques is called *multiple operationism,* operational definitions of a concept or variable that require a variety of measurement techniques for their implementation.[8]

OBTRUSIVE MEASUREMENT

Measurement techniques can be distinguished along many different dimensions. One major dichotomy of measurement techniques is that of obtrusive and unobtrusive measures.[9] *Obtrusive measurement* is that which intrudes on the environment, the setting, or the object of the measure. Such intrusion increases the potential for reactive effects, that is, the object being measured is affected by (or reacts to) the measurement process itself. For example, personal interviews with individuals are obtrusive, and the respondent may be affected by ways in which questions are asked, by the demeanor of the interviewer, and by ego-defensive mechanisms that trigger special responses.

A major portion of social science research is concerned with people, their attitudes, values, personalities, experiences, and behavior. The study of these personal characteristics relies heavily on obtrusive measurement techniques. Even within the obtrusive framework, however, there is a variety of approaches available that vary the measurement method error component. For example, the measurement of personal properties may proceed in a straightforward fashion, with the intent of the measurement known both to subject and observer. On the other hand, the intent of the measurement may be withheld from the subject or some deception may be exercised by the observer in measuring properties of the subject. Another measurement distinction involves the objectivity or subjectivity of the measurement stimulus. Questions that are asked may be objective in nature so that individuals would agree on their perception of the stimuli, although, of course, their responses would differ, according to their own opinions. However, subjective questions could be asked on which individuals differ, not only with respect to their responses, but with respect to their perception of the stimuli presented to them. Another distinction in obtrusive measurement techniques is between the free response form and the structured response form. The *free response* form permits the individual to formulate his own response, in his own words. *Structured response* forms provide the subject with response alternatives, from which one, and sometimes more than one, response is selected.

UNOBTRUSIVE MEASUREMENT

*Unobtrusive measurement* is that which does not intrude on the environment, the setting, or the object of the measure. It is nonreactive. For example, examination of a person's refuse or garbage is an unobtrusive way of gathering certain types of information that may not be elicited through obtrusive interview techniques.

A more thorough presentation of these varied measurement techniques is beyond the scope of this unit. A separate unit on unobtrusive measures is yet to come. A more detailed description of the free and structured response forms is undertaken in the unit on survey research. We move now from a general discussion of measurement techniques to a presentation of some specific techniques of indicator construction.

## Construction of Indicators

A wide variety of formats for structuring responses has been developed in the social sciences. We will present only some of the more common and significant techniques for constructing indicators. A distinction may be made between single-item indicators and multiple-item indicators. A *single-item indicator* consists of a single question, proposition, or other single stimulus. A *multiple-item indicator* contains multiple questions, propositions, or stimuli. Multiple-item indicators often are used to measure more fully and richly a concept or compound concept.

In addition to the single-item/multiple-item distinction, the construction of indicators also differs according to the level of measurement desired. The creation of classificatory or quantitative indicators is quite straightforward. Measurement at the classificatory level merely entails listing the various response categories. Examples are listing various religious denominations, geographic regions, categories of a typology, or other noncomparative, nonquantitative responses. The creation of quantitative indicators simply involves the assignment of numbers as provided by the operational definition.

It is at the comparative level of measurement where most effort and innovation have been directed in the construction of indicators, especially in the broad area of attitude measurement. The development of comparative indicators represents an effort to order the responses of individuals relative to each other along some sort of continuum or hierarchy. Since the number and sophistication of statistical manipulations that can be performed on data increase as the level of measurement moves from nominal through ratio, comparative (ordinal) measurement is generally preferable to classificatory (nominal) measurement.

### SINGLE-ITEM COMPARATIVE INDICATORS

Indicators with dichotomous response categories often can be conceptualized as comparative single-item indicators. If the categories are conceptualized as being discrete, noncontinuous categories of the indicator, then the dichotomy is considered to be classificatory. Whenever the dichotomous categories are conceptualized as continuous, polar components on a continuum, then the dichotomy may be designated as comparative. Using these criteria, it appears to us that there are very few dichotomies that cannot be conceptualized as comparative indicators.

Two fairly common forms of comparative single-item indicators are the Likert type response format[10] and Osgood's semantic differential.[11] The *Likert response format* consists of providing a stimulus in the form of a proposition or statement, with the specified response categories of: (a) strongly approve (agree, support, etc.); (b) approve; (c) undecided; (d) disapprove; (e) strongly disapprove (disagree, oppose, etc.). One modification of this technique expands the number of categories to seven in order to provide three different levels of intensity for each positive and negative viewpoint. Another modification has been to force some directional response by eliminating the neutral or undecided middle response.

The *semantic differential* employs bipolar adjectives, graphed along a continuum, with six or seven divisions within the continuum for individuals to indicate the intensity of their feeling toward either extreme of the bipolar set. For example,

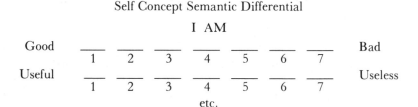

Both the Likert response style and the semantic differential are subject to a problem of response set bias. *Response set* refers to a tendency to respond in a systematic fashion, regardless of the content of the item. For example, acquiescent response set is the tendency to respond affirmatively or positively to an item, regardless of its content. Other response sets involve the tendency to use extreme ratings or classifications, avoid extreme ratings or classifications, give neutral responses, and respond in the direction of perceived socially desirable or acceptable responses.

Various techniques have been developed to overcome the various response set problems. For example, one forced-choice response format eliminates the neutral category in a response continuum and forces the subject to respond positively or negatively. This frustrates the tendency to give neutral responses. A somewhat different forced-choice format is used to overcome the tendency to give perceived socially desirable responses. The respondent is confronted with a choice between what often appears as two or more equally undesirable, inappropriate, or unrelated alternatives or (less often it seems) two or more equally desirable or acceptable alternatives. The tendency to respond primarily with socially desirable responses is frustrated by the presentation of at least two items presumably equal in perceived socially desirable content. One technique for detecting acquiescent response set is to reverse the wording of items that measure essentially the same property so that both approval and disapproval responses are necessary in order to provide a consistent response pattern based on the substance of the items.

MULTIPLE-ITEM COMPARATIVE INDICATORS

The use of multiple indicators to measure a concept serves to provide a fuller and richer operational definition of certain concepts. We will examine here two major kinds of multiple-item indicators: indexes and scales. The terms, indexes and scales, have been used rather loosely and even interchangeably in the sciences. We prefer to distinguish the two, however. An index may be defined as the combination of two or more indicators formed by the summation of numerals assigned to the response categories. A scale, on the other hand, may be defined as the combination of two or more indicators formed by an ordered response hierarchy of the indicators.

## Indexes

Here is an example of the way in which an index is created. The researcher wishes to create a measure of "trust in people." He does so by selecting three indicators that he feels validly measure the concept. The three questions are:

1. Generally speaking, would you say that most people can be trusted or that you can't be too careful in dealing with people?
   1—most people can be trusted
   0—can't be too careful
2. Would you say that most of the time, people try to be helpful, or that they are mostly just looking out for themselves?
   1—try to be helpful
   0—look out for themselves
3. Do you think that most people would try to take advantage of you if they got the chance or would they try to be fair?
   1—try to be fair
   0—take advantage

In each one of the questions, one of the responses is viewed as an indicator of trust in people. Those responses have been assigned the numeral 1. A person who gives all three of those responses receives the highest score for the measure, "trust in people." If the three measures are simply added together, then a person giving the trusting responses would receive a score of 3. An individual giving all nontrusting responses would receive a score of 0. Scores of 1 and 2 are somewhat more difficult to interpret. There are three different ways to receive either one of those two scores. This is a somewhat undesirable feature of some indexes that is not present in scales, as we will see somewhat later. Whenever necessary, it is possible to create an index with unique scores for each unique combination of categories. This may be necessary, for example, when the index is also considered to be a typology, formed by the cross-classification of two or more indicators. In many other instances, the researcher does not need to distinguish such uniqueness. In the example above, it probably is not especially important which item was answered in a trusting manner for a person with a score of 1.

Usually, an index should possess both a theoretical and an empirical justification for its existence. The items that make up the index are included on the basis of their theoretical relevance. The categories of the index (especially a typology) have systematic import. Empirically, it is desirable that each of the categories of the index contains cases. The creation of categories that do not exist empirically normally limits the utility of the index in prediction or explanation.

In most indexes, each of the indicators that comprise the index is given equal weight in deriving the index score. This is not a requirement of index construction, however. If there is a theoretical justification for weighting one of the indicators disproportionately, then it can be done. In the absence of any theoretically compelling reason, each indicator of the index should be counted equally.

Indexes are subject to the same validity and reliability assessments as other indicators since an index still represents an operational definition of a concept. Items of the index should contribute to the validity of the index. The individual items should converge with each other and the index as a whole. The index should be subject to the same tests for construct validity as other indicators.

### Scales

Scales also combine two or more measures. However, with scales the assignment of numerals does not occur through the mere summation of response scores. A scale contains an ordered response hierarchy of the indicators. The response hierarchy feature of a scale is probably best depicted by the Bogardus Social Distance Scale.[12] This particular scale is intended to measure the amount of social distance an individual is willing to accept between himself and persons of particular racial, ethnic, or social groups. We phrase the basic question in terms of our own special group of people.

"To which of the following categories would you admit professors of sociology?"

Would exclude from my country
As visitors only to my country
To citizenship in my country

To employment in my occupation
To my street as neighbors
To my club as personal chums
To close kinship by marriage

Each succeeding statement reduces the social distance between the respondent and sociology professors. It is the presumption of the scale that a person who responds negatively to a particular item will then continue to respond negatively to each succeeding item. A person who responds affirmatively to an item can be presumed to have responded affirmatively to any preceding item in the hierarchical arrangement. A scale score is assigned to an individual to mark the point at which affirmative responses give way to negative responses.

The most common scaling procedure in use today is called Guttman scaling.[13] Guttman scaling is a technique designed to test empirically whether measures selected by the researcher do in fact form a hierarchically ordered scale. For example, one could test whether the index of "trust in people" used just a moment ago could qualify as a scale. To the extent that the vast majority of individuals administered the questions responded in a consistently hierarchical fashion to the three items, it would tend to scale.

Construction of the Guttman Scale proceeds by first ordering the individual indicators on the basis of the frequency with which certain responses were given. For example, in one empirical study, the third question received the largest number of "trust" responses. The least number of "trust" responses were recorded for the first question. Identifying the order of the three items in relation to each other permits us to identify four consistent response styles, shown in Table 10–2.

The next step in establishing the scale is to check the response patterns of the individuals in the analysis. If all individuals administered the questions conform to one of these scale types, a perfect scale exists. In all likelihood, some persons will not conform to one of these four types. There may be some individuals who, for example, responded positively ("trustingly") to question 2 but

**Table 10–2.** EXAMPLE OF A PERFECT GUTTMAN SCALE FORMAT WITH FOUR SCALE TYPES

|  | Question 3 | Question 2 | Question 1 |
|---|---|---|---|
| Scale Type 4 | + | + | + |
| Scale Type 3 | + | + | − |
| Scale Type 2 | + | − | − |
| Scale Type 1 | − | − | − |

not to either question 1 or 3. This represents an inconsistency (error) in the scale. If the actual number of these inconsistencies exceeds 10 percent of the total number of responses given, then the items are adjudged not to form a scale. A second statistical criterion involves comparing actual inconsistencies with the total number of inconsistencies possible in the particular distribution at hand. Details concerning these statistics can be found in the scaling literature.[14]

It is important to recognize that a Guttman Scale is an empirical creation, generated from the specific data at hand. The indicators may have been selected initially because of theoretical or logical considerations, but the existence of a scale depends solely on whether a hierarchical pattern of responses is generated. The same indicators may form a scale with one set of data but not with another. However, if a set of indicators is found to scale with a variety of data sources, then the scale tends to gain greater validity and reliability.

## LEARNING AID

1. Multiple operationism involves operationally defining concepts with a _____ of measurement techniques.
2. What is the value of multiple operationism?
3. Obtrusive measurement is likely to produce reactive effects. Reactive effects describe situations in which _____

_____.

4. Construct a free response question and a structured question concerning an individual's activity in social groups and organizations.
5. The measurement technique that employs bipolar adjectives graphed along a continuum with six or seven divisions is called the _____.
6. The measurement technique that provides a statement and asks the respondent to strongly agree, agree, disagree, or strongly disagree is called the _____ response format.
7. Response set may be defined as _____

_____.

8. Distinguish between an index and a scale.
9. Create an index of local political knowledge.
10. The most common scaling procedure in use today is called _____ scaling.
11. If the actual number of Guttman Scale errors exceeds _____ percent of the total number of responses given, then the items are judged not to form a _____.

. . . . . . . . . . . . . . . . . . . . . . . . . . . . . . . . . . . . . . . . . . . . . . . . . . . . . . . . . .

1. variety
2. Every measurement technique has its own weakness or error component.

No single method of measurement is completely valid or reliable. Thus it is hazardous to base an inference on a single measurement technique. It is safer to use a variety of measurement techniques, each having different weaknesses or error components.

**3.** the object being measured is affected by (or reacts to) the measurement process itself.

**4.** Free response format example: "What social groups or organizations are you particularly active in?" Structured question format example: "How active would you say you are in social groups and organizations? Would you say that you are very active, somewhat active, or not very active at all?"

**5.** semantic differential

**6.** Likert

**7.** a tendency to respond in a systematic fashion, regardless of the content of the stimulus.

**8.** Both indexes and scales combine two or more measures into a more complex measure of a property. However, an index combines by summing the numerals of the response categories of the different indicators. A scale combines by establishing an ordered response hierarchy of the indicators.

**9.** Please answer the following questions by writing the answers in the blanks provided:

    a.   Who is presently the mayor of this city? _____

    b.   What is the length of the mayor's term of office? _____

    c.   What form of government does this city have: strong mayor, weak mayor, or council–manager? _____

    d.   Name one member of the local school board: _____

The index is created by assigning a numeral equal to the number of correct answers. For example, assign a value of 4 if all four items are correctly answered, a 3 if three are correctly answered, and so on. Although only one question is asked, the use of non–mutually exclusive categories presents four different indicators that measure some aspect of local political knowledge.

**10.** Guttman

**11.** ten, scale

## FOOTNOTES

1. Carl Hempel, *Philosophy of Natural Science,* (Englewood Cliffs, N.J.: Prentice-Hall, 1966) p. 96.

2. Claire Selltiz, et al., *Research Methods in Social Relations,* rev. ed. (New York: Holt, Rinehart and Winston, 1959), pp. 154–66; *Standards for Educational and Psychological Tests and Manuals* (Washington, D.C.: American Psychological Association, 1966), pp. 12–24.

3. Milton Rokeach, *The Open and Closed Mind* (New York: Basic Books, 1960), pp. 101–8.

4. Donald T. Campbell and Donald W. Fiske, "Convergent and Discriminant Validation by the Multitrait-Multimethod Matrix," *Psychological Bulletin* 56, no. 2 (March, 1959): 81–105.

5. *Standards for Educational and Psychological Tests and Manuals,* pp. 25–26; James L. Mursell, *Psychological Testing* (New York: Longmans, Green, and Co. 1947), pp. 40–52.

6. Campbell and Fiske, "Convergent and Discriminant Validation," 83.

7. A more detailed presentation of certain reliability measures can be found in J. P. Guilford and Benjamin Fruchter, *Fundamental Statistics in Psychology and Education,* 5th ed. (New York: McGraw-Hill, 1973), pp. 396–423.

8. The importance of multiple operationism is presented in Eugene J. Webb, et al., *Unobtrusive Measures: Nonreactive Research in the Scoial Sciences* (Chicago: Rand McNally, 1966), chap. 1.

9. See Webb, ibid., for a more thorough presentation.

10. Rensis Likert, "Technique for the Measurement of Attitudes," *Archives of Psychology* 22, no. 140 (1932): 1–55.

11. Charles Osgood, George J. Succi, and Percy Tannenbaum, *The Measurement of Meaning* (Urbana: University of Illinois Press, 1957).

12. Emory S. Bogardus, *Immigration and Race Attitudes* (Boston: D. C. Heath, 1928).

13. Samuel A. Stouffer, et al., *Measurement and Prediction* (Princeton, N.J.: Princeton University Press, 1950).

14. A single good source that presents articles dealing with the statistical and nonstatistical criteria for scales is *Attitude Measurement,* ed. Gene F. Summers (Rand McNally, 1970), chaps. 9, 10, and 11.

# 11
# Data Processing

# INTRODUCTION

## Rationale

Two of the basic goals of political and social inquiry are explanation and prediction. Explanation and prediction require the collection of information and the analysis of that information. However, there are certain activities that intervene between the collection of the information and its substantive analysis. The information must be stored in a fashion that permits repeated reference to it. Often, the information must be modified from its original form in order to facilitate storage and analysis. Finally, the information must be processed in ways that permit its substantive analysis. This entire set of intervening activities can be subsumed under the label "information processing."

In empirical inquiry, the collection of information usually entails measurement. Information that consists of measured observations is called *data*. *Data processing* may be defined as the storage, retrieval, and manipulation of data. By manipulation is meant that certain operations are performed on the data to modify their form or to facilitate their analysis.

The term "data processing" connotes computer processing to most of us. Today, such a connotation is not misleading. Computers play an ever-increasing role in the rapid and efficient processing of information. This is true also in social science research. The computer permits the processing of a much greater amount of information than a researcher can handle any other way. Furthermore, the computer permits more technical and sophisticated empirical analyses to be performed on the information than ever could be done before.

This unit will focus on computer data-processing techniques. The first section of the unit will concern storage of collected data on computer readable devices. Next, the language, composition, and operation of computers will be examined. Finally, attention will be given to the program languages that are used to feed instructions to the computer.

## Learning Objectives

After completing this unit, the student should be able to:

1. Define the following terms: data processing, case, code, computer hardware, computer software, bit, input, and computer program.

2. Explain the function of the following items: computer card, codebook, coding sheet, deck number, keypunch, verifier, counter–sorter, reproducer, interpreter, tabulator, analog computer, digital computer, and computer peripheral equipment.

231

3. Explain the major contributions of the computer in facilitating data analysis.

4. Describe the process of coding data from a survey questionnaire to a computer card.

5. Identify the elements of a codebook page.

6. Recall the coding conventions that facilitate rapid and efficient data processing.

7. Explain how a computer reads and stores numbers.

8. Identify the desirable features of a software package.

9. Identify and explain the functions of the units of the computer's central processor.

## DATA STORAGE

All political and social inquiry that attempts to describe, explain, or predict requires information processing. In traditional, nonempirical inquiry, the processing stage may be more subtle and less prominent than in empirical inquiry. Nevertheless, phenomena are observed, information is stored (even if only in note form), and the computer-like mind of the researcher manipulates the information to provide an analysis that adequately describes, explains, or predicts certain phenomena.

In empirical research, processing information (data) is much more elaborate. The preparation of data for the computer and the processing of data by the computer are used to supplement and enhance the analysis of information by the human mind, not to replace it. The goal of data processing is to move the data from the collection stage to the analysis stage as accurately, efficiently, and rapidly as possible.

Information may be collected for many different cases or observations on many different properties. The terms *case* and *observation* refer synonomously to the object or thing whose property is being observed. Thus, one empirical study may examine the roll call votes of congressmen in the House of Representatives. Each congressman represents one case or observation. Since there are 435 congressmen, the number of cases involved in this study is 435.

One major contribution of the computer in facilitating data analysis is its capacity to store and retrieve enormous amounts of information quickly. Another contribution is its ability to perform various manipulations of data, such as statistical procedures, quickly and accurately. If the votes of congressmen were collected on only 20 different bills, the total number of pieces of information gathered would be 20 × 435, or 8700. If votes on all bills, as well as informa-tion on properties of the bills and properties of the congressmen were added to the study, the amount of information collected defies comprehensive analysis without the aid of a computer.

## Coding Onto Computer Cards

To facilitate the computer processing of data, it is desirable to transform the in-formation into symbols, called *codes*. In empirical research, the process of assigning numerals to properties of things is a coding process. It is not necessary that codes be numeric symbols. Letters, words, and other symbols can be read by the computer. However, the use of numerals simplifies and speeds up considerably the processing of the data by the computer.

In social science research, the most common form of computer readable device used for initial data storage is the computer card. A variety of different computer cards is available, but the most popular one for social science data is shown in Figure 11–1. It consists of 80 vertical columns, with twelve different punching positions. Figure 11–1 demonstrates how numbers, letters, and certain symbols are coded on the card using an IBM 026 card-punching ma-chine.

The procedure for moving the data from its original storage form to a com-puter card usually occurs in two distinct steps. First, the data are transcribed onto coding sheets, sheets with 80 spaces across the page, one for each column of the computer card. Second, the computer cards are punched on a machine following the format given on the coding sheet. This process is demonstrated

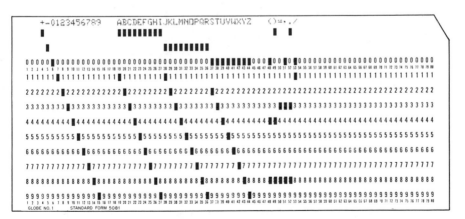

Figure 11-1. Computer Punch Card.

using as an example a page from a questionnaire that was used to collect information concerning political attitudes, voting behavior, and other related properties.

Figure 11–2 shows a page from an interview schedule of the Center for Political Studies, Institute for Social Research, at the University of Michigan. In Figure 11–2, notice that the initial question, E1, gives precoded responses to

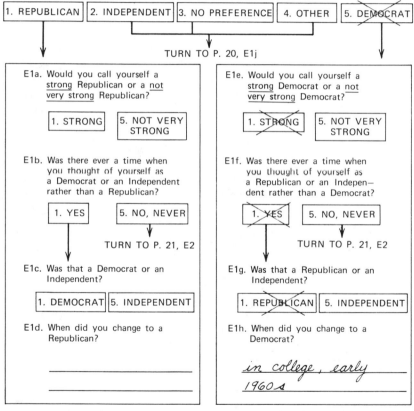

Figure 11-2. A page from a Survey Questionaire. Material supplied by the Center for Political Studies, Institute for Social Research, University of Michigan.

the question. The range of responses to the question are already anticipated and classified. Numerals have already been assigned. On the other hand, questions E1d and E1h are open-ended questions that are not precoded. For open-ended questions, the respondent's answers are written in by the interviewer. Later, the various responses to a question for all the cases are reviewed and analyzed with the intent of classifying the responses according to some comprehensive and functional scheme.

The questionnaire design directs the flow of the interview. Certain questions are contingent on answers given by the respondents. For example, in Figure 11–2 the initial response of "Democrat" leads to asking question E1e. The $X$s placed across the boxes in Figure 11–2 show how an interviewer may mark the interview schedule for a respondent identified as a strong Democrat who in college thought of himself as a Republican.

The coder is a person who transcribes the original information onto the coding sheets from which the data will be punched onto cards. In the case of a survey questionnaire, the coder operates from the questionnaire and from a codebook. The codebook provides instructions concerning how to code responses to various questions. The precoded responses can merely be directly copied onto the coding sheet from the questionnaire pages. However, the open-ended responses require the coder to classify the response according to the rules specified in the codebook.

The example of a Center for Political Studies codebook page presented in Figure 11–3 is not exactly the type from which a coder would work. This is a data user's codebook compiled for a set of data that already have been stored on cards and on computer tape. The data have been processed to the point of reporting frequencies of cases for each of the indicator responses. Nevertheless, in Figure 11–3 can be found the coding scheme developed for the responses to question E1h. Since an exact year was not reported in the original interview (see Figure 11–2), the code 62 is assigned as best representing the response that was given.

Using the codebook as a guide, the coder begins coding the responses from the questionnaire onto a coding sheet. In addition to the coded questionnaire responses, at least three other coded items appear on each card. One item is the study number, which identifies the project or study. Another is a case number, which identifies the particular case being coded. Finally, whenever more than one computer card for each case is needed to store the data, a deck number is assigned that identifies the card of a particular case. Deck 5 indicates that this information is stored on the fifth card of data for each case.

Figure 11–4 presents an illustration of a coding sheet and a computer card. Each one shows the three codes discussed in the previous paragraph and the listing of the items from the questionnaire in Figure 11–2. (The codes for other columns have been omitted to demonstrate more clearly the transcribing from

① VAR 0141                                                    ② DATA SET ID-'7010'
  ③ NAME-R'S PARTYID:R/I/NO/OTR/D ④ MD=GE 8
    ⑤ LOC  280 WIDTH 1           ⑥ DK  COL 14

                    ⑦ E1.  GENERALLY SPEAKING, DO YOU USUALLY THINK OF YOURSELF AS
                           A REPUBLICAN, A DEMOCRAT, AN INDEPENDENT, OR WHAT?
          - - - - - - - - - - - - - - - - - - - --- - - - - - - - - - - - - -
          ⑧             ⑨          ⑩
         632           1.       REPUBLICAN
         757           2.       INDEPENDENT
         206           3.       NO PREFERENCE
          18           4.       OTHER
        1089           5.       DEMOCRAT

                       8.       DK
           3           9.       NA


    VAR 0142                                                   DATA SET ID-'7010'
       NAME-IS R A STRONG DEM          MD=0 OR GE 8
       LOC   281 WIDTH  1              DK  5 COL 15

                    E1E.  WOULD YOU CALL YOURSELF A STRONG DEMOCRAT OR A NOT
                          VERY STRONG DEMOCRAT?
          - - - - - - - - - - - - - - - - - - - -- - - - - - - - - - - - - -
         675           1.       STRONG
        1039           5.       NOT VERY STRONG

           2           8.       DK
           5           9.       NA
         984           0.       INAP., CODED 2-4, 8 OR 9 IN Q. E1


    VAR 0146                                                   DATA SET ID-'7010'
       NAME-(DEM):WHEN CHANGE PTY   MD=0 OR GE 98
       LOC  285 WIDTH  2            DK  5 COL 19-20

                    --IF RESPONSE TO Q. E1 WAS "DEMOCRAT" AND RESPONSE TO Q. E1F
                      WAS "YES"--

                    E1H.  WHEN DID YOU CHANGE <FROM PRIOR PARTY IDENTIFICATION>
                          TO A DEMOCRAT?
          - - - - - - - - - - - - - - - - - - - - - - - - -- - - - - - - - - -
                    WHERE THE ACTUAL DATE WAS MENTIONED OR ASCERTAINED THE LAST
                TWO DIGITS ARE CODED.

                    01.      1901 OR ANY TIME PREVIOUS
                    02.      1902


                    70.      1970
                    72.      1972


236

WHERE THE ACTUAL DATE WAS NOT MENTIONED, BUT WHERE A RE-
SPONSE COULD BE IDENTIFIED WITH A PARTICULAR TERM OF OFFICE,
THE RESPONSE WAS CODED AS FOLLOWS:

| | |
|---|---|
| 03. | MCKINLEY AND ROOSEVELT (1901-1904) |
| 07. | T. ROOSEVELT (1905-1908) |
| 11. | TAFT (1909-1912) |
| 15. | WILSON - FIRST TERM (1913-1916) (NA WHICH TERM) |
| 19. | WILSON - SECOND TERM (1917-1920) |
| 23. | HARDING AND COOLIDGE (1921-1924) |
| 27. | COOLIDGE (1925-1928) |
| 31. | HOOVER (1929-1932) |
| 35. | F.D.R.- FIRST TERM (1933-1936) |
| 39. | F.D.R.- SECOND TERM (1937-1940) |
| 40. | F.D.R. NA WHEN |
| 43. | F.D.R.- THIRD TERM (1941-1944) |
| 47. | F.D.R. AND TRUMAN (1945-1948) |
| 51. | TRUMAN (1948-1952) |
| 55. | EISENHOWER (1953-1956) (NA WHICH TERM) |
| 59. | EISENHOWER (1957-1960) |
| 62. | KENNEDY AND JOHNSON (1961-1964) |
| 64. | JOHNSON (1965-1968) |
| 69. | NIXON (1969-1972) |
| | |
| 98. | DK |
| 99. | NA, NO CODEABLE INFORMATION |
| 00. | INAP., CODED 2, 3, 4, 8 OR 9 IN Q. E1: OR CODED 5, 8 OR 9 IN Q. E1B/Q. E1F; OR CODED 8 OR 9 IN Q.E1C/Q.E1G |

Figure 11-3.  Examples of a Data User's Codebook with a description
of the Entries. Material supplied by the Center for Political Studies,
Institute for Social Research, University of Michigan.

1.   Unique identification number assigned to each variable.

2.   An identification number assigned to this particular study.

3.   An abbreviated description name for the variable.

4.   Codes assigned to "missing data." Missing data include inappropriate, nonascertainable, or other nonresponsive classifications.

5.   Storage location for the variable on a computer tape, disk, or drum
and the number of coded digits or symbols for any one of the responses.
The width for VAR0141 is one column. Note that for VAR0146 the width
for the two digit responses is 2.

6.   Storage location for the variable on a computer card. In this
example, VAR0141 is stored on the fifth card (deck) of each case in
column 14.

7.   The complete text of the interview question or statement.

8.   The frequency of cases for each of the coded classifications.

9.   The codes for each response classification.

10.   The verbal description of the response classification.

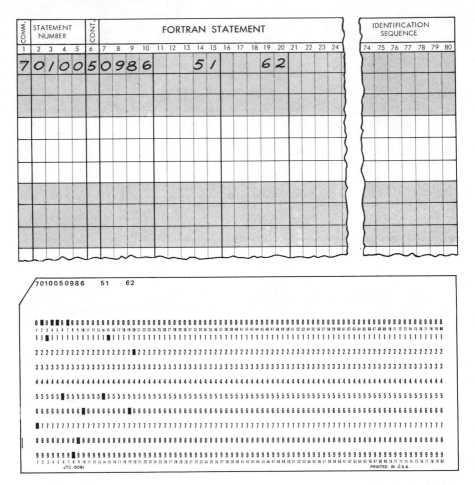

**Figure 11-4. Coding Sheet and Punched Computer Card.**

questionnaire to computer card.) Reference to the codebook (Figure 11–3) indicates that a "5" punch in column 14 designates a "Democrat" party identification. The "62" in columns 19 and 20 denotes a switch to "Democrat" in the Kennedy–Johnson era of 1961–1964.

## LEARNING AID

1. Two major contributions of the computer in facilitating data analysis are:
(a) _____
and (b) _____

**2.** The term *case* refers to _____.

**3.** The assignment of numerals to properties of things, as done in operational definitions, is called _____.

**4.** Identify at least four pieces of information that usually can be found in a data user's codebook.

**5.** The *deck number* identifies _____ _____ _____ .

**6.** Review the explanation of a codebook page given in Figure 11–3.

· · · · · · · · · · · · · · · · · · · · · · · · · · · · · · · · · · · · · · · · · · · · · · · · · · · ·

**1.** (a) the capacity to store and retrieve enormous amounts of information quickly, and (b) the ability to perform various manipulations of data quickly and accurately.

**2.** the object whose property is being observed.

**3.** coding

**4.** (a) Variable number; (b) Study number; (c) Variable name; (d) Missing data code; (e) Variable location for storage on computer tape, drum, or disk and width of the variable; (f) Variable location for storage on computer card; (g) Text of variable question or statement; (h) Frequency count for response categories; (i) Codes for response classifications; (j) Verbal response classifications.

**5.** the card number for a case.

**6.** See Figure 11–3.

## Coding Conventions

Although the computer is very versatile in accepting different codes, coding conventions do facilitate the rapid and efficient processing of data. The following conventions are some of the more important.

1. Use only numbers for designating coded classifications. This means that the use of symbols (+, −, etc.), letters, and blanks (no punch) should be avoided.

2. Punch only one number in a column. Some questions may permit multiple responses. Use separate columns for each response. Usually it is preferable to list multiple responses according to the primacy of the response. The first response is recorded first, the second response next, and so on.

3. Provide as complete and precise a coding scheme for the original data as possible. For example, classify age according to the actual age, not in age groupings.

4. Code consistently. If some variables have the same response categories, use the same codes for initial response classifications.

5. If more than one computer card of information is required for each case, provide each card with a deck number. The first card for each case is Deck 1;

the second card is Deck 2; and so forth. Be certain also to punch in an identification number on every card for each case.

## Alternative Coding Procedures

Efforts to bypass or expedite coding data onto computer cards have been made. Mark sensing sheets are used with multiple choice tests. The pencil marks on the sheet can be fed directly into a computer. Although mark sensing sheets have their place, the constraints imposed by precoded responses and a greater degree of unreliability in their use severely limit their utility.

Efforts to expedite coding data onto computer cards focus on eliminating the use of coding sheets. This is done simply by punching directly from the sheets on which the data are collected originally. In the case of a questionnaire, all items may be precoded or the codes may be filled in along the edge of the page. The bypassing of transcriptions onto coding sheets appears to reduce error by avoiding transcription errors while saving the time consumed by such transcriptions. However, card punching error increases with such direct punching, and it is considerably slower. The apparent advantages of bypassing the coding sheet transcription are more illusory than real.

## Computer Card Equipment

The prevalence of the computer card for data storage spawned the development of equipment to handle the various needs of computer card storage.

The *keypunch* is a machine that punches holes in a computer card to designate various numbers, letters, or symbols. The keypunch is operated by use of a keyboard that resembles that of a typewriter. The pattern of letters is the same, and the keypunch also has an upper and lower case. However, letters are punched only when the keyboard is set in the .lower case or alphabetic mode. Numbers are punched only when the keyboard is operated in the upper case or numeric mode. The keypunch contains several features that enhance its utility in performing the basic card punching function.

The *verifier* checks the accuracy of the initial keypunching operation. This check is made by "repunching" the cards. The difference between the keypunch and the verifier is that the verifier actually punches no holes in the cards. Instead, it detects if the card column being checked contains the proper punch (or blank). If the card column being checked does not contain the proper punch, the verifier indicates an error and prevents the card from proceeding to the next column. The machine operator is then able to check the accuracy of the punch to determine whether the error occurred on the initial keypunching or in the verifying check. If the error is in the punch made by the keypunch, then the verifier will mark the column containing the error, and the card proceeds to the next column.

The *counter–sorter* counts and sorts computer cards. The sorting operation permits a stack of computer cards to be separated into different receptacles or "pockets" of the machine according to the punch present in a particular column. Simultaneously, all cards processed through the machine are counted. Some counter–sorters contain a counter to tally the number of cards in each pocket. The counter–sorter is often used to provide a quick count of the total number of cards or of the distribution of cases among the various classifications of a variable. It also is used to order physically the cards according to their case identification number and deck number.

The *reproducer* permits the duplication of a set of punched cards. Reproducers also contain wiring boards that permit the punches in one set of cards to be relocated in different columns and punched into a blank set of cards. The reproducer still has some utility for social scientists, but computers have tended either to make such card duplication obsolete or to perform the same function with less trouble.

The *interpreter* prints the symbols of the card punches across the top of the computer card. Cards punched on a keypunch will not need the services of the interpreter, assuming that the "print" switch on the keypunch was turned on.

The *tabulator* prints out the contents of punched cards on paper. Having a record of what is punched on the cards is especially useful with respect to punched instructions to the computer. It permits an easier checking for errors and provides a copy of the instructions that can be repunched in the event the computer cards are lost.

## LEARNING AID

1. Although the computer is versatile in reading codes, it is desirable to use only _____ for designating coded classifications.
2. If a particular item permits multiple responses, the responses should be coded _____ .
3. In most social science research, mark sensing sheets are not used to speed up the coding and data storage process because _____.
4. What is a verifier machine?
5. For what purpose might the counter–sorter be used to sort?
6. The tabulator is designed to _____.
. . . . . . . . . . . . . . . . . . . . . . . . . . . . . . . . . . . . . . . . . . . . . . . . . . . . . . . . . . .

1. numerals.
2. in separate columns and in the order in which the responses were elicited.

**3.**  of the constraints imposed by precoded responses and a greater degree of unreliability in their use.
**4.**  A verifier checks the accuracy of the initial keypunching operation.
**5.**  The counter–sorter might be used to sort the cards into order, according to their case identification number and deck number.
**6.**  print out the contents of punched cards on paper.


## COMPUTER HARDWARE

The term *computer hardware* refers to the actual machinery of the computer. Two major types of computers are the analog computer and the digital computer. A third class of hybrid computers combines elements of the first two. An *analog computer* is designed to measure physical quantities, quantities that represent, by analogy, numbers. For example, the height of the mercury in a thermometer represents a particular numeric assignment concerning the temperature. Analog computers find their greatest use in scientific and industrial fields that require the monitoring and control of complex equipment and processes.

A *digital computer* is designed to count and perform various operations on the numbers or digits that are fed into the computer. The fact that numbers can be used also to represent letters and other symbols, however, expands the use of the digital computer far beyond what people usually regard as counting. Digital computers possess a greater capacity than analog computers for the storage of enormous amounts of data, for the logical processing of the data, and for accuracy in the results of mathematical operations. As you might have guessed, the digital computer is the one most commonly used by social scientists for their research.


### The Computer's Language

Digital computers operate with one of the simplest communications schemes available, one in which there are only two symbols—1 and 0. These are the two binary digits or *bits,* as they are more often called. Combinations of these bits are used by the computer to represent all the numbers, letters, and symbols that are fed into and sent out of the computer.

The computer does not actually read the numbers 1 and 0. Instead, electric current and magnetized materials are used to represent the numbers. A flow of current can represent a 1; its absence represents a 0. A positive charge is a 1; a negative charge is a 0. The inside of a computer memory device actually consists of tiny magnetic doughnut-shaped cores no larger than a pinhead strung on several criss-crossing wires. Each one of these cores holds a bit, either a positive or negative charge representing a 1 or 0. By stringing these cores in columns, very large numbers or even words may be stored in a column of bits.

Several numbering systems are available that use only the binary digits. Whereas the decimal system operates on a base 10 principle with a ones column, then a tens column, a hundreds column, and so on, basic binary operates on a base 2 with a ones column, a twos column, a fours column, an eights column, and so on. Table 11–1 demonstrates the basic binary numbering system. Most computers actually use some variant of this basic binary system in order to enhance the system's utility and efficiency.

Perhaps it has occurred to you that the data that are punched on computer

**Table 11–1.**  DECIMAL AND BINARY NUMBERING SYSTEMS

| Decimal | Binary |
|---|---|
| 0 | 0 |
| 1 | 1 |
| 2 | 10 |
| 3 | 11 |
| 4 | 100 |
| 5 | 101 |
| 6 | 110 |
| 7 | 111 |
| 8 | 1000 |
| 9 | 1001 |
| 10 | 1010 |
| 11 | 1011 |
| . | . |
| . | . |
| 16 | 10000 |
| . | . |
| . | . |
| . | . |
| 20 | 10100 |
| . | . |
| . | . |
| . | . |
| . | . |
| 129 | 10000001 |

cards are not coded in bits. If you think that this should make the computer card not readable by the computer, then you are technically correct. In order for the data on the computer card to be processed by the computer, it first must be translated into whatever binary-based system is used by the computer. This is accomplished by sending the cards through a card reader which, in effect, translates the punches into the computer's language. Similarly, once the computer has processed the data, the results are translated from the computer's language back into the language of the data.

## The Computer's Composition

Two basic types of equipment constitute a computer system—the central processor and the peripherals. The *central processor* is the actual computer. It contains four types of units. The *storage or memory unit* stores data and instructions in specified storage locations. The *arithmetic–logical unit* performs the arithmetic and data manipulation operations. The *control unit* keeps track of where the data are stored and executes the instructions given the computer. The *console* permits the computer to be operated by the computer operator.

The *peripheral equipment* is concerned with putting the information into the computer in the computer's language and translating the information from the computer back into readable form.

*Input* consists of retrieving data stored on some computer readable device and feeding them into the computer. Computer cards represent a somewhat inefficient and cumbersome input medium. It is generally preferable to store data in the binary-based language of the computer and on a device that can be read more quickly than cards. For example, data stored on a magnetic computer tape can be read by the computer over a hundred times faster than data stored on computer cards. Other prominent forms of data storage, both of which are faster to read from than computer tape, are the magnetized disk and the magnetized drum. Tape, disk, and drum all operate basically on the same principle. A spot on the device is magnetized to represent a 1 bit and is not magnetized to represent a 0 bit. These bits can be deposited in differing amounts of density, but 800 bits per inch on a computer tape is not unusual.

## The Computer's Operation

The computer operates at mind-boggling speed. It is an electronic device with no moving parts, and it sends its impulses at nearly the speed of light. The time in which it takes the computer to execute instructions or move a group of bits from one place to another in the computer is measured in nanoseconds, billionths of a second. The computer on which we currently are operating at our facility can process about two million instructions in a second.

The logic of the computer's operation is very simple. Computers are operated by computer programs. A *computer program* provides instructions and data for the computer. Each instruction and, as it is called for, each piece of data is assigned a memory storage location with an address that identifies its location. This operation can be illustrated by a simple problem. Let us instruct the computer to count the number of congressmen who are Republicans, Democrats, or any other partisan affiliation.

Instructions to the computer are punched on cards, as are the data. Together they are put into the card reader, which interprets the card punches into the computer's bit language and feeds the information into storage. Each

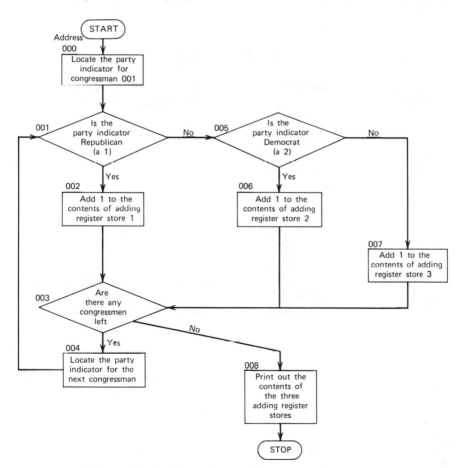

Figure 11-5.  Flowchart of Computer Program.

storage location is assigned an address, a number to identify the storage location. The control unit of the computer then causes the first instruction to be accessed and executed.

In Figure 11–5, a flowchart more clearly describes the logic of the program than a narrative can do. The arrows actually represent instructions to the computer to go to a particular address to perform the instruction requested. The data may or may not be located in the computer's core storage. More often than not, the social scientist's data may be stored on a drum or disk for use during the operation of the program.

The arithmetic–logical unit of the computer contains registers. A *register* is a special storage location designed to perform a specified function. In this example, instructions provide that if a certain condition is satisfied, the adding register will add 1 to the contents already accumulated and store the sum.

## LEARNING AID

1. In a somewhat simplistic sense, we may say that analog computers are designed to _____ (count/measure), and digital computers are designed to _____ (count/measure).

2. Digital computers operate with only two basic symbols, which are called _____.

3. In order for the punches on a computer card to be processed by the computer, it first must be _____.

4. The computer's central processor consists of four different units. What are they?

5. Computer cards _____ (are/are not) the most efficient form of storing data for use by a computer.

6. What is a computer program?

7. Although a computer operates only one instruction at a time on one piece of data at a time, it gains its speed from its ability to execute _____ (hundreds, thousands, millions, billions) of instructions in a single second.

. . . . . . . . . . . . . . . . . . . . . . . . . . . . . . . . . . . . . . . . . . . . . . . . . . . . . . . . . . . . . .

1. measure, count.

2. bits or binary digits.

3. processed through a card reader, which translates into the computer's language.

4. storage, arithmetic–logical, control, console.

5. are not

6. A computer program provides instructions and data for the computer.

7. millions.

## COMPUTER SOFTWARE

In contrast to the computer hardware, *computer software* refers to the language and symbol representations used to provide instructions and information to the computer. In the example given in Figure 11–5, narrative instructions were given which, in reality, cannot be given directly to the computer. Software is developing to the point where instructions to the computer can be presented in fairly natural language. However, even this more natural language must utilize a strict terminology and a strict format of presentation.

Most university computer facilities now possess statistical packages for social scientists that dispense with the need to master the somewhat abstract program languages such as FORTRAN and COBOL. These social science–oriented packages permit a complex statistical procedure such as a factor analysis to be performed simply by inputing the instruction FACTOR and specifying which variables should be incorporated into the analysis. The computer searches through the appropriate storage device for the term FACTOR. Under that heading, a whole list of instructions is stored that eventually is translated into the computer's language and acted on.

Most computer programs contain three basic components. The *job control language (JCL) cards* are designed to gain access to and departure from the specific computer being used. JCL cards provide certain information concerning the identity of the user, an account number for billing purposes, identification for the specific program being run, estimates of time and length of output. Certain instructions may be included in the JCL cards to assure that the information necessary to the program is available and to ensure that the run is terminated properly.

The second component consists of some *program language control cards,* which permit the desired storage, retrieval, or manipulation of data to occur. The control cards are written in the syntax of the program package being used.

The third component of a run consists of the *data file.* A data file contains a defined set of data that is stored on some sort of computer readable device. The program either must provide the data along with the JCL and control cards, or it must inform the computer of the storage location for the data.

There are certain features a software computer package needs in order to have maximum utility for the social scientist. It must permit the processing and analysis of large amounts of data, both in terms of the number of cases and the number of variables. It must provide for considerable modification of the data. Within a single variable, it should be possible to reassign numerals to different classifications, combine separate classifications together, and omit certain classifications from inclusion in a particular operation. Mathematical and logical operations among the different variables should be possible. The ability to have operations performed only on subgroups in the data file is essential. A wide variety of statistical operations should be available in the package. Finally, the syntax employed by the package should be simple to understand and to use.

## LEARNING AID

1.  Computer software refers to _____ .
2.  The three components that constitute a computer program are: _____, _____, and _____.
3.  Identify at least four functions of the job control language cards.
4.  Identify four different features a software system should possess.

. . . . . . . . . . . . . . . . . . . . . . . . . . . . . . . . . . . . . . . . . . . . . . . . . . . . . . .

1.  the language and symbol representations used to provide instructions and information to the computer.
2.  job control language cards, program language control cards, data file.
3.  identify the user, identify the specific program being run, provide an account number for billing, estimate the time the program will take to run, estimate the length of output from the program.
4.  See the last paragraph in the section.

# 12
# Descriptive Data Analysis

# INTRODUCTION

## Rationale

The essence of empirical research is the gathering and analysis of data. Data consist of nothing more than information, information that has been measured. The measurement process is described in Unit 10. Later units will detail some of the processes by which information is collected. The purpose of the next two units is to present the statistical techniques of analyzing the information that is collected.

This unit deals especially with various techniques for describing the data. Collectively, these techniques are referred to as descriptive statistics. The term "statistics," however, refers more specifically to certain mathematical techniques that are employed to organize the data in order to facilitate interpretation. The concern of this unit is less with the mathematical computations than with the comprehension and interpretation of the results of various statistical operations.

## Learning Objectives

After completing this unit, the student should be able to:

1. Identify and distinguish among the following:

   a. univariate, bivariate, and multivariate distributions;

   b. mode, median, and mean;

   c. linear regression, partial correlation, multiple regression, and multiple correlation;

   d. control effects, relative effects, and conjoint effects.

2. Compute and interpret the following:

   a. ratio, proportion, rate, percentage, and percentage change;

   b. mode, median, and mean;

   c. a percentaged bivariate table.

3. Understand and explain the following concepts: central tendency, variation, original variation, explained variation, unexplained variation, and prediction.

4. Define and interpret the regression coefficient and the partial regression coefficient.

5. Describe the general manner in which measures of association are computed and interpreted.

251

## UNIVARIATE ANALYSIS

This unit examines statistical techniques for describing a set of data. The term *data* refers to the measured observations of a set of things. The classification of the set of things is designated by the term *unit of observation,* and it refers to people, objects, events, or any other thing whose property is measured. The term *observations* denotes the collectivity of things whose property is measured. In the next two units, the term "variable" will be used synonomously with the term "indicator." The use of "variable" is predominant in statistical literature. Furthermore, the term "variable" serves to emphasize the fact that the measured observations for a particular property must vary; they cannot all be the same. If they are all the same, then the property is a constant, not a variable. In statistics, a variable not only must have *two or more* mutually exclusive categories or values provided for in the definition, but two or more of these categories or values actually must contain observations.

The term *categories* generally will be used in Units 12 and 13 to refer to the measured divisions of a variable, regardless of the variable's level of measurement. Thus, the values or scores of a quantitative or comparative variable and the classifications of a classificatory or comparative variable will be encompassed by the reference to the categories of a variable.

Earlier a distinction was made between univariate and multivariate distributions. It is now desirable to refine that distinction to produce a tripartite division of univariate (one variable), bivariate (two variables), and multivariate (three or more variables) distributions. The application of statistics to data is based on this distinction. Data description techniques will be presented in turn for each of these three types of data distributions.

### Univariate Distributions

At least three different methods are used in the actual display of univariate distributions. The *raw distribution* is used whenever it is desired to identify the measurement for each individual observation. For example, voting turnout and election results often are presented on a district by district basis (Table 12–1).

The presentation of data in this raw form is informative concerning each individual observation, but it frustrates attempts to analyze certain patterns or characteristics of the distribution. To achieve this latter objective, the data normally are arranged in a frequency distribution. A *frequency distribution* lists the categories of the variable and the number of observations that possess that particular characteristic (Table 12–2).

The long list of different percentages for the voting turnout variable suggests another technique for presenting quantitative distributions, namely, grouping

**Table 12-1** RAW DISTRIBUTIONS FOR TWO VARIABLES

| Congressional District | Percentage Turnout | Party of Winner |
|:---:|:---:|:---:|
| Alabama #1 | 44.0 | Republican |
| Alabama #2 | 45.3 | Republican |
| Alabama #3 | 37.6 | Democrat |
| . | . | . |
| . | . | . |
| etc. | etc. | etc. |
| . | . | . |
| . | . | . |
| Wyoming | 65.0 | Democrat |

the values into intervals. Such a method is the *grouped frequency distribution*. This method is employed whenever the number of unique values in the indicator is considered too large to list individually or whenever the grouping of different values into intervals facilitates comprehension of the data distribution. Table 12–3 shows two display techniques.

The difference between these two grouped frequency distributions demonstrates the distinction between quantitative and comparative level measurement. Quantitative measurement requires equal intervals or measurement units. The distribution on the left in Table 12–3 has equal intervals. The distribution on the right does not. The uppermost and lowermost intervals of the right distribution contain, by implication, 30 units of the indicator each. The other intervals contain only 10 units (if you think it's nine, count them).

**Table 12-2** TWO FREQUENCY DISTRIBUTIONS

| Percentage Turnout | f | Party of Winner | f |
|:---:|:---:|:---|:---:|
| 22.4 | 1 | Republican | 191 |
| 24.1 | 1 | Democratic | 244 |
| 26.7 | 2 | Total ($N$) | (435) |
| . | | | |
| . | | | |
| etc. | | | |
| . | | | |
| . | | | |
| 88.6 | 1 | | |
| ($N$) | (435) | | |

**Table 12-3** TWO GROUPED FREQUENCY DISTRIBUTIONS

| Percentage Turnout | f | Percentage Turnout | f |
|---|---|---|---|
| 80–89% | 3 | 70% and over | 12 |
| 70–79 | 9 | 60–69 | 184 |
| 60–69 | 184 | 50–59 | 115 |
| 50–59 | 115 | 40–49 | 87 |
| 40–49 | 87 | 30–39 | 28 |
| 30–39 | 28 | Below 30% | 9 |
| 20–29 | 7 | (N) | (435) |
| 10–19 | 2 | | |
| (N) | (435) | | |

Often, the uppermost category does not even possess an implied limit. For example, the use of "over $25,000" as the uppermost income bracket in a grouped frequency distribution prohibits the distribution from being analyzed by use of statistics requiring either an interval or ratio level of measurement.

## Relative Frequencies

In many social science studies, the number of observations is quite large, in the hundreds or thousands. Interpreting and comparing frequency counts can be difficult, especially when data distributions with different numbers of observations are compared. *Relative frequencies* provide a basis for the interpretation and comparison of frequencies by relating a frequency to some other frequency. The relationship between the two frequencies provides a standard for interpretation and comparison.

The *ratio* compares the frequency of one or more combined categories to that of one or more other categories. Interpretation of the resulting fraction is enhanced by reducing the fraction to the lowest common denominator or by dividing the numerator by the denominator to produce a denominator of 1. For example, in the "Party of Winner" of Table 12–2, the ratio of Democrats to Republicans is 244 to 191, written as 244/191, which reduces to about 9/7 or 1.28/1.

A *proportion* is a special ratio that divides the frequency of one or more combined variable categories by the total number of observations in the distribution. The total number of observations is equal to the total number of frequencies and is referred to as the $N$. Thus, the proportion of Democrats in Table 12–2 is 244/435 = 0.56.

**Table 12-4**  PERCENTAGE DISTRIBUTIONS OF PARTY FOR EACH HOUSE OF CONGRESS

| House of Representatives | | Senate | |
|---|---|---|---|
| Republican | 44% | Republican | 42% |
| Democrat | 56 | Democrat | 56 |
| (N) | (435) | Other | 2 |
| | | (N) | (100) |

The *rate* is a proportion that is multiplied by a number, which is designed to facilitate the interpretation of the proportion. For example, the birth rate is computed by calculating the number of live births as a proportion of the country's population and multiplying the proportion by 1,000. In 1970, the number of live births in the United States was approximately 3,731,000. The population was about 204,875,000. The proportion of live births to population is 0.0182. Multiplying by 1,000 gives the birth rate of 18.2 per thousand population. The proportion is multiplied by a particular number in order to facilitate interpretation. It is customary in creating a rate to select a base number that will produce a two- or three-digit rate number. Crime rates in the United States, for example, use a base of 100,000.

Rates provide a basis for making comparisons. Birth rates of different nations or for the same nation over time can be compared meaningfully, regardless of the population difference. The most common rate of all is the percentage. A *percentage* is a proportion that is multiplied by a base of 100. It is customary to report univariate frequency distributions in percentage forms whenever $N$ exceeds 30. This facilitates the comprehension of the data and enhances comparison with other data distributions, especially those with different $N$s. For example, the percentaged distributions in Table 12-4 give a greater comprehension concerning the partisan distribution of seats in the House and an immediate comparison with the distribution in the Senate.

*Percentage change* is another type of relative frequency that converts to percentage form the amount of change in two reports of numbers over time. Percentage change is computed in the following fashion:

*Percentage Change*

$$\frac{n_2 - n_1}{n_1} (100)$$

where $n_1$ = beginning number
$n_2$ = terminal number

The number of live births in the United States decreased from 4,258,000 in 1960 to 3,731,000 in 1970. This represents a percentage decrase of 12.4%.

$$\frac{3,731,000 - 4,258,000}{4,258,000} (100) = -12.4$$

Changes in the number of births are interesting, but changes in the birth rate can be more revealing. The birth rate declined from 23.7 in 1960 to 18.2 in 1970, a percentage decrease of 23.2%

## LEARNING AID

1. The classification of the set of things whose properties are measured is called a _____ .

2. "Congressional District" is an example of _____ (data/an observation/a unit of observation).

3. "Alabama #3" is an example of _____ (data/an observation/a unit of observation).

4. The absence of variation in an indicator produces a _____.

5. If grades are posted for the purpose of informing each student of his or her grade, a _____ (raw/frequency/grouped frequency) distribution should be used.

6. A grouped frequency distribution of numeric values measures only at the comparative level if _____.

7. In the grouped frequency distribution on "percentage turnout" presented in Table 12–3, what proportion of congressional districts report a turnout of 50 percent and over?

8. In distribution 2 of Table 12–7, what is the ratio of Protestants to non-Protestants?

9. In 1970, the United States population was about 203,806,000. The number of violent crimes that year was 734,000. What is the crime rate per hundred thousand population for 1970?

10. In 1960, the crime rate was 159 per 100,000. What is the percentage change in the crime rate between 1960 and 1970?

. . . . . . . . . . . . . . . . . . . . . . . . . . . . . . . . . . . . . . . . . . . . . . . . . . . . . . .

1. unit of observation.
2. a unit of observation.
3. an observation.
4. constant.
5. raw

**6.**  the intervals are unequal either by count or by implication.

**7.**  0.715.  (311/435 = 0.715.)

**8.**  2/1.  (10 Protestants to 5 non-Protestants = 10/5 = 2/1)

**9.**  360 per 100,000.  $\dfrac{734000}{203806000}$ (100,000) = 360

**10.**  +126%.  $\dfrac{360 - 159}{159}$ (100) = +126

## Central Tendency

Certain convenient measures have been developed to summarize univariate distributions, facilitate their interpretation and comparison, and enhance their utility. One way in which it is useful to summarize univariate distributions is to report the most typical or representative classification of the distribution. Central tendency is the term used to describe this concept of representativeness, typicalness, or centrality.

There are different ways of defining representativeness. The most representative category may be considered to be the one that occurs most frequently in a distribution. Such a category is called the *mode*. In the frequency distribution of the "Party of Winner" in Table 12–2, the modal category is "Democratic." It is the most frequently recurring category, the most representative or typical observation from that data distribution. In the grouped frequency distribution for voting turnout, the modal interval is 60–69% (see Table 12–3).

Another way of interpreting the representativeness or central tendency of a distribution is to determine the classification or the observation that occurs at the middle point among the observations. Such a classification is called the *median*. The median (mdn) requires that the categories of a measure be ordered. This demands measurement at the comparative or quantitative level. The median is determined by locating the middle observation in a distribution so that half of the observations have classifications equal to or greater than the middle observation and half of the observations have classifications equal to or lower than the middle observation.

In Table 12–2 a median cannot be computed on the "Party of Winner" variable, because it is a classificatory variable, not possessing ordered categories. A median could be computed for "percentage turnout" in that table if all the data were present. For an $N$ of 435, the median is the score of the 218th observation. There are 217 observations with the same or higher score and 217 with the same or lower score. In Table 12–3 the 218th observation is in the interval "50–59%." The exact score is obscured by the grouping of scores into intervals. A more precise number can be computed through an interpolation process, not shown here.

A third method of defining representativeness or central tendency involves the computation of an arithmetic average. It is called the arithmetic mean, or simply, the mean. It requires an assumption that measurement units are equidistant, a requirement of quantitative measurement. The *mean* ($\bar{X}$) of a variable is computed by summing the scores for all observations and dividing that sum by the total number of observations. In a raw distribution, simply add together the scores of all observations and divide that sum by the number of observations ($\Sigma X/N$). In a frequency distribution, the sum of the scores is obtained by multiplying each score listed by the frequency with which it occurs. The sum of these products is equal to the sum of the observed scores. Then, divide by the number of observations ($\Sigma fX/N$). In a grouped frequency distribution, the scores of the individual observations are no longer known. In this situation, it is customary to use the midpoint of the interval as the score for all of the observations in the interval and then proceed to compute the mean, as with a frequency distribution ($\Sigma fm/N$).

The three measures of central tendency can differ considerably in identifying the most representative category of the same distribution. The most appropriate measure is the one that best represents the central tendency in the distribution. Table 12–5 presents three different distributions that demonstrate some of the difficulties in central tendency selection.

The mean generally is restricted to use with quantitative data. Moreover, the mean is used most appropriately in unimodal distributions that do not contain extreme scores toward one end of the distribution. The rightmost distribution in Table 12–5 demonstrates how a bimodal distribution (one with two modes) can produce a mean that falls virtually in the middle of nowhere, hardly a typical score. The middle distribution in Table 12–5 demonstrates how the mean is influenced by an extreme score. Such scores distort the mean as a representative measure of the distribution, while leaving the mode and median relatively unaffected.

The median may be used either with quantitative or comparative data. It is appropriate in almost any unimodal distribution, particularly those where the mean is distorted by extreme scores. The median is somewhat less useful whenever the mean is especially appropriate, because the mean is amenable to greater mathematical computations than the median. Like the mean, the median is normally not a good measure of central tendency in bimodal or multimodal distributions.

The mode may be used with any level of measurement. However, in quantitative distributions, the mode may have to be based on a cluster of scores since the same exact scores may not be repeated. The first distribution in Table 12–5 illustrates this point. The definition of the mode as the most frequently recurring category should not be interpreted too literally. The mode is especially ap-

**Table 12–5**  THREE RAW INCOME DISTRIBUTIONS WITH CENTRAL TENDENCY MEASURES

| Income Distribution 1 | Income Distribution 2 | Income Distribution 3 |
|---|---|---|
| 25,000 | 100,000 | 32,000 |
| 22,000 | 15,000 | 32,000 |
| 19,000 | 14,000 | 32,000 |
| 18,000 | 13,000 | 16,000 |
| 17,000 | 11,000 | 11,000 |
| 14,000 | 10,000 | 11,000 |
| 11,000 | 10,000 | 11,000 |
| | | |
| $\bar{X} =$ 18,000 | $\bar{X} =$ 24,714 | $\bar{X} =$ 20,714 |
| mdn = 18,000 | mdn = 13,000 | mdn = 16,000 |
| mode = 17,000– | mode = 10,000 | modes =32,000 |
| 19,000 | | 11,000 |

propriate whenever there is more than one mode. The multimodal nature of the distribution should be made known in order to portray accurately the central tendencies in the distribution.

## LEARNING AID

1. The mode may be defined as _____.
2. A median or mean may not be computed on the "Party of Winner" variable because _____

_____.

3. Name three factors that condition the appropriate use of the mean as a central tendency measure.
4. Determine the mean, median, and mode of the following frequency distribution.

| Variable Value (X) | f |
|---|---|
| 4 | 12 |
| 3 | 3 |
| 2 | 4 |
| 1 | 11 |

**5.** For problem 4, which measure of central tendency represents best the central tendency of the distribution? _____

. . . . . . . . . . . . . . . . . . . . . . . . . . . . . . . . . . . . . . . . . . . . . . . . . . . .

**1.** the category that occurs most frequently.

**2.** neither the mean nor median may be computed on a classificatory variable.

**3.** The appropriate use of the mean requires quantitative level data, a unimodal distribution, and no extreme scores toward one end of the distribution.

**4.** Mean = 2.53: The formula for the mean of a frequency distribution is $\Sigma fX/N$. Applying this formula, $\Sigma fX = (12 \times 4) + (3 \times 3) + (4 \times 2) + (11 \times 1) = 76$ and $N = 12 + 3 + 4 + 11 = 30$. $\bar{X} = 76/30 = 2.53$.

Median = 2.5: The half-way point among 30 frequencies is between the 15th and 16th frequencies. The 15th frequency has a score of 2; the 16th a score of 3. Splitting the difference, we obtain 2.5.

Mode = 4 and 1: Technically, the modal category is 4, but the distribution is clearly bimodal, and that fact should be reported.

**5.** the modes. The mean and median report central tendencies between the two modes, where very few observations are found. This is an example of the mode as the most appropriate central tendency measure in a bimodal distribution.

## Variation

The term variation denotes a very special characteristic and important concept in statistics. *Variation* refers to differences among the various measured observations. The absence of variation in an indicator produces a constant; all the observations share the same trait. Maximum variation in a measure differs according to the level of measurement. In a classificatory variable, maximum variation involves the equal distribution of observations among each of the categories (see Table 12–6).

**Table 12–6** MINIMUM AND MAXIMUM VARIATION IN A CLASSIFICATORY VARIABLE

| Minimum (No) Variation | | Maximum Variation | |
|---|---|---|---|
| Religion | f | Religion | f |
| Protestant | 15 | Protestant | 5 |
| Catholic | 0 | Catholic | 5 |
| Jewish | 0 | Jewish | 5 |

**Table 12–7**  TWO DISTRIBUTIONS OF THE SAME
CLASSIFICATORY VARIABLE

| Distribution 1 | | Distribution 2 | |
|---|---|---|---|
| Religion | f | Religion | f |
| Protestant | 10 | Protestant | 10 |
| Catholic | 5 | Catholic | 3 |
| Jewish | 0 | Jewish | 2 |

Measures have been developed to summarize the degree of variation present in a data distribution. In general, such measures serve a twofold function. One function of most variation measures is to indicate how well the central tendency measure represents the central tendency in the data distribution. The lower the value of the variation measure, the more representative the central tendency measure. An appropriate variation measure should always accompany a central tendency measure. This is especially desirable whenever two distributions of the same variable are compared.

A second function of a variation measure may be to summarize the dispersion of the observations throughout the categories in the distribution. Again, the lower the value of the variation measure, the less variation present; the higher the measure, the greater is the variation. Variation measures can be interpreted in various substantive ways, such as measures of consensus, density, or other variation-based concepts.

CLASSIFICATORY VARIABLES

Variation is defined in many different ways. For classificatory variables, one simply can note the proportion of the observations in the nonmodal categories of a variable. This is the technique employed by the *variation ratio* ($V$). $V$ is calculated by the formula

*Variation Ratio*

$$V = 1 - \frac{f_{mode}}{N}$$

$f_{mode}$ = frequency of the mode
$N$ = number of observations

Subtracting the proportion of modal observations from 1 leaves the proportion of nonmodal observations. In both distributions in Table 12–7 below, the variation ratio is

$$V = 1 - f_{mode}/N = 1 - 10/15 = 5/15 = .33$$

In Table 12–6 above, the variation ratios are .00 and .67, respectively. (Despite the three modes in the maximum variation distribution, the variation ratio requires that only one category be treated as a mode. Consequently, $V = 1 - 5/15 = .67$.)

Another technique defines variation in terms of pairs of observations with different classifications. For example, in Distribution 1 of Table 12–7, there are 10 Protestants, each of whom has a different classification than each of five Catholics. Since each Protestant has a different classification from each of five Catholics, the number of pairs of observations with different classifications is 10 × 5, or 50. For Distribution 2, the number of different pairs is 56. (There are 30 Protestant/Catholic pairs, 20 Protestant/Jewish pairs, and six Catholic/Jewish pairs.) This technique reveals greater variation in the second distribution, variation left undetected by the variation ratio.

The "different pairs" technique of measuring variation is used in the *index of qualitative variation* (IQV). IQV is computed by comparing the empirical data distribution with a distribution of the same $N$, which contains maximum variation. In a maximum variation distribution, the frequency for each category is determined by dividing the $N$ by the number of variable categories. A maximum variation distribution for Table 12–7 data is presented in Table 12–6. The maximum variation table produces 75 pairs of observations with different scores. IQV is the ratio of actual variation to maximum variation. For the two distributions in Table 12–7, this is $50/75 = .67$ and $56/75 = .75$, respectively.

## COMPARATIVE VARIABLES

Variation measures of comparative variables are concerned with the clustering of observations around the median. Such measures involve determining the range of scores for various subsets of the distribution. The *range* is a variation measure that designates the difference between the highest and lowest scores. With a comparative indicator, this difference may simply be the number of ordered categories over which the distribution ranges. Although a range is useful in gathering an overview of the variation in a distribution, more information can be gathered on the variation among categories within the distribution by computing certain inter-ranges. For example, the *inter-quartile range* designates the range of scores within which the middle 50% of the observations are found, 25% on either side of the median. The *inter-quintile range* designates the middle 60%, and the *inter-decile range* identifies the range of the middle 80%, 40% on either side of the median.

## QUANTITATIVE VARIABLES

At the quantitative level of measurement, variation is determined by computing the magnitude by which the scores deviate from the mean. The process is somewhat complicated by the fact that the sum of deviations from the mean is zero. That is to say, if the mean is subtracted from the score for each observation in the distribution and the differences are added up, the sum always will be zero. Two basic techniques are employed to circumvent this feature. One is to disregard pluses and minuses and simply sum the absolute deviations from the mean. Dividing that sum by $N$ produces the average amount that a score in the distribution deviates from the mean. A different technique with statistically superior qualities is to square each deviation from the mean and sum the squared deviations. Dividing the sum of the squared deviations by $N$ gives the average squared deviation from the mean, a measure called the *variance*. The square root of the variance produces another measure termed the *standard deviation*. Although the intuitive interpretation of the variance and the standard deviation may seem obscure, they possess desirable mathematical properties that make them very important measures of variation for quantitative variables.

## Univariate Comparisons

The utility of a univariate distribution is severely limited because it lacks a standard or perspective by which to evaluate or compare the given distribution of frequencies. Such perspective is provided in two ways. A given univariate distribution may be compared with one or more distributions for the same variable under different circumstances or conditions. For example, the distribution of party affiliation in the House may be compared with that in the Senate, or with that from the House for the previous election. A second way is to compare a univariate distribution with itself among categories of one or more other variables. This comparison is accomplished by subdividing the univariate distribution among the different categories of one or more variables. This latter comparison produces a bivariate distribution, the next topic of discussion.

### LEARNING AID

1.  Describe the two functions of variation measures.
2.  How many pairs of observations have different classifications on the party distribution in the Senate presented in Table 12–4? (Since $N = 100$, the percentages may be treated as frequencies.)
3.  The inter-quartile range designates the range of values within which the middle _____% of the observations are found, _____% on either side of the _____.
4.  Two techniques to overcome the fact that the sum of deviations from the mean is _____ are: _____ and _____.

**5.** Of the two techniques given in the previous question, the statistically superior one is _____, and it is used for the calculation of the _____.

**6.** Perspective may be given to univariate distributions by _____ _____ .

**7.** One substantive interpretation for a measure of variation on a variable measuring differences in public opinion on a political issue is _____.

. . . . . . . . . . . . . . . . . . . . . . . . . . . . . . . . . . . . . . . . . . . . . . . . . . . . .

**1.** Variation measures measure how well the central tendency measure represents the central tendency in the distribution. Variation measures also summarize the dispersion of the observations throughout the classifications or values in the distribution.

**2.** 2,548.
$$42 \times 56 = 2352$$
$$42 \times \phantom{0}2 = \phantom{00}84$$
$$56 \times \phantom{0}2 = \underline{\phantom{0}112}$$
$$2548$$

**3.** 50%; 25%; median.

**4.** zero; sum the absolute deviations from the mean or sum the squared deviations from the mean.

**5.** summing the squared deviations from the mean; variance and standard deviation.

**6.** comparing the distribution with one or more distributions for the same variable under different circumstances or conditions or by comparing the distribution with itself among categoreis of one or more other variables.

**7.** that of a measure of consensus.

## BIVARIATE ANALYSIS

*Bivariate distributions* identify the distribution of a set of observations conjointly on two variables.

### The Cross-Classification Table

One basic format for portraying bivariate distributions is the cross-classification table. The table is created by listing the categories of one variable across the top of the table and the categories of the other variable along the side. The cells of the table contain the frequency count for observations possessing both classifications designated by the intersection of one category from each variable.

As with univariate distributions, cross-classifications are usually percentaged to enhance comprehension. The manner in which tables are percentaged depends on the purpose of the bivariate data analysis. The most common purpose of bivariate data analysis in the social sciences is to assess the impact of an independent variable on a dependent variable. Recall from Unit 6 that dependent variables are concepts that are to be explained and predicted and that occur as a consequence of other variables. Independent variables are concepts used to explain and predict other concepts and occur antecedent to the dependent variable.

In order to explain or predict the dependent variable, the distribution of the dependent variable must be compared across each category of the independent variable. *Percentaging the table, then, requires computing percentages for the dependent variable distribution separately for each category of the independent variable.* For example, Table 12–8 presents a hypothetical frequency distribution that examines alcohol usage and sex.[1] Alcohol usage is the dependent variable, the "effect" variable; sex is the independent variable, the "cause" variable (see Unit 6).

**Table 12–8** A BIVARIATE DISTRIBUTION OF ALCOHOL USAGE AND SEX

|  | Male | Female | Total |
|---|---|---|---|
| nondrinkers | 55 | 78 | 133 |
| mostly beer | 105 | 28 | 133 |
| mostly wine | 35 | 34 | 69 |
| mostly hard liquor | 55 | 60 | 115 |
| Total | 250 | 200 | 450 |

The successive steps in percentaging the table are:

1.   Determine which variable is the dependent variable and *percentage the dependent variable distribution.* The dependent variable distribution is the "Total" row or column that totals the frequency count for each dependent variable category.

|  | Male | Female | Total |
|---|---|---|---|
| nondrinkers |  |  | 29.6% |
| mostly beer |  |  | 29.6 |
| mostly wine |  |  | 15.3 |
| mostly hard liquor |  |  | 25.6 |
| Total |  |  | 100.1 |
| (N) | (250) | (200) | (450) |

The frequency of each dependent variable category is now expressed as a percentage of the combined number of observations in those categories. Consequently, the percentages add up to 100%. Notice also the slight change in the format of presenting frequency totals for the independent variable categories, in parentheses with the heading ($N$). By first percentaging the dependent variable, the direction is established in which the other percentages are calculated. Since the dependent variable categories are listed vertically, in a column, percentaging occurs within each column. If the dependent variable categories had been listed across the top of the table, percentaging would have occurred across the rows.

2.   Percentage the dependent variable distribution for the first independent variable category. Be certain to divide each cell frequency by the total frequency *of the independent variable category*, (e.g., 55/250).

|  | Male | Female | Total |
|---|---|---|---|
| nondrinkers | 22.0% |  | 29.6% |
| mostly beer | 42.0 |  | 29.6 |
| mostly wine | 14.0 |  | 15.3 |
| mostly hard liquor | 22.0 |  | 25.6 |
| Total | 100.0 |  | 100.1 |
| ($N$) | (250) | (200) | (450) |

3.   Percentage the dependent variable distribution for each of any remaining independent variable categories.

|  | Male | Female | Total |
|---|---|---|---|
| nondrinkers | 22.0% | 39.0% | 29.6% |
| mostly beer | 42.0 | 14.0 | 29.6 |
| mostly wine | 14.0 | 17.0 | 15.3 |
| mostly hard liquor | 22.0 | 30.0 | 25.6 |
| Total | 100.0 | 100.0 | 100.1 |
| ($N$) | (250) | (200) | (450) |

If the dependent variable distribution is percentaged for each category of the independent variable, as demonstrated, then any percentage in the bivariate part of the table reports what percentage of the observations in the independent variable category are classified as that particular dependent variable category. For example, 39% of the women are classified as "nondrinkers." Comparisons between independent variable categories interpret the impact of the independent variable on the dependent variable. For example, whereas 39% of the women are "nondrinkers," only 22% of the men are so classified, a difference of 17%. The interpretation is that women are much more likely than men to be nondrinkers. A comparison of men and women on the "mostly beer" classification shows that three times the proportion of men as women are "mostly beer" drinkers (42% to 14%).

Begin reading a table by reading the title. Titles normally identify the variables in the table. It is especially important to know whether the table is univariate, bivariate, or multivariate. If the table presents a bivariate distribution, determine if dependent and independent variables are specified and if the dependent variable distribution is percentaged for each independent variable category. It is customary for the independent variable to be aligned across the top of the table, its categories forming the columns of the table. However, the social science literature is replete with examples to the contrary. Be alert for such exceptions.

## LEARNING AID

1. Identify the dependent and independent variables in the table below:

The Degree of Racial Prejudice by Sex

|  |  | Degree of Racial Prejudice | | | |
|---|---|---|---|---|---|
|  |  | Low | Medium | High | Total |
|  | Male | 40 | 110 | 50 | 200 |
| Sex | Female | 30 | 70 | 50 | 150 |
|  | Total | 70 | 180 | 100 | 350 |

2. Percentage the above distribution so that the impact of the independent variable on the dependent variable may be assessed.
3. What is the meaning of the percentage in the cell that conjoins low prejudice and male sex?
4. What is the percentage difference between males and females on medium prejudice?
5. Which sex is more likely to demonstrate high prejudice?
. . . . . . . . . . . . . . . . . . . . . . . . . . . . . . . . . . . . . . . . . . . . . . . . . . . . . . . .

1. The dependent variable is "Degree of Racial Prejudice;" the independent variable is "Sex." For these two variables, sex would have to be considered the "cause" and racial prejudice the "effect." If necessary, review Unit 6 concerning dependent and independent variables.

**2.**

| | | Low | Medium | High | Total | (N) |
|---|---|---|---|---|---|---|
| | | | | Degree of Racial Prejudice | | |
| Sex | Male | 20% | 55 | 25 | 100% | (200) |
| | Female | 20% | 47 | 33 | 100% | (150) |
| | Total | 20% | 51 | 29 | 100% | (350) |

Here is an example of a table that is percentaged across rather than down. The dependent variable categories run across the top of the table. The direction of percentaging across is established by percentaging the dependent variable first, across the bottom row.

**3.** Twenty percent of the males are classified as "Low" on racial prejudice.

**4.** There is an 8% difference (55% − 47% = 8%), with males more likely than females to be classified as "Medium" on racial prejudice.

**5.** Females are. Despite the fact that an equal number of males and females are classified "High" on racial prejudice, the percentages reveal that women are more likely than men, in this hypothetical example, to be classified "High."

### Explanation Using Measures of Association

The empirical relationship between two indicators is often summarized or measured by statistical measures of association. Association can be interpreted in different ways, but generally an association or relationship between two variables means that a position or score on one variable appears conjointly with a position or score on the other variable in a disproportionate number of instances.

The concept of association is demonstrated in Table 12–9. In the cross-classification table on the left, no association exists between the two variables; there is no relationship between them. The position "Dems" is not conjoined disproportionately with either position on the voting variable. An equal

**Table 12–9  VOTES ON TWO BILLS BY PARTY OF SENATOR**

| | | Party of Senator | | | | | Party of Senator | | |
|---|---|---|---|---|---|---|---|---|---|
| | | Dems | Reps | Total | | | Dems | Reps | Total |
| Vote on S2516 | Yes | 30 | 20 | 50 | | Vote on S1444  Yes | 60 | 0 | 60 |
| | No | 30 | 20 | 50 | | No | 0 | 40 | 40 |

number of Democrats voted yes and no. The same is true for the Republicans. Conversely, the "Yes" and "No" voters contain equivalent proportions of Republicans and Democrats. Forty percent of both types of voters were Republicans and 60% of both were Democrats. In the table on the right, perfect association is evident as all Democrats conjoin with "Yes" voting and all Republicans with "No" voting.

Explanation uses one variable to account for or explain the variation in the other variable. For example, variation is present in the variable "Vote on S1444" in Table 12–9. In fact, there is a variation ratio of .40 ($V = 1 - 60/100$). Introduction of the "Party of Senator," however, eliminates the variation in "Vote on S1444." We say that "Party of Senator" explains or accounts for all the variation in "Vote on S1444." This determination can be made by examining the variation on "Vote on S1444" within each category of the independent variable. There is no more variation. All Democrats voted "Yes;" all Republicans voted "No."

The amount of variation in the dependent variable alone is called the *original variation,* or the total variation. The amount of variation remaining after the independent variable is introduced is called the *unexplained variation.* The difference between the original variation and the unexplained variation is called the *explained variation.* Explained variation is the amount of variation in the dependent variable that disappears with the introduction of the independent variable.

In general, measures of association are computed by the following formula

MEASURE OF ASSOCIATION

$$\frac{\text{original} - \text{unexplained}}{\text{original}} = \frac{\text{explained}}{\text{original}} = \begin{array}{c}\text{proportion of}\\\text{original variation}\\\text{accounted for}\end{array}$$

The numeric coefficient for the measure of association can be interpreted as the proportion of original variation in the dependent variable explained or accounted for by the independent variable. On occasion the process is reversed and the dependent variable is used to "explain" the variation in the independent variable. In either case, the measure of association is described as *asymmetrical*—one variable accounts for variation in another variable.

Some measures of association are *symmetrical.* The original variation is a composite of the separate variations for each variable. In this case, the explained variation is the difference between the original variation less the amount of joint variation in the bivariate distribution.

The asymmetrical association technique can be demonstrated by using the variation ratio on the data in Table 12–9 and Table 12–8. This demonstration is not intended to provide computational skills. However, the reader should be able to follow the logic of determining original and unexplained variation and its application to the general measure of association formula.

In Table 12–9, the variation ratio for the dependent variable "Vote on S2516" is .50 ($V = 1 - 50/100 = .50$). The effect of the independent variable on this original variation is determined by computing the variation ratio for the dependent variable distribution within each category of the independent variable. In both cases, $V = .50$. (For Dems., $V = 1 - 30/60 = .50$; for Reps., $V = 1 - 20/40 = .50$.) The amount of variation remaining for "Vote on S2516" (the unexplained variation) is an average of the variation ratios for each independent variable category, .50 in this case. The original variation (0.50) less the remaining or unexplained variation (0.50) leaves an explained variation of .00. Zero divided by anything is zero; there is no association. Following this same technique yields a 1 for "Party" and "Vote on S1444", perfect association.

In Table 12–8, the original variation on "alcohol usage" is .704 ($V = 1 - 133/450 = .704$). Among males, the variation ratio is .580 ($V = 1 - 105/250 = .580$); among females, .610 ($V = 1 - 78/200 = .610$). A weighted average[2] of the $V$s within the two independent variable categories yields an unexplained variation of .593. Applying the measure of association formula presented above, we have:

$$\frac{\text{original} - \text{unexplained}}{\text{original}} = \frac{.704 - .593}{.704} = \frac{.111}{.704} = .158$$

The measure of association coefficient is .158. About 16% of the variation in "alcohol usage" is accounted for by sex. This particular measure of association using the variation ratio is called lambda.

Since there are different variation measures for each level of measurement, it should come as no surprise that there are different association measures appropriate to the different levels of measurement. One feature of association measures for comparative and quantitative variables is a specification of the direction of an association between two or more variables. A *positive association* is one in which higher scores or classifications on one variable are conjoined disproportionately with higher scores or classifications on the other variable. A *negative association* is one in which higher scores or classifications on one variable are conjoined disproportionately with lower scores or classifications on the other variable. For most of these measures, this directional association coefficient must be squared to obtain a measure of the amount of the proportional reduction in variation.

There are many different measures of association. For your reference, Appendix B presents some of the more common ones. Also listed are the level of measurement requirements, whether the measure of association is symmetrical or asymmetrical, and whether the association coefficient can be interpreted as the proportion of original variation accounted for.

## LEARNING AID

1.  A positive association between two variables is one in which higher classifications or scores on one variable are conjoined disproportionately with _____.

2.  For an asymmetrical measure of association, the amount of variation in the dependent variable that disappears with the introduction of the independent variable is called the _____ variation.

3.  In general, measures of association can be computed by dividing the _____ by the _____.

4.  For an asymmetrical measure of association, the unexplained variation designates the amount of variation _____.

5.  Confronted with two bivariate distributions in which a symmetrical measure of association is −.40 in one distribution and .30 in the other, in which bivariate distribution is the bivariate association stronger? What is the basis for your response?

6.  A bivariate distribution in which there is no association between the two variables should have a measure of association coefficient of _____.

. . . . . . . . . . . . . . . . . . . . . . . . . . . . . . . . . . . . . . . . . . . . . . . . . . . . . . . . . . . . . . . . . .

1.  higher scores or classifications on the other variable.
2.  explained
3.  explained variation; original variation.
4.  remaining in the dependent variable after the independent variable is introduced.
5.  The bivariate distribution with the association coefficient of −.40 exhibits the stronger relationship. The direction of the association (positive or negative) has no effect on the strength of the association. The higher the absolute value of the association measure coefficient, the stronger the association between the two variables.
6.  zero.

## Prediction

Prediction involves an effort to guess the classification or value of an observation for a particular variable. Whereas explanation, using measures of association, is based primarily on analyzing and explaining variation, prediction is a technique based on central tendency. Prediction and explanation are not unrelated. For example, if all the variation in a dependent variable is accounted for by an independent variable, then the independent variable is usually a perfect predictor of the dependent variable. However, the measure of association does not predict. It can only indicate how accurate or reliable a prediction might be. The proportion of variation that is left unexplained by the bivariate relationship can be interpreted as a measure of error in the prediction.

The prediction technique, and its relation to explanation, can be shown with reference to the classificatory data presented on alcohol usage and sex in Table 12–8. If only the univariate distribution of alcohol usage is known, then that distribution serves as the only empirically established basis for a prediction. Different predictive schemes are available. Guesses could be patterned after the distribution, so that 30% of the guesses would be of the "nondrinker classification," 30% for the "mostly beer" classification, and so on. Alternatively, guesses could be made completely on the basis of random choice without regard to the distribution. However, the method that would maximize systematically the number of correct guesses is to guess the modal category of the distribution in every instance. Since "alcohol usage" has two modes ("mostly beer" and "nondrinker"), either one can be used. Guessing that a person is primarily a beer drinker has about a 30% chance of being correct (or a 70% chance of being wrong).

Using only a univariate distribution for prediction purposes is uncommon. In everyday life, most of us make predictions that involve assumptions about relationships between the property being guessed and factors that are associated with the property. In trying to guess whether a person was rich or poor, most of us would look for certain cues or attributes that we associate with being rich or poor. Such associated attributes improve the chance of guessing correctly.

Empirical analysis bases prediction on established empirical relationships between the variable to be guessed and other variables. If two variables are related, then the guessing is improved.

In Table 12–8, sex is related to alcohol usage. The mode is still the best guess, but now the mode within each independent variable category can be used. For a man, the best guess is that he drinks "mostly beer." Such a guess is correct 42% of the time for that set of data (and for any population adequately represented by the data). For women, the "nondrinker" guess minimizes error. The lambda coefficient computed earlier is interpreted as the proportion of variation in the dependent variable accounted for by the independent variable. With a compatible prediction technique, the same measure can be interpreted in an error reduction manner. The lambda of 0.158 means that errors in guessing alcohol usage by use of the mode can be reduced 15.8% by using sex as a predictor.

In a quantitative variable, variation is measured by the variance. The variance is the sum of the squared deviations from the mean divided by $N$. If any number other than the mean were used for computing the squared deviations, the variance would be greater. This fact means that efforts to predict the scores in a quantitative univariate distribution will minimize variance from the predictor value, if that predictor score is the mean.

An important technique for the prediction of quantitative variables using a predictor variable is regression analysis. *Regression analysis* specifies the relationship between two variables and calculates a predictive ratio between them. This ratio, the *regression coefficient,* measures the amount of change in the score of the guessed variable for an increase of one unit in the score of the predictor variable. Regression is demonstrated by the following example. A persistent phenomenon in electoral politics is the loss suffered by the party of the president in House seats during nonpresidential election years. Between the election years of 1950 and 1974, the losses range from 5 in 1962 to 64 in 1950. The mean loss of seats over this period is about 33; the variance is 478. The use of the mean to guess each of the election year losses is not particularly accurate, as demonstrated in Table 12–10.

Although many factors probably affect the outcomes of such elections, one factor may be the popularity of the president during that election year. The popularity of the president perhaps serves as a barometer of public satisfaction with the state of the nation, and the fortunes of the president's party closely parallel those of the president.

Quantitative bivariate distributions are rarely presented in table form since more than a few different scores are involved. A *scattergram* (see Fig. 12–1) provides a graphic display of the joint scores held by an observation on the two variables in the distribution. In a scattergram, the scores of the predictor variable (usually the independent variable) are arrayed along the horizontal or $X$ axis.

**Table 12–10  THE MEAN AS PREDICTOR**

| Number of Seats Lost ($Y$) | Mean Seat Loss ($\bar{Y}$) | $(Y - \bar{Y})$ | $(Y - \bar{Y})^2$ |
|:---:|:---:|:---:|:---:|
| 64 | 33 | 31 | 961 |
| 49 | 33 | 16 | 256 |
| 47 | 33 | 14 | 196 |
| 43 | 33 | 10 | 100 |
| 12 | 33 | −21 | 441 |
| 8 | 33 | −25 | 625 |
| 5 | 33 | −28 | 784 |

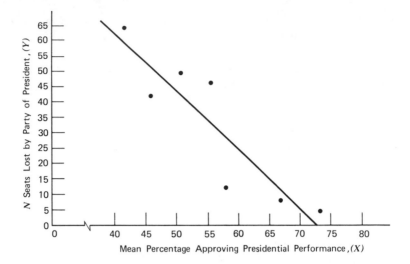

**Figure 12–1. A Scattergram and Regression Line of the Number of House Seats Lost by the President's Party in Nonpresidential Election Years and the Mean Percentage Who Approve of the President's Job Performance During the Year**

The scores of the variable to be predicted are listed along the vertical or $Y$ axis. Each dot in the scattergram represents the joint scores of an observation. For example, when the presidential popularity averaged 73%, only five seats were lost ($X = 73$; $Y = 5$). Note that in the scattergram, the scores of the independent variable range only from 42 to 73. For this reason that part of the scattergram ranging from about 5 to 40 on the $X$ axis is deleted.

Scattergrams provide a very visual image of a bivariate relationship. The most commonly used regression technique is linear regression. Bivariate *linear regression* provides the calculation of a single straight line that passes through the two dimensional scattergram of the bivariate distribution so that the variance of the joint observations from the line is minimized. In the same sense that the mean minimizes the variance in a univariate distribution, the regression line minimizes variance in a bivariate linear relationship. The sum of the squared $Y$ deviations from this line is less than for any other straight line that could be drawn through the data.

The regression coefficient ($b$) is equal to the slope of the line and is interpreted as the amount of change in $Y$ for each unit increase in $X$. In this example, $b = -1.92$. Verbally, an increase of 1% in approval of presidential performance results in a decrease of 1.92 seats lost by the presidential party.

Once the point at which the line intercepts the $Y$ axis is known, the value can be predicted for any given score of $X$. The intercept point is identified by the symbol $a$ (alpha). In this example, $a = 140.43$.

The computation of a $Y$ value for any given $X$ value represents a prediction of $Y$, given $X$. Predictions are made using the formula

Regression Prediction Formula

$$Y' = a + bX$$

where $Y'$ = predicted value of $Y$;
$\quad a$ = alpha, the intercept point;
$\quad b$ = regression coefficient;
$\quad X$ = given score of the predictor variable

The seat loss prediction $(Y')$ when presidential popularity averages 42 $(X = 42)$ is about 60.

$$Y' = a + bX = 140.43 + (-1.92)(42) = 140.43 + (-80.64) - 59.79$$

Table 12–11 compares the predictions for "presidential party seat loss" for the mean and linear regression prediction techniques. The regression predictions $(Y')$ are much closer to the actual seat loss $(Y)$ than is the mean prediction $(\bar{Y})$. The squared deviations in the last two columns reflect this difference. Summing the squared deviations from the regression line and dividing by the $N$ of 7 gives a variance of about 98. The squared deviations from the mean reveal the original variation in seat loss to be about 480. The regression technique provides more accurate predictor scores and reduces the original variation by almost 80%.

**Table 12–11**   MEAN AND LINEAR REGRESSION PREDICTION

| Number of Seats Lost $(Y)$ | Mean Prediction $(\bar{Y})$ | Regression Prediction $(Y')$ | Deviation$^2$ From Mean $(Y-\bar{Y})^2$ | Deviation$^2$ From $Y'$ $(Y-Y')^2$ |
|---|---|---|---|---|
| 64 | 33 | 60 | 961 | 16 |
| 49 | 33 | 41 | 256 | 64 |
| 47 | 33 | 33 | 196 | 196 |
| 43 | 33 | 52 | 100 | 81 |
| 12 | 33 | 29 | 441 | 289 |
| 8 | 33 | 12 | 625 | 16 |
| 5 | 33 | 0 | 784 | 25 |

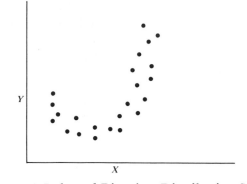

**Figure 12–2.   A J-shaped Bivariate Distribution Scattergram**

Linear regression is inappropriate for some distributions. For example, some distributions are J-shaped or N-shaped (see Fig. 12–2). In such distributions, linear regression is misleading. Curvilinear regression must then be employed to minimize predictive error.

### LEARNING AID

1.  Whereas explanation, using measures of association, is based primarily on analyzing the _____ of a distribution, prediction is based on the use of _____.

2.  The major goal of prediction is to _____.
3.  In a classificatory distribution, the best guess is _____.
4.  In prediction, a measure of association can be interpreted as a measure of _____.

5.  Assume that the regression coefficient between voting turnout and median education (in years) for Congressional districts is 2.8. What is the meaning of that 2.8 coefficient?
6.  For the data in the previous problem, assume a = 25. Applying the linear regression formula of $Y' = a + bX$, what voter turnout is predicted when the median education in the district is 11 years?

. . . . . . . . . . . . . . . . . . . . . . . . . . . . . . . . . . . . . . . . . . . . . . . . . . . . . . . . . . . . . . . . . . . . . .

1.  variation; central tendency
2.  minimize error, predict accurately and so on.
3.  the mode
4.  error reduction

**5.** For each unit increase in median education, voting turnout in a district will increase by 2.8%.

**6.** 55.8%. $Y' = 25 + (2.8)(11) = 25 + (30.8) = 55.8$

## MULTIVARIATE ANALYSIS

Univariate analysis is often inadequate because it provides no comparison or perspective from which to evaluate or explain the distribution. Bivariate analysis is often inadequate because it provides only a partial, perhaps spurious, explanation of the dependent variable distribution. *Multivariate analysis* overcomes these problems to some extent through the simultaneous analysis of three or more variables, conceptualized as one dependent variable and two or more independent variables.

The introduction of additional variable(s) to the original bivariate relationship permits an analysis of three types of effects:

1. *control effects*—The additional variable(s) serve to test the validity of the bivariate relationship and to specify conditions under which the relationship between two variables is strengthened or weakened.

2. *relative effects*—The additional variable(s) serve to assess the relative separate impact of each independent variable, while controlling the effects of the other independent variables.

3. *conjoint effects*—The additional variable(s) serve to determine the combined effect of the independent variables on the dependent variable.

The bivariate data in Table 12–12 tend to support the hypothesis that working-class status is more conducive to civil rights support than is middle-class status. However, as we learned in Units 7 and 9 alternative hypotheses should be tested. They may serve to confirm or disconfirm the original research hypothesis.

**Table 12–12**  CIVIL RIGHTS SUPPORT BY SOCIAL CLASS*

|  |  | Middle Class | Working Class |
|---|---|---|---|
| Civil | High | 37% | 45% |
| Rights | Low | 63 | 55 |
| Support | (N) | (120) | (120) |

* Adapted from Table 4–7 from *The Logic of Survey Analysis,* by Morris Rosenberg, (©) 1968 by Basic Books, Inc., Publishers, New York.

One alternative hypothesis to that "confirmed" by Table 12–12 is that support for civil rights is considerably more prevalent among nonwhites than whites. Furthermore, the predominance of nonwhites in the working class tends to obscure the fact that middle-class status is actually more likely to foster support for civil rights than working-class status. Table 12–13 presents the data.

The comparison between middle class and working class separately for each racial group permits an analysis of control effects. In this hypothetical example, the relationship between social class and civil rights support actually reverses when race is controlled. Among both nonwhites and whites, middle-class respondents are more likely to score high on the civil rights support indicator. This finding has the effect of disconfirming the original hypothesis.

Note that Table 12–13 also permits a comparison of whites and nonwhites on civil rights support while controlling for social class. Among middle class respondents, 70% of the nonwhites and 30% of the whites score high. For working-class people, the figures are 50% and 20%, respectively. Nonwhite support for civil rights is much more predominant than support among whites, controlling for social class.

Relative effects and conjoint effects also can be gleaned from Table 12–13. An analysis would show, for example, that race has a greater impact on civil rights support than does social class. Moreover, the combination of nonwhite race and middle-class status produces a very strong likelihood of civil rights support, whereas the white working-class position is most likely to foster low support. The calculation of relative effects and conjoint effects is demonstrated in Appendix C.

Statistical techniques are available that permit the same type of explanation and prediction processes presented for bivariate relationships. For most measures of association it is possible to compute what is called a *partial* association coefficient. Such measures retain their explanation of variation in-

**Table 12–13** CIVIL RIGHTS SUPPORT BY SOCIAL CLASS AND RACE*

|  |  | Nonwhites | | Whites | |
|---|---|---|---|---|---|
|  |  | Middle Class | Working Class | Middle Class | Working Class |
| Civil | High | 70% | 50% | 30% | 20% |
| Rights | Low | 30 | 50 | 70 | 80 |
| Support | (N) | (20) | (100) | (100) | (20) |

* Reprinted from Table 4–8 from *The Logic of Survey Analysis,* by Morris Rosenberg, (©) 1968 by Basic Books, Inc., Publishers, New York.

terpretation. Thus, an asymmetrical partial coefficient may indicate the proportion of original variation in the dependent variable accounted for by an independent variable, while controlling that variation accounted for by other independent variables in the analysis. Partial association measures are quite useful in interpreting control effects and comparing relative effects.

*Multiple linear regression* permits the establishment of the predictive technique outlined in the previous section on prediction. A *partial regression coefficient* measures the amount of change in the predicted variable for a unit increase in the predictor variable, while the effects of other predictor variables are controlled. The ability to introduce several variables into the prediction scheme vastly enhances the accuracy and utility of regression predictive techniques.

Finally, *multiple association coefficients* measure the amount of original variation accounted for by all the variables introduced and simultaneously controlled for. The multiple coefficient permits an assessment of the conjoint effect of the independent variables on a dependent variable.

A fuller explanation of multivariate analysis is presented in Appendix C. Special attention is given to interpreting different types of control effects. More detail is also given to understanding relative effects and conjoint effects.

## LEARNING AID

**1.** Multivariate analysis may be used to analyze three different types of effects. These three effects are: (a) _____; (b) _____; and (c) _____.

**2.** Distinguish among these three types of effects.

**3.** A partial association coefficient measures association between _____ (two/several) variables at a time, while the effects of the other variables in the analysis are _____.

**4.** The partial regression coefficient is interpreted as _____ _____.

**5.** Multiple association coefficients measure _____ _____.

. . . . . . . . . . . . . . . . . . . . . . . . . . . . . . . . . . . . . . . . . . . . . . . . . . . . . . .

**1.** control effects; relative effects; conjoint effects.

**2.** Control effects examine the validity of the bivariate relationship and specify conditions under which the relationship between two variables is strengthened or weakened.

Relative effects measure the relative separate impact of each independent variable, while controlling the effects of the other independent variables.

Conjoint effects determine the combined effect of the independent variables on the dependent variable.

**3.** two; controlled.

**4.** the amount of change in the predicted variable for a unit increase in the predictor variable, while the effects of the other predictor variables are controlled.

**5.** the amount of original variation accounted for by all of the variables introduced and simultaneously controlled for.

## FOOTNOTES

1. The percentage distributions on this table are based on data from a study by Hugh J. Parry and Ira H. Cisin, as summarized by Edward M. Brecher in *Licit and Illicit Drugs* (Boston: Little, Brown and Company, 1972), p. 478.

2. Since there are more males than females, the males' V of .580 is given a bit more weight in averaging the two Vs.

# 13
# Inferential Data Analysis

# INTRODUCTION

## Rationale

The previous unit demonstrated how researchers use statistics to summarize and describe data distributions. The other major component in empirical data analysis is called inferential data analysis. *Inferential data analysis* involves probabilistic judgments about the application of statistical descriptions to populations of things. These "statistical descriptions" may include almost any of the descriptive statistics presented in the previous unit. Some of the more common descriptive statistics used in inferential data analysis are means, proportions, and variances.

*Population* and *universe* are two terms used synonomously to refer to the total collection of things that constitute the focus of the study. A *sample,* on the other hand, consists of a subset of a population. Statistical descriptions of populations are called *population parameters*. Statistical descriptions of samples are called *sample statistics*. For example, the mean of a sample is a statistic; the mean of a population is a parameter.

The basis for inferential data analysis is probability. This unit first examines probability and special probability distributions. Then attention shifts to two major types of inferential data analysis—estimation and hypothesis testing.

## Learning Objectives

After completing this unit, the student should be able to:

1.  Define the following:

    a.  inferential data analysis;

    b.  population, universe, sample;

    c.  population parameter, sample statistic;

    d.  estimation, statistical test of a hypothesis.

2.  Explain and demonstrate the use of a sampling distribution, especially the normal distribution.

3.  Compute and demonstrate the use of:

    a.  a standard error of the sampling distribution;

    b.  a confidence interval;

    c.  a $z$ score in the statistical test of a hypothesis.

4. Know the meaning of the following:

    a. null hypothesis;

    b. to accept a null hypothesis, to reject a null hypothesis;

    c. "not statistically significant," "statistically significant";

    d. two-tail test, one-tail test.

5. Identify the four major categories of null hypothesis tests.

6. Explain some specific functions for which each of these four categories of tests is employed.

7. Understand the function of a t-test, analysis of variance, and chi square.

## SAMPLING DISTRIBUTIONS

Inferential data analysis involves probabilistic judgments about the application of statistical descriptions to populations of things. The probabilistic judgments are made by locating the statistical description in a probability distribution known as a sampling distribution.

A *sampling distribution* is a data distribution of a particular statistic for all possible data distributions of the same size. For example, the mean of a sample is a statistic that summarizes the central tendency of a distribution. Another sample that is the same size and from the same population will produce a mean also. The same process can be repeated until all possible samples of that size and from that population are obtained. The means from all these samples form a data distribution of their own, a sampling distribution of means.

In reality, a sampling distribution is not an empirical creation. It is a creation of deductive mathematical logic. Perhaps the simplest sampling distribution is the binomial sampling distribution for equally probable events. The binomial distribution deals with dichotomous attributes. The binomial distribution presented here further specifies a distribution that stipulates that either one of the two categories is equally likely to occur.

Coin flipping is often depicted as an example of such a binomial distribution. Presumably the probability of obtaining a "heads" is the same as obtaining a "tails," namely one out of two chances or .5. The binomial probability distribution is easy to calculate. The logic of the calculation is demonstrated in Figure 13–1. For the first coin flip, only two equally probable events can occur, a heads and a tails. Regardless of whether a heads or a tails is obtained on the first flip, the probability for a heads, or alternatively for a tails, on any subsequent flip will remain at .5. However, after the second flip, four different flipping experiences will have been possible. The lines in the diagram identify the four possibilities: two heads, a heads and a tails, a tails and a heads, and two tails. Note that the middle two occurrences produce the same outcome—the occurrence in two flips of one heads and one tails: Out of the four different possibilities, then, two produce the same outcome. Thus, the probability of that outcome is 2/4 or .5. The probability of two heads is 1/4 or .25. The probability of two tails in two flips is 1/4 or .25.

The third flip adds two more possibilities to each of the four previous ones. By summing up identical outcomes, the probabilities of those outcomes can be determined. For example, of the eight unique ways that three coin flips can produce, three of the outcomes involve obtaining two heads and one tails. Thus, the probability of obtaining two heads and one tails in three flips is 3/8 or .375.

Figure 13–1 is actually a binomial sampling distribution for $N = 3$ when the

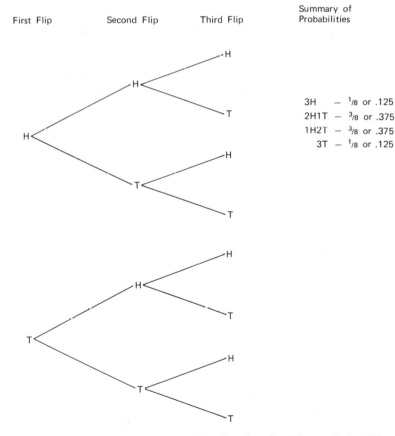

Figure 13-1. A Probability Distribution for Three Coin Flips.

| Frequency of Occurrence of Heads | probability of the frequency |
|:---:|:---:|
| 0 | .001 |
| 1 | .010 |
| 2 | .044 |
| 3 | .117 |
| 4 | .205 |
| 5 | .246 |
| 6 | .205 |
| 7 | .117 |
| 8 | .044 |
| 9 | .010 |
| 10 | .001 |

**Figure 13–2.   A Binomial Sampling Distribution, $N = 10$, $P = .5$**

probability of an event is .5 ($P = .5$). Of course, the use of a mathematical formula obviates the use of a tree diagram to determine the probabilities for the binomial distribution. Figure 13–2 presents a binomial sampling distribution for $N = 10$ when $P = .5$.

The sampling distribution is used to identify the probabilities of obtaining certain statistical descriptions in data distributions. The binomial distribution in Figure 13–2 can be used to assess the probability of obtaining a particular frequency of occurrence by random chance whenever $N = 10$ and $P = .5$. For example, an employer hires 10 people, supposedly on an equal opportunity basis. An equal number of men and women had applied for the openings. No appreciable sex differences in qualifications and suitability for the jobs can be detected. Only two women are hired as opposed to eight men. Now, what is the probability, given these conditions, that no more than two women would be hired on the basis of nondiscriminant random hiring? The binomial distribution in Figure 13–2 reveals that the probability of hiring no more than two women by chance is only about 5.5%. (Add the probabilities for 2, 1, and 0 to obtain the answer.) Given this information, would you begin to suspect that sex discrimination may have played a part in the hiring procedures?

The sampling distribution provides a new perspective to descriptive statistics. No longer is a particular statistic merely a description of some data distribution. It is also a single observation in a distribution of its own—the sampling distribution for that statistic. This fact is very important for the inferential data analysis technique known as estimation, our next topic of discussion.

## LEARNING AID

1.   Inferential data analysis involves _____ judgments about the application of _____ to _____.
2.   A sampling distribution _____ (is/is not) a probability distribution.
3.   In ten random flips of an unbiased coin, the probability of obtaining exactly five heads and five tails is _____.
4.   In a binomial sampling distribution for $N = 10$ and $P = .5$, the probability of a particular event occurring more than six times is _____.
5.   What is the importance of a sampling distribution to inferential data analysis?

. . . . . . . . . . . . . . . . . . . . . . . . . . . . . . . . . . . . . . . . . . . . . . . . . . . . . . . . . . . . .

1.   probabilistic, statistical descriptions, populations of things.
2.   is
3.   .246
4.   .172. Add the probabilities of 7, 8, 9, and 10.
5.   The probabilistic judgments that form the basis for inferential data analysis are made by locating the statistical description in a sampling distribution.

## ESTIMATION

One major aspect of inferential data analysis is the estimation of population parameters by using the descriptive statistics from a sample of the population. *Estimation* is the generalization of a statistical description of a sample to the appropriate population.

Accurate estimation requires a sample that is representative of the population from which it is drawn and a relatively low variation in the sampling distribution. The selection of a representative sample helps to avoid systematic or biased error inherent within the sample itself. Techniques of sampling will be presented in Unit 15. For now, it is sufficient to note that most inferential data analysis is based on the assumption of a random sample. A random sample is one in which each and every member of the population has as equiprobable chance of being selected in the sample.

The presence of a random sample does not eliminate the random error that accompanies any sample of a population. Although the error cannot be eliminated, at least it can be measured. Consequently, it is possible to calculate a margin of error in the estimation of population parameters from sample statistics.

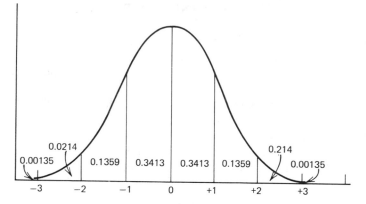

**Figure 13-3.   Normal Curve, Showing Proportions of the Distribution with Specified Standard Deviation Units from the Mean. Adopted from George A. Ferguson, *Statistical Analysis in Psychology and Education*, (New York: McGraw-Hill, 1959) p. 81.**

Estimation is based on a unique feature of the sampling distribution of many statistical descriptions, such as the mean, proportion, and others. For relatively large samples, the sampling distribution of a statistical description approximates a normal distribution with a mean equal to the population parameter of the description. Moreover, the standard deviation of the sampling distribution (called the standard error) is equal to the standard deviation of the population divided by the square root of the sample size.

The *normal distribution* is a unique probability distribution that is symmetrical and unimodal. This means that the mean, median, and mode all coincide. The normal distribution also possesses certain precise mathematical properties that enhance its utility for statistical inference. For example, 50% (*i.e.*, .5000) of the distribution lies above the mean and 50% lies below the mean. In addition, between the mean and one standard deviation unit are 34.13% of the observations in the distribution.

A graphic presentation of the normal distribution, called the normal curve, is presented in Figure 13–3. Table 13–1 presents proportions of the normal distribution associated with various standard deviation distances from the mean. These standard deviation scores, which represent standard deviation units from the mean, are called *z* scores. *z scores* express the difference between an observation and its mean in terms of standard deviation units. For example, if the standard deviation of a distribution is 5, then whenever the difference between the score of an observation and the mean is also 5, they are one standard deviation apart. The $z$ score of the observation would be 1. The formula for $z$ is

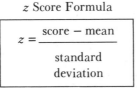

$z$ Score Formula

$$z = \frac{\text{score} - \text{mean}}{\text{standard deviation}}$$

In Table 13–1 $z$ scores are listed down the side in the first column with the second decimal digit across the top row. The body of the table reports the proportion of observations contained between the mean and the designated $z$ score. Thus, in a normal distribution, the proportion of observations contained between the mean and two standard deviation units ($z = 2$) is .4772. To determine the proportion of observations between a $-2$ and $+2$ standard deviation units, we add .4772 and .4772 to obtain .9544.

To determine the proportion of observations above a positive $z$ score (or below a negative $z$ score), subtract the area listed in Table 13–1 from .5000. Thus, the proportion of observations above a $z$ score of 1.5 (or below $-1.5$) is .5000 less .4332, which is .0668.

A somewhat different problem is to determine the $z$ score associated with a specified proportion of the distribution. For example, the middle 50% of the observations are located approximately between _____. The answer is $-.67$ and $+.67$. It is found by searching in Table 13–1 for the proportion of observations specified between the mean and the sought-after $z$ score. In this case, the middle 50% means 25% or .2500 on either side of the mean. Perusal of the body of Table 13–1 reveals no .2500, but .2486 comes the closest. Having found the specified area, the $z$ score that delineates this much area is obtained, in this example about .67.

Estimation is an effort to predict accurately the population parameter of a particular statistical description. The accuracy of the statistical description is determined largely by the amount of variation present in the data distribution. The probability that the sample statistic accurately reflects the population parameter can be determined with reference to the sampling distribution. Keep in mind that the mean of the sampling distribution is equal to the population parameter and that the sampling distribution is distributed normally for large samples.

To provide a concrete example, assume that a pollster conducts a survey for a senatorial candidate and determines that 51% of those who intend to vote indicate a preference for that candidate. The 51% is a statistical description of the sample. The 51% also represents a single observation in a sampling distribution of proportions of that sample size (assume $N = 400$) concerning the pro-

### Table 13-1 AREAS FOR A STANDARD NORMAL DISTRIBUTION[a]

An entry in the table is the area under the curve, between $z = 0$ and a positive value of $z$. Areas for negative values of $z$ are obtained by symmetry.

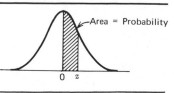

| | | | | Second Decimal Place of $z$ | | | | | |
|---|---|---|---|---|---|---|---|---|---|
| ↓$z$ | .00 | .01 | .02 | .03 | .04 | .05 | .06 | .07 | .08 | .09 |
| 0.0 | .0000 | .0040 | .0080 | .0120 | .0160 | .0199 | .0239 | .0279 | .0319 | .0359 |
| 0.1 | .0398 | .0438 | .0478 | .0517 | .0557 | .0596 | .0636 | .0675 | .0714 | .0753 |
| 0.2 | .0793 | .0832 | .0871 | .0910 | .0948 | .0987 | .1026 | .1064 | .1103 | .1141 |
| 0.3 | .1179 | .1217 | .1255 | .1293 | .1331 | .1368 | .1406 | .1443 | .1480 | .1517 |
| 0.4 | .1554 | .1591 | .1628 | .1664 | .1700 | .1736 | .1772 | .1808 | .1844 | .1879 |
| 0.5 | .1915 | .1950 | .1985 | .2019 | .2054 | .2088 | .2123 | .2157 | .2190 | .2224 |
| 0.6 | .2257 | .2291 | .2324 | .2357 | .2389 | .2422 | .2454 | .2486 | .2517 | .2549 |
| 0.7 | .2580 | .2611 | .2642 | .2673 | .2703 | .2734 | .2764 | .2794 | .2823 | .2852 |
| 0.8 | .2881 | .2910 | .2939 | .2967 | .2995 | .3023 | .3051 | .3078 | .3106 | .3133 |
| 0.9 | .3159 | .3186 | .3212 | .3238 | .3264 | .3289 | .3315 | .3340 | .3365 | .3389 |
| 1.0 | .3413 | .3438 | .3461 | .3485 | .3508 | .3531 | .3554 | .3577 | .3599 | .3621 |
| 1.1 | .3643 | .3665 | .3686 | .3708 | .3729 | .3749 | .3770 | .3790 | .3810 | .3830 |
| 1.2 | .3849 | .3869 | .3888 | .3907 | .3925 | .3944 | .3962 | .3980 | .3997 | .4015 |
| 1.3 | .4032 | .4049 | .4066 | .4082 | .4099 | .4115 | .4131 | .4147 | .4162 | .4177 |
| 1.4 | .4192 | .4207 | .4222 | .4236 | .4251 | .4265 | .4279 | .4292 | .4306 | .4319 |

portion who intend to vote and who support the candidate in question.

The concern of the candidate is with the population parameter and how accurately the 51% found in the sample estimates the parameter. Since the sampling distribution is distributed normally with a mean equal to the population parameter, the probability that the 51% is within one standard deviation of the population parameter is 68.26%. Since the population parameter is unknown, it makes more sense to turn the statement around. There is a 68.26% chance that the population parameter is within one standard deviation of the sample proportion.

Unfortunately, the standard deviation of either the population or the sampling distribution is also unknown. However, the standard deviation of the

## Table 13-1 (*Continued*)

| $\xrightarrow{z}$ | .00 | .01 | .02 | .03 | .04 | .05 | .06 | .07 | .08 | .09 |
|---|---|---|---|---|---|---|---|---|---|---|
| 1.5 | .4332 | .4345 | .4357 | .4370 | .4382 | .4394 | .4406 | .4418 | .4429 | .4441 |
| 1.6 | .4452 | .4463 | .4474 | .4484 | .4495 | .4505 | .4515 | .4525 | .4535 | .4545 |
| 1.7 | .4554 | .4564 | .4573 | .4582 | .4591 | .4599 | .4608 | .4616 | .4625 | .4633 |
| 1.8 | .4641 | .4649 | .4656 | .4664 | .4671 | .4678 | .4686 | .4693 | .4699 | .4706 |
| 1.9 | .4713 | .4719 | .4726 | .4732 | .4738 | .4744 | .4750 | .4756 | .4761 | .4767 |
| | | | | | | | | | | |
| 2.0 | .4772 | .4778 | .4783 | .4788 | .4793 | .4798 | .4803 | .4808 | .4812 | .4817 |
| 2.1 | .4821 | .4826 | .4830 | .4834 | .4838 | .4842 | .4846 | .4850 | .4854 | .4857 |
| 2.2 | .4861 | .4864 | .4868 | .4871 | .4875 | .4878 | .4881 | .4884 | .4887 | .4890 |
| 2.3 | .4893 | .4896 | .4898 | .4901 | .4904 | .4906 | .4909 | .4911 | .4913 | .4916 |
| 2.4 | .4918 | .4920 | .4922 | .4925 | .4927 | .4929 | .4931 | .4932 | .4934 | .4936 |
| | | | | | | | | | | |
| 2.5 | .4938 | .4940 | .4941 | .4943 | .4945 | .4946 | .4948 | .4949 | .4951 | .4952 |
| 2.6 | .4953 | .4955 | .4956 | .4957 | .4959 | .4960 | .4961 | .4962 | .4963 | .4964 |
| 2.7 | .4965 | .4966 | .4967 | .4968 | .4969 | .4970 | .4971 | .4972 | .4973 | .4974 |
| 2.8 | .4974 | .4975 | .4976 | .4977 | .4977 | .4978 | .4979 | .4979 | .4980 | .4981 |
| 2.9 | .4981 | .4982 | .4982 | .4983 | .4984 | .4984 | .4985 | .4985 | .4986 | .4986 |
| | | | | | | | | | | |
| 3.0 | .4987 | .4987 | .4987 | .4988 | .4988 | .4989 | .4989 | .4989 | .4990 | .4990 |

[a] From *Introductory Statistics* by T. H. Wonnacott and R. J. Wonnacott. Copyright © 1969, 1972 by *John Wiley & Sons, Inc. Reprinted by permission of the publisher.*

sample may be used to estimate the standard deviation of the sampling distribution. The term *standard error* is used to refer to the standard deviation of a sampling distribution.

The estimate of the standard error of a proportion is equal to

Standard Error of a Proportion

$$SE_p = \sqrt{\frac{p_s(1-p_s)}{N}}$$

where $p_s$ = the sample proportion,
$N$ = the sample size.

In the election survey example, $p_s = .51$ and $N = 400$. The standard error of the proportion $(SE_p)$ is equal to .025.

The standard error now can be used to construct an error interval around the sample proportion. The width of the interval depends on how much confidence is desired concerning whether or not the population parameter is contained within the interval. Such an interval is called a *confidence interval*.

It already has been noted that there is a 68.26% chance that the population proportion is within $\pm 1$ standard error on either side of the sample proportion. Creating an interval of one standard error on either side of the sample proportion establishes an interval that ranges from 48.5% to 53.5% (51% $\pm$ one standard error of 2.5%). In other words, the candidate can be assured that there is a 68.26% chance that somewhere between 48.5% and 53.5% of those who plan to vote support him at the moment. In this particular example, the candidate is told little more than the fact that he is going to either win or lose, but not by much.

Most social science researchers are not content to be only 68% confident in their estimations. Confidence intervals of 90% or 95% are more common. The formula for a confidence interval is

Confidence Interval

$$p_s + z\,(SE_p)$$

where $p_s$ = the sample proportion;
   $z$ = the $z$ score associated with the width of
       the desired confidence interval;
   $SE_p$ = the standard error of the proportion.

A confidence interval of 90% distributes half of the interval on either side of the sample statistic, in this case 45%. Table 13–1 reveals that the $z$ score associated with 45% (i.e., .4500) of the normal curve between the mean of the sampling distribution and the $z$ lies between 1.64 and 1.65. Thus, the width of a 90% confidence interval is $p_s \pm 1.64\,(SE_p)$. Filling the formula for a confidence interval, we get

$$.51 \pm 1.64\,(.025)$$
$$.51 \pm .041$$
$$.469 - .551$$

There is a 90% probability that the interval of 46.9% to 55.1% includes the population percentage.

Of course, the sample statistic used to estimate need not be a proportion or percentage. A population mean can be estimated just as easily by use of the sample mean. In this case, the standard error of the mean $(SE_{\bar{x}})$ is equal to the sample standard deviation $(s)$ divided by the square root of the sample size less 1 $(\sqrt{N-1})$; $SE_{\bar{x}} = s/\sqrt{N-1}$.

If the size of the sample is not large, say, less than 60, then certain biases distort the normality of the sampling distribution. Other sets of distributions are more appropriate in such circumstances. Thus, when using sample means to estimate population means, the t-distributions are more appropriate. When using sample proportions to estimate population proportions, the binomial distributions are more appropriate. Statistics texts should be consulted for reference to those sampling distributions.[1]

## LEARNING AID

1. Estimation may be defined as _____ .
2. In general, inferential data analysis is based on the assumption that samples are _____ .
3. For relatively large samples, the sampling distribution of a proportion is distributed _____ .
4. In a normal distribution, what proportion of observations can be expected to fall within the interval from $-2$ to $+1$ standard errors from the mean?
5. In a normal distribution, the middle 80% of the observations fall within $\pm$ _____ standard errors of the mean.
6. Construct a 95% confidence interval about a sample proportion when $p_s = .60$ and $SE_p = .02$.

. . . . . . . . . . . . . . . . . . . . . . . . . . . . . . . . . . . . . . . . . . . . . . . . . . . . . . . . . . .

1. the generalization of a statistical description of a sample to the appropriate population.
2. randomly selected.
3. normally.
4. 81.85%: From the mean of 0 to a $-2$ lies .4772 of the distribution. From the mean to $+1$ is .3413 of the curve. Add these two together to get .8185.
5. 1.28 (approximately): The middle 80% incorporates 40% on either side of the mean. A search for .4000 in the area part of Table 13–1 reveals .3997, the closest thing to .4000. The $z$ score associated with the .3997 is 1.28.
6. .5608 to .6392: The 95% confidence interval splits 47.5% of the interval on either side of the sample proportion. Table 13–1 reveals a $z$ of 1.96 to be associated with an area of .4750. Filling in the formula gives .60 $\pm$ 1.96 (.02) = .60 $\pm$ .0392.

## STATISTICAL TESTS OF HYPOTHESES

In Unit 8 it was noted that a hypothesis cannot be verified because the affirmation of the test implication supportive of the hypothesis is affirming the consequent, an invalid argument. In Unit 9 strategies were presented that are designed to strengthen the likelihood that a hypothesis is true. The ability of a hypothesis to withstand multiple and varied tests without disconfirmation is such a strategy. Another is the use of the crucial test to disconfirm rival or alternative hypotheses. These two strategies should both be employed, because the weakness of one is the strength of the other. The strength of the multiple and varied tests is that they deal directly with the hypothesis in question. The weakness is that they ignore any test of competing or alternative hypotheses. The crucial test does the opposite; it attempts to confirm a hypothesis by eliminating alternative hypotheses rather than directly testing the original hypothesis.

There is, however, one crucial test that deals rather directly with the original hypothesis. Although a hypothesis cannot be verified, it is possible to validly falsify the denial of the assertion made in a hypothesis. For example, we may be unable to verify that individualism in social groups leads to higher suicide rates, but we can falsify that individualism in social groups does not lead to higher suicide rates. An important part of this denial of the original hypothesis, however, is the corollary hypothesis that the assertion in the original hypothesis is a random chance occurrence. Thus, an alternative hypothesis is tested, but it is one bearing very directly on the original hypothesis.

### The Null Hypothesis

The original hypothesis (called the research hypothesis) makes an assertion. The *null hypothesis* denies the assertion stated in the research hypothesis with the assumption that the assertion is a random chance occurrence. The test implication for the null hypothesis is that any statistical description that supports the research hypothesis is a random chance occurrence. The probability that this test implication is true is determined by converting the statistical description to a score in an appropropriate probability distribution, such as $z$ in a normal curve. Thus, a probabilistic basis is provided for the acceptance or rejection of the test implication and thereby of the null hypothesis. The denial of the test implication that the description is due to chance falsifies the null hypothesis. This is a situation of denying the consequent, a valid argument form.

The distinction between the research hypothesis test and null hypothesis test can be demonstrated by form and example.

### Test of a Research Hypothesis

| H–D Form | Example |
|---|---|
| (1) *H*. | (1) A higher degree of individualism (*IND*) in a social group causes higher suicide rates (*SR*) in that group. |
| (2) If *H*, then *I*. | (2) If (*IND* causes *SR*) and assuming that Protestants (*P*) have higher *IND,* then (*P* have higher *SR*). |
| (3) *I* is true. | (3) *P* have higher *SR*. |

| | |
|---|---|
| (4) *H* is confirmed. (invalid) | (4) *IND* causes *SR*. |

### Test of a Null Hypothesis (H₀)

| H–D Form | Example |
|---|---|
| (1) *H*₀. | (1) A higher degree of individualism (*IND*) in a social group does not cause higher suicide rates (*SR*) in that group; any such connection is due to random chance. |
| (2) If *H*, then *I*. | (2) If (*IND* does not cause *SR*) and assuming that Protestants (*P*) have higher *IND,* then (*P* have higher *SR*) is due to chance. |
| (3) *I* is false. | (3) (*P* have higher *SR*) is not due to chance. |

| | |
|---|---|
| (4) *H*₀ is falsified. (valid) | (4) (*IND* does not cause *SR*) is false. |

Since we are concerned with demonstrating how confirming evidence in support of a research hypothesis is gathered, these examples display the test result necessary to support the research hypothesis. The null hypothesis test provides better support for the research hypothesis because it simultaneously confirms the research hypothesis test implication (*P* have higher *SR*) and eliminates the alternative hypothesis that (*P* have higher *SR*) is due to chance. It is important to recognize, however, that the test of a null hypothesis does not obviate the use of multiple and varied tests, additional crucial tests, or any check for insufficient and biased statistics. Almost all generalizations in the social sciences are statistical rather than universal in nature. *Statistical tests of null hypotheses* provide a probabilistic basis for asserting that certain statistical descriptions are not due to random chance. If random error or chance can be ruled out as an explanation for a particular phenomenon, then other more theoretically relevant explanations can be sought.

In practice, researchers speak of accepting or rejecting the null hypothesis. To *accept the null hypothesis* is to accept the possibility that the statistical description is a chance occurrence. Whenever a null hypothesis is accepted, the statistical description is said to be *not statistically significant*. To *reject the null hypothesis* is to assert that the statistical description is not a function of random error or chance. The statistical description is described as being *statistically significant*.

In statistical tests of hypotheses, the probability of the chance occurrence of the statistical description is determined by locating the statistic in an appropriate sampling distribution. The customary probability cutting point is at 5% (.05). Thus, the null hypothesis is accepted if there is more than a 5% chance of its being correct (P > .05). The null hypothesis is rejected whenever the probability of being correct is less than or equal to .05 (P <= .05). If P = .05, it is said to be significant at the .05 level.

Different significance levels may be adopted for rejecting null hypotheses. For this reason, it is customary to report the actual probability level rather than impose some significance level on the reader. For example, P = .03 is preferable to P < .05.

Statistical tests of null hypotheses can never rule out the possibility of a chance occurrence of a statistical description. A .05 probability level still leaves a 5% chance of making a mistake by rejecting a null hypothesis that is, in fact, correct. This particular type of error is referred to by statisticians as Type I error. This error type is shown in the Figure 13–4 matrix. The other type of error, Type II, is the acceptance of a null hypothesis that is, in fact, incorrect.

Although there is no way of knowing if either error is committed, the probability of committing either one can be adjusted. Unfortunately the two types of error are inversely related. To reduce the probability of one error type is to increase the probability of the other error type. A researcher who uses the .01 probability level rather than .05 as the criterion for rejecting a null hypothesis will reduce the number of correct null hypotheses that are rejected.

| | | The null hypothesis is | |
| --- | --- | --- | --- |
| | | Accepted | Rejected |
| The null hypothesis is | Correct | | Type I error |
| | Incorrect | Type II error | |

**Figure 13–4. The Acceptance or Rejection of Correct and Incorrect Null Hypotheses**

However, such a move simultaneously increases the number of incorrect null hypotheses that are accepted.

The .01 or even the .05 probability levels may seem stringent criteria for rejecting the likelihood of a chance occurrence. If scientists err, however, they usually wish to do so in a manner that will not suggest a substantive finding when random error can account for the result. For this reason, scientists are more concerned with Type I error, rejecting a null hypothesis that in fact is correct.

## One- and Two-Tail Tests of Hypotheses

A null hypothesis may be considered a denial of an assertion made in a research hypothesis. A research hypothesis may state, for example, that gender is related to alcohol usage. The null hypothesis then states that the two are unrelated, that there is no difference between the sexes on alcohol usage, that any difference exhibited is due simply to chance. The null hypothesis is then tested to determine the probability that the relationship is due to chance.

The determination of that probability, however, is dependent on whether the research hypothesis being denied is directional or nondirectional. The hypothesis that gender is related to alcohol usage is a nondirectional hypothesis. It expresses no concern with whether males or females are more likely to be either users or nonusers of alcohol. The null hypothesis asserts that the sampling distribution of the statistical description that measures the sex difference has a mean of zero, indicating no difference between the sexes on alcohol usage. Determining the probability that this statistical description is a chance occurrence requires what is called a two-tail statistical test.

A *two-tail test* is one in which the research hypothesis is nondirectional. There is no concern with whether the statistical description is above or below the mean of the sampling distribution. The only concern is whether the statistical description is sufficiently different from the mean of the sampling distribution to warrant the conclusion that the difference is not due to random chance. Thus, the selection, for example, of a .05 probability level for rejecting a null hypothesis consists of .025 of the distribution from both tails. In a normal distribution, a two-tail test requires that the difference between a statistical description and the mean of the sampling distribution must equal or exceed $\pm 1.96$ standard errors in order to be rejected as a random chance occurrence.

An example of a directional hypothesis is the specification that women are more likely than men to be nondrinkers. The null hypothesis is that women are not more likely than men to be nondrinkers, that any statistical description which shows a higher proportion of women as nondrinkers is due to chance. Determination of this probability requires what is called a one-tail test.

A *one-tail test* is one in which the research hypothesis is directional. Concern focuses either on whether the statistical description is above the mean of the sampling distribution or on whether it is below the mean, but not both. The researcher is concerned with rejecting the null hypothesis only if the statistical description deviates from the mean of a sampling distribution in a specified direction. If the .05 probability level is used, all 5% is concentrated in one tail of the distribution. In a normal distribution, then, the difference between a statistical description and the mean of the sampling distribution must equal or exceed only 1.64 standard errors in the specified direction in order to be rejected as a random chance occurrence.

## LEARNING AID

**1.** Statistical tests of hypotheses provide a _____ basis for asserting that certain statistical descriptions are due to _____.
**2.** To accept the null hypothesis is to accept the possibility that the statistical description is _____.
**3.** To reject the null hypothesis is to assert that the statistical description is

_____.

**4.** If a statistical description is determined to be statistically significant, then the null hypothesis is _____ (accepted/rejected).
**5.** To alter the probability level for rejecting the null hypothesis from .01 to .05 will _____ (increase/reduce) the chance of accepting an incorrect null hypothesis and _____ (increase/reduce) the chance of rejecting a correct null hypothesis.
**6.** Using the normal distribution table given in Table 13–1, indicate the $z$-score required to reject a null hypothesis at the 0.1 level for a one-tail test.
**7.** A two-tail test is one in which the research hypothesis is _____ (directional/nondirectional).
**8.** Testing the null hypothesis is preferable to testing the research hypothesis because _____

_____.

. . . . . . . . . . . . . . . . . . . . . . . . . . . . . . . . . . . . . . . . . . . . . . . . . . . . . . . . . . . . .

**1.** probabilistic, random error or chance (random chance).
**2.** a chance occurrence.
**3.** not a function of random error or chance.
**4.** rejected.
**5.** reduce, increase
**6.** approximately 1.28: The .1 level means that .1000 of the curve area is located between the $z$ score and the tail of the distribution. Thus, .4000 of the curve area is located between the mean and the $z$. To find the $z$, locate .4000 in

the area part of Table 13–1. The closest figure is .3997, associated with a $z$ score of 1.28.

7. nondirectional.

8. the null hypothesis simultaneously confirms the research hypothesis test implication and eliminates the alternative hypothesis that the test implication is due to chance. Moreover, it does this with a valid form of argument (denying the consequent) in contrast to the invalid confirmation in the test of a research hypothesis.

## Four Major Categories of Null Hypothesis Tests

A variety of statistical tests have been developed to test a wide range of null hypotheses. We will identify four major categories of null hypotheses, each one of which may employ a variety of specific statistical tests and sampling distributions.

1.  The difference between a sample statistic and a known or hypothesized population parameter is due to chance.

In certain instances, some population parameters may already be known. Nevertheless, a sample of the population may be drawn in order to gather additional information concerning properties whose parameters are not known. The representativeness of the sample may be checked by comparing the difference between a key population parameter and the statistical description of the property in the sample. Rejection of the null hypothesis in this case leads to the conclusion that the sample may be biased, with the consequence that the sample statistics may not be very accurate estimators of the population parameters.

Educational attainment is one property that might be checked for population/sample discrepancies. By subtracting the population parameter from the sample statistic, the difference between the two is determined. Dividing this difference by the standard error of the sampling distribution converts the difference to a $z$ score. Comparison with the probabilities listed in the appropriate sampling distribution provides a probability level that the difference is due to chance.

If the sample is a large sample ($>$ 60), then the normal distribution is suitable for comparing means or proportions. If the sample is not large, special t-distributions must be consulted for the sampling distribution of the mean. For the sampling distribution of a proportion, the binomial distributions are appropriate.

As an example, assume that a sample of 400 revealed that 24% of the respondents attained more than a high school education. A census of the population already has revealed that only 20% of the population have attained more than a high school education. What is the probability that the difference between the two figures is due to random chance?

The probability is found by converting the difference between the two scores to a $z$ score. This requires first the computation of the standard error of the sampling distribution.

$$SE_p = \sqrt{\frac{p_\mu(1 - p)}{N}}$$

$$SE_p = \sqrt{\frac{.20\,(1 - .20)}{400}}$$

$$SE_p = \sqrt{\frac{.16}{400}}$$

$$SE_p = .02$$

Now we can convert the difference between the sample statistic and population parameter into a $z$ score. The general formula, given earlier, is: (score − mean)/standard deviation. In this instance, the score is the sample proportion, the mean is the population proportion (the mean of the sampling distribution), and the standard deviation is the standard error of the proportion.

$$z = \frac{p_s - p_\mu}{SE_p}$$

$$z = \frac{.24 - .20}{.02}$$

$$z = +2$$

The actual probability that the difference between .24 and .20 is due to chance depends on whether a one-tail or two-tail test is employed. In this example, a one-tail test concerns the probability of obtaining a score at least two standard errors above the mean (or below the mean, but not both). This probability is the proportion of a normal curve above a $z$ score of 2. Thus, subtract the Table 13–1 value of .4772 from .5000 to obtain .0228.

Whenever the direction of the difference is not relevant, a two-tail test is appropriate. In this example, a two-tail test assesses the probability that the sample proportion deviates *plus or minus* two standard errors from the mean. Therefore, the probability obtained for a one-tail test simply can be doubled to obtain the two-tail probability for the same $z$ score. In this example of educational attainment, a two-tail test is appropriate since no concern with direction is expressed or implied. The probability that the .04 difference was due to chance is .0456.

More often than not, the population parameter will not be known. However, a parameter may be hypothesized or stipulated. For example, the senatorial candidate, whose election survey was used in an earlier example, may stipulate a 55% support percentage in the population before certain decreases in campaign expenditures will be permitted. A statistical test is then in order to determine the probability that the difference between the sample statistic of 51% and the stipulated parameter of 55% is due to random chance.

2. The difference between sample statistics or between population parameters of two groups is due to chance.

There are sampling distributions of differences between statistical descriptions. Moreover, these sampling distributions of differences approximate a normal distribution under certain circumstances. Basically, if the data distributions of the two groups are relatively large ($> 60$), if the two groups are independent of each other, and in the case of samples, if the two groups are constituted through random sampling techniques, then the normal distribution can be used for determining probabilities. Of course, the mean of this sampling distribution of the difference is equal to the difference of the population parameters. The standard deviation of the sampling distribution is called the standard error of the difference. In general, it is computed as an average of the standard deviations of each data distribution divided by the square root of the $N$ for that distribution.

Testing for the chance occurrence of the difference between two statistical descriptions is a very common type of inferential data analysis. One of the most common uses is to compare the statistical descriptions of two groups to determine if they differ on a particular property. The difference test indicates the probability that the difference may be due to random chance. If the difference is not due to chance, then perhaps other more theoretically relevant explanations can account for the difference.

A difference test is used often with experimental research designs. This is because more caution is exercised in experiments to ensure independent randomly selected groups. For example, we have taught a course covering the material in this book in which students were randomly assigned to two different instructional techniques. A difference-of-means test was employed on the mean test performances for the two groups. Since the $N$'s in the two groups were about 40, we utilized a t-test. A *t-test* is simply the appropriate utilization of a t-distribution in a statistical test of a hypothesis. The t value derived is a standard deviation score that provides, in this case, the probability of obtaining a difference of that magnitude by random chance.

Contrary to certain folk wisdom, statistical tests of hypotheses may be used to test the difference between two population parameters.[2] Inferential statistics is often defined as the inference of population parameters from sample statistics. Our definition is less restrictive (see the Rationale section). Statistical tests of hypotheses determine the probability that a statistical description is a random chance occurrence. The difference between two population parameters is subject to random variations just as sample statistics are subject to random error.

An example of a comparison between population parameters is the comparison of voter turnout means in states with a strong two-party structure and states with a weak two-party structure. If the difference in voter turnout between these two groups can be matched by comparisons of randomly assigned groups of states, then the difference between the strong and weak two-party states is not especially intriguing. However, if a test of statistical significance indicates a random chance probability of less than .05, then the randomness explanation for the difference can be ruled out with a reasonable degree of certainty. Then the theoretical relevance of the group distinction can take on added meaning.

Up to this point, the difference test has required independent data distributions. Often, however, an investigator wishes to compare differences between statistical descriptions for the same group or for two groups matched carefully on certain properties. In the strictest sense, a difference test is inappropriate for such a situation. However, if the differences between the pairs of statistical observations are treated as a single observation, then a test can be used that checks the difference between a statistical description of the differences and zero. The zero serves as a stipulated population parameter since the mean of randomly assigned differences is zero. The statistical test is the one employed for the first type of hypothesis described in this section.

## LEARNING AID

1. One major type of statistical test of a hypothesis is that which tests whether the difference between a sample statistic and _____.

2. A t-test refers to any statistical test that _____

_____.

3. The t-distributions are used primarily whenever _____

_____.

4. The standard error of the difference refers to _____

_____.

**5.** Statistical tests of hypotheses _____ (are/are not) used appropriately on differences between population parameters.

· · · · · · · · · · · · · · · · · · · · · · · · · · · · · · · · · · · · · · · · · · · · · · · · · · · · · · · ·

**1.** a known or hypothesized population parameter is due to chance.
**2.** appropriately uses the t-distributions in a statistical test.
**3.** the $N$'s of the data distributions are relatively small ($< 60$) and when the sampling distribution involve means.
**4.** the standard deviation of the sampling distribution of the difference.
**5.** are


## Four Major Categories of Null Hypothesis Tests (Continued)

3. The differences among sample statistics or population parameters among three or more groups are due to chance.

Determining whether the differences among the statistical descriptions for three or more groups are due to chance involves more than just an extension of the difference tests between two groups. One of the most common statistical tests for three or more groups is the *analysis-of-variance*. It serves as an indirect test for a difference among means.

As the name indicates, the analysis-of-variance measures differences in variances. Two independent measures of the population variance are computed from the three or more data distributions. One of the measures always results in an unbiased estimate of the population variance. The other estimate is derived by using the means of each group as individual observations. If the means are from different sampling distributions, their estimate of the population variance will enlarge and produce a biased estimate of the variance.

Analysis-of-variance calculates a ratio ($F$) of the mean estimate of variance to the other unbiased estimate. As the ratio increases in magnitude, the probability that the differences among the groups are a random occurrence decreases. Comparison of the $F$ ratio to the appropriate sampling distribution gives the probability of a random chance occurrence.

Analysis-of-variance can be employed in multivariate distributions as well as the bivariate. The two-way analysis-of-variance, three-way analysis-of-variance, and the analysis of covariance are all labels of multivariate analysis-of-variance techniques. Alternatives to the analysis-of-variance also are available. Consult a statistics text for reference to these statistical tests.[3]

4. The relationship between two or more variables is due to chance.

Measures of association are designed to measure the strength of the relationship between two or more variables. However, it requires a statistical test of a hypothesis to determine the probability that the magnitude of the association measure is a chance occurrence. Several measures of association are capable of

### Table 13-2  TWO TABLES OF ALCOHOL USAGE BY SEX

| | Actual Empirical Distribution | | | | Hypothetical Distribution of "No Relationship" | | |
| --- | --- | --- | --- | --- | --- | --- | --- |
| | Male | Female | Total | | Male | Female | Total |
| nondrinkers | 22.0% | 39.0% | 29.6% | nondrinkers | 29.6% | 29.6% | 29.6% |
| mostly beer | 42.0 | 14.0 | 29.6 | mostly beer | 29.6 | 29.6 | 29.6 |
| wine | 14.0 | 17.0 | 15.3 | wine | 15.3 | 15.3 | 15.3 |
| hard liquor | 22.0 | 30.0 | 25.6 | hard liquor | 25.6 | 25.6 | 25.6 |
| (N) | (250) | (200) | (450) | (N) | (250) | (200) | (450) |

having statistical significance tests computed that test the hypothesis that the association measure is a chance occurrence. Such a test indicates only the probability that the association measures differs from zero, the condition of no relationship. Tests can be employed to determine the probability that the association measure differs from a stipulated association level by chance, but this is rarely done.

One of the most famous of all statistical tests of hypotheses is the chi square. *Chi square* ($\chi^2$) is a one-tail test that measures the probability that any departures in an actual distribution from a stipulated probability distribution is due to chance. Although $\chi^2$ can be calculated on a univariate distribution, it is computed most commonly on bivariate distributions. In the bivariate case, $\chi^2$ compares each cell of the empirical bivariate distribution with the corresponding cell in the hypothetical bivariate distribution that would exist if the two variables were unrelated. Recall from Unit 12 that no relationship between two variables exists whenever the percentaged distribution of the dependent variable is duplicated within each category of the independent variable.

Chi square can be demonstrated using some data from the previous unit on alcohol usage and gender. The data are recreated here on the left side of Table 13-2. On the right side in Table 13-2 is the hypothetical table of no relationship.

Chi square is computed from the following formula:

$\chi^2$ Formula

$$\chi^2 = \sum \frac{(O - E)^2}{E}$$

where $O$ = observed cell frequency
$E$ = expected cell frequency
$\Sigma$ = the sum of

Chi square must be computed using the frequencies of the table rather than the percentages. (Percentages are shown in Table 13–2 to contrast more vividly a "no relationship" table with an actual empirical bivariate distribution.) For example, the observed cell frequency ($O$) for the upper left hand cell is 55 ($O$ = 0.22 × 250 = 55). The expected frequency ($E$) for the same cell is 74 ($E$ = 0.296 × 250 = 74). The difference between $O$ and $E$ is then squared and divided by $E$. This procedure is followed for each cell in the table (excluding any "Total" cells), and the quotients are then summed to obtain the $\chi^2$ value. In this example, $\chi^2 = 43.67$.

Since $\chi^2$ has its own set of sampling distributions, a $\chi^2$ table must be consulted to determine the probability of obtaining a $\chi^2$ of that magnitude by chance. In this example, P < .001. The null hypothesis that the relationship between these two variables is due to chance is therefore rejected.

## LEARNING AID

1.  Identify the four types of hypotheses that are tested in inferential data analysis and that were presented in the last two subsections.
2.  The analysis-of-variance is designed to test the hypothesis that _____ .
3.  Although the analysis-of-variance does analyze the variances of different groups, indirectly it is testing the differences among the _____ of the groups.
4.  Usually, a test of significance for a measure of association measures the probability that the association measure _____

_____ .

5.  Chi square is a test of the hypothesis that _____

_____ .

. . . . . . . . . . . . . . . . . . . . . . . . . . . . . . . . . . . . . . . . . . . . . . . . . . . . . . . . . . . . . .

1.  (a) The difference between a sample statistic and a known or hypothesized population parameter is due to chance. (b) The difference between sample statistics or between population parameters of two groups is due to chance. (c) The differences among sample statistics or population parameters among three or more groups are due to chance. (d) The relationship between two or more variables is due to chance.
2.  the differences among sample means or population means among three or more groups are due to chance.
3.  means
4.  differs significantly from zero *or* that the magnitude of the association measure is a chance occurrence.
5.  the relationship between two or more variables is due to chance.

## FOOTNOTES

1. One statistics text with a very comprehensive set of sampling distribution tables is Wilfrid J. Dixon and Frank J. Massey, *Introduction to Statistical Analysis* (New York: McGraw-Hill, 1969).
2. For various opinions on the subject, see Denton E. Morrison and Ramon E. Henkel, eds., *The Significance Test Controversy—A Reader* (Chicago: Aldine, 1970).
3. One of the better texts is Hubert M. Blalock, Jr., *Social Statistics* (New York: McGraw-Hill, 1972). Another text, especially strong on statistical tests of hypotheses, is John T. Roscoe, *Fundamental Research Statistics* (New York: Holt, Rinehart, & Winston, 1969).

# 14
# Experimental Research*

* The information in this unit relies heavily on the work of Donald Campbell, who has contributed more to the development of experimental research in the social sciences than perhaps anyone else. See Donald T. Campbell and Julian Stanley, *Experimental and Quasi-Experimental Research* (Chicago: Rand McNally and Co., 1963); Donald Campbell, "Reforms as Experiments," *American Psychologist* 24 (April, 1969): 409–29; and D. T. Campbell, "Factors Relevant to the Validity of Experiments in Social Settings," *Psychological Bulletin* 54 (July 1957), 297–312.

# INTRODUCTION

## Rationale

Knowing the logic of experimentation is basic to understanding social science. Science is concerned with establishing reliable explanations and predictions. To explain and predict is to know cause–effect relations. A strong approach to gathering information relevant to causal inference is experimental research. Experimentation is not only a natural science tool. It has an increasing number of applications in the social sciences, ranging from the study of the effects of propaganda on political attitudes to simulations, mass media experiments, election campaign experiments, negative income tax experiments, Head Start experiments, and wage and price control evaluations.

This unit will help to prepare us for the unit on survey research. In the present unit, attention will focus initially on the factors that affect the validity of an experiment. Then eleven different kinds of experimental designs will be examined within the context of three experimental techniques. Finally, an attempt will be made to evaluate the adequacy of a variety of experimental designs in social science.

## Learning Objectives

After completing this unit, the student should be able to:

1. Name, define, and identify the fifteen factors affecting the internal and external validity of experiments.

2. Explain how the three requirements of causal inference are achieved by experimental design.

3. Reproduce the Experimental Design Matrix.

4. Name and explain three techniques for varying experimental designs.

5. Define and diagram the basic experimental designs.

6. Evaluate the major weaknesses and strengths of the basic and modified experimental designs.

7. Name, diagram, analyze, and evaluate examples of experimental designs appearing in the social science literature.

## EXPERIMENTAL VALIDITY

### Treatment and Control Groups

In experimental research the investigator controls the occurrence of the independent variable and then observes changes or differences in the dependent variable. We learned earlier that this control maximizes the three criteria required for inferring causality: temporal precedence (the independent variable precedes the dependent variable in time), constant conjunction (the independent and dependent variables are regularly associated), and nonspuriousness (variables other than the independent variable are not the cause of the dependent variable).

Later a number of experimental designs will be presented and evaluated in terms of their causal evidence. Many of these designs employ two types of groups. One group of units (which may be persons, groups, nations, and so on) is subjected to some stimulus or treatment and is called the *treatment* or *experimental group*. Another group of units is not subjected to the stimulus or treatment and is called the *control* or *comparison group*. Here are examples of two experiments that will illustrate these concepts and facilitate the discussion in the next section.

Example 1:

A Pretest–Posttest Canvassing Experiment

A political scientist asks what the effect is of door-to-door canvassing by a legislative candidate on the voting turnout of the registered voters in the 1976 election.

From a 1974 list of the voters in the district, the researcher randomly selects 400 names. He checks the poll lists to see how many of these people turned out to vote in 1974.

He personally canvasses each of the houses of these 400 persons. The canvass involves introducing himself, presenting his position on issues, and asking the person for support in the campaign. After the 1976 election, he observes the poll lists to see how many of these people turned out to vote.

He infers the effect of canvassing by comparing the proportion of the 400 names who turned out to vote in 1974 before the canvass with the proportion who turned out to vote in 1976 after the canvass.

Example 2:

## A Pretest–Posttest Control Group Canvassing Experiment

A political scientist asks what the effect is of door-to-door canvassing by a legislative candidate on the voting turnout of the registered voters in the 1976 election.

From a 1974 registration list of the voters in the district, the researcher randomly selects 400 names. He randomly assigns 200 registered voters to the canvassing condition. This is the treatment or experimental group. He randomly assigns 200 registered voters to the noncanvassing condition, which is the control or comparison group.

He personally canvasses each of the houses of the 200 persons in the treatment condition.

After the 1976 election, he observes the poll lists to determine the proportion of persons in both groups turning out to vote.

He infers the effect of canvassing by comparing the proportion of voters in the treatment condition with the proportion of voters in the control condition.

## LEARNING AID

1. In experimental research the investigator controls the occurrence of the _____ variable and then observes changes or differences in the _____ variable.

2. In the canvassing experiment the investigator controls the occurrence of _____ (canvassing/voting turnout) and then observes changes or differences in _____ (canvassing/voting turnout).

3. Thus, the independent variable in this experiment is _____, and the dependent variable is _____.

4. The 200 persons assigned to the canvassing condition in the second example are called the _____ group, whereas those assigned to the noncanvassing condition are called the _____ group.

5. Three criteria necessary for establishing causality are:
   a. _____
   b. _____
   c. _____

6. Since the experimenter can control the introduction of the independent variable, he has evidence that the independent variable _____ the dependent variable in time.

7. Since the experimenter can compare the status of the dependent variable before and after the independent variable is introduced or in a treatment and a

control group, he has evidence that the independent and dependent variables are regularly _____.

8. Since the experimenter can control many confounding variables by experimental design, he has evidence that variables other than the independent variable are not the _____ of the dependent variable.

. . . . . . . . . . . . . . . . . . . . . . . . . . . . . . . . . . . . . . . . . . . . . . . . . . . . . . . . . .

1. independent, dependent
2. canvassing, voting turnout
3. canvassing, voting turnout
4. treatment or experimental, control or comparison
5. temporal precedence, constant conjunction, nonspuriousness
6. precedes
7. associated (related)
8. cause

## Internal and External Validity

The strengths and weaknesses of experimental designs can be identified by checking for internal and external validity. *Internal validity* is a check for experimental effect. It asks whether the experimental treatment (the independent variable) had a significant effect on the outcome of the dependent variable. Did door-to-door canvassing in fact have an effect on voting turnout in the political experiment? *External validity,* on the other hand, is a check for generalizability. It asks whether the effect can be generalized to other populations, treatment variables, or settings. Can the effect of an experiment conducted in one precinct be generalized to the American voting population? Can the results of a door-to-door canvassing experiment be generalized to a telephone canvassing treatment? Can the effect of an experiment on turning out to vote be generalized to other indicators of political participation?

Internal validity analyzes experimental effect. Did the treatment produce the effect or did something else cause it? If variables other than the independent variable are causes of the dependent variable, then the relationship between the independent and dependent variables is spurious or false. To test for internal validity is a partial test of spuriousness. Nine factors have been identified as contending alternative explanations for the effect. If these factors are left uncontrolled, they could produce effects confounded with the experimental stimulus and thereby make the results difficult to interpret. Aiming for unambiguous conclusions about treatment effects, the investigator tries to rule out these nine alternative hypotheses by controlling them in the design of the experiment. The factors that might threaten internal validity include the following "HIS MISTER" variables:

H   istory
I   nstability
S   election

M   aturation
I   nstrumentation
S   election-maturation interaction
T   esting effects
E   experimental mortality
R   egression effects

## LEARNING AID

1.  Whereas internal validity is a check for _____, external validity is a check for _____.
2.  The "HIS MISTER" factors affect the _____ validity of an experiment.
3.  Test your recall of the factors affecting internal validity by listing them on a piece of paper.

. . . . . . . . . . . . . . . . . . . . . . . . . . . . . . . . . . . . . . . . . . . . . . . . . . . . . . . . .

1.  experimental effect, generalizability
2.  internal
3.  history, instability, selection, maturation, instrumentation, selection–maturation interaction, testing effects, experimental mortality, and regression effects.

## Internal Validity: "His Mister" Factors

HISTORY

*History* involves the occurrence of specific events in addition to the experimental variable.

History is left uncontrolled in the pretest–posttest canvassing experiment. The time gap between the first and second observations is two years. This leaves plenty of opportunity for the occurrence of many events in addition to canvassing to affect voting turnout, such as changes in voting registration procedures or the influence of a high stimulus presidential campaign in 1976 but not in 1974.

INSTABILITY

*Instability* refers to random sampling and measurement error. The result of such random variation in samples and measurements can be the false appearance of effects ("pseudoeffects") on the dependent variable. The use of statistical tests of significance can be used to assess the probability that instability rather than the independent variable is the source of the effects on the dependent variable.

a. Instability is uncontrolled in the pretest–posttest control group experiment. The differences between the treatment and control groups may be explained by random sampling error, such as an oversampling in the treatment condition of older registered voters who are more likely to turn out to vote.

b. If the clerks at the polls are randomly inconsistent in checking off the voters' names, then the turnout measures would be inaccurate.

SELECTION

*Selection* refers to nonrandom errors in the sampling of units. The units are the persons or groups being analyzed. The systematic over- or underrepresentation of certain characteristics or traits can produce biases that affect the status of the dependent variable.

a. Selection is uncontrolled in the pretest–posttest control group canvassing experiment if older people are systematically sampled and assigned to the treatment or the control group.

b. In the 1936 election the *Literary Digest* public opinion poll predicted a landslide victory of the Republican Alf Landon over Franklin Roosevelt. The sample was selected with the use of telephone directories. During the depression many lower income people did not have telephones and therefore were excluded from the sample. Consequently the sample systematically overrepresented the wealthy, who also tended to be Republican and support Alf Landon.

c. If the effectiveness of a social action program is evaluated by introducing it in one city and comparing results with another city where the program is not introduced, differences in results might be explained by selection factors; the cities might have differed anyway in income, racial, social, or other factors even without the occurrence of the program.

MATURATION

*Maturation* refers to natural changes in the units that evolve with the passage of time. Fatigue, aging, and boredom are examples of maturational factors.

Maturation is uncontrolled in the pretest–posttest canvassing experiment. If the 1976 posttest group turns out in higher proportions than it did in 1974, the cause may not be canvassing but age. The voters were older and therefore more likely to turn out to vote in the 1976 election.

*Instrumentation* designates changes in the measuring instrument or the method of observation.

a.   If an opinion pollster changes interviewers, coders, or question wording in a posttest interview, instrumentation may explain differences between the pretest and posttest scores and not the independent variable.

b.   In cross-cultural studies instrumentation errors may be present in translating the interview schedule into different languages.

c.   If a crime index is calculated differently in 1970 than in 1960, then the investigator must attempt to control for instrumentation errors in evaluating a crime reduction program.

SELECTION–MATURATION  INTERACTION

*Selection–maturation interaction* refers to the nonrandom sampling of units that results in different rates of maturation between the groups. In other words, selection biases interact with or lead to additional maturational biases.

A political scientist attempts to study the effects of his propaganda course. He selects his senior level propaganda class as the treatment group and his freshman level American Government course as a control group. He finds greater propaganda resistance in his senior level propaganda course than in his freshman level American Government course. He concludes that his propaganda course produces resistance to propaganda. He neglects, however, to consider the possibility of selection–maturation interaction. His selection of seniors for the treatment group may result in different maturational characteristics (such as increasing critical awareness) and can explain the dependent variable rather than the effect of the course.

TESTING  EFFECTS

*Testing effects* occur when the process of taking a test or being observed affects the outcome of a second test or observation. It can include the effects of publishing the results of a poll or a social indicator on subsequent polls or indicators.

a.   Testing effects are minimized in the canvassing experiment only if the poll lists are observed and subjects are not interviewed about their voting turnout in 1974.

b.   Persons who are respondents in public opinion polls are more likely to turn out to vote than persons not interviewed. The process of interviewing sensitizes the respondents to political information, and they are more likely to behave differently on a posttest.

EXPERIMENTAL  MORTALITY

*Experimental mortality* refers to the nonrandom loss of units resulting in differences between the groups.

If a higher proportion of older voters move away and drop out of the control group in the pretest–posttest control group canvassing experiment, then differences in turnout rates may be caused by experimental mortality and not by canvassing.

### REGRESSION EFFECTS

*Regression effects* occur when units are selected for treatment on the basis of their extremity producing pseudoshifts in scores. A unit's score tends to vary over time. Sometimes its score is high; other times its score is low. Over a period of time, it has an average tendency indicated by the mean. Whenever an extremely high or low scoring unit is selected for treatment, we find that the next score on the unit tends to be closer to the average tendency for the unit. The score, in other words, tends to shift or "regress" toward the mean, the average tendency. Regression effects, occurring when units are selected for treatment on the basis of their extremity, then, are likely to produce differences between the pretest and posttest groups. And thus, regression effects may be mistaken for treatment effects.

a. If a legislative district is selected for the canvassing treatment because it had an extremely low voting turnout rate in 1974, then in 1976 its turnout rate is likely to shift upward in the direction of its average turnout rate. The upward shift in rates is likely to be a regression effect, but investigators may falsely identify it as the effect of canvassing.

b. Crime rates do fluctuate, being higher in some years and lower in others. An innovative criminal justice program is most likely to be put into effect when the crime rates are extremely high. When the posttest crime rates are observed, they are found to have decreased. The evaluator might fallaciously conclude that the program is successful without ruling out the hypothesis of regression effects. Perhaps a difference between pretest and posttest rates would appear since the pretest is based on the most extreme rate and then compared with some other rate, the posttest, which probably would be lower and closer to the average crime rate in a period of fluctuating rates. The evaluator sees a drop in crime rates, concludes that the "treatment" works, and confuses program effect with regression effect.

c. Compensatory educational programs such as Head Start are made available to the children who are most needy. The control group is selected from untreated children of the same community. Often this untreated population is on the average more able than the experimental group. Regression effects can occur when the two groups are compared, and the compensatory program may appear to have harmful rather than helpful effects on children.

## LEARNING AID

1. History involves the occurrence of specific _____ in addition to the _____ variable.
2. Instability involves random _____ and _____ error.
3. Selection involves _____ (random, nonrandom) errors in the sampling of units.
4. Maturation consists of _____ changes in units that evolve with the passage of _____.
5. Instrumentation designates changes in the _____ instrument or the method of _____.
6. Selection-maturation interaction refers to the nonrandom _____ of units that results in different rates of _____ between groups.
7. Testing effects occur when the process of taking a _____ or being _____ affects the outcome of the _____ test or observation.
8. Experimental mortality refers to nonrandom _____ of units resulting in differences between the groups.
9. Regression effects occur when units are selected for treatment on the basis of their _____ producing pseudo_____ in scores.
10. Internal validity is a check for experimental _____.
11. Test your recall by naming the nine factors affecting internal validity.

. . . . . . . . . . . . . . . . . . . . . . . . . . . . . . . . . . . . . . . . . . . . . . . . . . . . . . . . . . . . . . . . . . .

1. events, experimental (independent)
2. sampling, measurement
3. nonrandom
4. natural, time
5. measuring, observation
6. sampling, maturation
7. test, observed, second
8. loss
9. extremity, shifts
10. effect
11. history, instability, selection, maturation, instrumentation, selection–maturation interaction, testing effects, experimental mortality, regression effects.


## External Validity: "SMIIRR" Factors

External validity, you will recall, is a check for generalizability. To test for external validity is to ask whether the treatment effect can be generalized to other populations, treatment variables, or settings. Six factors can threaten or "SMIIRR" the external validity of political experiments:

## SMIIRR FACTORS

*S*   election–treatment interaction
*M*   ultiple treatment interference
*I*    rrelevant treatment replicability
*I*    rrelevant measure responsiveness
*R*   eactive testing
*R*   eactive arrangements

Test your recall now by trying to name the six factors affecting external validity.

### SELECTION TREATMENT INTERACTION

*Selection-treatment interaction* is a lack of generalizability to a population where nonrandom sampling of units produces unrepresentative treatment effects.

a.   Canvassing effects may be observed by taking before and after interviews. A biased selection of respondents, however, may be obtained if different kinds of persons refuse to be interviewed or are not at home. The nonrandom selection of units then may interact with the treatment to produce effects unrepresentative of the population as a whole.

b.   If a compensatory education program is designed for disadvantaged minority children and all the children selected for participation are Indians, the program's treatment effects may be unrepresentative of the disadvantaged minority population.

### MULTIPLE TREATMENT INTERFERENCE

*Multiple treatment interference* is a lack of generalizability to the effects of single treatments or where a treatment is reapplied to the same units or where more than one treatment is applied simultaneously.

If door-to-door canvassing is repeated several times before the election or if telephone canvassing is applied in addition to door-to-door canvassing, then it is difficult to make generalizations about the effects of single or separate treatments.

### IRRELEVANT TREATMENT REPLICABILITY

*Irrelevant treatment replicability* is a lack of generalizability to a treatment where a treatment is not fully reproduced ("replicated"). A treatment is a complex combination of stimuli, and the replication of the treatment that fails to include those components actually responsible for the effects may produce unrepresentative treatment effects.

Door-to-door canvassing is a complex activity encompassing a number of components: the candidate, message content, style of presentation, recipient, and so on. If in a replication of the experiment a party worker does the canvassing instead of the candidate and the presence of the candidate is responsible for producing treatment effects, irrelevant treatments are replicated and the expected effects will probably not occur.

### IRRELEVANT MEASURE RESPONSIVENESS

*Irrelevant measure responsiveness* is a lack of generalizability of measures where each measure contains its own irrelevant components and sources of error that may produce apparent effects.

Measuring turnout by identifying names checked on poll lists may include errors related to the spelling, giving, and recording of names. Measuring turnout by asking respondents if they recall voting or by posting observers at the polls carries other irrelevant components and sources of error. Each of these measures is complex and includes irrelevant components that may produce pseudoeffects.

### REACTIVE TESTING

*Reactive testing* is a lack of generalizability to unpretested populations, where the pretest affects a second test.

The measurement of turnout in the canvassing experiment is nonreactive since observing poll lists would not affect the subject's responsiveness to the canvass. If, instead, turnout is measured by interviewing before the after canvass, the respondent's sensitivity to the election might be increased and affect his responsiveness to the canvass. This would limit the generalizability of the effects to populations pretested as this one.

### REACTIVE ARRANGEMENTS

*Reactive arrangements* is a lack of generalizability to other settings, where experimental conditions are atypical of conditions of regular application of the treatments.

If the canvassing experiment is conducted in a setting atypical of those in which canvassing is generally conducted, its treatment effects may be unrepresentative of other settings.

## LEARNING AID

1. Name the nine factors affecting interval validity.
2. Name the six factors affecting external validity.

**3.** Whereas internal validity is a check for experimental _____, external validity is a check for _____.

**4.** Selection treatment interaction is a lack of generalizability to a population where _____ sampling of respondents produces unrepresentative _____ effects.

**5.** Multiple treatment interference is a lack of generalizability to a population where _____ treatment, (where more than one _____ is applied simultaneously) or where a treatment is reapplied to the same units.

**6.** Irrelevant treatment replicability is a lack of generalizability where a treatment is not fully _____.

**7.** Irrelevant measure responsiveness is a lack of generalizability where the method of _____ carries _____ components and sources of _____ producing apparent effects.

**8.** Reactive testing is a lack of generalizability to _____ populations.

**9.** Reactive arrangements is a lack of generalizability to other _____.

**10.** Once more, name the six factors affecting external validity.

**11.** What are those nine factors affecting external validity?

. . . . . . . . . . . . . . . . . . . . . . . . . . . . . . . . . . . . . . . . . . . . . . . . . . . . . . . . . . . . . .

**1.** History, instability, selection, maturation, instrumentation, selection–maturation interaction, testing effects, experimental mortality, regression effects.

**2.** Selection treatment interaction, multiple treatment interference, irrelevant treatment replicability, irrelevant measure responsiveness, reactive testing, reactive arrangements

**3.** effect, generalizability

**4.** nonrandom, treatment

**5.** single, treatment

**6.** reproduced (replicated)

**7.** observation (measurement), irrelevant, error

**8.** unpretested

**9.** settings

**10.** see question 2.

**11.** Although the rain stays mainly on the plain, see question 1.

## EXPERIMENTAL DESIGN

Deciding on an experimental design is usually not as easy as simply selecting the "perfect" one. The experimenter is usually in a situation where resources are limited, so he has to decide which design maximizes causal evidence and minimizes resource usage. He has to decide, for example, whether it is more important to determine that the stimulus has an effect or to generalize to varied populations. This is the internal–external validity dilemma. What is gained by maximizing internal validity is usually lost at the expense of external validity, and vice versa. Even within internal or external validity, the experimenter must decide which factors pose the most serious threats and which designs provide the most effective controls for these threats. Thus, deciding on a design is complex. It involves simultaneous consideration of the requirements of causal inference, resource availability, and experimental design.

In the causation unit the student learned that three criteria must be satisfied to infer that the independent variable is the "cause" of the dependent variable. These criteria are: (1) temporal precedence ($IV$ precedes $DV$ in time), (2) constant conjunction ($IV$ is regularly associated or paired with DV), and (3) nonspuriousness (a variable other than IV is not the cause of $DV$).

Experimental research is an important social science method because it maximizes the evidence on these criteria. To establish temporal precedence, the experimenter controls the introduction of the independent variable ($X$) so that he knows it occurs prior to an observation of the dependent variable ($O$). Constant conjunction is determined by observing whether the introduction of the independent variable ($X$) is associated with a change in the dependent variable ($O$). Nonspuriousness is approached but never totally established by incorporating in the design such techniques as randomization to eliminate the most likely alternative causes (the internal validity factors).

The experimenter has three techniques for varying or constructing alternative experimental designs: (1) adding same group observations, (2) adding comparison group observations, and (3) adding control group observations.

"The Experimental Design Matrix," shown in Table 14–1, illustrates nine designs generated by varying the three techniques previously mentioned. The diagram of each design in the table will be examined later in this section. For now, however, the student should learn that "$X$" represents the occurrence of the stimulus or the independent variable. "$O$" represents an observation of the

**Table 14–1. EXPERIMENTAL DESIGN MATRIX**

|  | One Group | Comparison Group | Control Group |
|---|---|---|---|
| Posttest | $X\ O$ | $X\ O$ | $R\ X\ O$ |
|  |  | $\overline{\phantom{XX}}\ O$ | $R\quad O$ |
| Pretest-Posttest | $O\ X\ O$ | $O\ X\ O$ | $R\ O\ X\ O$ |
|  |  | $\overline{\phantom{OO}}\ O\quad O$ | $R\ O\quad O$ |
| Time Series | $O\ O\ O\ X\ O\ O\ O$ | $O\ O\ O\ X\ O\ O\ O$ | $R\ O\ O\ O\ X\ O\ O\ O$ |
|  |  | $O\ O\ O\quad O\ O\ O$ | $R\ O\ O\ O\quad O\ O\ O$ |

dependent variable. The dimension of time is symbolized by space moving from left to right. "*O*'s" on the same line represent observations of the same group at different points in time. "O's" on different lines reflect observations of different groups. "*R*" represents random selection of a group and random assignment of the group to *X* or to a non-*X* condition. Observations prior to *X* are called "pretests," and those after *X* are "posttests." The name of a design consists of two parts, the time order of the observation and the type of group. Accordingly, the design in the upper left cell of the matrix is referred to as the "Posttest One Group," while the one in the lower right cell is called the "Time Series Control Group."

The student should understand the role of the three techniques in the matrix. Adding observations of the same group is represented by moving from the top row to a lower row (such as going from the Posttest One Group to the Pretest–Posttest One Group and finally to the Time Series One Group). Adding comparison group observations is represented by moving from the first column to the second column (such as going from the Posttest One Group to the Posttest Comparison Group, or from the Pretest–Posttest One Group to the Pretest–Posttest Comparison Group). Adding control group observations is represented by going from column one or two to column three (such as going from the Posttest Comparison Group to the Posttest Control Group). With this overview of the alternative design techniques, we will now examine these nine basic designs.

## LEARNING AID

**1.** The problem of deciding whether it is more important to determine the effect of the stimulus than to generalize the effect to various populations is called the _____ dilemma.

**2.** The three criteria for causal inference are: _____, _____, and _____.

**3.** To establish temporal precedence, the investigator introduces the _____ variable prior to the observation of the _____ variable.

**4.** Constant conjunction is determined by observing whether the introduction of the independent variable is associated with a _____ in the dependent variable.

**5.** Nonspuriousness is approached with such techniques as _____.

**6.** Reproduce the Experimental Design Matrix.

**7.** Name the three techniques for varying experimental designs.

. . . . . . . . . . . . . . . . . . . . . . . . . . . . . . . . . . . . . . . . . . . . . . . . . . . . . . . . . .

**1.** internal–external validity

**2.** temporal precedence, constant conjunction, nonspuriousness

**3.** independent, dependent
**4.** change
**5.** randomization
**6.** see text
**7.** adding same group observations, adding comparison group observations, adding control group observations

## Designs Adding Same Group Observations

POSTTEST ONE GROUP

The simplest and weakest of all experimental designs is the *Posttest One Group,* where units (individuals or groups) are observed (*O*) after being exposed to some stimulus, treatment or event (*X*).

Form:

| One Group | | |
|---|---|---|
| Posttest | *X* | *O* |

Example:

After registered voters are canvassed (*X*) by the candidate, their voting turnout is observed by checking poll lists or by interviewing.

This design is totally inadequate since it does not effectively control for even one internal validity factor. At least one formal comparison of the group with another group not exposed to *X* or with the same group at a time prior to *X* is necessary for any type of scientific analysis. Thus, causal inference cannot be inferred legitimately from designs of this type.

PRETEST–POSTTEST ONE GROUP

By adding an observation of the same group prior to the occurrence of *X* to the Posttest One Group, we obtain a design called the *Pretest–Posttest One Group,* in which one group is observed before and after exposure to *X*.

Form:

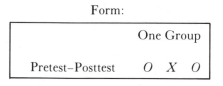

| One Group | | | |
|---|---|---|---|
| Pretest–Posttest | *O* | *X* | *O* |

Example:

A group of voters is observed (*O*) by interviewing before and after exposure to the campaign canvass (*X*).

Adding a pretest observation provides information for temporal precedence and constant conjunction. In addition, it establishes some control over:

*Experimental mortality (nonrandom loss of units) can be detected and thereby controlled by counting the number of units observed in the pretest absent from the posttest.*

The addition of a pretest observation, however, increases the threat of two internal validity factors:

*Instrumentation (changes in the measuring instrument or method of observation) becomes more serious if interviewers become more fatigued or experienced at the posttest than at the pretest.*

*Testing Effects (pretest effects on posttest behavior) is introduced because a pretest is brought into the design.*

Adding a pretest observation also increases the external validity problem of reactive testing (generalization to unpretested populations). Thus, the student should recognize that associated with the gains of adding a pretest are certain costs and the experimenter has to make hard judgments concerning the gravity of various threats to both internal and external validity when deciding on an experimental design.

This design is an improvement over the Posttest One Group, but it is still very weak. It at least has one formal comparison. It controls for selection, selection–maturation interaction, and experimental mortality. Left uncontrolled are history, maturation, testing effects, and instrumentation. If it is feasible, a stronger design should be selected.

TIME SERIES ONE GROUP

By adding a series of observations of the same group to the Pretest–Posttest One Group, we obtain the *Time Series One Group*. In this design one group is observed periodically (hence "time series") before and after exposure to $X$.

| Form: | Example: |
|---|---|
| One Group<br><br>Time Series   $O \; O \; O \; X \; O \; O \; O$ | A series of repeated observations of voting turnout may be taken on a sample of voters before and after exposure to the canvass. |

Adding multiple pre- and posttest observations of the same group provides even stronger controls over selection, selection–maturation interaction, and experimental mortality than the Pretest–Posttest One Group. Moreover, the Time Series One Group establishes some measure of control over:

*Maturation (natural change) can be ruled out if the rate of change in the time series is constant before X occurs but shifts dramatically after X is introduced.*

*Instrumentation (changes in the measuring instrument or observation) can be ruled out since it is unlikely that these changes would occur in the time series exactly when the treatment is introduced. If the observers are aware of the experimental hypothesis, however, their anticipation of expected results may affect the measurement procedure and produce pseudoconfirmation of the hypothesis.*

*Testing effects (pretest effects on posttest behavior) can be eliminated if it can be safely assumed that it is unlikely for testing effects to occur exactly when the treatment is introduced into the time series.*

The Time Series One Group has had a measure of success in the physical sciences and has potential for the social sciences. Its primary weakness is its lack of control over history. Before the results of this design are accepted as definitive, it should be replicated in a number of different settings so as to improve confidence in external validity.

## LEARNING AID

**1.** Define, diagram and identify the Posttest One Group, Pretest–Posttest One Group, and Time Series One Group.

**2.** The Posttest One Group is totally inadequate because it lacks even one formal _____.

**3.** Adding a pretest to the Posttest One Group controls _____ but produces a problem with _____ and _____.

**4.** Adding multiple pre- and posttests to the Pretest–Posttest One Group controls _____, _____, and _____.

**5.** Maturation, instrumentation, and testing effects are eliminated as serious threats in the Time Series One Group if these changes are unlikely to occur in the time series exactly when the independent variable is _____.

. . . . . . . . . . . . . . . . . . . . . . . . . . . . . . . . . . . . . . . . . . . . . . . . . . . . . . . . . . . . . . .

**1.** See text
**2.** comparison
**3.** experimental mortality, instrumentation, testing effects
**4.** maturation, instrumentation, and testing effects
**5.** introduced

## Designs Adding Comparison Group Observations

A group that is neither randomly selected and assigned nor exposed to $X$ is called a *comparison group*. A group that is randomly selected, assigned, and exposed to $X$ is called a *control group*. Random selection and assignment of units are important because they provide good reason for believing that there is no difference between the treatment and control groups prior to the introduction of $X$. In other words, without randomization, pretest equivalency cannot be assumed. Without equivalency, the investigator has no way of knowing whether the posttest treatment group differs from the posttest conparison group because the former is exposed to $X$ and the latter is not or because the groups were different to begin with. So, randomization produces control groups that establish equivalency, which makes for a stronger experimental test; and nonrandomization produces comparison groups that do not establish equivalency, which provides a weaker experimental test.

POSTTEST COMPARISON GROUP

By adding a comparison group to the Posttest One Group, we obtain the *Posttest Comparison Group*, in which nonrandomly selected and assigned treatment and comparison groups are observed after $X$ occurs. The comparison group design is diagramed with dashes between the rows of the groups.

Form:

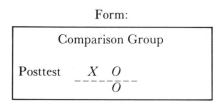

Example:

A nonrandomly selected and assigned group exposed to the campaign canvass is compared with a nonrandomly selected and assigned group not exposed to the canvass.

The addition of a comparison group to the Posttest One Group brings history under some measure of control, since specific events in addition to $X$ occur both to the treatment and comparison groups and would not account for treatment–comparison group differences. Adding a comparison group, however, increases the threat of selection and selection–maturation interaction.

This design is a relatively weak approach to causal inference. Its most serious flaws are selection, experimental mortality, and selection–maturation interaction. It does, however, control to some extent the factors of history, testing effects, and instrumentation. This design is superior to the Posttest One

Group and the Pretest–Posttest One Group but is certainly inferior to the Time Series One Group.

PRETEST–POSTTEST COMPARISON GROUP

A comparison group added to the Pretest–Posttest One Group creates the *Pretest–Posttest Comparison Group,* in which treatment and comparison groups are observed before and after $X$ occurs.

Form:

| Pretest–Posttest | $O$ | $X$ | $O$ |
|---|---|---|---|
| | $O$ | | $O$ |

Example:

Before and after observations of a nonrandomly assigned group that is canvassed is compared with before and after observations of a nonrandomly assigned group that is not canvassed.

In comparison to the Pretest–Posttest One Group, this design achieves control over:

*History (specific events in addition to X) affects both groups and would not account for posttest treatment and comparison group differences.*

*Maturation (natural changes) would occur in both groups and therefore would not account for differences between treatment and comparison groups.*

*Instrumentation (changes in the measuring instrument or method of observation) would affect both groups alike and therefore would not explain treatment–comparison group differences.*

*Testing effects (pretest effects on posttest behavior) occur in both groups and therefore would not explain treatment–comparison group differences.*

The addition of a comparison group to the Pretest–Posttest One Group has two costs:

*Selection (nonrandom sampling errors may produce differences between the two nonrandomly selected and assigned groups.*

*Selection–maturation interaction (nonrandom sampling of units producing different rates of natural change) may produce differences between the two nonrandomly selected and assigned groups.*

The Pretest–Posttest Comparison Group is widely used in social science where many politically interesting groups consist of naturally assembled collectivities such as precincts, cities, states, nations and other units that cannot be randomly assigned treatments. This design controls for history, maturation, testing effects, and instrumentation in an effective manner but lacks control over instability, selection, selection–maturation interaction, and regression effects. This design is stronger than the Pretest–Posttest One Group and the Posttest Comparison Group but is inferior to the Time Series One Group.

TIME SERIES COMPARISON GROUP

By adding a comparison group to the Time Series One Group, the *Time Series Comparison Group* is obtained, in which a treatment and a comparison group are observed periodically before and after $X$ occurs.

Form:

| | Comparison Group |
|---|---|
| Time Series | $O\ O\ O\ X\ O\ O\ O$ |
| | $O\ O\ O\ \ \ \ O\ O\ O$ |

Example:

A series of before and after observations of a nonrandomly selected and assigned group that is exposed to the canvass is compared with a series of before and after observations of a nonrandomly selected and assigned group that is not exposed to the canvass.

Adding the comparison group to the Time Series One Group has the effect of controlling for history because specific events affecting the treatment group also affect the comparison group and therefore would not explain differences between the groups. Adding the comparison group does not produce adverse effects.

This is a relatively powerful design. It achieves some control over each of the internal validity factors. It is superior to the Time Series One Group or the Pretest–Posttest Comparison Group.

**LEARNING AID**

**1.** Define, diagram, and identify the Posttest Comparison Group, Pretest–Posttest Comparison Group, and Time Series Comparison Group.

**2.** Randomization establishes (pretest/posttest) equivalency between the treatment and _____ groups.

3. Adding a comparison group to the Posttest One Group controls for _____ but increases the threat of _____ and _____.

4. History is controlled to some extent in all three comparison group designs because specific events in addition to $X$ would affect _____ the treatment and control groups, and therefore, would not explain differences found between the _____ and _____ groups.

5. Selection and selection–maturation interaction are serious threats in comparison group designs because the groups are not _____ assigned.

6. When groups are randomly assigned to treatment and nontreatment conditions, there is evidence for pretest _____ between the groups.

7. If pretest equivalency between the groups cannot be established, then the groups may have differed regardless of whether _____ was introduced.

. . . . . . . . . . . . . . . . . . . . . . . . . . . . . . . . . . . . . . . . . . . . . . . . . . . . . . . . .

1. see text
2. pretest, control
3. history, selection, selection–maturation interaction
4. both, treatment, control
5. randomly
6. equivalency
7. $X$ (the treatment)

## Designs Adding a Control Group

A *control group* is a group that is randomly selected, assigned, and exposed to the treatment $(X)$. Random selection and assignment establish pretest equivalency between the treatment and control groups and therefore strengthen the experimental test. Control groups are diagrammatically represented by "$R$'s" (randomization) and by the absence of dashes between the rows.

POSTTEST CONTROL GROUP

By adding a control group (i.e., by randomizing) rather than by adding a comparison group to the Posttest One Group, we obtain the *Posttest Control Group,* in which randomly selected and assigned treatment and control groups are observed after $X$ occurs.

Form:                                                              Example:

| Control Group | | |
| --- | --- | --- |
| | $R$ | $X$ $O$ |
| Posttest | $R$ | $O$ |

A randomly selected and assigned group is exposed to the canvass and is compared with a randomly selected and assigned group not exposed to the canvass.

There are five advantages of the Posttest Control Group over the Posttest Comparison Group:

*Instability (random sampling error) can be detected and controlled by tests of statistical significance.*

*Selection (nonrandom sampling error) is controlled by random selection and assignment.*

*Maturation (natural change) is controlled in that it would occur to both randomly selected and assigned groups.*

*Selection–maturation interaction (nonrandom sampling of units producing different rates of natural change) is controlled by random selection and assignment of the groups.*

*Experimental mortality (nonrandom loss of units) can be detected by counting the loss rate for each group and testing whether the difference between groups in loss is statistically significant.*

The Posttest Control Group has no disadvantages with respect to internal validity. This design is one of the most efficient and powerful experimental approaches. It controls each of the factors of internal validity, and it is particularly effective with testing effects since no pretests are taken. It even gains some control over selection–treatment interaction (by randomizing) and testing effects and reactive testing (by having no pretests) in the realm of external validity. However, this design does lack the capability of measuring change from the time prior to $X$ to that after $X$, which is often desirable information to secure.

PRETEST–POSTTEST CONTROL GROUP

By adding a control group rather than a comparison group to the Pretest–Posttest One Group, we arrive at the *Pretest–Posttest Control Group* in which a treatment and a control group are observed before and after $X$ occurs.

Form:

|  | Control Group | | |
| --- | --- | --- | --- |
| *Pretest–Posttest* | $R$  $O$ | $X$ | $O$ |
|  | $R$  $O$ |  | $O$ |

Example:

The before and after observations of a randomly selected and assigned group exposed to the canvass are compared with the before and after observations of a randomly selected and assigned group not exposed to the canvass.

The Pretest–Posttest Control Group has four internal validity advantages over the Pretest–Posttest Comparison Group:

*Instability (random sampling error) is detectable by tests of statistical significance.*

*Selection (nonrandom sampling error) is controlled by randomly selecting and assigning both groups.*

*Selection–maturation interaction (nonrandom sampling of units producing different rates of natural change) is controlled by randomization.*

*Regression effects (pseudoshifts in scores produced by selection on the basis of score extremity) are controlled by random selection and assignment techniques.*

The Pretest–Posttest Control Group is a powerful design controlling all nine internal validity factors. Requiring a pretest, however, it may not be feasible in many field situations. With a pretest, reactive testing (generalization to unpretested populations) is its most serious external validity shortcoming.

TIME SERIES CONTROL GROUP

By adding a control group rather than a comparison group to the Time Series One Group, we obtain the *Time Series Control Group*. In this design, randomly selected and assigned treatment and control groups are observed periodically before and after $X$ occurs.

Form:

|  | Control Group | | |
|---|---|---|---|
| Time Series | $R \ O \ O \ O \ X \ O \ O \ O$ | | |
|  | $R \ O \ O \ O \quad\ \ O \ O \ O$ | | |

Example:

A series of before and after observations of a randomly selected and assigned group that is exposed to the canvass is compared with a series of before and after observations of a nonrandomly selected and assigned group that is not exposed to the canvass.

Adding a control group rather than a comparison group to the Time Series One Group provides stronger control over history, instability, selection, selection–maturation interaction, and regression effects. The Time Series Control Group is a powerful design providing effective control over all the internal validity factors. Since random assignment of the groups is not feasible in many social science field situations, this design is applied less frequently than the Time Series Comparison Group.

## LEARNING AID

**1.** Define, diagram, and identify the Posttest Control Group, Pretest–Posttest Control Group, and Time Series Control Group.
**2.** The advantage of control group designs lies in their control over _____, _____, and _____.
**3.** The virtue of a posttest type of design over a pretest–posttest type of design in the realm of internal validity is _____ and in the realm of external validity is _____.

. . . . . . . . . . . . . . . . . . . . . . . . . . . . . . . . . . . . . . . . . . .

**1.** See text
**2.** instability, selection, selection–maturation interaction
**3.** testing effects, reactive testing

## Modified Designs

The previous nine experimental designs do not exhaust the alternative approaches to experimentation. They do, however, describe the most basic and common designs in social research. Two other designs should be mentioned because they illustrate alterations in the basic designs. They are the Separate Pretest–Posttest Control Group and the Solomon Four Group.

### SEPARATE PRETEST–POSTTEST CONTROL GROUP

In this design a control group is observed before exposure to treatment, and a separate randomly selected and assigned group is observed after exposure to $X$.

Form:

|  | Control Group | | |
|---|---|---|---|
| Separate | | | |
| Pretest | $R$ | $O$ | $(X)$ |
| Posttest | $R$ | $X$ | $O$ |

Example:

One random sample is randomly assigned to the control condition of a pretest observation and an $X$, whereas the other random sample is randomly assigned to the campaign canvass and the posttest observation.

This design modifies the Pretest–Posttest One Group design by conducting the pretest and the posttest on separate randomly selected and assigned groups. The advantages of this design over the Pretest–Posttest One Group involve avoiding testing effects (pretest effects on posttest behavior) and reactive testing (generalizing to unpretested populations). In many social research situations, it is difficult to obtain subjects who will cooperate with both a pretest and a post-test. This design requires participation in only one. A treatment is applied to the pretest group even though no posttest observation is taken to avoid the threat of selection (differences in cooperativeness and accessibility between groups).

The Separate Pretest–Posttest Control Group is superior to the Pretest–Posttest One Group. Its main weaknesses are lack of control over history and experimental mortality. Its major strength lies in its control over testing effects and reactive testing. It is a relatively practical design for many social and political situations.

SOLOMON FOUR GROUP

This design starts with the Pretest–Posttest Control Group and adds the Post-test Control Group. In what is called the Solomon Four Group, a treatment and a control group are observed before and after $X$, whereas a treatment and a control group are observed after $X$ occurs.

|  |  |  |  |
|---|---|---|---|
| **Form:** | | | **Example:** |

Form:

```
Four Group

R   O₁   X   O₂
R   O₃        O₄
R        X   O₅
R            O₆
```

$$
\begin{array}{llll}
R & O_1 & X & O_2 \\
R & O_3 &   & O_4 \\
R &     & X & O_5 \\
R &     &   & O_6
\end{array}
$$

Example:

Four groups are randomly selected and assigned to one of four conditions: (1) observations before and after exposure to the canvass, (2) observations before and after nonexposure to the canvass, (3) observations after exposure to the canvass, and (4) observations after nonexposure to the canvass.

The Solomon Four Group is a highly sophisticated experimental design. Although its six required observations are costly in terms of time and energy, it effectively controls for testing effects and reactive testing. It more effectively controls for all internal validity factors than any other design. Internal validity can be tested with four separate replications: the experimental effect should be stronger in $O_2$ than in $O_1$, in $O_2$ than in $O_4$, in $O_5$ than in $O_6$, and in $O_5$ than in $O_3$. If the time and financial costs can be met, then this design is rated as the strongest general design for social and political research. If the costs cannot be met, then the Posttest Control Group or the Time Series Control Group should be used.

## LEARNING AID

**1.** Define, diagram, and identify the Separate Pretest–Posttest Control Group and the Solomon Four Group.
**2.** The Separate Pretest–Posttest Control Group provides effective control over the internal validity factor, _____, and the external validity factor, _____.
**3.** A treatment is applied to the pretest in the Separate Pretest–Posttest Control Group to avoid the threat of _____.
**4.** The Separate Pretest–Posttest Control Group lacks control over _____ and _____.
**5.** The Solomon Four Group is a combination of two designs: _____ and _____.
**6.** The Solomon Four Group requires _____ observations but can test internal validity with _____ separate replications.

. . . . . . . . . . . . . . . . . . . . . . . . . . . . . . . . . . . . . . . . . . . . . . . . . . . . .

**1.** See text
**2.** testing effects, reactive testing
**3.** selection
**4.** history, experimental mortality
**5.** Pretest–Posttest Control Group, Posttest Control Group
**6.** six, four

### Internal Validity Matrix

Before concluding the discussion of experimental research, the student should learn the use of Table 14–2, "The Internal Validity Matrix." In this table, each of the basic and modified designs we previously examined is listed and evaluated according to whether it controls each of the nine factors of internal validity. Whenever a design controls a validity factor, a plus (+) is entered in the appropriate row and column of the matrix. Whenever a factor is left uncontrolled, a minus (–) is entered. Whenever a factor is irrelevant to a design or whenever there is insufficient information about a factor, nothing is entered in the cell.

**Table 14–2.** INTERNAL VALIDITY MATRIX

| Designs: | History | Instability | Selection | Maturation | Instrumentation | Selection–Maturation/Interaction | Testing Effects | Experimental Mortality | Regression Effects |
|---|---|---|---|---|---|---|---|---|---|
| 1. Posttest One Group | − | | | − | − | | | | − |
| 2. Pretest–Posttest One Group | − | − | + | − | − | | | + | − |
| 3. Time Series One Group | − | + | + | + | + | + | + | + | + |
| 4. Posttest Comparison Group | + | − | − | − | + | − | + | − | + |
| 5. Pretest–Posttest Comparison Group | + | − | − | + | + | − | + | + | − |
| 6. Time Series Comparison Group | + | + | + | + | + | + | + | + | + |
| 7. Posttest Control Group | + | + | + | + | + | + | + | + | + |
| 8. Pretest–Posttest Control Group | + | + | + | + | + | + | + | + | + |
| 9. Time Series Control Group | + | + | + | + | + | + | + | + | + |
| 10. Separate Pretest–Posttest Control Group | − | + | + | + | − | + | + | − | + |
| 11. Solomon Four Group | + | + | + | + | + | + | + | + | + |

The purpose of presenting Table 14–2 is to show the strengths and weaknesses of a design in relation to other designs. The student should neither memorize such a table nor use it reflexively as a reference source without thinking through the logic of validity control on a factor by factor basis. The Internal Validity Matrix is merely a guideline to the validity factors and is not a hard-and--fast list of absolutes. This table, in other words, should not substitute for the student's own thinking about the interpretation of a particular design.

## SUMMARY LEARNING AID

**1.** Be able to name and define the fifteen factors affecting the internal and external validity of experiments.

**2.** Be able to define and diagram each of the experimental designs.

**3.** Be able to use the internal validity matrix to evaluate various experimental designs.

**4.** Be able to name, diagram, analyze (identify the major validity factors), and evaluate an experimental design such as the following.

   a. In September, 1947, the United Nations launched a massive information campaign in Cincinnati, Ohio, to demonstrate how a community could become informed on world affairs. The campaign lasted for six months and consisted of distributing films, literature, circulars, radio programs, radio spots, seminars, and speakers for service clubs. Social scientists were interested in determining the effect of the information campaign on the citizens' interest, information, and opinions about the United Nations. The experimental design involved interviewing a random cross-section of the community before the campaign and interviewing a different random cross-section after the campaign ended. During the six-month period, the "cold war" with the Soviet Union was greatly intensified and was widely reported in the newspapers. At the end of the educational campaign, the researchers found little change in the citizens' interest, information, and opinion about the United Nations. The researchers concluded that information must be functional or made interesting to the ordinary man, so he can see how it affects his own affairs.[1]

   b. On January 1, 1958 the European Economic Community (EEC)— composed of France, Germany, Italy, Belgium, Netherlands, and Luxembourg—came into effect. These six countries joined together to pursue common policies in a wide variety of substantive areas, among which were the lowering of internal (within EEC) tariffs, the merging of external tariffs to provide and maintain a common tariff wall with respect to third countries, and the pursuit of common policies in several functional areas such as agriculture and transport. Caporaso and Pelowski were interested in determining what effects the formation of the EEC had on trade patterns.[2] One measure of trade patterns is a country's exports to the EEC as a proportion of its exports to the rest of the world (exports to EEC/exports to world). The researchers focused on Germany's exports to the EEC as a proportion of its world exports and examined the data at annual intervals from 1955 to 1965. The graph shows a small increase in the indicator immediately after the formation of the EEC, followed by a decrease and then an average rise in trade figures for the rest of the time points.

   c. In mid-August, 1971, President Nixon inaugurated a new economic policy aimed at checking inflation, stimulating business, and restoring confidence in the dollar abroad. All of this was to be accomplished by a series of steps, starting with a 90-day freeze on wages, prices, rents and dividends, plus the imposition of a 10% tax on imports, an end to the excise tax on autos, a tax cut for individuals, and a suspension of gold payments. The freeze then was lifted, more flexible control machinery was set up, and by the year's end the dollar was devalued, the import surcharge removed, and taxes cut. Suppose a political scientist is interested in examining the effectiveness of wage–price controls. He observes that the cost of living was up 3.8% before controls but up only 2.5% one year after controls. He sees that the average size of pay increases negotiated by unions was 10% before controls and 7.5% one year afterward. The rate of unemployment was 5.9% before and 5.5% one year after.

d. A high school government instructor is disappointed about the content of his basic American Government course, which is required of all Seniors. The course content is structured around a traditional textbook, strongly oriented toward a historical-descriptive-institutional emphasis. He decides to implement a new approach that uses paperbacks rather than a text in addition to role playing, simulation games, guest speakers, and films. He believes that the new course will produce students who know as much basic information as in the traditional course, plus students who are more interested in politics and who have a greater capacity to analyze political phenomena critically and realistically. In order to compare approaches, the instructor arranges to have the students randomly assigned to the four sections of the course he teaches. He intends to teach two courses by the traditional technique and two by the innovative technique. Tests are developed to measure such things as political information, political interest, political analysis skills, and political activity. One class using each approach is tested prior to the course; the other two are not given such tests. At the end of the course, tests are administered to all students concerning the items mentioned. The class with the innovative technique that was pretested scored highest on every part of the final test. The traditional class that was pretested scored next highest on each part of the test. The other innovative class scored third highest, except for scoring lowest on political information. The other traditional class scored lowest on all items, except it scored third highest on political information.

. . . . . . . . . . . . . . . . . . . . . . . . . . . . . . . . . . . . . . . . . . . . . . . . . . . . . . . . . . . . . . . . . .

**1.** The fifteen factors may be defined as follows:

INTERNAL VALIDITY:
1. *History* involves the occurrence of specific events in addition to the experimental variable.
2. *Instability* refers to random sampling and measurement error.

3. *Selection* refers to systematic error in the sampling of units.
4. *Maturation* involves natural changes in units that evolve with the passage of time.
5. *Instrumentation* designates changes in the measuring instrument or the method of observation.
6. *Selection–maturation interaction* refers to nonrandom sampling of units, which also results in different rates of maturation between groups.
7. *Testing effects* occur when the process of taking a test or being observed affects the second test or observation.
8. *Experimental mortality* refers to the nonrandom loss of units resulting in differences between groups.
9. *Regression effects* occur when units are selected for treatment on the basis of their extremity producing pseudoshifts in scores.

EXTERNAL VALIDITY:

1. *Selection treatment interaction* is a lack of generalizability to a population where nonrandom sampling of units produces unrepresentative treatment effects.
2. *Multiple treatment interference* is a lack of generalizability to the effects of a single treatment where more than one treatment is applied simultaneously or where a treatment is reapplied to the same units.
3. *Irrelevant treatment replicability* is a lack of generalizability to a treatment where a treatment is not fully reproduced.
4. *Irrelevant measure responsiveness* is a lack of generalizability of measures where each measure contains its own irrelevant components and sources of error, which may produce apparent effects.
5. *Reactive testing* is a lack of generalizability to unpretested populations, where the pretest affects a second test.
6. *Reactive arrangements* is a lack of generalizability to other settings, where experimental conditions are atypical of conditions of regular application of the treatments.

**2.** See Table 14–1.
**3.** See Table 14–2.
**4a.** *Name:* This design most closely approximates the separate Pretest–Posttest Control Group design. A control group is randomly selected and observed before exposure to a treatment. In this case the treatment is the same as the treatment given to the treatment group, but this should not affect the logic of the design. A separate but equivalent group is exposed to the treatment and is then observed.

*Diagram:* R  O  (X)
R      X   O

*Analysis:*  The main strength of this design lies in its controlling for instability and testing effects. History and multiple treatment interference appear to be its major deficiencies. History in particular should be considered a threat to validity since the researchers indicated that the "cold war" intervened and intensified during the course of the experiment. Intensification of the war rather than the information campaign could have caused a change. Care should be exercised about generalizing the effectiveness of any single component of the treatment. The information campaign consisted of multiple treatments (films, lectures, radio spots, etc.). To generalize to the effectiveness of any one treatment is to commit multiple treatment interference. Experimental mortality, in addition, should be considered a possible threat if evidence indicates that a large number of persons moved in or out of the city during the six-month campaign. Finally, selection treatment interaction should be considered if the researchers generalize their findings about the effects of the treatment on residents of Cincinnati to citizens in general. It is possible that Cincinnati residents respond to the treatment differently from another population to which we may wish to generalize.

*Evaluation:*  The separate Pretest–Posttest Control Group is a relatively efficient and powerful design. Requiring only two observations and contact with a unit only once, it is suitable for many social and political settings. The Posttest Comparison Group design uses only two observations but is significantly inferior to the design selected by the researchers. The Pretest–Posttest One Group is also a two-observation design but is essentially weaker in the factors of instability, testing effects, and reactive testing. The Posttest Control Group is a two-observation design and is more powerful than the present design. The major problem with using the Posttest Control Group design in this situation is the inability of the researchers to randomly assign the treatment to some members of the community and to randomly withhold it from others. The separate Pretest–Posttest Control Group design appears to have been an appropriate selection by the researchers.

**4b.**  *Name:*  This experiment employs the Time Series One Group design. Germany's trade patterns are observed for three years before and seven years after the formation of the EEC.

*Diagram:*   O   O   O   O   X   O   O   O   O   O   O   O

*Analysis:*  Lack of control over history and external validity are the most serious deficiencies of the Time Series One Group design. The researchers should consider whether other events such as monetary changes, the 1958 recession, or other events may have intervened to disturb the "experiment." Researchers also must take care in generalizing from Germany's experience to the experience of EEC (selection treatment interaction) and from their measure of trade patterns to other measures of trade patterns (irrelevant measure responsiveness). The researchers must rule out the possibility that the trend line of the data resembles that of the normal economic development (maturation) of an industrialized nation such as Germany. Finally, they should consider whether pretreatment variability in the time series is as great as posttreatment variability (instability). The researchers checked this with tests of statistical significance and found that indeed the random variability of the time series was great enough to account for the occurrence of the upswing after the formation of the EEC.

*Evaluation:* The Time Series One Group design is greatly superior to the Posttest One Group and the Pretest–Posttest One Group designs. Since the formation of the EEC was an international phenomenon, the assignment of the treatment was beyond the control of the researchers. Thus, designs involving random assignment of the treatment to the units are not feasible. The Time Series Comparison Group is more powerful than the Time Series One Group. Why did the researchers not use this design? If the alternative hypothesis of instability had been rejected, then they might have compared Germany's trend line with that of a "comparable" non–EEC country. The instability hypothesis was accepted, and it was not necessary to go any further. The time series comparison group design, however, would have been an even stronger design for deciding whether the formation of the EEC had an effect on trade patterns.

**4c.** *Name:* Pretest–Posttest One Group design.

*Diagram:* O X O

*Analysis:* The most serious weaknesses of this design are history, instability, maturation, regression effects, and multiple treatment interference. Other events such as changes in fiscal policy, money supply, and trade deficits may have contributed to the observed change. The charge may not be significant; it could be within the range of random fluctuation or variability (instability). The change could be part of the natural development of the economy rather than a treatment effect (maturation). Particular attention should be focused on the possible explanation that the program was put into effect when inflation was extremely high and that the observed changes are really pseudo-shifts in the direction of the normal or average inflation rate (regression effects). Finally, recognizing that the new economic program consisted of a number of different treatments, the investigators should be cautious in generalizing about the effectiveness of the wage and price control component (multiple treatment interference).

*Evaluation:* The Pretest–Posttest One Group design is a relatively weak basis for a causal inference. The investigators could have easily devised a time series one group design. They could certainly have added three or more pretreatment observations and perhaps one or more posttreatment observations. Even if they were not able to add any more posttreatment observations, a modified Time Series One Group design could have more effectively controlled for instability, maturation, and regression effects than the Pretest–Posttest One Group design.

**4d.** *Name:* This design is the Solomon Four Group design. Subjects are assigned randomly to four different test conditions. One pair of groups is administered both pretests and posttests; the other pair is given only posttests. One group from each pair is exposed to the experimental treatment.

*Design:* $R \quad O_1 \quad X \quad O_2$
$R \quad O_3 \qquad\; O_4$
$R \qquad\;\; X \quad O_5$
$R \qquad\qquad O_6$

*Analysis:* The Solomon Four Group is one of the most sophisticated experimental designs. All internal validity factors are controlled. In this particular setting, there is some danger that the experimental treatments (namely, the innovative courses) and their absence (namely, the traditional courses) are taught in a consistent fashion by the instructor. This hampers the generalizability of the study, since it might be difficult to duplicate any technique at another time. Generalizability is hampered also by the student population that the instructor must deal with. The findings indicate that $O_2$ and $O_4$ both exceed $O_5$ and $O_6$. However, the fact that $O_2 > O_4$ suggests the possibility that $O_2$ and $O_4$ were inflated artificially somewhat by the use of pretests, $O_1$ and $O_3$. The fact that $O_2 > O_4$ and $O_5 > O_6$, with one exception, supports the hypotheses. It was hypothesized that, with respect to political information, $O_2 = O_4$ and $O_5 = O_6$. In fact, an anomaly occurred; $O_2 > O_4$ and $O_5 < O_6$. This suggests the possibility of an interaction between the pretest, $O_1$, and the treatment for that group. One possible interpretation is that the pretest keys students to picking up the traditional information, which subsequently is supplemented by factors in the innovative approach.

*Evaluation:* This design requires the ability to randomize selection into four different groups. This is often hard to achieve in many social settings. Problems also may arise with respect to ensuring duplication of the experimental treatment in two different groups. Nevertheless, this design offers validity checks and controls and information found in no other design.

## FOOTNOTES

1. S. Star and H. Hughes, "Report on an Educational Campaign: The Cincinnati Plan for the United Nations," *American Journal of Sociology* 55 (1950): 389–403.
2. J. Caporaso and A. Pelowski, "Economic and Political Integration in Europe: A Time-Series Quasi-Experimental Analysis," *American Political Science Review* 65 (June 1971): 418–33.

# 15
# Survey Research

# INTRODUCTION

## Rationale

*Survey research* is a method of collecting standardized information by interviewing a sample representative of some population. Survey research is today probably the most prevalent data collection technique in the social sciences. Survey research is commonly used to ascertain public opinion on political issues and candidates. It is used to determine consumer preferences for new products. Governmental agencies use surveys to identify human needs, resources, and reactions to governmental programs. Surveys also are used by social scientists to collect standardized information so that generalizations about individual behavior may be formulated and tested. This unit examines the logic of survey research as it applies to the social sciences.

Survey research has two major strengths. First, it makes possible the collection of vast amounts of information on large numbers of people. Second, survey research information is accurate within specifiable ranges of sampling error. It is possible to specify how accurate a sample is likely to be and to improve accuracy by adjusting sample size or design.

Survey research also has several weaknesses. First, survey research is demanding of time and money. A large statewide survey may take several months to complete, and the cost may approach $20 or more per personal interview. Second, the survey is a reactive research technique, that is, the respondent is being presented with a stimulus and his reactions are observed. The interviewing situation, moreover, may create an unnatural atmosphere with which the respondent may cope by creating idealized or artificial answers. Third, survey research is a complicated technique requiring a great deal of knowledge on the part of the investigator.

We may conveniently divide the process of survey research into eight stages:

1. Specifying research objectives.
2. Choosing the survey design.
3. Selecting the sample.
4. Designing the questionnaire.
5. Interviewing the sample.
6. Processing the data.
7. Analyzing the results.
8. Writing the report.

There is not enough space available in this unit to examine each of the above stages of survey research. We will focus on four important stages: choosing the survey design, selecting the sample, designing the questionnaire, and interviewing. Information concerning the other phases are partially treated in the units of this text relating to problem formulation, data processing, and data analysis.

## LEARNING AID

1. Survey research is a method of collecting _____ information by interviewing a _____ representative of some _____.
2. Name the strengths and weaknesses of survey research.
3. Name the eight phases of survey research.

. . . . . . . . . . . . . . . . . . . . . . . . . . . . . . . . . . . . . . . . . . . . . . . . . . . . . . . . . .

1. standardized, sample, population
2. See text
3. See text

## Learning Objectives

After completing this unit, the student should be able to:

1. Define and identify survey research, unweighted cross-sectional designs, weighted cross-sectional designs, contrasting sample designs, recall designs, cohort analyses of cross-sectional surveys, cohort surveys, trend surveys, panel surveys, nonprobability samples, accidental samples, quota samples, judgmental samples, probability samples, simple random samples, systematic samples, stratified samples, cluster samples, total sampling error, sampling bias, random sampling error, closed-ended questions, open-ended questions, rapport, and probing.
2. Identify the strengths and weaknesses of survey research.
3. Identify the eight stages of survey research.
4. State and use the formula for estimating the sampling error for proportions for various sample sizes.
5. State and use the formula for determing sample size.
6. Identify the advantages and disadvantages of personal interviews and mail questionnaires.
7. Name and apply the rules governing the construction of questionnaire items.
8. Identify the guidelines for preparing for and conducting personal interviews.

## SURVEY DESIGN

Surveys may be cross-sectional or longitudinal. *Cross-sectional surveys* conduct observations at one point in time. *Longitudinal surveys,* on the other hand, conduct observations at two or more points in time.[1]

### Cross-Sectional Designs

Surveys which conduct observations in only one cross-section of time may be divided into three types: unweighted cross-sectional surveys, weighted cross-sectional surveys, and contrasting sample surveys.

UNWEIGHTED CROSS-SECTIONAL SURVEYS

A survey is *unweighted* if every element in the population has the same chance of being included in the sample. In unweighted surveys, the characteristics in the sample are supposed to be in proportion to the characteristics in the population. In other words, if 10% of the population is black, then about 10% of the sample should also consist of black persons. Unweighted cross-sectional surveys may be diagramed as follows:

| Form: | Example: |
|---|---|
| $R_u \quad O$ | A national sample of registered voters taken in September, 1976. |

where "$R$" represents random sampling, "$O$" stands for the observation, and subscript "$u$" refers to an unweighted sample.

When the primary purpose of a survey is to describe the characteristics of a population, unweighted surveys are ordinarily employed. Political campaign surveys are often unweighted because campaign managers want an accurate description of the political attitudes of some population.

WEIGHTED CROSS-SECTIONAL SURVEYS

A survey is *weighted* if some elements in the population are deliberately overrepresented in the sample. In weighted surveys, the sample characteristics are not in proportion to population characteristics. If 10% of the population is black, then blacks may be deliberately "oversampled" so that perhaps 50% of the sample consists of black persons. Weighted cross-sectional surveys are diagramed in this manner:

Form:

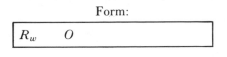

Example:

Blacks are oversampled so that they comprise 50% of the sample but 10% of the population.

where $R$ represents random sampling, subscript $w$ refers to a weighted sample, and $O$ symbolizes the observation or the interviewing of the sample at one point in time.

When the primary purpose of a survey is to analyze differences between subgroups in a population, then weighted cross-sectional surveys are frequently employed. If a subgroup constitutes a small fraction of the total population, then an unweighted sample would yield too few cases for statistical analysis. Accordingly, the smallest subgroup under consideration is often "weighted" or overrepresented in the sample so that a sufficient number of cases is obtained for analysis.

Obviously, a researcher cannot generalize directly to population characteristics from weighted sample data since the sample is not proportionate to the population. The investigator, however, may reweight the sample or exclude the oversample from analysis if he wants to estimate population characteristics.

CONTRASTING SAMPLE SURVEYS

Although many research problems are effectively approached with a survey of an entire population, some problems are approached more efficiently by drawing samples that contrast in the variable under consideration. An investigator, for example, may study the differences between elite and mass political participation by drawing a sample of party leaders and comparing it with a sample of the mass electorate. Surveys that sample from two or more subgroups or populations are called *contrasting sample surveys*. They take the following form:

Form:

$$
\begin{array}{ll}
R_1 & O \\
R_2 & O \\
R_3 & O \\
\cdot & \\
\cdot & \\
R_n & O
\end{array}
$$

Example:

Party leader sample.
Mass electorate sample.

where $R$ refers to random sampling; subscripts 1, 2, 3, . . . $n$ represent different subgroups or populations, and $O$ stands for the observation of the sample.

## Longitudinal Designs

*Longitudinal designs* conduct observations at two or more points in time. There are two major types: cohort and panel.

### COHORT SURVEYS

A *cohort* is the set of all people born at the same time. Another word for cohort is "generation." People born between 1900 and 1910 constitute a cohort or generation. People born between 1911 and 1920 form another cohort, and so forth. Social scientists study cohorts because cohorts indicate phases of maturation or classes of common experiences (depressions, wars, and so on). This knowledge sheds further light on many questions about social and political change. Some political scientists, for example, have found that age is related to conservatism, that is, older people are more conservative and younger people are less conservative. Is this finding a function on the one hand of *maturation,* of young people being wild and reckless but becoming more conservative with increasing responsibility and age, or on the other hand, of *generation,* of the older generation being more conservative having gone through the school of "hard knocks" with strict upbringing, the Depression, and World War II and of the younger generation being less conservative having grown up with JFK, Vietnam, protest marches, drugs, and Watergate? Cohort studies help to answer such interesting but complex questions about political and social change.

*Cohort surveys* are observations of a specific cohort (age group) at two or more points in time. For example, an investigator may conduct a cohort survey on the age–conservatism problem by observing a sample of college freshmen in 1972, observing another sample of the same population in 1976 when the students are seniors, and continuing periodic samplings of the same group. Here is a diagram of a cohort survey:

| | Form: | | | Example: |
|---|---|---|---|---|

| $R_c$ | $O$ | | | 1972, freshman sample |
|---|---|---|---|---|
| $R_c$ | | $O$ | | 1976, senior sample |
| $R_c$ | | | $O$ | 1980, four years after graduation |
| $R_c$ | | | | $O$ | etc. |

where $R$ is a random sample, subscript $c$ is the cohort from which the sample is drawn, and $O$ is the observation (survey).

Cohort surveys are useful longitudinal designs because they help to answer such questions as whether the relationship between age and conservatism is attributable more to maturation or generation. Suppose an investigator conducts five cohort surveys, with those born in 1900 forming the first cohort, those born in 1920, the second cohort, 1930, the third, 1940, the fourth, and 1950, the sixth. Suppose also the investigator were able to draw a sample and interview persons from each of these cohorts every five years until the cohort disappears (through death of the members). This type of cohort data suggests several test implications. If the "maturational theory" of the age–conservatism relationship is true, then conservative attitudes should increase as people get older regardless of their generation or cohort. On the other hand, if the "generation theory" is correct, then conservative attitudes should not increase as persons get older but be uniformly high in some cohorts and uniformly low in other cohorts. If, as a third rival theory, maturation and generation are not mutually exclusive but combine in their effect, then we might expect to observe increasing conservative attitudes with increasing age in all the cohorts but faster rates of change in some cohorts than others. Thus, cohort surveys provide many possibilities for systematic analysis of political and social change.

PANEL SURVEYS

*Panel surveys* involve observing the same sample at two or more points in time. The sample in this case is called the "panel." An example of a panel survey is an election survey in which the same individuals are reinterviewed in May, July, September, and November to determine when voting preferences form and change. The panel survey is diagramed as follows:

Form:                                          Example:

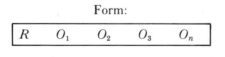

Election survey in which the same persons are reinterviewed two or more times.

where $R$ stands for random sampling and $O_1$, $O_2$, $O_3$, ... $O_n$ represent repeated observations or interviews of the same individuals.

The panel survey is the most effective and sophisticated approach to the study of social and political change. It explains total change at the individual level, something trend surveys cannot do. We will illustrate how total change can be identified in a panel study with what is called a "turnover table," which is shown in Table 15–1.

### Table 15-1.  TURNOVER TABLE

|        |            | $O_1$       |             |        |
|--------|------------|-------------|-------------|--------|
|        |            | Prefer Dem. | Prefer Rep. | Total  |
| $O_2$  | Prefer Dem. | 40%        | 15%         | 55%    |
|        | Prefer Rep. | 5          | 40          | 45     |
|        | Total      | 45%         | 55%         | 100%   |

Table 15–1 is a panel survey of candidate preferences at two points in time ($O_1$ and $O_2$). The upper left hand cell (40%) shows persons who prefer the Democratic candidate at both times of the survey; the lower right hand cell (40%) shows persons stable in their Republican candidate preferences. The upper right hand cell (15%) consists of those persons who preferred the Republican candidate at first observation and then changed to preferring the Democratic candidate, whereas the lower left cell (5%) includes those who initially preferred the Democrat but changed to the Republican candidate. The turnover table shows that 80% (40% plus 40%) of the preferences were stable. It shows a total change of 20% (5% plus 15%), with a net change of 10% (15% minus 5%). Thus, panel surveys not only provide information on net change but also information on total individual change, which is important to know if the investigator wants to identify who is likely to change in what directions and under what conditions. Approximating the experimental design called the Time Series One Group, the panel survey controls for most of the internal validity factors. However, it does lack control over history and experimental mortality. Experimental mortality is called "attrition" in the survey research language. Attrition is particularly a problem with panel surveys because it is so difficult to make sure that every individual is interviewed at each point in time. With people not at home, being on vacation, refusing to cooperate further, and so on, experimental mortality or what we call attrition becomes a serious problem for the investigator. Sometimes the attrition rate is so high there are not enough cases to perform statistical analyses. Sometimes the attrition rate is high enough so that there is serious question as to whether selection enters into the interpretation of the results. Panel surveys are expensive and time consuming, so they are found only infrequently in the social science literature. Yet panel surveys are the most powerful tool we have for analyzing social and political change using survey techniques.

## Quasi-longitudinal Designs

Designs that are longitudinal conduct observations at two or more points in time. Quasi-longitudinal designs are not legitimately longitudinal but approximate in varying degrees observations at or about two or more points in time.

### RECALL SURVEYS

*Recall surveys* conduct an observation at one point in time and have respondents remember information to establish a prior observation. They are practically useless as evidence for inferring causality. Nevertheless, they occasionally appear in the literature. For example, after the United States recognized China an investigator may want to study the impact of recognition on attitudes toward China. The investigator takes a survey of present attitudes and also asks respondents to recall their attitudes before recognition of China. The investigator then compares the remembered attitudes with present attitudes to determine how much they have changed. Recall surveys take the following form:

Form:

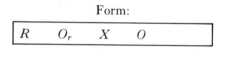
$$R \quad O_r \quad X \quad O$$

Example:

After the recognition of China $(X)$, a survey is conducted of present $(O)$ attitudes and attitudes recalled $(O_r)$ from the past.

where $R$ refers to random sampling, $O_r$ stands for recollection of prior attitudes or perceptions, and $O$ represents observation of present attitudes and perceptions.

The recall survey is the weakest kind of longitudinal design. It is longitudinal only in the sense that it attempts to establish two data points. It attempts to approximate the pretest–posttest one group design by recalling the pretest observation. In reality a recall survey is a cross-sectional survey attempting to approximate a longitudinal survey. Lacking control over history, maturation, and experimental mortality, recall designs provide a very weak basis for causal inferences. In addition, memory decay and distortion are forms of the maturational factor that is particularly likely to contribute to survey invalidity.

### COHORT ANALYSES OF CROSS-SECTIONAL SURVEYS

Like recall surveys, cohort analyses of cross-sectional surveys attempt to approximate longitudinal data with a cross-sectional observation. *Cohort analyses of cross-sectional surveys* show the distribution of a dependent variable on the age groupings (cohorts) in a survey at one point in time. For example, the age–conservatism relationship may be examined by using a cross-sectional survey containing the variables age and attitude toward conservatism. These variables are cross-classified in Table 15–2.

**Table 15–2.** CONSERVATISM BY AGE

|  |  | Age | | | |
|---|---|---|---|---|---|
|  |  | 18–34 | 35–50 | 51–65 | 65+ |
| Conservatism | Low | 65% | 45% | 25% | 15% |
|  | Medium | 20 | 30 | 30 | 20 |
|  | High | 15 | 25 | 45 | 65 |
|  |  | 100% | 100% | 100% | 100% |

Table 15–2 shows that age is strongly related to conservative attitudes. Whereas 15% of the 18–34 year old group (cohort) is conservative, 65% of the 65 and over cohort is conservative. This cohort analysis of conservatism with a cross-sectional survey demonstrates the relationship between the variables, but it does not explain why the relationship occurs, that is, whether maturation or generation (environment) is responsible for the relationship. Unless valid indicators for these factors can be found in the survey and used as control variables, cohort analysis of a cross-sectional survey cannot proceed much further than the description of a relationship. Cohort surveys take the following form:

Form:

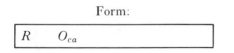

Example:

A cross-sectional survey with age cohort: 18–34, 35–50, 51–65, and over 65.

where $R$ is random sampling, $O$ is a cross-sectional observation, and the subscript *ca* refers to cohort analysis.

TREND SURVEYS

*Trend surveys* sample a population at two or more points in time. The population is the same but different samples are drawn for different observations. Periodic Gallup polls of national attitudes are examples of trend surveys. In describing attitudes toward presidential candidates, Gallup takes a different national sample in May, July, September, and November. Trend surveys are similar to cohort surveys in that both involve repeated samples of the same population. They differ, however, in that trend surveys sample all cohorts at each period of observation but cohort surveys repeatedly sample one cohort through time. Trend surveys may be diagramed in the following manner:

|  |  | Form: | | | Example: |
|---|---|---|---|---|---|
| $R$ | $O_1$ | | | | Periodic national Gallup polls |
| $R$ | | $O_2$ | | | |
| $R$ | | | $O_3$ | | |
| $R$ | | | | $O_n$ | |

where $R$ represents random sampling and $O_1$, $O_2$, $O_3$, . . .$O_n$ are different samples of the same population taken in sequence.

Trend surveys are useful for describing changes. Two trend surveys, for example, vividly illustrate gains and losses for candidates. Table 15–3 shows how a Democratic candidate gained and a Republican candidate lost support between two surveys, $O_1$ and $O_2$.

**Table 15–3.  A TREND SURVEY**

|  |  | $O_1$ (May) | $O_2$ (July) | Net Change |
|---|---|---|---|---|
| Preferences for: | Dem. | 45% | 55% | +10% |
|  | Rep. | 55 | 45 | −10% |
|  |  | 100% | 100% |  |

Having plotted the trend, the investigator may ask what caused the change. The investigator may hypothesize, for example, that the Democrats gained 10 percentage points because they began to appeal more to the working class. This hypothesis may be tested with the data shown in Table 15–4.

Table 15–4 shows that the net increase for Democrats between $O_1$ and $O_2$ can be accounted for by net shifts in the preferences of working class persons. Whereas the net change for the middle class was negligible, working class attitudes shifted 20% in the direction of the Democratic candidate. Thus, trend surveys provide a good picture of net change, the trend in the data, and a cursory glimpse of the factors behind the change.

Trend surveys have two main limitations. First, although they describe *net*

**Table 15-4.** CANDIDATE PREFERENCE BY WORKING CLASS FOR $O_1$ AND $O_2$

| | | | | Social Class | | | |
|---|---|---|---|---|---|---|---|
| | | Working Class | | | Middle Class | | |
| | | $O_1$ | $O_2$ | Net Change | $O_1$ | $O_2$ | Net Change |
| Preferences | Dem. | 40% | 60% | +20% | 49% | 50% | +1% |
| for: | Rep. | 60 | 40 | −20% | 51 | 50 | −1% |
| | | 100% | 100% | | 100% | 100% | |

*change,* they do not describe *total change* at the individual level. For example, the net change for the Democratic candidate among the middle class is a 1% gain, as shown in Table 15-4. This does not mean that only 1% of the respondents changed their preferences. This figure shows only the final balance. It could be that at $O_2$ 5% of those who preferred the Democratic candidate at $O_1$ shifted their preferences to the Republican candidate and 6% of those who preferred the Republican candidate at $O_1$ shifted their preferences to the Democratic candidate. This means there was a total change of 11%, leaving a net change of 1%. Thus, total change can exceed net change by a significant amount, but trend studies cannot pick up this type of information. Panel surveys do permit detection of total change at the individual level. A second limitation of trend surveys is lack of control over history as a factor of survey invalidity. Notice that trend surveys are similar to Separate Pretest–Posttest Control Group designs, which also lack control over history.

## LEARNING AID

1. A survey is _____ if some elements in the population are over-represented in the sample.
2. _____ surveys sample a population at two or more points in time.
3. Surveys that sample from two or more subgroups or populations are called _____.
4. A survey is _____ if every element in the population has the same chance of being included in the _____.
5. Surveys conducting an observation at one point in time and having respondents remember information to establish a prior observation are called _____ surveys.

**6.** A _____ is the set of all people born at the same time.

**7.** Surveys showing the distribution of a dependent variable on age groupings in a survey at one point in time are _____.

**8.** _____ surveys are observations of a specific age group at two or more points in time.

**9.** _____ surveys involve observing the same sample two or more points in time.

**10.** Whereas _____ surveys can indicate only net change, _____ surveys indicate not only net change but also total change at the individual level.

IDENTIFY AND DIAGRAM THE FOLLOWING SURVEY DESIGNS:

**11.** In *Communism, Conformity, and Civil Liberties,* Samuel Stouffer attempted to study how persons' images of communists are related to their willingness to deprive nonconformists of civil rights. He analyzes differences in tolerance of nonconformity by drawing a national sample of the population and a supplementary sample of local community leaders in the summer of 1954.

**12.** *In Children and Politics,* Fred Greenstein studied the development of childrens' feelings about political authority by administering a paper-and-pencil questionnaire to 659 New Haven fourth through eighth grade school children in 1958. He analyzed the political attitudes of the school children by grade in school.

**13.** In *The Political Life of American Teachers,* Harmon Zeigler analyzed the factors influencing the political behavior of high school teachers by interviewing 803 high school teachers living in Oregon. The sample was a stratified, random one in which the teaching population of medium and small towns was oversampled to provide a more equal distribution than would have otherwise occurred because of the heavy concentration of Oregon's population in metropolitan areas.

**14.** In *Personality and Social Change,* Theodore Newcomb studied the influence of the college environment on the political attitudes of the entire student body of Bennington College, which consisted of 600 women. He interviewed the 600 women each year from 1935 to 1939 and once again about fifteen years later.

**15.** In *The American Voter,* Campbell, Converse, Miller, and Stokes examined attitudes of American voters toward presidential candidates Eisenhower and Stevenson by conducting national samples of registered voters in 1952 and again in 1956.

**16.** An investigator examined the process of attitude change by interviewing 600 Republicans after President Nixon departed from office. The investigator asked about the respondents' past perceptions of Nixon along with their current predispositions.

**17.** Lou Harris conducts a national survey of registered voters in September of 1976.

. . . . . . . . . . . . . . . . . . . . . . . . . . . . . . . . . . . . . . . . . . . . . . . . . . . . . . . . . . . .

1. weighted
2. trend
3. contrasting sample surveys
4. unweighted, sample
5. recall
6. cohort
7. cohort analyses of cross-sectional surveys
8. cohort
9. panel
10. trend, panel
11. contrasting samples survey, $R \quad O$
$\qquad R \quad O$
12. cohort analyses of cross-sectional survey, $R \quad O_{ca}$
13. weighted cross-sectional survey, $R_w \quad O$
14. panel survey, $R \, O_1, \, O_2, \, O_3, \, O_4, \ldots \ldots \ldots O_{19}$
15. trend survey, $R \, O_1$
$\qquad R \quad O_2$
16. recall survey, $R \qquad O_r \, X \, O$
17. unweighted cross-sectional survey, $R_u \, O$

## SURVEY SAMPLING

In this section we will examine various kinds of sampling designs.[2] *Sampling* is the procedure by which the characteristics of a large number of elements called a *"population"* are inferred from a smaller number of elements called a *"sample."* The characteristics of populations are referred to as *parameters*; the characteristics of samples are called *statistics*. These distinctions are illustrated in Figure 15–1.

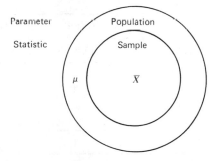

Parameter — Population

Statistic — Sample

$\mu$ — $\bar{X}$

**Figure 15–1. Parameters and Statistics**

## Nonprobability Samples

*Nonprobability samples* do not specify the probability of each element of the population being included in the sample. Nonprobability samples are convenient and economical, but they risk the fallacy of biased statistics, the error of making an inductive generalization on the basis of unrepresentative observations. There are three types of nonprobability samples: accidental, quota, and judgmental.

### ACCIDENTAL SAMPLES

An *accidental sample* consists of selecting the most available elements in the population. It is a very unreliable method of sampling, providing no way of evaluating how much bias is introduced into the sample. Examples of accidental samples include: street corner, classroom, and grocery store surveys. Television commentators and journalists often conduct surveys of this type and mistakenly label them as "random" surveys. Accidental samples are inadequate procedures for selecting units of observation and should not be used in scientific research.

### QUOTA SAMPLES

In *quota samples,* interviewers select a certain number of respondents fitting the characteristics (quota) that describe a population. Sex, age, and income are frequently used as "quota controls" since information about them for various populations is readily available in census reports. Determining the proportions for each of the characteristics, the researcher assigns a quota to each interviewer, such as the one shown in Table 15–5. Accordingly, the interviewer is instructed to bring back 20 interviews of respondents fitting the characteristics described in the table. Quota samples are quick and inexpensive to take but are

**Table 15–5.**  AN EXAMPLE OF AN INTERVIEWER'S QUOTA

| | Income | | | | | | |
|---|---|---|---|---|---|---|---|
| | Under $10,000 | | $10,000–20,000 | | Over $20,000 | | |
| Age: | Male | Female | Male | Female | Male | Female | Total |
| 20–29 | 1 | — | — | 1 | 1 | 1 | 4 |
| 30–44 | — | 1 | — | 1 | 3 | 1 | 6 |
| 45–64 | — | — | 1 | 1 | 2 | 3 | 7 |
| 65+ | — | — | — | — | 1 | 2 | 3 |
| Total | 1 | 1 | 1 | 3 | 7 | 7 | 20 |

often unreliable because of the subjective method the interviewer uses to select respondents.

JUDGMENTAL SAMPLES

In *judgmental samples,* the researcher selects those cases he thinks are typical of the population he is trying to describe. Judgmental samples are sometimes used to pretest questionnaires, by selecting different kinds of people who are likely to vary in terms of responses and reactions to the measuring instrument. Judgmental samples are also used sometimes in election forecasting, where bellwether precincts are selected for purposes of predicting election outcomes.

Judgmental samples have the advantages of speed and economy. However, they lack sampling error estimates and any objective basis for sampling elements of a population. Like other types of nonprobability samples, judgmental samples pose unknown risks to the fallacy of biased statistics and are not admissible for purposes of scientific research, except possibly for the pretesting of questionnaires.

## Probability Samples

*Probability samples* specify the probability of each element of the population being included in the sample. Probability samples are highly desirable bacause they permit the estimation of sampling error. Four types of probability samples will be discussed: simple random, systematic, stratified, and clustered samples.

SIMPLE RANDOM SAMPLES

*Simple random samples* give every element and every possible combination of elements in the population an equal chance of being selected. Simple random samples are selected by assigning a unique number to each element in the population and then drawing the sample through the random selection of numbers. Such numbers may be selected by some type of lottery device or by random numbers generated from a computer or by use of a table of random numbers. The method of random sampling by the use of a table is done by assigning a number to each element in the population, opening the table to any page, placing a finger on any number, and proceeding down columns or across rows of the table selecting the sample from the required set of digits appearing next to each other.

Simple random samples are desirable but often impractical. Many populations are too large for enumerating each element. Also researchers may not be able to obtain accurate lists identifying each of the elements for many populations. For these reasons, other forms of probability samples are often used instead of simple random samples.

In *systematic samples,* every $K$th element in a total list is selected for inclusion in the sample. If the list contains 50,000 elements and the investigator desires a sample of 500, he will select every one hundredth element from the population (50,000/500 = 100). The standard distance between elements in the population selected for the sample is called the *sampling interval.* The investigator starts the selection with a random start by drawing a random number in the first interval (between 1 and 100 in this example) and selecting elements at systematic intervals throughout the population. The *sampling fraction* is the proportion of the elements in the population that are samples. The sampling fraction for this example is one–one hundredth (500/50,000 = 1/100).

Systematic samples have the advantage of not requiring the enumeration of each element in the population. The interval selection process can even be simplified using approximating measurement devices. If a sample is being taken from a file of voter registration cards, the researcher can count out the cards for an interval, measure it with a ruler, and use that distance as the interval selection device. In this way, the researcher does not need to count out each population element in determining the intervals.

Systematic samples should be used only when the elements in the population are not grouped in some systematic fashion. If a systematic sample is selected from a population of married persons where the husband is listed first and the wife second, then only husbands or only wives would be drawn in the sample. To avoid any possible bias researchers should examine population lists to determine whether elements are arranged in any particular order before a systematic sample is selected.

STRATIFIED SAMPLES

In *stratified samples,* the population is divided into two or more groups called strata, and simple random samples are taken from each stratum and combined to form the total sample. A political researcher in conducting a statewide campaign survey may stratify on party registration. He does so by drawing random samples of Democrats, Republicans, Other, and Independents (see Figure 15–2).

Stratified samples are either proportional or disproportional. *Proportionally stratified samples* are simply unweighted samples, that is, the number of elements selected in each stratum is proportional to the size of the stratum relative to the size of the population. In other words, larger samples are taken from larger strata and smaller samples are taken from smaller strata. In a proportionally stratified sample, 10% of the total sample should be selected from a county (a stratum) that represents 10% of the registered voters in the state. *Disproportionally stratified samples* are weighted samples, that is, the number of elements selected in each stratum is not proportional to the size of that stratum

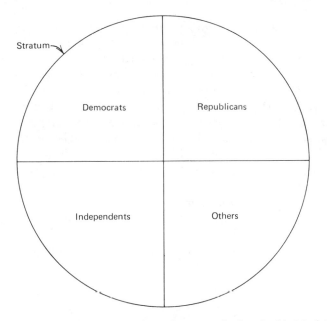

**Figure 15-2. A Stratified Sample. The population is divided into four strata such as Democrats, Republicans, Independents, and Other. A random sample is then taken from *each* stratum.**

relative to the size of the population. Larger samples may be selected from smaller strata than what one would expect based on the size of the strata. In a disproportionally stratified sample, 10% of the total sample may be selected from a county which represents only one percent of the registered voters in the state. Disproportionally stratified samples are taken for analysis purposes and must be reweighted if generalizations are to be made about the characteristics of the total population.

Stratified samples are often desirable because they reduce sampling error. In fact, stratified samples are often more accurate than simple random samples. Stratification reduces sampling error by using knowledge about the population. If party registration and county of residence are important variables and if the researcher knows party registration in each county, then he can stratify on these two variables and reduce the sampling error to zero for these two variables. Thus, the investigator ensures that these groups are correctly represented in the sample.

CLUSTER SAMPLES

The preceding probability designs have assumed the existence of a list of population elements. Many interesting social and political populations, however, cannot be easily listed for sampling purposes. In such cases, cluster sampling is often employed. In *cluster sampling,* the investigator divides the population into a large number of groupings called clusters, draws a sample (simple random or stratified) of clusters, lists each of the elements in each of the sampled clusters, and draws a simple random or stratified sample of elements from each cluster. Since cluster sampling usually involves sampling at two or more levels, it is also called *multistage cluster sampling* (see Figure 15–3).

An example of a multistage cluster sample may be taken from a survey of a city. The population of a city resides on city blocks, which can be treated as clusters. A sample of city blocks can be drawn (the first stage of sampling) and a list of individual households can be created for each sampled block. A subsample of households can then be drawn from the lists (second stage of sampling). Finally, the persons in each household can be listed and randomly sampled (third stage).

The advantages of cluster sampling include not having to list every element

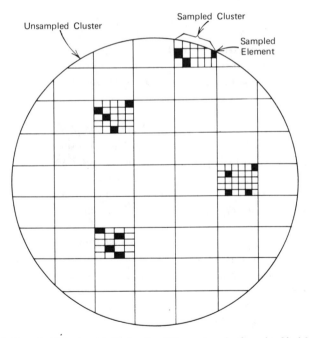

**Figure 15–3. A Clustered Sample. The population is divided into a large number of clusters. A random sample of clusters is drawn. Each of the elements (e.g., households) in the sampled clusters is listed. Finally, a random sample of elements is drawn from the sampled clusters.**

in the population and reducing travel time (since interviewers can concentrate their efforts in small or "clustered" areas). The major disadvantage of multi-stage sampling is that each stage of sampling contributes to the total sampling error, which sometimes can be rather large.

## LEARNING AID

1.  The characteristics of samples are _____ and the characteristics of populations are _____.
2.  _____ samples specify the probability of each element of the population being included in the sample.
3.  The three types of nonprobability samples are: _____, _____, and _____.
4.  In judgmental samples, the researcher selects those cases that he thinks are _____ of the population he is trying to describe.
5.  An accidental sample consists of selecting the most _____ elements in the population.
6.  In quota samples, _____ select a certain number of respondents fitting the characteristics that describe a population.
7.  Simple random samples give every element and every _____ of elements an _____ chance of being selected.
8.  In systematic samples, every _____ element in a total list is selected for inclusion in the sample.
9.  The proportion of elements in the population selected for inclusion in the sample is called the _____.
10.  In stratified samples, the population is divided into two or more strata and _____ samples are taken from each strata and combined to form the total sample.
11.  Weighted stratified samples are called _____ stratified samples, and unweighted stratified samples are called _____ stratified samples.
12.  In cluster sampling, the investigator divides the population into a (large/small) number of groupings called _____, draws a sample of _____, lists the _____ in each of the clusters, and draws a sample from each cluster.
13.  The interviewers are given great latitude in deciding who the respondents will be in (systematic/quota/stratified) sampling.
14.  The population is divided into groups, and random samples are taken in each group in (quota/stratified) sampling.
15.  Identify the kind of sample in each of the following designs:
     a.  A researcher wants to study ethnic elites, so he or she selects those black, chicano, and Indian persons identified as leaders in newspapers and magazines.

b.  A researcher takes a sample of 30,000 students at a state university by taking the student directory and selecting every one-hundredth name after a random start.

c.  A researcher wants to forecast the election results, so he or she goes to one precinct on election day and asks how people voted.

d.  An investigator takes a sample of national attitudes by dividing the nation into four sections: north, south, east, and west. He then takes random samples from each of these areas.

e.  An investigator takes a campaign sample by instructing interviewers to bring back a set of interviews having the following characteristics: 55% Republicans, 30% Democrats, and 15% Independent; 50% male and 50% female; and 90% white and 10% non-white.

f.  An investigator surveys opinions toward urban renewal in a community by dividing the city into city blocks, taking a random sample of blocks, and sampling the households.

g.  Student opinion at a state university is studied by obtaining a list of student identification numbers and selecting a sample of numbers from a table of random numbers.

h.  In a community where 90% of the population is white and 10% is black, a researcher studying racial relations divides the population into whites and blacks and draws 50% of the total sample from the white population and 50% from the black population.

. . . . . . . . . . . . . . . . . . . . . . . . . . . . . . . . . . . . . . . . . . . . . . . . . . . . . . . . . . . .

1. statistics, parameters
2. probability
3. accidental, quota, judgmental
4. typical
5. available
6. interviewers
7. combination, equal
8. $K$th
9. sampling fraction
10. simple random samples
11. disproportionally, proportionally
12. large, clusters, clusters, elements
13. quota
14. stratified
15. (a) judgmental, (b) systematic, (c) accidental, (d) stratified, (e) quota, (f) multistage cluster sampling, (g) sample random, (h) disproportionally stratified

## Sampling Error and Sample Size

The difference between the sample statistic and the population parameter is called *total sampling error*. If 58% of a population are registered as Democrats but 52% of a sample are registered as Democrats, then the difference between 58 and 52 reflects total sampling error. Total sampling error consists of two components: sampling bias and random sampling error.

---

Total sampling error = sampling bias + random sampling error

---

*Sampling bias* is the difference between the statistic and the parameter attributable to systematic errors resulting from the design of the sample. Nonprobability samples result in systematic selection errors. If a sample is drawn using an accidental sample survey design, such as a grocery store survey, then sampling bias is likely to occur as a result of the sample design. The particular grocery store may be more accessible to registered Republicans than Democrats and therefore account for some of the difference between the statistic and the parameter.

Sampling bias cannot be controlled. Increasing sample size does not reduce systematic errors resulting from an inadequate sample design. Sampling bias is also very difficult, if not impossible, to estimate, so that adjustments cannot be made in interpreting inferences about populations. The most effective way of dealing with sampling bias is to avoid it in the first place by designing samples that do not result in systematic selection errors. If probability and random sampling techniques are properly used, sampling bias can be eliminated as a factor contributing to total sampling error. Although sampling bias can be avoided through the use of probability samples, random sampling still remains as a source of total sampling error. Since random sampling error can be estimated and controlled, it is not as serious as sampling bias.

*Random sampling error* is the difference between the statistic and the parameter attributable to random variation in samples. Since different random samples of the same population will yield different sample statistics, differences between statistics and parameters can partially be explained by random sampling variations. These are variations resulting from the fact that samples rather than populations are being observed. The student will recall that since population parameters are normally not known, sampling error must be estimated. Figure 15–4 illustrates the variation of statistics from four different samples and the true population value in a study of attitudes toward the legalization of marijuana.

Random sampling error is estimated with the standard error formula, usually at the 95% confidence level. One formula is used for proportions and another one for means. To estimate the sampling error of a mean, the standard

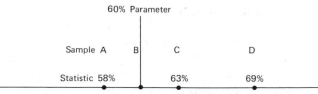

Figure 15–4.   Random Sampling Error

error formula is used:

Sampling Error for Means

$$SE_{\bar{x}} = \pm 2 \frac{s}{\sqrt{n}}$$

where $SE_x$ is the sampling error, or standard error (the terms can be used interchangeably), "2" is the approximate standard or z score for the 95% confidence level, "s" is the standard deviation of the sample, and "$n$" is the sample size.

Since sampling error is most frequently estimated with proportions, we will go into more detail with it recognizing that the logic of estimating the sampling error of a mean parallels that of estimating the sampling error of a proportion. The following formula should be used to estimate the sampling error of a proportion:

Sampling Error for Proportions

$$SE_p = \pm 2 \sqrt{\frac{p(1 - p)}{n}}$$

where $SE_p$ is the sampling error, 2 is the approximate standard or z score for the 95% confidence level, $\sqrt{\phantom{x}}$ is a square root sign, $p$ is the sample proportion and $n$ is the sample size.

The above formula shows sampling error to be a function of three factors: (1) the confidence level, 2; (2) dispersion in the population, $p$ $(1 - p)$; and (3) sample size, $n$. We will discuss each of these factors.

CONFIDENCE LEVEL

The standard score or z score at the 95% level is 1.96; but it is normally rounded up to 2 for ease of calculation. Rounding up also makes the estimate of sampling error even slightly more conservative. We will accept the 95% level as the conventional level in social science and treat 2 as a constant. The confidence level, of course, could be increased to the 99% level where $z = 2.6$. Since 2.6 is greater than 2, sampling error is increased by increasing the confidence level from 95% to 99% level. In other words, increased confidence is gained at the expense of making more vague or general types of statements. To repeat, we will set the confidence level at 95% and treat $z = 2$ as a constant.

## DISPERSION

The numerator in the formula, $p(1 - p)$, is an estimate of the dispersion in the population. If the population is heterogeneous, the numerator becomes larger. Heterogeneity is at a maximum when $p = .5$. For example, if 50% of a student sample favors legalization of marijuana and 50% opposes it, then the numerator is at a maximum and becomes $.5(1 - 0.5) = (.5)(.5) = .25$. The larger the numerator, that is, the greater the dispersion, then the more sampling error increases.

Conversely, the more homogeneous the population, the smaller the numerator and the sampling error become. A totally homogeneous population occurs when $p = 1$. If all the students favor legalization, then the numerator is at a minimum and becomes $1(1 - 1) = 1(0) = 0$. The smaller the numerator becomes, the smaller the fraction becomes. When the fraction becomes smaller, then sampling error also becomes smaller. So, as homogeneity increases, sampling error decreases.

In this text, we will assume $p = .5$. This assumes maximum dispersion in the population, an assumption that again makes the estimate of sampling error slightly more conservative and facilitates calculation for the student.

## SAMPLE SIZE

The size of the sample is depicted in the denominator of the formula. If the denominator increases, simpling error decreases. Thus, increasing the size of the sample will have the effect of reducing the sampling error. Increasing sample size is how random sampling error can be controlled, as we noted earlier. The location of $n$ under the square root sign at the 95% level implies that by reducing sampling error by one-half the sample size must be increased fourfold. Table 15–6 shows that to reduce sampling error from 2% to 1% the sample size must be increased from 2500 to 10,000, an increase of four times the sample size.

It is interesting to note that sampling accuracy (sampling error) is a function of the size of the sample and not the size of the population. Thus, a sample size of 400 will have a sampling error of 5% in a population of size 50,000 or 500,000 or 500,000,000. The size of the population does not affect sampling accuracy so long as the sampling fraction (sample size/population size) is less

**Table 15–6.  SAMPLING ERROR AND SAMPLE SIZE**[a]

| Sampling Error | Sample Size |
|:---:|:---:|
| ± 1% | 10,000 |
| ± 2 | 2,500 |
| ± 3 | 1,111 |
| ± 4 | 625 |
| ± 5 | 400 |
| ± 6 | 278 |
| ± 7 | 204 |
| ± 8 | 156 |
| ± 9 | 124 |
| ±10 | 100 |

[a] Assumes 95% confidence level ($z = 2$), $p = .5$, and a simple random sample.

than 10%. If the sampling fraction exceeds 10%, then population size becomes a relevant factor in reducing sampling error, and another factor should be added to the formula.[3]

CALCULATING SAMPLING ERROR

It is important to be able to use the sampling error formula to estimate the sampling error for various sample sizes. When planning a project, researchers often need different sized samples. The steps for solving two problems are illustrated below:

| STEPS | EXAMPLE 1 | EXAMPLE 2 |
|---|---|---|
| 1.  State the problem. | What is the sampling error for a sample size of 100 at the 95% confidence level and $p = .05$? | What is the sampling error for a sample size of 400 at the 95% confidence level and $p = .05$? |
| 2.  State the formula. | $SE_p = \pm 2\sqrt{\dfrac{p(1-p)}{n}}$ | $SE_p = \pm 2\sqrt{\dfrac{p(1-p)}{n}}$ |
| 3.  Fill in known values. | $SE_p = \pm 2\sqrt{\dfrac{(.5)\,(.5)}{100}}$ | $SE_p = \pm 2\sqrt{\dfrac{(.5)\,(.5)}{400}}$ |
| 4.  Extract the square root. | $SE_p = \pm 2\left(\dfrac{.5}{10}\right)$ | $SE_p = \pm 2\left(\dfrac{.5}{20}\right)$ |
| 5.  Divide. | $SE_p = \pm 2\,(.05)$ | $SE_p = \pm 2\,(.025)$ |

| | EXAMPLE 1 | EXAMPLE 2 |
|---|---|---|
| 6. Multiply. | $SE_p = \pm.10$ | $SE_p = \pm.05$ |
| 7. Convert to % by multiplying by 100. | $SE_p = \pm 10\%$ | $SE_p = \pm 5\%$ |
| 8. Interpretation. | With a sample of 100 there is a 95% probability that the interval from .1 below the sample proportion to .1 above it will contain the population proportion. | With a sample of 400, there is a 95% probability that the interval from .05 below the sample proportion to .05 above it will contain the population proportion. |

By increasing the sample size fourfold (from 100 to 400), the sampling error is reduced one-half (from 10% to 5%).

CALCULATING SAMPLE SIZE

Both political participants and researchers often ask how large a sample is needed for some kind of public opinion poll. To answer such questions, the student should be able to use the sampling error formula to compute the sample size for a given amount of sampling error. First we must solve for $n$, the sample size.

| STEPS | EXAMPLE 1 | EXAMPLE 2 |
|---|---|---|
| 1. State the problem. | What is the sample size for sampling error of $\pm 10\%$ at the 95% confidence level with $p = .5$? | What is the sample size for sampling error of $\pm 5\%$ at the 95% confidence level with $p = .5$? |
| 2. State the formula. | $SE_p = 2\sqrt{\dfrac{p(1-p)}{n}}$ | $SE_p = 2\sqrt{\dfrac{p(1-p)}{n}}$ |
| 3. Fill in known values. | $.1 = 2\sqrt{\dfrac{(.5)(.5)}{n}}$ | $.05 = 2\sqrt{\dfrac{(.5)(.5)}{n}}$ |
| 4. Square both sides. | $.01 = 4\dfrac{(.5)(.5)}{n}$ | $.0025 = 4\dfrac{(.5)(.5)}{n}$ |
| 5. Multiply. | $.01 = 4\dfrac{(.25)}{n}$ | $.0025 = 4\dfrac{(.25)}{n}$ |
| 6. Multiply both sides by $n$. | $.01n = 4\,(.25)$ | $.0025n = 4\,(.25)$ |

| | | |
|---|---|---|
| 7. Multiply. | $.01n = 1$ | $.0025n = 1$ |
| 8. Divide. | $n = 100$ | $n = 400$ |

The student should notice again that to reduce sampling error by one-half (from 10% to 5%) sample size must be increased four times (from 100 to 400).

The student should also notice in step 7 that the left side of the equation always reduces to the square of the sampling error (stated as a proportion, not as a percentage), and the right-hand side always reduces to 1. So, the student can shortcut the computation by dividing 1 by the square of the sampling error.

Sample Size

$$n = \frac{1}{SE_p{}^2}$$

| STEPS | EXAMPLE |
|---|---|
| 1. Problem | What sample size is required for sampling error at $+4\%$? |
| 2. Formula | $n = \dfrac{1}{SE_p{}^2}$ |
| 3. Fill in values. | $n = \dfrac{1}{(.04)^2}$ |
| 4. Square denominator. | $n = \dfrac{1}{.0016}$ |
| 5. Divide. | $n = 625$ |

## LEARNING AID

1. The difference between the sample statistic and the population parameter is called _____.

2. Total sampling error consists of two parts: _____ and _____.

3. The difference between the statistic and the parameter attributable to systematic errors resulting from the design of the _____ is called _____.

4. The difference between the statistic and the parameter attributable to _____ variation in samples is called _____.

5. State the formula for the sampling error of proportions.

6. In the sampling error formula, dispersion is indicated by the symbols _____, sample size is represented by _____, and the confidence level is indicated by _____.

7. Sampling error decreases as the confidence level (increases/decreases), dispersion (increases/decreases), and sample size (increases/decreases).

8. Sampling accuracy is primarily a function of the size of the (population/ sample).

9. To reduce sampling error by one-half, the sample size must be increased _____ times.

10. To the nearest tenth of a percentage, what is the sampling error for a sample size of 900 at the 95% confidence level with $p = 0.5$? Show work.

11. State the calculating formula for determining sample size.

12. What sample size is necessary to obtain $+5.5\%$ sampling error at the 95% confidence level with $p = 0.5$? Show work.

· · · · · · · · · · · · · · · · · · · · · · · · · · · · · · · · · · · · · · · · · · · · · · · · · · · · · · · ·

1. total sampling error
2. sampling bias, random sampling error
3. sample, sampling bias
4. random, random sampling error
5. $SE_p = \pm 2 \dfrac{p(1-p)}{n}$
6. $p(1-p), n, 2$
7. decreases, decreases, increases
8. sample
9. four

10. $SE_p = \pm 2 \sqrt{\dfrac{p(1-p)}{n}}$

$\quad = \pm 2 \sqrt{\dfrac{(.5)(.5)}{900}}$

$\quad = \pm 2$

$\quad = \pm 2\,(.0167)$
$\quad = \pm .0334$
$\quad = \pm 3.3\%$

11. $n = \dfrac{1}{SE_p{}^2}$

12. $n = \dfrac{1}{SE_p{}^2}$

$\quad = \dfrac{1}{(.055)^2}$

$\quad = \dfrac{1}{.003}$

$\quad = 333$

## QUESTIONNAIRE DESIGN

Constructing a questionnaire is both an art and a science. It involves five steps:
(1) specifying the informational objectives, (2) selecting the type of questionnaire, (3) writing the first draft, (4) pretesting the questionnaire, and (5) revis-
ing the questionnaire. Since we will touch on only some of the basic principles,
the student may wish to consult a more thorough treatment before constructing
his own questionnaire.[4] In this section, we shall examine types of questionnaires and principles of question wording and sequencing.

## TYPES OF QUESTIONNAIRES

### Personal Interview and Self-Administered

The word "questionnaire" is used to refer to either a personal interview
schedule in which an interviewer asks questions and records answers or a self-
administered questionnaire in which the respondent completes the task by
himself. Table 15–7 shows the advantages and disadvantages associated with
each type.

### Closed- and Open-Ended

Questionnaires also may be distinguished by the structuring of the questions
and responses. Highly structured items are called "closed-ended questions."

In *closed-ended questions,* the respondent is asked to select his answer from a
list of alternatives provided by the interviewer.

Closed-Ended Question:

"What do you think is the most serious problem facing the United States today? Would you say racial relations, poverty, inflation, the environment,
crime, unemployment, drugs, or what?" (23)

Racial relations . . . . . . . . . . . . . . . . . . . . . . . . . . . . . . . . . . . . . . . . . . . . . . . . .1
Poverty . . . . . . . . . . . . . . . . . . . . . . . . . . . . . . . . . . . . . . . . . . . . . . . . . . . . . . .2
Inflation . . . . . . . . . . . . . . . . . . . . . . . . . . . . . . . . . . . . . . . . . . . . . . . . . . . . . . .3
Environment . . . . . . . . . . . . . . . . . . . . . . . . . . . . . . . . . . . . . . . . . . . . . . . . . . . .4
Crime . . . . . . . . . . . . . . . . . . . . . . . . . . . . . . . . . . . . . . . . . . . . . . . . . . . . . . . . . .5
Unemployment . . . . . . . . . . . . . . . . . . . . . . . . . . . . . . . . . . . . . . . . . . . . . . . . . .6
Drugs . . . . . . . . . . . . . . . . . . . . . . . . . . . . . . . . . . . . . . . . . . . . . . . . . . . . . . . . . .7
Other . . . . . . . . . . . . . . . . . . . . . . . . . . . . . . . . . . . . . . . . . . . . . . . . . . . . . . . . . .8

Table 15–7.  PERSONAL INTERVIEWS AND SELF-ADMINISTERED QUESTIONNAIRES

|  | Personal Interview | Self-Administered Questionnaire |
|---|---|---|
| *Advantages* | 1.  Does not assume literate and interested population. <br> 2.  Higher response rates. <br> 3.  More flexible. <br> 4.  Better for complex and controversial topics. <br> 5.  Honesty and competency of respondent can be appraised. | 1.  Requires less skill from interviewers. <br><br> 2.  Less expensive. <br><br> 3.  Can be mailed. <br> 4.  Standardized administration is easy. <br><br> 5.  Respondent has time to study responses more carefully. |
| *Disadvantages* | 1.  Requires more skill from interviewers to administer. <br> 2.  More expensive. <br><br> 3.  Cannot be mailed. <br> 4.  Cannot be administered to groups. <br><br> 5.  Standardized administration is difficult. <br> 6.  Respondents must give quick answers. | 1.  Assumes literate and interested population. <br><br> 2.  Lower response rates. <br> 3.  Less flexible. <br> 4.  Worse for complex and controversial topics. <br> 5.  Honesty and competency of respondents cannot be appraised. |

The response categories should be both *exhaustive* (include all alternatives) and *mutually exclusive* (an answer should be classifiable in only one category). Closed-ended questions are useful when the researcher knows enough about the topic to intelligently structure the alternatives. Closed-ended questions are advantageous because they standardize responses and facilitate data processing. In the above example, the column (23) and punch assignments (1 to 8) are indicated. This is called *precoding* and allows the key puncher to punch directly from the questionnaire.

Less structured items are called "open-ended questions." In *open-ended questions*, the respondent is asked to provide the answer to the question without reference to alternative answers.

Open-Ended Question:

"What do you think is the most serious problem facing the United States today?"

When the topic is complex or when relevant dimensions are unknown, then open-ended questions are more appropriate than closed-ended questions. When a new subject is under investigation, many researchers start their study with a set of intensive, open-ended interviews so that they can gain the knowledge to construct a reliable and valid closed-ended type of interview schedule.

## Question Wording

The phrasing of questions is fraught with difficulties for survey researchers. Here are some of the more important guidelines for constructing questionnaire items:

1. *Questions should not contain equivocal terms.* When items are ambiguous and lead to different interpretations by different people, then the fallacy of equivocation is committed. Questions should be written in clear, specific, and simple language so that double meanings will be minimized and intersubjective understanding will be maximized.

| Poor: | Improved: |
|---|---|
| Do you think that nonconformists should be tolerated or not? | Do you think an admitted Communist who wants to make a speech in your community should be allowed to speak, or not? |

2. *Questions should not be complex or double-barreled.* The fallacy of the complex question, it may be recalled, consists of asking for a yes or no answer

to a question involving a number of parts. The counterpart to this in survey research is called the double-barreled question.

|  Poor:  |  Improved:  |
|---|---|
|  Are you for Republicans and prosperity, or not?  |  Are you for Republicans, or not? Are you for prosperity, or not?  |

3. *Questions should not contain biased or emotionally loaded terms.* Inclusion of terms with positive or negative connotations often influences the acceptance or rejection of a proposition. Although it may be impossible to find absolutely neutral terms, the researcher should design questions so that the words themselves do not predispose respondents towards one alternative rather than another.

|  Poor:  |  Improved:  |
|---|---|
|  Do you favor nationalizing the railroads, or not?  |  Do you favor public ownership of the railroads, or not?  |
|  Do you favor or oppose the child-killing bill?  |  Do you favor or oppose the bill ending pregnancy before the twelfth week?  |

4. *Questions should not contain biased response alternatives.* Just as the words in the question can influence the response, the structure of the alternatives can also constitute a bias. In the example below, one option (increasing presidential power) is split three ways, whereas the alternative (reducing presidential power) is undivided and is likely to show a higher frequency count than the divided opposition.

|  Poor:  |  Improved:  |
|---|---|
|  Do you think the power of the presidency should be increased in foreign policy, increased in domestic policy, increased in foreign and domestic policy or should it be reduced?  |  Do you think that the power of the presidency should be increased or reduced?  |

5. *Questions should not seek technical information that the respondent cannot answer.* This problem is often encountered when researchers formulate questions for children in political socialization research or when questionnaires are given to uneducated persons. It can also occur when the subject matter is simply too technical for the average respondent.

Poor:

Which do you think is more effective
in solving urban problems, bloc grants
or categorical grants-in-aid?

6. *Questions should not be stated in the negative direction.* Sometimes this is unavoidable. Negative questions, however, tend to confuse or mislead respondents who do not listen or read carefully.

Poor:                                              Improved:

Marijuana should not be decrimi-        Marijuana should be decriminalized.
nalized.

## Question Sequencing

The order in which items are placed in the questionnaire influences the response to the question. If a closed-ended question precedes an open-ended one relating to the same topic, then the information contained in the closed-ended item is likely to influence the response to the open-ended item. Accordingly, open-ended questions normally precede closed-ended items.

Question sequencing is also dependent on whether the researcher is conducting a personal interview or a self-administered questionnaire. In a personal interview, the researcher attempts to gain rapport with the respondent by first asking nonthreatening questions, usually demographic items, and then leading to more controversial items. In self-administered questionnaires, however, questions likely to engage and interest the respondent should come first, leading to the controversial and concluding with demographic items.

### LEARNING AID

1. Name four advantages of the personal interview.
2. Name four advantages of the self-administered questionnaire.

3. In _____ questions, the respondent is asked to provide the answer without reference to alternative answers; in _____ questions, however, the respondent is asked to select his answer from a list of alternatives provided by the interviewer.

4. Name four rules for the construction of questionnaire items.

5. Closed-ended items should normally (precede/follow) open-ended items relating to the same topic.

6. Identify the rule the following questionnaire items violate:
   a. Do you favor or oppose the racist policy of birth control?
   b. Do you support the busing of school children and equality of educational opportunity, or not?
   c. Do you favor prohibiting birth control, or not?
   d. Do you think that inflation should be reduced by cutting governmental spending?
   e. Do you think that by cutting the prime rate four points the condition of stagflation will be improved or worsened?
   f. Do you think that Vietnam War deserters should be treated with justice, or not?

. . . . . . . . . . . . . . . . . . . . . . . . . . . . . . . . . . . . . . . . . . . . . . . . . . . . . . . . . . . . . . . . . . . . .

1. See Table 15-7
2. See Table 15-7
3. open-ended, closed-ended
4. See text.
5. follow
6. (a) biased terms, (b) complex or double-barreled question, (c) negative question, (d) biased alternatives (other options were excluded), (e) technical question, (f) equivocal terms (both deserters and Veterans of Foreign Wars could agree with this item because of their different interpretations of what is "just.").

## INTERVIEWING

In this section, we will examine some of the rules governing the collection of data through interviewing techniques.[5] This section discusses how to prepare for the interview and how to conduct it.

### Preparing for the Interview

GAINING RAPPORT

The primary objective of the interviewer is to gain rapport with the respondent. *Rapport* is the personal relationship between the interviewer and respondent characterized by confidence and understanding. The interviewer helps to establish rapport by showing interest in the respondent as a person, by being friendly and conversational, and by letting the respondent know what is expected of him or her. The respondent should feel completely free to express any feeling or viewpoint without sensing any kind of pressure, coercion, reaction, or preference from the interviewer.

APPEARANCE

Normally, the interviewer should dress in clothes that are fairly neutral. The interviewer's appearance should not be striking or "far out."

BEHAVIOR

The interviewer should be pleasant toward the respondent and neutral in his or her opinions. The interviewer should be friendly without being too casual or intimate. The respondent should feel comfortable in the presence of the interviewer. The interviewer should also be neutral and impartial with respect to opinions. The interviewer should not give any cue, whether by word, action or gesture that indicates surprise, pleasure or disapproval with any answer. The role of the interviewer is to ask questions and record answers accurately, not to evaluate the answers.

PRACTICE

The interviewer can put the respondent at ease only if the interviewer is at ease himself. The interviewer is at ease only if he or she has mastery over the interview schedule. Mastery and confidence are obtained by practicing the interview situation in a supervised training session with other interviewers, by rehearsing at home, and by trying some interviews in the field. The interviewer should know the interview schedule backward and forward, so that the interview sounds like a natural conversation and not like someone is reading from a script, stumbling over words and instructions in a monotone voice.

## Conducting the Interview

ASKING QUESTIONS

The interview schedule is constructed so as to provide exactly the same stimulus to each respondent. Accordingly, the interviewer should ask the questions exactly as they are worded in the questionnaire. Every question specified in the questionnaire should be asked, and the questions should be asked in the same order as presented in the questionnaire. Finally, the questions should be asked in a relaxed and informal atmosphere. The respondent should not feel as though he or she is under cross-examination but should feel secure in expressing any thought or attitude.

When open-ended questions are asked, some respondents reply with unclear, incomplete, or irrelevant answers. When this occurs, interviewers need to obtain clear, complete, and relevant answers by stimulating the respondent to provide more information. This is called "probing." *Probing* is a technique used by interviewers to stimulate discussion and to obtain more information.

Interviewers may use a number of different probing techniques to elicit fuller and clearer responses from the respondents. First, the interviewer can *reinforce* the respondent's answer ("Yes," or "That's interesting," or "I see.") and encourage the respondent to talk further. The interviewer also can *pause,* letting the respondent know that the interviewer thinks he has just begun to answer the question and is waiting for the rest of the answer. Third, *repeating the question or reply* often stimulates the respondent to provide additional information. Finally, *asking a neutral question* ("Could you tell me a little more about that?" or "I'm not sure what your had in mind," or "Why do you think that is so?") often elicits more complete answers.

RECORDING ANSWERS

The interviewer should record the answers using the respondent's own words. No attempt should be made to summarize, paraphrase, or correct the grammar of an answer. The interview should represent a picture of what was said and how it was said. Note taking is facilitated by finding where the interviewer can write comfortably, by writing as soon as the respondent begins answering, and by entering only the key words and leaving out articles and prepositions.

## LEARNING AID

1. "Rapport" is the personal relationship between the interviewer and respondent characterized by _____ and _____.

2. The interviewer should dress in clothes (similar to/different from) the people he or she will be interviewing.

3. The interviewer should be _____ and _____ with respect to opinions.

4. Mastery and confidence are obtained by _____ the interview situation in a supervised training session with other interviewers.

5. The interviewer should ask questions exactly as they are _____ in the questionnaire.

6. _____ is a technique used by interviewers to stimulate discussion and to obtain more information.

7.  Name four techniques of probing.

8.  Good interviewers (do/do not) summarize, paraphrase, or correct the grammar of the respondent's answer.

. . . . . . . . . . . . . . . . . . . . . . . . . . . . . . . . . . . . . . . . . . . . . . . . . . . . .

1.  confidence, understanding
2.  similar to
3.  neutral, impartial
4.  practicing
5.  worded
6.  probing
7.  (a) reinforcing, (b) pausing, (c) repeating the question or reply, (d) asking a neutral question
8.  do not


## FOOTNOTES

1.  See Earl Babbie, *Survey Research Methods* (Belmont, Cal.: Wadsworth, 1973), pp. 62-70; Charles Glock, ed., *Survey Research in the Social Sciences* (New York: Russell Sage Foundation, 1967), pp. 42-57; Angus Campbell and George Katone, "The Sample Survey," in Leon Festinger and Daniel Katz, eds., *Research Methods in the Behaviorial Sciences* (New York: Holt, Rinehart, & Winston, 1966), pp. 21-30.

2.  See Claire Selltiz, et al., *Research Methods in Social Relations* (New York: Holt, Rinehart and Winston, 1959), pp. 509-45; Earl Babbie, *Survey Research Methods,* pp. 73-108; C. A. Moser, *Survey Methods in Social Investigation* (London: Heinemann, 1958), pp. 66-144; and Leslie Kish, *Survey Sampling* (New York: John Wiley, 1967).

3.  The sampling error formula should be multiplied by $\dfrac{N-n}{N-1}$, where $N$ is the size of the population and $n$ is the size of the sample. If the entire population is the sample, then this factor becomes 0 and so does sampling error.

4.  Selltiz, *Research Methods in Social Relations,* pp. 546-74; Charles Backstrom and Gerald Hursh, *Survey Research* (Evanston, Ill.: Northwestern University Press, 1963), pp. 67-128; and Babbie, *Survey Research Methods,* pp. 131-70.

5.  See Raymond Gorden, *Interviewing* (Homewood, Ill.: Dorsey Press, 1969); Babbie, *Survey Research,* pp. 171-185; Robert Kahn and Charles Cannell, *The Dynamics of Interviewing* (New York: John Wiley, 1967); Backstrom and Hursh, *Survey Research,* pp. 134-44; and Survey Research Center, *Interviewer's Manual* (Ann Arbor, Mich.: Institute of Social Research, 1969).

# 16
# Unobtrusive Research

# INTRODUCTION

## Rationale

In Unit 10, Measurement, we distinguished between obtrusive and unobtrusive research.[1] In *obtrusive research,* the method of observation significantly changes the natural settings and outcomes. The subjects, reacting to the process of observation and measurement, distort and change their natural actions. Experimental and survey research are the most important forms of obtrusive research in the social sciences. Their obtrusiveness creates such special internal and external validity problems as testing effects, instrumentation, reactive testing, and reactive arrangements. To avoid such validity threats some investigators have turned to *unobtrusive research,* in which the method of observation and measurement does not significantly affect the natural settings and outcomes. Unobtrusive research, in other words, is nonreactive research.

In this unit two major types of unobtrusive research will be examined: content analysis and participant research. *Content analysis,* to be discussed first, is a method of observing and analyzing the content of communications. *Participant observation,* to be discussed next, is a method of observing behavior by living in the field and sharing in the experiences of those observed. Different forms of participant observation vary in their degree of unobtrusiveness. We classify participant observation as unobtrusive because it is conducted in natural settings by natural forms of human interaction and because it is less obtrusive in general than experimental and survey research.

## Learning Objectives

After completing this unit, the student should be able to:

1. Define and identify: obtrusive and unobtrusive research, content analysis, unitizing, representational and instrumental models, mutually exclusive, collectively exhaustive.
2. Name and explain the six stages of content analysis.
3. Name and explain the four guides to category construction.
4. Unitize sentences.
5. Name and identify the four kinds of units of analysis.
6. Explain when computers are superior to manual methods of content analysis.
7. Define and identify: participant observation, respondent and informant

interviewing, complete participant, participant-as-observer, observer-as-participant, complete observer, going native.

8. Name the various research techniques employed by participant observation.

9. Name and explain the five stages of participant observation.

10. Name and explain the four participant observer roles.

11. Name and explain the four stages of the constant comparative method of analysis.

12. Name and explain the factors most seriously threatening the internal and external validity of participant observation.

13. Discuss the major advantages and limitations of participant observation research.

## CONTENT ANALYSIS

### Definition

*Content analysis* is an objective research technique for inferring the characteristics, causes, and effects of communications.[2] The communications may consist of films, TV, diplomatic messages, books, speeches, letters, or various other types of language signs and artifacts. In its simplest form, content analysis involves a specification of the documents to be observed (e.g., propaganda messages), construction of a set of categories into which the messages are classified or "coded" (e.g., name calling, glittering generalities, bandwagon, and so on), and an ennumeration of the instances of these categories in the messages. It is an "objective" research technique only to the extent that the procedures are explicit enough so that the same results are obtained by other analysts using the same procedures.

As the definition suggests, content analysis is used *to infer the characteristics of communications*. For example, the messages produced by two or more sources may be compared (such as the content of Democratic and Republican Party platforms). Moreover, messages may be studied over time (such as trend studies of party platforms). Messages from a single source may be compared in different situations (campaign speeches in own-party versus other-party audiences). Finally, messages may be analyzed by relating two or more variables in the text (the incidence of references to governmental expansion and advocacy of increased taxation or deficit spending).

Second, content analysis is used *to infer the causes or antecedents of com-*

*munications.* From content analysis such psychological characteristics of the communicator as personality, attitudes, and motivations are inferred. The intentions of foreign policy decision makers, for example, have been studied by examining diplomatic documents.[3] Also, inferences about the causes of varying degrees of achievement motivation among nations have been drawn using content analysis.[4] However, using content analysis to make inferences about attitudes and personality traits is hazardous and should be used only as a last resort and then should be used with great caution.

A methodological issue confronting researchers conducting studies of this type is whether the content of messages can be taken at face value in making inferences about the attitudes and motives of communicators. The question is whether the words in the message represent ("representational model") the author's beliefs or whether the words are instruments ("instrumental model") of influence. If the latter situation is the case, then faulty inferences about attitudes and values can be drawn when the content analysis takes the words at face value. To avoid faulty inferences of this type, content analysts often require corroborating evidence from other independent sources.

Third, content analysis is used *to infer the effects of communications.* Political and social scientists attempt to study the effects of propaganda, campaign speeches, and biased news media stories on attitudes, values, and behavior. However, just as it is hazardous to assume a one-to-one correspondence between the message and the motive, it is also dangerous to assume a correspondence between the message and the effect. Persons are different, and they interpret and assimilate information differently. Thus, effects cannot be assumed just because individuals are exposed to messages; they must be inferred by corroboration through independent evidence. The investigator, for example, may corroborate the effects of a message by examining subsequent messages and responses.

## Procedure

Content analysis involves six stages: (1) formulating the problem, (2) defining the population, (3) categorizing the population, (4) identifying the unit of analysis, (5) sampling the population, and (6) analyzing the data. Each stage will be elaborated on with an example taken from Richard Merritt's study of the development of American consciousness, *Symbols of American Community 1735–1775.*[5]

FORMULATING THE PROBLEM

Research normally begins with the asking of some question. We previously noted that content analysis is particularly relevant to questions concerning the characteristics, causes, and effects of various types of communications. Richard Merritt, for instance, asked what types of processes led to a unified American community. How important were such dramatic events as the Stamp Act crisis, or the creation of common political institutions, or long-run patterns of communication? Specifically, when did Americans begin to pay more attention to local events than to European wars and English court gossip? When did they begin to refer to themselves more often in terms of being American than being Anglo-American or British? Thus, the purpose of Merritt's research was to measure the development of national consciousness in the American colonies during the four decades prior to the American Revolution.

DEFINING THE POPULATION

The next step is to define or identify the population of content to be analyzed. Merritt decided to limit the scope of study to the years 1735–1775. Before 1735, there were very few newspapers in the colonies, and only incomplete files of these newspapers were available in libraries. Furthermore, the period from 1735 to 1775 contained the most important formative events prior to the Revolution. Merritt further decided to select for analysis newspapers located in the five largest population clusters in the colonies. Seven newspapers finally were selected for analysis based on three criteria: (1) continuity of the newspaper from 1735 to 1775, (2) availability and completeness of the newspaper library files, and (3) prestige of the newspaper.

CATEGORIZING THE POPULATION

The quality of content analysis depends primarily on the quality of the categories used to classify the elements in the population of content. Four principles guide the construction of content categories: (1) mutual exclusiveness, (2) collective exhaustiveness, (3) validity, and (4) reliability.

A category is *mutually exclusive* if an element can be classified into one and only one category. If elements can be classified into more than one category, then either the operational definitions of the categories are not precise and specific enough or the categories are based on more than one dimension of classification. Merritt classifies common identity into six mutually exclusive categories:

1.  Symbols of explicit British common identity ("British North America," "British colonists")
2.  Symbols of identification with the British Crown ("His Majesty's colonies," "crown colonies")
3.  Symbols of implicit British common identity ("colonies," "provinces")
4.  Symbols of implicit American common identity ("continent," "country," "American colonists")

5. Symbols of explicit American common identity ("America," "Americans")

6. Other symbols

To the extent that a word or symbol is classifiable into one of the six categories the scheme of categories is said to be mutually exclusive.

A category is *collectively exhaustive* if the elements of the content population are classifiable into one of the categories of the scheme. The set of categories is incomplete if a word cannot be placed into one of the categories. Merritt's categories fulfill this principle by including the residual category entitled, "Other symbols."

A category is *valid* if it measures what it is intended to measure. Categories should adequately reflect the investigator's research questions. Merritt's categories are valid if the occurrence of place names accurately reflects nationalism. If the frequency of occurrence of place names more adequately reflects the occurrence of newsworthy events than the growth of common identity, then the measure is not a valid index of nationalism.

A category is *reliable* if there is agreement by different coders in classifying elements in the content population. To check on the reliability of the coders, Merritt used a simple percentage agreement index called the *coefficient of reliability*:

$$CR = \frac{2A}{N_1 + N_2}$$

where $CR$ is the ratio of coding agreements to the total number of coding decisions, $A$ is the number of coding decisions on which two judges are in agreement, and "$N_1$" and "$N_2$" refer to the number of coding decisions made by judges 1 and 2, respectively. Merritt's coefficient of reliability was high, varying from 0.92 to 0.96. In other words, the coders agreed on how the content items should be classified between 92% and 96% of the time.

IDENTIFYING THE UNIT OF ANALYSIS

Once the categories have been defined, the content analyst must decide what unit of analysis is the object of categorization. There are three common units of analysis: (1) single words, (2) themes, and (3) items.

*Single words* are the smallest units of analysis. The investigator counts the frequency of appearance of certain types of words within communications. Merritt, for example, counted the frequency of occurrence of American place and people names in the colonial press to study the development of American nationalism.

*Themes* are single assertions about some subject. Since sentences are usually compound assertions about a subject, they are usually analyzed into their component themes. This process of reducing sentences to thematic units is called *unitizing*. For example, "The pig police are fascist murderers" is a sentence that is unitized as follows:

> The POLICE are pigs.
> The POLICE are fascists.
> The POLICE are murderers.

Thus, the sentences is analyzed or unitized into three themes. The themes can then be coded more reliably into whatever category scheme is being used.

*Items* such as entire books, articles, messages, or TV programs sometimes serve as units of analysis. Usually reliability in coding is quite low when entire items are used as the unit of analysis, because items are generally complex and ambiguous. In analyzing propaganda as journalistic bias, analysts may count such spatial characteristics as size of headlines, placement of story, total column inches of a story, and the size and number of pictures. As for film, radio, and TV bias, time of coverage for a particular viewpoint or individual may also be used as a unit of analysis.

SAMPLING THE POPULATION

When the population of content and the unit of analysis are identified, the investigator must determine whether the entire population of content or a sample of it should be observed. Since the volume of information in content populations is frequently too large for complete inspection, samples are normally taken and inferences are made about population characteristics.

The logic of sampling in content analysis is the same as that in survey research. Unit 15, therefore, provides more information about sampling designs and formulas for estimating sampling error and sample size. Instead of randomly selecting persons or census tracts, which is normally done in survey research, communications (books, speeches, articles, etc.) are selected in content analysis. Multistage samples are often taken in content analysis, starting with the random selection of the communication and proceeding to the random (sometimes systematic random) sampling of pages, paragraphs, or sentences within the text. In TV, radio, and motion picture research time is frequently used as the sampling unit. Observations, for example, may be taken every ten minutes (systematic random sample). Since the volume of information is normally very extensive, sampling techniques are commonly used in studies employing content analysis.

Merritt's population of content extends over 40 years in seven newspapers. He obviously could not perform a content analysis on every issue of each newspaper. He therefore used a random sample of one issue per quarter (or four per year) from each of the selected set of newspapers. Thus, Merritt drew a stratified random sample by dividing the year into four strata (quarters) and randomly selecting one issue from each of the newspapers each quarter of the years from 1735 to 1775. The content analysis then included all the new items in each issue sampled, omitting only advertisements.

ANALYZING THE DATA

Frequency and contingency analysis are the most frequently used methods of analyzing content analysis data. *Frequency analysis* is simply an enumeration of the frequency with which the categories occur in the text being analyzed. Merritt, for example, simply counted the frequency of place and community symbols. He found that the colonists' interest in things and places American grew significantly, as did their self-perception as members of the American rather than the British political community, long before the occurrence of such dramatic events as the Stamp Act Congress of 1765.

*Contingency analysis* indicates how often a symbolic unit appears in conjunction with other symbolic units. Contingency analysis, for instance, has been performed on wartime diaries kept by Nazi propaganda minister Joseph Goebbels.[6] A frequency count revealed 21 categories of symbols. Next, contingency matrices were constructed showing the probability that each pair of content categories would appear in the same passage selected from the diaries.

## Computerized Content Analysis

Computers are normally used in most types of quantitative research to facilitate the analysis of the data. Computers assist in the calculation of measures of central tendency, dispersion, association, and so forth. They are used this way in content analysis research. Computers, however, are also used in content analysis research to facilitate the collection, processing, storage, and retrieval of the data. Computer programs, for example, can count the frequency with which a symbol appears in a text. These are called *word count programs.*[7] After key punching the text onto IBM cards, word count programs are used to generate word frequencies on the computer printout. Providing there are no key punching errors, word count programs perform frequency counts at high speeds with perfect reliability. A second type of computer program, called *dictionary programs,* such as the popular "General Inquirer Program," uses a preconceived dictionary system in which the text is first punched onto IBM cards and then the words in the text are automatically looked up in the computer dictionary and coded, counted, retrieved, manipulated, and transformed according to the analyst's instructions.[8]

Although computers have provided great assistance in content analysis research, they are not always superior to manual methods. The student should learn to recognize the conditions under which the computer is more or less applicable to a content analysis problem.[9] Generally, computers are more useful when:

1. The unit of analysis consists of words.
2. The number of variables and categories is large.
3. The data are used in many different analyses.

On the other hand, manual techniques are more useful when:

1. The unit of analysis consists of space/time characteristics, where simpler methods, such as a ruler or stopwatch, provide precise answers at a low cost.
2. A small amount of information is taken from each of many different documents.
3. The data are used for just one analysis and will not be used on other analyses.

## LEARNING AID

1. Content analysis is an objective research technique for inferring the _____, _____, and _____ of communications.
2. A methodological issue is whether words reflect the author's beliefs (called the _____ model) or whether words are used to influence other people (called the _____ model).
3. Name the six stages of content analysis research.
4. Name the four principles of category construction.
5. A category is mutually exclusive if an element can be classified into _____ category.
6. An investigator attempts to categorize the population of nations with these categories: capitalist, democratic, totalitarian, and socialist. This set of categories violates the principle of _____ because the classification is based on two dimensions (political and economic systems). Thus, a nation may not be classifiable into one and only one _____.
7. If a nation cannot be classified in one of the categories in the scheme presented in the previous question, then it violates the principle of _____.
8. A category is _____ if it measures what it is _____ to measure.
9. A category is _____ if there is agreement by different coders in classifying the elements in the population.
10. Name three kinds of units of analysis.
11. Unitize the following sentence: "The underdeveloped Arab nations skillfully used the oil embargo to generate economic resources."

**12.** Explain when computers are superior to manual methods of content analysis.

. . . . . . . . . . . . . . . . . . . . . . . . . . . . . . . . . . . . . . . . . . . . . . . . .

**1.** characteristics, causes, effects
**2.** representational, instrumental
**3.** (a) formulating the problem, (b) defining the population, (c) categorizing the population, (d) identifying the unit of analysis, (e) sampling the population, and (f) analyzing the data.
**4.** (a) mutual exclusiveness, (b) collective exhaustiveness, (c) validity, and (d) reliability
**5.** one and only one
**6.** mutual exclusiveness, category
**7.** collective exhaustiveness
**8.** valid, intended
**9.** reliable
**10.** (a) single words, (b) themes, and (c) items.
**11.**  a.  The ARAB NATIONS are underdeveloped.
  b.  The ARAB NATIONS are skillful.
  c.  The ARAB NATIONS used the oil embargo.
  d.  The ARAB NATIONS generated economic resources.
**12.** See text.

## PARTICIPANT OBSERVATION

### Definition

*Participant observation* is a combination of research techniques, including sharing in the daily lives of those being studied, for the systematic description of behavior in social settings. The definition requires some elaboration. First, it stipulates that participant observation combines a number of research techniques.[10] Specifically, it may include any of the following:

1.  *Direct observation,* by personally viewing the social and political activities of people.

2.  *Respondent interviewing,* by asking persons with whom the researcher has not developed a close relationship about their feelings, perceptions, motives, attitudes, and behaviors.

3.  *Informant interviewing,* by asking persons with whom the researcher has developed a close and trusting relationship about their own feelings, percpetions, attitudes, motives, and behaviors and about those of others whom they know particularly well.

4. *Document analysis,* by studying available statistics, records, newspaper accounts, and reports relevant to the behavior under study.

5. *Direct participation,* by personally engaging in the day-to-day experiences of those being studied.

An important aspect of participant observation is direct participation. This technique assumes that a researcher must share as intimately as possible the life and activities of those he studies if he wants to really know and understand them. Participant observers may involve themselves by becoming members of a gang, living with a tribe of Indians for an extended period of time, joining a radical movement, or participating in a demonstration. By taking part in relevant activities, the participant observer shares the symbolic world, the meanings, of those he studies and acquires some understanding of their subjective experiences. Through a combination of observation, participation, and introspection, the participant observer thinks he can more readily interpret the meaning of his subjects' statements and actions.

Second, the definition stipulates that the purpose of participant observation is systematic description of behavior. Participant observers frequently focus on topics about which little is known. So, their objective usually is to reliably and validly describe some behavior. They go into the field to formulate concepts and generate new hypotheses. The results of their analyses may be a conceptual approach or a propositional inventory. Many participant observers are content to stop with descriptions, whereas others suggest informal explanations or explanation sketches of the behavior they observe. Participant observers generally do not engage in more formal hypothesis testing or deductive–nomological explanation.

Finally, the definition indicates that the observed behavior takes place in social settings. That is, it takes place in settings where people interact on a face-to-face basis. Participant observation is used to study behavior in groups, such as in primitive societies, deviant subcultures, complex organizations, social movements, communities, and informal groups.

## Procedure

Participant observation consists of the following stages: (1) formulating problems and working hypotheses, (2) entering the field, (3) recording and analyzing observations, (4) refining the analysis and observations, and (5) assessing internal and external validity. Each of these stages will be discussed in turn.

### FORMULATING THE PROBLEMS AND WORKING HYPOTHESES

In experimental and survey research the investigator generally goes into the field with the problem well defined and hypotheses operationalized. In participant observation research, however, the investigator does not enter the field with predetermined problems and hypotheses. Instead, he begins with only a general definition of the problem and a set of tentative hypotheses with which to begin work. The participant observer develops much of his research design in the field as he is participating, observing, recording observations, and analyzing various actions. As research progresses, the design is often reformulated and then refined as more observations are taken and interpreted.

To illustrate the five stages of participant observation or what also has come to be known as "field research," we draw from a study of an Air Force training program.[11] The general purpose of the study was to understand the motives and attitudes of airmen in the course of their training. The problem the researchers focused on was that airmen entered the service with attitudes favorable or at least neutral to the Air Force but during the course of the program often turned against the Air Force. Specifically, the investigators asked: What are the processes through which the airman's attitude and behavior toward the service change from positive to negative?

The researchers reviewed the relevant literature and formulated the following working hypotheses: (1) membership in the American culture predisposes the airman to both conforming the nonconforming behavior, (2) the Air Force consists of a formal subculture embodied by the official rules and regulations and an informal subculture involving unofficial expectations of behavior, (3) the airman would be socialized into both the informal as well as the formal structure of the service, and (4) the informal subculture increases tendencies toward nonconforming behavior already present in the recruitee.

ENTERING THE FIELD

This stage requires the participant observer to make three decisions: what setting should he enter, what observational role should he play, and how does he establish initial contacts in the field. With respect to the first question, the field setting is determined both by the formulation of the problem and the investigator's accessibility to a setting. The nature of the problem in the military training program, for example, study more of less specifies the setting in which the research takes place. Air Force sponsorship of the study made a number of settings accessible to the researchers.

Once the participant observer is in the field, he must decide what role to enact. He may choose one of four observer roles:[12]

1. *Complete participant,* where the field worker conceals his true identity and purpose from those he observes. The major problem with this role is the tendency for the fieldworker to "*go native,*" that is, to gradually overidentify with those he studies so that the objectivity of his observations is impaired. To guard against "going native," complete observers often leave the field for a period of time to cool off and reflect more dispassionately about their reactions and shifts in their perspectives. The military training study employed the role of a complete participant. One of the fieldworkers assumed a new identity and

was "enlisted" by high ranking Air Force personnel. A new personality with a cover story was developed to maximize rapport with other trainees. The fieldworker spent the weekends he had off with the other research team members trying to "cool off" and to reestablish in his mind the objectives of the study.

2. *Participant-as-observer,* where the field worker makes his investigative role known to those he observes. The participant-as-observer role is commonly used in community studies in which the fieldworker spends more time participating and developing relationships with informants than observing. The "going native" threat is also a problem with this type of role.

3. *Observer-as-participant,* where the field worker conducts only one visit or interview with the respondent. The relationship is brief and highly formalized. It minimizes the problem of going native, but it maximizes problems of mutual misunderstandings between the observer and respondent. An example of the observer-as-participant role is the survey research interviewer who visits the respondent only once and does not develop a close relationship with him.

4. *Complete observer,* where the fieldworker does not interact with those he observes. He observes people at a distance without their knowledge. If he cannot observe something directly, he may interview knowledgeable people called "informants" who can tell him what occurs. He may even use some type of mechanical recording device such as a tape recorder to take even more complete observations. Although the role of complete observer minimizes the going native problem, it maximizes the opposite problem of ethnocentrism, which occurs when the fieldworker misunderstands the observed because he can view them only from his own cultural perspective and because he cannot interact meaningfully with them.

The final field entry decision that the fieldworker must make is to determine how initial field contacts are to be made.[13] The fieldworker should not jump immediately into the field meeting people cold. He should use existing relationships with people who trust him to establish contacts with those he wants to observe. In addition, he should work from persons of higher authority and status downward toward those in the field. The fieldworker should understand that the "gatekeepers" of his field entry are interested in how the proposed observations may help and hurt those who are to be observed. Thus, the fieldworker needs to formulate plausible yet honest explanations that make sense to those whose cooperation he seeks. The fieldworker should take plenty of time to gain acceptance by those he is observing and not be overeager to collect initial data. Establishing initial contacts in the field is a critical stage in participant observation and should be carefully planned by the investigators.

RECORDING AND ANALYZING OBSERVATIONS

In experimental and survey research the process of data collection is separated from data analysis. In participant observation, however, the two processes are interwoven.[14] The participant observer goes into the field with only general notions about what he is seeking. As he shares the experiences of those he observes and as he records observations of these events, the fieldworker begins to develop generalizations and explanations about observed behavior. One of the most important duties of the fieldworker is to carefully record such observations and interpretations. Notes are usually not taken in the presence of those he is observing, for the process of note taking tends to destroy the naturalness of interaction between the fieldworker and the observed. The fieldworker, therefore, must train himself to make mental notes, remembering such items as who was present, who said what to whom, what the environment was like, and what was the sequence of events. Sometimes the participant observer can inconspicuously jot down a few key phrases to help his memory when he completes his daily report. The full daily report should be completed each night and certainly no later than the next morning. The fieldworker should plan to spend almost as much time writing his notes as observing in the field.

These records are most conveniently completed on a typewriter with several carbon copies. The fieldworker should let the ideas and the observations flow through his mind, and he should type madly, not worrying about mistakes and grammar. The fieldworker should try to record descriptions of events and behavior in very specific and concrete terms. Inferences and interpretations of what is happening may be placed in special memos. As the fieldworker develops his observations, he begins to think about the major themes of the study. Then, topics that may consist of 10 to 20 pages in the final report and subtopics that consist of only a few pages begin to crystallize in his mind. As the researcher compiles numerous observations, he may begin to classify or index the fieldnotes by various topics for easy reference. By reproducing multiple copies of the information, he may classify the information in file folders according to topic. He may index it by recording the topics and locations for each report. Since the diary is the basis for all inferences, particular care should be taken in developing skills in remembering and writing notes.

In the military training study, the fieldworker consolidated his notes each evening. On weekends when he could leave the base, he transcribed a more complete account on a dictating machine. He then met with the other team members for eight to 10 hours to discuss the previous report, focusing particularly on the analysis, meaning, and interpretation of various events. Team discussion of the reports generated new insights and hypotheses, which were subsequently pursued and tested with more observations and analysis.

REFINING THE ANALYSIS AND OBSERVATIONS

After the recording and preliminary analysis of observed incidents, research continues both by sharpening the categories and concepts and by taking critical observations that pose more severe tests on the initial hypotheses. In this way, conceptualization becomes more focused, theoretical, and testable. To illustrate this phase of research, we shall rely on the *"constant comparative method of analysis,"* developed by Barney Glaser.[15] This method of analysis consists of four parts: (1) comparing incidents applicable to each category, (2) integrating categories and their properties, (3) delimiting the theory, and (4) writing the theory.

## Comparing incidents applicable to each category

Each incident (statement or action) is coded in as many different categories as possible. Each incident is compared with every other incident coded in the same category. After a number of incidents are coded in the same category, the investigator begins to think there are important differences among them. He conceptualizes new underlying properties and hypotheses. When such ideas flash into his mind, the researcher should stop coding and write a memo on his thoughts. By discussing these ideas with other team members, other ideas often can be generated. George McCall vividly portrays this process:

*"Nurses X and Y seemed to be spending quite a bit of time today just chatting with the young boy in 7C who is thought to be dying of cancer."*

*"Nurse S was unusually prompt in responding to buzzes from the lawyer in 4G. He appears to be in terminal phase, but no particular emergency in most of his calls. Nurse S is usually so cavalier about answering these things."*

*"Many of the nurses again observed dropping into 7C, with little medical purpose for many of the visits."*

*"More pitiful cries audible in hall from the geriatric case in 7K. Though he seems to be slipping pretty fast, nurses seem reluctant to answer his calls, which don't strike me as particularly cranky."*

*"Nurse D made two special trips to the kitchen today to get ice cream for 4J. The fellow is parched and enjoys the cold stuff. Nurse D is particularly concerned about his poor prognosis and worries about what might become of his large family—six kids. Family is evidently in very shaky financial condition, as wife is reported unable to work."*

*Having pulled together these incidents bearing upon differences in nurses' mobilization for patients, the researcher may see a common thread running through them. The special concern of nurses for a young boy, a professional, and a man with heavy family responsibilities, as contrasted with the lack of concern for a worn-out geriatric case, may suggest to the researcher the proposition that patients whose death would represent unusual social loss receive greater responsiveness from the nursing staff.*

*The researcher then endeavors to sharpen his definitions of the constructs of "social loss" and "responsiveness." As these definitions become elaborated, he compares them with each of the relevant incidents to determine the "goodness of it" between definition and incident. He may, for example, initially define social loss primarily in terms of socio-economic status, but discover, in attempt-*

*ing to apply this definition to his collection of incidents, that his proposition ac-
counts for more incidents if he defines social loss primarily on the basis of youth
and only secondarily on socio-economic status. In this fashion, his changing
definitions of the construct may lead him to reclassify the incidents, deciding
that some particular incident which at first seemed similar to the others does
not share the properties of the emerging construct and is thus irrelevant to the
proposition.*[16]

## Integrating categories and their properties

As the comparative coding process continues, the analytical focus changes from
comparing incidents with incidents to comparing properties of categories with
properties of categories. Glaser describes the difference:

*For example, in comparing incident with incident we discovered the property
that nurses are constantly recalculating a patient's social loss as they learn
more about him. From then on each incident on calculation was compared to
accumulated knowledge on calculating, not to all other incidents of calculation.
Thus, once we found that age was the most important characteristic in calculating social loss, we could discern how age affected the recalculation of social loss
as the nurses found out more about the patient's education. We found that
education was most important in calculating the social loss of a middle year
adult, since at this time in life education was likely to be of most social worth.
This example also shows that the accumulated knowledge on a property of the
category—because of constant comparison—readily starts to become integrated;
that is, related in many diverse ways, resulting in a unified whole.*[17]

Thus, analysis rises from the specific and concrete to a higher level of abstraction, where properties are systematically related to other properties and where
hypotheses are linked to other hypotheses.

## Delimiting the theory

The data collection and analysis progress simultaneously, and the investigators
usually begin to feel inundated by the sheer quantity of fieldnotes, incidents,
categories, and hypotheses. By focusing on more general characteristics and
hypotheses, many categories can be subsumed under more general categories,
hypotheses subsumed or explained by more general hypotheses. As the analysis
becomes more theoretical, many categories and terms can be reduced. In turn,
the analyst can focus more on observing and comparing incidents applicable to
a small set of categories. He can then concentrate on taking critical observations that most severely test his theory. By delimiting the theory, the analyst
economizes on the effort that needs to be expended in the field, since it forces
him to spend his time on data relevant only to his categories. Without such
delimitation, the researcher is likely to become bogged down in his data and
waste resources.

## Writing the theory

At this point the investigator has data coded into categories, a series of memos, and a set of interrelated propostions that we call a theory. The major themes (section titles) of the research paper are contained in the memos discussing the content of the most important categories. To write the "theory," the researcher collates and analyzes the memos on each category, using the coded data for illustrating or testing a hypothesis.

The research on the military training program progressed roughly through these four stages of constant comparative analysis. In reporting on their findings, the authors focused particularly on the theme of "patterned evasions" among trainees:

*As had been anticipated, the trainees' images of the Air Force and of themselves changed in the course of their experiences. In the strange world of basic training the men looked to their instructors, exclusively at first, for leadership and explanations of their day-by-day activities. Then, as the training took shape, as the trainees saw themselves becoming airmen, as they began to understand the structure of their environment, they learned how to meet the multitude of requirements with which they were faced. There then began an unending search for shortcuts, methods by which one job could be done more quickly so as to allow more time for doing a second, third, and fourth. In seeking shortcuts, the trainees learned that some things were never checked up on even though they were officially required, and others did not have to be done as long as the appearance of doing them was demonstrated. There were instances when it seemed that the "Air Force" expected the trainees to indulge in these "patterned evasions," and one who had learned the "trick" behind the requirement did not need to feel any guilt.* [18]

### ASSESSING INTERNAL AND EXTERNAL VALIDITY

Inferences in participant observation are subject to the same validity threats as experiments and surveys. Whereas internal validity asks whether the observations represent real differences, external validity asks whether the observations can be generalized to other populations and settings. The factors most threatening to the internal validity of participant observation include: (1) history, (2) selection, (3) maturation, (4) instrumentation, (5) testing effects, (6) experimental mortality, and (7) regression effects.

## History

History involves specific events intervening between the first and last observations. A historical factor in the military training study might be the adoption of a volunteer army policy by Congress during the training program. Current drafted trainees may develop even more negative attitudes toward the Air Force not because of the program but because of specific external events.

## Selection

Selection refers to nonrandom errors in the selection of units (informants or respondents). The observer may systematically select informants with characteristics atypical of the population. He may selectively perceive, retain, and interpret certain kinds of statements and incidents.

## Maturation

Maturation refers to natural changes in informants and respondents. When participant observers remain in the field (such as with a tribe) for a long period of time, maturation can be particularly troublesome.

## Instrumentation

Instrumentation involve changes in the method of observation. If the fieldworker "goes native," his perceptions and attitudes change. If he does not record these shifts in his daily notes, such biases may go undetected.

## Testing effects

Testing effects occur when the process of being observed affects the outcome of a later observation. Although participant observation is less obtrusive than experimentation and survey research, it still involves some intervention in the field. To observe behavior the fieldworker establishes close relationships with informants. The relationship itself may change the behavior of the observed. The observer should record in his fieldnotes any evidence of informants reacting to the process of being observed.

## Experimental mortality

Experimental mortality refers to nonrandom loss of units (informants). It is easily measured. The fieldworker simply records in his notebook who died, moved away, retired, and so forth for the various reasons.

## Regression effects

Regression effects occur when extreme units (informants) are selected for observation and false shifts occur in observations from an earlier time to a later time. Participant observation researchers are particularly interested in extreme cases—deviants, radicals, criminals, subcultures, and so on. Therefore, fieldworkers should be very sensitive to the possibility of the regression fallacy occurring in the course of interpreting changes in behavior.

External validity concerns the problem of generalizing the observations to other populations, treatments, settings, and measures. The factors most seriously threatening the external validity of participant observation inferences are: selection–treatment interaction, reactive testing, and reactive arrangements.

### Selection–treatment interaction

Selection–treatment interaction involves generalizing unrepresentative treatment effects to other populations. Since biases may be involved in the selection of the cases, the results of observation may not be generalizable to other populations. The content of the military training program, for example, may not be representative of military training programs in general; so the observation of "patterned evasions" may not be generalizable to other training programs. The fieldworker should enter in his notebook descriptions of the characteristics of those he observes so that these can be compared with characteristics of the population to which he is generalizing.

### Reactive testing

Reactive testing is a lack of generalizability to unpretested (unobserved) populations. If testing effects is a serious internal validity problem in a study, then the investigator should be concerned about whether his results can be generalized to populations that have not been observed.

### Reactive arrangements

Reactive arrangements are a lack of generalizability to other settings. The fieldworker should detail characteristics of the setting so that these can be compared with characteristics of other settings to which the results may be generalized. Becker recommends three procedures relevant to controlling reactive arrangements.[19] They suggest first that observations be recorded in the notebook in terms of whether the fieldworker was alone with the subject or whether the subject was in the company of a group. If subjects are alone, they may say things opposed to group opinion; but in the presence of a group, they may conform to group norms. The setting may change the results and, therefore, should be recorded in the notebook. Second, records should be kept as to whether the statements were volunteered by the subject or whether they were solicited by the observer. Third, a record should be kept of the observer's role in a group he is observing—whether he is a complete participant, participant-as-observer, observer-as-participant, or complete observer.

## Advantages and Limitations

Participant observation has a number of positive features.[20] First, the researcher can reformulate the problem and hypotheses as research progresses. Experimentation and survey research, on the other hand, require standardization of stimuli and data collection, so problem reformulation in the field is highly restricted. Second, the researcher is better able to develop a valid technique of observation, because field experience reveals poor categories and questions. Third, the researcher is better able to generate and test new insights and hypotheses. Finally, participant observation places the most qualified people in contact with the data in the field at a lower cost than survey research.

Its major limitations are two. First, it is difficult to conduct statistical tests on participant observation evidence because of the nonstandardized manner in which data are collected. Second, selective perception and bias are likely to occur because of the personal relationships the fieldworker establishes in the field and because of the subjective nature of many of the interpretations placed on the data.

## LEARNING AID

1. Participant observation is a combination of research techniques, including _____ in the daily lives of those being studied, for the systematic _____ of _____.

2. Participant observation may consist of any of the following research techniques: (a) _____ (b) _____ (c) _____ (d) _____ (e) _____.

3. Name and explain the five stages of participant observation:
   a. _____
   b. _____
   c. _____
   d. _____
   e. _____

4. Name and explain the four participant observer roles:
   a. _____
   b. _____
   c. _____
   d. _____

5. Name and explain the four stages of the constant comparative method of analysis:
   a. _____
   b. _____
   c. _____
   d. _____

6. Name and explain the factors most seriously threatening the internal validity of participant observation:
   a. _____
   b. _____
   c. _____
   d. _____

e. _____

f. _____

g. _____

7.  Name and explain the factors most seriously threatening the external validity of participant observation:

a. _____

b. _____

c. _____

8.  Discuss the major advantages of participant observation:

a. _____

b. _____

c. _____

d. _____

9.  Discuss the major disadvantages of participant observation:

a. _____

b. _____

· · · · · · · · · · · · · · · · · · · · · · · · · · · · · · · · · · · · · · · · · · · · · · · · · · · · · · · · · ·

**1.** sharing (engaging, participating), description, behavior

**2.** (a) direct observation, (b) respondent interviewing, (c) informant interviewing, (d) document analysis, and (e) direct participation

**3.** See text for explanation. (a) formulating problems and working hypotheses, (b) entering the field, (c) recording and analyzing observations, (d) refining the analysis and observations, (e) assessing internal and external validity

**4.** (a) complete participant, (b) participant-as-observer, (c) observer-as-participant, (d) complete observer. See text for explanation of roles.

**5.** See text for explanation. (a) comparing incidents applicable to each category, (b) integrating categories and their properties, (c) delimiting the theory, (d) writing the theory.

**6.** See text for explanation. (a) history, (b) selection, (c) maturation, (d) instrumentation, (e) testing effects, (f) experimental mortality, (g) regression effects

**7.** See text for explanation. (a) selection–treatment interaction, (b) reactive testing, (c) reactive arrangements

**8.** See text.

**9.** See text.

## FOOTNOTES

1.  Eugene Webb, Donald Campbell, Richard Schwartz, and Lee Sechrest, *Unobtrusive Measures: Nonreactive Research in the Social Sciences* (Chicago: Rand McNally, 1966).

2. This section on content analysis relies heavily on Ole Holsti, *Content Analysis for the Social Sciences and Humanities* (Reading, Mass.: Addison-Wesley, 1969).

3. Dina Zinnes, R. C. North, and H. Koch, "Capability, Threat and the Outbreak of War," in J. N. Rosenau, ed., *International Politics and Foreign Policy* (New York: Free Press, 1961), pp. 469–82.

4. David McClelland, *The Achieving Society* (Princeton: Van Nostrand, 1961).

5. Richard Merritt, *Symbols of American Community 1735–1775* (New Haven: Yale University Press, 1966).

6. Reported in Charles Osgood, "The Representational Model and Relevant Research Methods," in I. de S. Pool, *Trends in Content Analysis* (Urbana: University of Illinois Press, 1959), pp. 69–71.

7. Holsti, *Content Analysis for the Social Science and Humanities,* pp. 154–56.

8. Phillip Stone, et al., *The General Inquirer* (Cambridge: M.I.T. Press, 1966).

9. Holsti, *Content Analysis for the Social Sciences and Humanities,* pp. 151–52.

10. George McCall and J. L. Simmons, Eds., *Issues in Participant Observation* (Reading, Mass.: Addison-Wesley, 1969), pp. 1–5, 61–64.

11. M. Sullivan, S. Queen, and R. Patrick, "Participant Observation as Employed in the Study of a Military Training Program," *American Sociological Review* 23 (1958): 660–67.

12. Raymond Gold, "Rules in Sociological Field Observations," *Social Forces* 36 (1958): 217–23.

13. See J. Dean, R. Eichhorn, and L. Dean, "Establishing Field Relations," in *An Introduction to Social Research,* ed. John Doby (New York: Appleton-Century-Crofts, 1967), 2nd ed., 281–183; and John Lofland, *Analyzing Social Settings* (Belmont: Wadsworth, 1971), p. 95.

14. See Lofland, *Analyzing Social Settings,* pp. 101–109, and McCall and Simmons, *Issues in Participant Observation,* pp. 73–75.

15. Barney Glaser, *"The Constant Comparative Method of Qualitative Analysis,"* *Social Problems* 12 (1965): 436–45.

16. George McCall, "The Problem of Indicators in Participant Observation Research," *Issues in Participant Observation,* ed. by George McCall and J. Simmons (Reading: Addison-Wesley, 1969), p. 233. Copyright 1969 by Addison-Wesley. Reprinted by permission of the publisher.

17. Glaser, "The Constant Comparative Method of Qualitative Analysis," 440.

18. Sullivan, Queen, and Patrick, "Participant Observation as Employed in the Study of a Military Training Program," 665.

19. Howard Becker, "Problems of Inference and Proof in Participant Observations," *American Sociological Review* 23 (December, 1958): 652–50.

20. John Dean, et al., "Limitations and Advantages of Unstructured Methods," *An Introduction to Social Research,* ed. John Doby (New York: Appleton-Century-Crofts), 2nd ed., pp. 274–79.

# 17
# The Ethics of Political and Social Inquiry

# INTRODUCTION

Political and social inquiry is often conducted in the midst of public controversy. This is not to be unexpected, for the results of research often serve the interests of some and threaten the interests of others. Thus, power-seekers recognize that knowledge is an important source of power. Sometimes knowledge is used to legitimate the use and abuse of power. Other times knowledge has the function of increasing the capability to change and control events. Regardless of how knowledge is used, competitors for power occasionally attempt to suppress, control, or support knowledge when it serves their interests. Consequently, pressures are applied directly and indirectly to social scientists because they are perceived as the gatekeepers of social scientific information.

In the process of seeking, transmitting, and using knowledge, social scientists confront many difficult ethical questions.[1] Seeking knowledge, the ultimate goal for social scientists, often conflicts with such other values as human dignity, privacy, national security, and so forth. Seeking knowledge may also conflict with the standards of conduct established by professional associations and governments. Social scientists cannot avoid these difficult choices affecting the integrity of their research and perhaps their own personal welfare. In this unit we will examine seven such ethical issues for social scientists: (1) deception, (2) treatment of subjects, (3) confidentiality, (4) invasion of privacy, (5) governmental intervention, (6) scholarship, and (7) advocacy. In discussing each issue, we will also present related strandards of conduct adopted by various social science associations.[2] The accompanying Learning Aids consist of essay questions (with no answers) that involve the students making the value judgments that professional social scientists must make in the course of their research.

# DECEPTION

Deception has been frequently employed in social science research. In fact, it is now almost a standard feature of social psychological experiments. Social scientists and their professional organizations, however, have begun to question the moral and methodological implications of research designs employing deception-laden techniques.[3] We will examine their responses to this issue, but first we will turn to the basic types of deception occurring in social science: covert observation, deception experiments, deception surveys, and professional misrepresentation.

## Covert Observation

*Covert Observation* involves investigators using another identity as they gather data and participate in the daily lives of their subjects. For example, Festinger, Riecken, and Schacter infiltrated an unorthodox religious group by posing as converts.[4] The little group of true believers firmly believed that floods and a cataclysm would destroy the earth on December 21. The researchers joined the group to study the effects of the disconfirmation of strongly held beliefs on group members. Prior to the eve of the predicted catastrophe, some members of the group were observed to give up their jobs and possessions. On the eve of the event the group gathered at the house of the leader who declared that a visitor from the Planet Clarion would arrive at midnight to escort them to safety by way of a flying saucer. When the disaster failed to occur, the group considered and rejected various explanations. Finally at 4:45 A.M. the leader emerged from another room and announced she had received a message to the effect that since the little group of believers had spread so much light God decided to call off the catastrophe. The authors justified covert observation as the only feasible technique for studying this unusual event.

In another instance Scott McNall studied how, why, and through what processes people joined radical right groups by covertly observing an anticommunist organization in a large Pacific Northwest city.[5] Because of the suspiciousness of the members of the organization, the investigator assumed the role of a potential recruit or believer for a period of about three years. He was called on to demonstrate his support by repeating the dogma, distributing leaflets, selling materials, stuffing envelopes, and so on. The investigator indicated that participant observation was the best way of studying the organization and that a strictly survey research approach could not get at the internal dynamics of the group. At no time did he challenge their ideas, argue with them, or criticize their life style. The researcher concluded that the members of the organization tended to be downwardly mobile and concentrated in the lower social classes, older people, alienated with authoritarian leanings, located in an area characterized by high rates of social disorganization and low social status, members in fundamentalist churches, and living close to the organization.

Humphreys conducted a study of men who engage in restroom sex ("tearoom trade") by posing as a homosexual.[6] He argued that the topic was a significant and legitimate one for sociologists since the majority of arrests on homosexual charges resulted from meetings in public restrooms. Because of the nature of the situation, he maintained he had to become a covert participant observer of furtive and felonious acts:

*Fortunately, the very fear and suspicion of tearoom participants produces a mechanism that makes such observation possible: a third man (generally one who obtains voyeuristic pleasure from his duties) serves as a lookout, moving back and forth from door to windows. Such a "watchqueen," as he is labeled in the homosexual argot, coughs when a police car stops nearby or when a stranger approaches. He nods affirmatively when he recognizes a man entering as being a "regular." Having been taught the watchqueen role by a cooperating respondent, I played that part faithfully while observing hundreds of acts of fellatio. After developing a systematic observation sheet, I recorded fifty of these encounters (involving 53 sexual acts) in great detail. These records were compared with another 30 made by a cooperating respondent who was himself a sexual participant. . . . By passing as a deviant, I had observed their sexual behavior without disturbing it. Now, I was faced with interviewing these men (often in the presence of their wives) without destroying them. Fortunately, I held another research job which placed me in the position of preparing the interview schedule for a social health survey of a random selection of male subjects throughout the community. With permission from the survey's directors, I could add my sample to the larger group (thus enhancing their anonymity) and interview them as part of the social health survey.[7]*

Covert observation has, therefore, been used in a number of social science research designs. Later, we will discuss their moral and methodological implications. We will now turn to the second kind of deception employed in social and political research.

## Deception Experiments

*Deception experiments* involve letting a person believe that he is acting as the experimenter or the accomplice of the experimenter when he is in fact serving as the subject.[8] In Milgram's experiments on obedience, the subjects were led to believe that they were participating in a learning study and were instructed to administer increasingly severe shocks to another person who did not learn the appropriate word–pair associations.[9] The victim was, of course, the accomplice of the experimenter and did not really receive any shocks. The accomplice responded according to a predetermined schedule and increasingly protested the shocks and cried out in pain. As the experiment proceeded, the naïve subject was commanded to administer increasingly more intense shocks to the victim, even to the point of reaching the level marked "Danger: Severe Shock." The procedure created extreme levels of nervous tension in subjects including sweating, trembling, stuttering, and nervous laughter. Obedience was operationally defined as the maximum intensity shock the subject was willing to administer before he refused to participate further. Milgram found that of the 40 subjects, 26 obeyed the orders of the experimenter to the end, proceeding to punish the victim until they reached the maximum shock labeled 450 volts, two steps beyond the designation, "Dander: Severe Shock." Milgram considered the obedience experiment to be significant because it shed light on why people obeyed orders they considered to be wrong. Experiments such as this one, it is claimed, may help to explain why millions of Jews were slaughtered on command and why participants in Watergate obeyed orders.

## Deception Surveys

*Deception surveys* involve the concealment of the true purposes of the researcher. In most cases deception is used because it is feared that knowledge of the purpose will affect the answers respondents provide. If, for example, interviewers introduce themselves as conducting a study of prejudice, the respondent is likely to try not to sound prejudiced. If the welfare department sponsors a study and interviewers indicate the purpose of the study is to determine how much welfare money is misspent, then a recipient's responses are likely to be modified to guard against the loss of benefits. Thus, to enhance the reliability of their studies, survey researchers may deceive respondents as to the true purposes of the investigation. Babbie states that the researcher is obliged to be honest with his respondents concerning both the sponsor and the auspices of the study. However, with regard to the purposes Babbie proposes:

*(1) The researcher should tell nothing about the purpose of the study that is likely to affect the reliability of responses. (2) At the same time, he should tell respondents whatever he can about purposes where such information will not likely affect responses. (3) Explanations of purpose should be kept general rather than specific. (4) The researcher should never offer fictitious reasons for the study.*[10]

## Professional Misrepresentation

*Professional misrepresentation* occurs when social scientists claim false qualifications, affiliations, and objectives. One form of professional misrepresentation occurs when a social scientist operates as a consultant in an area in which he lacks technical competence. When social scientists testify in court, their competency is particularly subjected to scrutiny and test. A second form of misrepresentation occurs when a social scientist uses his professional standing as a cloak for gathering intelligence information and for conducting clandestine intelligence operations in other countries. Deceptive use of scholarly status has also been employed by social scientists in the United States. Persons posing as political science students or scholars have been planted on the staffs of opposing candidates for public office allegedly for the purpose of collecting material of a research character.[11] A third form of professional misrepresentation occurs when social scientists fail to disclose fully all sources of financial support for their research. Special conditions and relationships with the sponsor can affect the conduct, interpretation, and release of the study for publication. Disclosure of financial sources, therefore, is relevant for editors for judging its inclusion in a professional journal.

The use of deception has been a matter of controversy for social scientists. There has been agreement, however, on the use of professional misrepresentation. For example, the American Sociological Association states:

*The sociologist should recognize his own limitations and when appropriate, seek more expert assistance or decline to undertake research beyond his competence. He must not misrepresent his own abilities, or the competence of his staff to conduct a particular research project.*[12]

The American Political Science Association more specifically states that the individual:

1. Must avoid any deception or misrepresentation concerning his personal involvement or the involvement of respondents or subjects, or use research as a cover for intelligence work.

2. Refrain from using his professional status to obtain data and research materials for purposes other than scholarship.

3. With respect to research abroad, should not concurrently accept any additional support from agencies of the government for purposes that cannot be disclosed.[13]

Covert observation, deception experiments, and deception surveys are more controversial among social scientists than professional misrepresentation. Standards concerning these actions have not been incorporated into the codes of ethnics of the American Sociological Association, American Psychological Association, or the American Association for Public Opinion Research. The reluctance to state restrictions implies that these are not simple issues. They often involve balancing the interests of the advancement of knowledge against some other value such as privacy or the thoughtful treatment of those who supply the data. Some argue that if all deception is eliminated from research the loss would be great, for many experiments and surveys about human behavior would be impossible. On the other hand, if deception is routinely used, the public will lose its näiveté about experiments and come to distrust totally experiments and what experimenters specify as their purposes. Under such circumstances, experiments would lose their validity. In short, social science cannot and should not be based on massive deception.

Instead, Kelman maintains that social scientists should: (1) become more aware of the negative implications of deception and use it only when justified (lack of feasible alternatives and significance of topic) and not as a matter of habit; (2) explore ways of counteracting and minimizing negative consequences of deception when it is used (postexperimental feedback to the subject about what the experiment was about); and (3) develop new experimental techniques that dispense with deception but rely on the subject's positive motivations (e.g., role playing).[14]

## LEARNING AID

1. List, define, and give examples of the four types of deception found in social science research.
2. Do you propose the complete elimination of deception under all circumstances in social and political inquiry, or do you think some circumstances justify the use of deception? Formulate a standard of conduct and be able to defend it.

## TREATMENT OF SUBJECTS

The treatment of subjects has been an issue for some time in the medical profession. The question frequently centers on whether a drug should be denied to those selected to be in a control group and how they should be selected. Campbell discusses the problem:

*Consider the heroic Salk poliomyelitis vaccine trials in which some children were given the vaccine while others were given an inert saline placebo injection—and in which many more of these placebo controls would die than would have if they had been given the vaccine. Creation of these placebo controls would have been morally, psychologically, and socially impossible had there been enough vaccine for all. As it was, due to the scarcity, most children that year had to go without the vaccine anyway. The creation of experimental and control groups was the highly moral allocation of that scarcity so as to enable us to learn the true efficacy of the supposed good. . . . The political stance furthering social experimentation here is the recognition of randomization as the most democratic and moral means of allocating scarce resources (and scarce hazardous duties), plus the moral imperative to further utilize the randomization so that society may indeed learn true value of the supposed boon.*[15]

Another example occurred in which no such scarcity of the product existed. In 1972 the U.S. Public Health Service terminated a program in which a group of syphilis victims was denied proper medical treatment for the disease during a 40-year federal experiment.[16] The syphilis experiment, called the "Tuskegee

Study," began in 1932 in Tuskegee, Alabama, an area having the highest syphilis rate in the nation at that time. The discovery of penicillin as a cure for syphilis occurred 10 years after the beginning of the study and was not generally available until five years after that. Treatment in the 1930s consisted primarily of doses of arsenic and mercury. Of the 600 original participants in the study, one-third showed no signs of having syphilis whereas the others had contracted it. Half of the men with syphilis were given the arsenic–mercury treatment, but the other half, about 200 men, received no treatment for the syphilis at all, even after penicilin was discovered as a cure for syphilis. A number of persons died as a direct result of untreated syphilis since the beginning of the study. The federal government subsequently approved a $37,500 settlement for each survivor and $15,000 for the estates of deceased participants.

No comparable physical "horror stories" to our knowledge have yet befallen the social sciences. However, controversy has occurred over the proper treatment of subjects in psychological experiments. The issue involves how much stress and loss of dignity is justifiable in experiments. A few years ago, Milgram's experiment on obedience was at the center of the controversy. Baumrind in particular criticized Milgram for subjecting people to extreme stress:

*I do regard the emotional distrubance described by Milgram as potentially harmful because it could easily effect an alteration in the subject's self-image or ability to trust adult authorities in the future. It is potentially harmful to a subject to commit, in the course of an experiment, acts which he himself considers unworthy, particularly when he has been entrapped into committing such acts by an individual he has reason to trust. The subject's personal responsibility for his actions is not erased because the experimenter reveals to him the means which he used to stimulate these actions. The subject realizes that he would have hurt the victim if the current were on. The realization that he also made a fool of himself by accepting the experimental set results in additional loss of self-esteem. Moreover, the subject finds it difficult to express his anger outwardly after the experimenter in a self-acceptant but friendly manner reveals the hoax.*[17]

In reply to Baumrind's criticism, Milgram argued:

*In review, the facts are these: (a) At the outset, there was the problem of studying obedience by means of a simple experimental procedure. The results could not be foreseen before the experiment was carried out. (b) Although the experiment generated momentary stress in some subjects, this stress dissipated quickly and was not injurious. (c) Dehoax and follow-up procedures were carried out to insure the subjects' well-being. (d) These procedures were assessed through questionnaire and psychiatric studies and were found to be effective. (e) Additional steps were taken to enhance the value of the laboratory experience for participants, for example, submitting to each subject a careful report on the experimental program. (f) The subjects themselves strongly endorse the experiment, and indicate satisfaction at having participated.*[18]

Each student will have to judge the issue for himself. The American Sociological Association prescribes that all research should avoid causing personal harm to subjects used in research. The American Psychological Association has the most complete set of standards relating to the treatment of subjects:

*Principle 16.   Research Precautions.   The psychologist assumes obligations for the welfare of his research subjects, both animal and human.*

 a.   *Only when a problem is of scientific significance and it is not practicable to investigate it in any other way is the psychologist justified in exposing research subjects, whether children or adults, to physical or emotional stress as part of an investigation.*

 b.   *When a reasonable possibility of injurious aftereffects exists, research is conducted only when the subjects or their responsible agents are fully informed of this possibility and agree to participate nevertheless.*

 c.   *The psychologist seriously considers the possibility of harmful aftereffects and avoids them or removes them as soon as permitted by the design of the experiment.*[19]

## LEARNING AID

**1.**   Do you agree or disagree with Campbell that "randomization is the most democratic and moral means of allocating scarce resources"? Defend your view.
**2.**   State the ethical issue concerning the treatment of subjects.
**3.**   Specify the principles adopted by professional associations for regulating abuses of treatment to subjects. Do you think they are adequate to meet the problem or not? If not, specify how they are inadequate and how they can be improved.

## CONFIDENTIALITY

Confidentiality is often confused with anonymity although they are distinct operations. *Anonymity* occurs when the researcher himself cannot identify a given person's response.[20] Anonymity exists, for example, in a mail survey where identification numbers are not placed on the questionnaire. Anonymity is sometimes used where it is felt that it will increase the accuracy of the responses and where the researchers do not want to be in a position of being asked for names of sexual deviants, drug offenders, or whatever. *Confidentiality* occurs when the researcher can identify a given person's response, but he promises the person he will not do so. Confidentiality, therefore, is different from anonymity, and the two terms should not be used interchangeably.

Confidentiality also should not be granted casually to a repondent, for it carries serious legal questions for the researcher. Confidentiality is promised by the researcher with no legal authority whatsoever. Although the Federal Rules of Evidence recognize and define privileges between lawyers and clients, husbands and wives, psychotherapists and patients and so forth, no such privileged relationship is legally recognized for the researcher and respondent. Confidentiality, therefore, must be maintained by the researcher himself. The researcher and his records can be subpoenaed by various government investigative bodies and grand juries, and the researcher can be ordered to reveal and identify his sources and the content of the information in his research. If he refuses to obey the order, he risks imprisonment up to 180 days for one act of contempt of court.

James Carroll's analysis of the Popkin case demonstrates the seriousness and complexity of confidentiality for social scientists.[21] Samuel Popkin was a 30-year-old assistant professor of government at Harvard. He was a serious scholar on Vietnam, having published a number of articles and books on the subject. In 1971 two F.B.I. agents visited him asking many questions about the personal habits and characteristics of Daniel Ellsberg and about the Pentagon Papers. Subsequently, he was subpoenaed to appear before a federal grand jury. Popkin and 24 other political and social scientists filed a motion for an order protecting him from an inquiry concerning information obtained by him in his capacity as a scholar, author, and teacher. His motion was denied, and he was then granted limited immunity from prosecution and ordered to testify. Popkin was asked 126 questions by the grand jury, but he refused to answer seven questions involving his opinion concerning who possessed the Pentagon Papers, the identity of persons who furnished him information that enabled him to form an opinion as to who possessed the papers, the identity of persons having knowledge of who participated in the Pentagon Papers study, and whether he discussed the Papers with Daniel Ellsberg. For refusing to answer these questions Popkin was ordered in contempt of court and was imprisoned in the federal section of the Norfolk County jail in Dedham, Massachusetts. The Popkin case involved a conflict between different forms of the public's right to know. On the one hand, the public acting through a grand jury has a right to inquire into the conditions of society and to determine whether there is probable cause to believe an individual has committed a crime. On the other hand, the public has a right to know the results of research inquiring into the conditions of society and the operations of government. Carroll summarizes Popkin's argument as follows:

*Informed and free choice by knowledgeable citizens is the fundamental basis of a free society. The opportunity to exercise informed choice depends on a free flow of information to the public from individuals and organizations engaged in research and publishing. This free flow of information often depends on the right of researchers and reporters to assure confidentiality to sources. Without such assurances elected officials, members of bureaucracy, dissidents, social deviants, and other members of the public will refuse to divulge information that may be important to the effective exercise of public choice. Sources will be inhibited by timidity, fear of embarrassment, and fear of reprisal. The shutting off of confidential information concerning the conditions of society and the operations of government could make the public excessively or totally dependent on official governmental versions of "the truth." For these reasons a researcher should not be ordered to divulge confidential sources and data to a grand jury or similar body except on the basis of a finding by the presiding judge that the government has demonstrated that the researcher has information that is relevant to a specific probable violation of law, that the information cannot be obtained by alternative means less destructive of First Amendment rights, and that the government has demonstrated a compelling and overriding interest in the information.*[22]

As a result of the Popkin case the American Political Science Association has adopted the following principle:

*The scholar has an ethical obligation to make a full and complete disclosure of all non-confidential sources involved in his or her research so that his or her work can be tested or replicated. The scholar, as a citizen, has an obligation to cooperate with grand juries, other law enforcement agencies, and institutional officials. He or she also has a professional duty not to divulge the identity of confidential sources of information or data developed in the course of research, whether to governmental or non-governmental officials or bodies, even though in the present state of American law he or she runs the risk of suffering some sort of penalty. Since the protection of confidentiality of sources is often essential in social science research, and since the continued growth of such research is clearly in the public interest, scholars have an obligation to seek to change the law so that the confidentiality of sources of information may be safeguarded. Scholars must, however, exercise appropriate restraint in making claims as to the confidential nature of their sources, and resolve all reasonable doubts in favor of full disclosure.*[23]

The response by the American Sociological Association is as follows:

*Confidential information provided by a research subject must be treated as such by the sociologist. Even though research information is not a privileged communication under the law, the sociologist must, as far as possible, protect subjects and informants. Any promises made to such persons must be honored. However, provided that he respects the assurances he has given his subjects, the sociologist has no obligation to withhold information of misconduct of individuals or organizations.*

*If an informant or other subject should wish, however, he can formally release the researcher of a promise of confidentiality. The provisions of this section apply to all members of research organizations (i.e., interviewers, coders, clerical staff, etc.), and it is the responsibility of the chief investigators to see that they are instructed in the necessity and importance of maintaining the confidentiality of the data. The obligation of the sociologist includes the use and storage of original data to which a subject's name is attached. When requested, the identity of an organization or subject must be adequately disguised in publication.*[24]

## LEARNING AID

**1.** Examine the legal and ethical questions of confidentiality with particular reference to the Popkin case.

**2.** Under what circumstances, if any, does a researcher have a duty to promise a source of information not to reveal the identity of the source and the content of what is learned?

**3.** Under what circumstances, if any, should a researcher reveal the identity of a source and the information developed in confidence?

## INVASION OF PRIVACY

Privacy is, of course, one of the most cherished rights in a free society, and social scientists often find themselves intruding on this privacy when they collect their data. The value conflict then occurs between the need for privacy and the need for knowledge. Individual privacy may be violated by at least three types of social science research techniques.[25] First, *self-descriptions* elicited by interviews, questionnaires, and personality tests may be so carefully designed that they may trap the individual into making public those facts and feelings about himself or others that he otherwise would not want disclosed. A privacy issue arises additionally if the individual does not participate willingly, or if he participates without knowledge that information is being elicited from him, or if he does not understand the use of the information, or if he is duped or coerced into participation. Second, *direct observations and recording of individual behavior* may intrude on privacy as in the cases of covert participant observation or observation through a one-way mirror or observation using eavesdropping techniques. Third, *descriptions by informants or the use of secondary data* may also violate privacy. Examples include eliciting information from children about their parents' relationship, using institutional records compiled for one purpose (e.g., a sociological study of poor people) for another purpose (welfare agency information about the behavior of their clients), or digging through wastepaper baskets and trash cans for discarded information.

The most famous case involving invasion of privacy in social science research is the Wichita Jury Recording Case.[26] In 1952 researchers at the University of Chicago undertook a $400,000 research grant funded by the Ford Foundation to study the nature and operation of the jury system. They undertook the study because of the increasing debate over the effectiveness of juries. Some people maintained that the jury system was supportive of civil rights and was the cornerstone of the American judicial system. Others criticized the fitness of jury trials for some types of litigation. A number of reforms were advocated. The researchers felt that the debate of the jury system involved many untested assumptions about the operation of juries and that more information about how juries work was needed.

The Chicago researcher initially formulated a research design that involved interviewing jurors and conducting simulated trials and jury proceedings. Consulting lawyers thought that interviewing jurors was a flawed procedure because jurors often forget what occurred in the jury room and sometimes even shape the information so that it sounds more socially acceptable. The lawyers suggested the possibility of obtaining consent for obtaining exact information of jury deliberations by installing tape recordings in the jury rooms. The researchers pursued the idea and began discussions with a U.S. District Court judge. Before consent would be granted they had to develop an elaborate procedure for guarding the recorders, exclusion of recordings in criminal cases, the assurance of no publicity until after the completion of the research, editing of the transcripts by the judge, and destruction of the original transcripts under the supervision of the judge. The Chief Judge of the U.S. State Court of Appeals ultimately approved of the research being carried out provided that the jurors were informed. Subsequently, the researchers obtained consent to record a limited number of trials without the knowledge of the jurors. After about a year of data collection, reports about the research surfaced and the public reacted against it. Public hearings were held by the Internal Security Subcommittee of the Senate Commitee on the Judiciary. The members of the subcommittee attacked the researchers' invasion of privacy and their affront to the judicial system. The subcommittee appeared even more interested in showing this as another example of the communist subversive threat to the internal security of the United States. Bills were introduced in both houses of Congress, and the result was that President Eisenhower signed into law a measure prohibiting, under penalty of a $1,000 fine and/or one year in prison, the recording of jury deliberations of federal petit or grand juries for any purpose whatsoever.

## LEARNING AID

1. Explain the ways in which social science research techniques may constitute an invasion of privacy.
2. Recount the Wichita Jury Recording Case. Do you agree or disagree that a law prohibiting jury recordings was justified? Defend your position.

## GOVERNMENTAL INTERVENTION

Since knowledge is power and since governments are concerned with the control of power, governments sometimes attempt to regulate the search for knowledge. Regulation may involve financial support for some kinds of research and nonsupport for others. Nonsupport of research may extend to the passage of laws prohibiting certain methods of research. Scientists have often been at odds with the law. Galileo, for example, felt the heavy hand of a government fearful of the implications of his research. On the other hand, scientists may be willing or unwilling instruments of state power through the development of useful tools or by supporting governmental policy with results of research. In this section, we shall examine how governments may intervene in social scientific inquiry, how the norms of science may come into conflict with the norms of government, and how social scientists have reacted to threats of governmental censorship of social scientific research.

Governmental initiation of the Tuskegee Syphilis Study and then governmental termination of the study in 1972 have already been discussed. We also described the approval by federal court judges of the Wichita Jury Study and then Congressional hearings and the enactment of a law prohibiting the use of recorders in jury deliberations. We turn now to a third case of governmental intervention in social scientific inquiry, Project Camelot.

Project Camelot was a social science research program formulated in late 1964 by the Department of Defense.[27] A number of high ranking Army officers were concerned about the guerrilla wars and revolutions occurring in Cuba, Vietnam, and the Congo. They realized that the conventional and nuclear war weapons were of limited use in this new type of combat. They began to ask why this type of "hardware" cannot be used effectively and whether social science can provide any useful "software" alternatives.

A well-known Latin American specialist was chosen as the director of the project. The objectives of the research were to measure and forecast the causes of insurgencies and revolutions in the underdeveloped countries and to find ways of coping effectively with them. As the name implies, the purpose of Project Camelot was to find ways of creating and maintaining peaceful and orderly societies.

The U.S. Army contracted with the Special Operations Research Organization of American University to the amount of $6 million to be spent over three or four years. A recruiting letter was sent to important scholars all over the world inviting them to participate in a multimillion dollar study to "make it possible to predict and influence politically significant aspects of social change in the developing nations of the world." A number of famous scholars in sociology, political science, economics, and psychology responded favorably and subsequently helped to develop the technical aspects of the research design.

Only seven months after its creation, Project Camelot was abruptly cancelled by the government in June, 1965. We will describe some of the events leading to its termination. An assistant professor of anthropology at Pittsburgh planned a trip to Chile and asked the research director for involvement in the project. Being a former citizen of Chile, he was asked to prepare a report concerning the possibilities of cooperation from Chilean scholars for a modest fee. Despite the limitations placed on his involvement, the anthropologist conveyed the impression to Chilean scholars that he was an official of Project Camelot and had the authority to make proposals to prospective participants. In the course of a meeting with the officials of the University of Chile, he was challenged to describe the ultimate aims of the project, its sponsors, and military implications.

At about the same time a Norwegian sociologist in Chile doing research received an invitation to participate in a Camelot planning session for $2,000. The sociologist refused the invitation because he could not accept the role of the U.S Army as a sponsoring agent in a study of counter-insurgency. Subsequently, he called the nature of Camelot to the attention of Chilean intellectuals, the left-wing press, and members of the Chilean Senate. The Chilean leftists bitterly attacked the American researchers, the project, and the United States. The American Ambassador to Chile, not having been informed by the Department of Defense about the existence of Project Camelot, became furious and called for its cancellation. Meanwhile, back in Washington, tensions between the Department of State and the Department of Defense grew. A number of United States senators demanded hearings about the project in the Foreign Relations Committee, and the House of Representatives also scheduled hearings in the Foreign Affairs Committee.

President Johnson finally interceded and announced the termination of Project Camelot. He decided in favor of the State Department and issued an executive order that no government sponsorship of foreign area research should be undertaken that in the judgment of the Secretary of State would adversely affect United States foreign relations. Presently, the State Department screens and judges all federally-financed research projects conducted in other countries.

Jessie Bernard, a participant in Project Camelot, summarizes what she thinks are the major ethical issues raised by the project:

*The major issues of concern to social scientists resulting from the cancellation of the project appear to be: 1) the responsibility of social scientists for the use made of their findings; 2) the ethical problems involved in funding; and 3) censorship.*

*1) What are the moral or social responsibilities of the social-scientist researcher with respect to the uses of the results of his work. This question was raised with reference to Project CAMELOT, as it has also been raised with atomic research. . . . Some argued that the findings could be used to foment revolutions . . . ; others, that they could be used to repress them. . . . Project CAMELOT was especially "vulnerable" because findings were to be unclassified, hence available to "bad guys" as well as "good guys."*

*Since all scientific findings can be used by "bad guys" as well as by "good guys," the question arises as to whether the problems set for Project CAMELOT should be researched at all. Or, if researched, should they be classified, "undercover," and available only to the sponsor?*

*2) . . . the second question is, By whom should the research be done? A number of people believed the problems should be researched . . . but that the research should not be funded by the Department of Defense. Perhaps by the United Nations or by foundations. Even, however, if funded by a peace research organization, the findings could still be used by both "good" and "bad guys." The first issue raised remains unresolved.*

*Since such research requires a large staff and a great deal of money, it may be that the major problem is how it should be organized. Perhaps a totally new concept is needed in the field of the organization of science in politically sensitive areas. A concept which would make the findings nonsuspect.*

*3) On August 5, an Executive Order was issued requiring all research in foreign countries which use federal funds to be cleared by the Department of State. Censorship implications of this Order constitute a fundamental issue for social scientists. The implementation of this Order is, therefore, a major concern for them. They will certainly wish to be consulted in the setting up of guidelines.*[28]

Horowitz concluded that censorship was perhaps the most serious ethical issue raised by Camelot:

*In conclusion, two important points must be clearly kept in mind and clearly apart. First, Project Camelot was intellectually, and from my own perspective, ideologically unsound. However, and more significantly, Camelot was not cancelled because of its faulty intellectual approaches. Instead, its cancellation came as an act of government censorship and an expression of the contempt for social science so prevalent among those who need it most. Thus it was political expedience, rather than its lack of scientific merit, that led to the demise of Camelot because it threatened to rock State Department relations with Latin America.*

*Second, giving the State Department the right to screen and approve government-funded social science research projects on other countries, as the President has ordered, is a supreme act of censorship. Among the agencies that grant funds for such research are the National Institutes of Mental Health, the National Science Foundation, the National Aeronautics and Space Agency, and the Office of Education. Why should the State Department have veto power over the scientific pursuits of men and projects funded by these and other agencies in order to satisfy the policy needs—or policy failures—of the moment? President Johnson's directive is a gross violation of the autonomous nature of science.*[29]

The American Anthropological Association reacted to this governmental directive of research grant overview by stating that the review procedures offered a dangerous potential for censorship of research.[30] The American Political Science Association recommended that funding agencies adopt the following principles:

*Rule 9. Financial sponsors of research have the responsibility for avoiding actions that would call into question the integrity of American academic institutions as centers of independent teaching and research. They should not sponsor research as a cover for intelligence activities.*

*Rule 10. Openness concerning material support of research is a basic principle of scholarship. In making grants for research, government and non-government sponsors should openly acknowledge research support and require that the grantee indicate in any published research financed by their grants the relevant sources of financial support. Where anonymity is requested by a non-governmental grantor and does not endanger the integrity of research, the character of the sponsorship rather than the identity of the grantor should be noted.*

*Rule 11. Political science research supported by government grants should be unclassified.*

*Rule 12. After a research grant has been made, the grantor shall not impose any restriction on or require any clearance of research methods, procedures, or content.*[31]

## LEARNING AID

**1.** Review the case of Project Camelot and the ethical issues it raised for social science.
**2.** How did the professional associations react to Project Camelot? Do you think that their action was sufficient or not?

## SCHOLARSHIP

In the academic community there is agreement about plagiarism, distorting findings, and claiming undue credit. The principles articulated by some organizations will be presented. The American Sociological Association, for example, states:

*6. Presentation of Research Findings. The sociologist must present his findings honestly and without distortion. There should be no omission of data from a research report which might significantly modify the interpretation of findings.*

*8. Acknowledgment of Research Collaboration and Assistance. The sociologist must report fully all sources of financial support in his research publications and any special relations to the sponsor that might affect the interpretation of findings.*[32]

The American Psychological Association specifies more explicitly principles regarding publication credits:

*a. Major contributions of a professional character, made by several persons to a common project, are recognized by joint authorship. The experimenter or author who has made the principal contribution to a publication is identified as the first listed.*

*b. Minor contributions of a professional character, extensive clerical or similar nonprofessional assistance, and other minor contributions are acknowledged in footnotes or in an introductory statement.*

*c. Acknowledgment through specific citations is made for unpublished as well as published material that has directly influenced the research or writing.*[33]

Rule 20 of the American Political Science Association states that with respect to publication of the results of research the individual researcher:

*a. bears sole responsibility for publication;*

*b. should disclose relevant sources of financial support, but in cases where anonymity is justified and does not endanger the integrity of research, by noting the character of the sponsorship;*

*c.   should indicate any material condition imposed by his financial sponsors or others on his research and publication;*
*d.   should conscientiously acknowledge any assistance he receives in conducting research.*[34]

Furthermore, the American Political Science Association stipulates in Rule 1 a principle governing a troublesome aspect of the relationship between teachers and students:

*A faculty member must not expropriate the academic work of his students. As a dissertation adviser, he is not entitled to claim joint authorship with a student of a thesis or dissertation. The teacher cannot represent himself as the author of independent student research; and research assistance, paid or unpaid, requires full acknowledgement.*[35]

The American Association for Public Opinion Research has devised a set of standards for reporting poll results. Eight items of information should be included in all news reports concerning public opinion polls:

1.   Identity of who sponsored the survey.
2.   The exact wording of questions asked.
3.   A definition of the population actually sampled.
4.   Size of sample. For mail surveys, this should include both the number of questionnaires mailed out and the number returned.
5.   An indication of what allowance should be made for sampling error.
6.   Which results are based on parts of the sample, rather than the total sample, for example, likely voters only, those aware of an event, those who answered other questions in a certain way, and the like.
7.   Whether interviewing was done personally, by telephone, by mail or on street corners.
8.   Timing of the interviewing in relation to relevant events.[36]

## LEARNING AID

**1.**   State and explain the principles devised by professional associations for maintaining the integrity of scholarly research.

## ADVOCACY

Because of their subject matter, social scientists are likely to engage in such political activities as making speeches, signing statements for newspaper publication, holding office in a party, managing political campaigns, running for office, and so forth. They may participate politically either because they have deep convictions about issues or because involvement provides understanding and insight into the subject matter that may not be acquired any other way. Regardless of their motives, professionally trained social scientists are confronted with several ethical problems. How far should they go in trying to influence public opinion and policy? When is advocacy incompatible with the function of university teaching? Are they giving the impression that their views are being supported by research findings? How scrupulously must they assess a candidate or a position before endorsement for a newspaper or television advertisement? These are difficult questions. We shall examine some of the guidelines developed by the professions.

The American Psychological Association, for example, concerns itself with the making of public statements:

*Principle 5. Public Statements.   Modesty, scientific caution, and due regard for the limits of present knowledge characterize all statements of psychologists who supply information to the public, either directly or indirectly.*

a.  *Psychologists who interpret the science of psychology or the services of psychologists to clients or to the general public have an obligation to report fairly and accurately. Exaggeration, sensationalism, superficiality, and other kinds of misrepresentation are avoided.*[37]

The American Political Science Association makes the following recommendation:

*Rule 6.   The college or university teacher is a citizen, and like other citizens, he should be free to engage in political activities insofar as he can do so consistently with his obligations as a teacher and scholar. Effective service as a faculty member is often compatible with certain types of political activity, for example, holding a part-time office in a political party or serving as a citizen of a governmental advisory board. Where a professor engages in full-time political activity, such as service in a state legislature, he should, as a rule, seek a leave of absence from his institution. Since political activity by academic political scientists is both legitimate and socially important, universities and colleges should have institutional arrangements to permit such activity, including reduction in the faculty member's work-load or leave of absence, subject to equitable adjustment of compensation when necessary.*[38]

Finally, the American Association of University Professors provides the statement:

*1.   The Professor, guided by a deep conviction of the worth and dignity of the advancement of knowledge, recognizes the special responsibilities placed upon him. His primary responsibility to his subject is to seek and to state the truth as he sees it. To this end he devotes his energies to developing and improving his scholarly competence. He accepts the obligation to exercise critical self-discipline and judgment in using, extending, and transmitting knowledge. He practices intellectual honesty. Although he may follow subsidiary interests, these interests must never seriously hamper or compromise his freedom of inquiry.*[39]

## LEARNING AID

**1.** What kinds of radical political activity, if any, do you think are incompatible with the standards of conduct established by the professional associations?

**2.** Do you think the professional associations attempt to regulate the political activity of academic social scientists too much, not enough, or just about right. Take a position and defend your viewpoint.

## FOOTNOTES

1. For a summary of such issues see Nicholas Hobbs, "Ethical Issues in the Social Sciences," *International Encyclopedia of the Social Sciences,* 5, 160–66.
2. This section refers to the following codes: "Ethical Standards of Psychologists," *American Psychologist* 18 (1963): 56–60, "Toward A Code of Ethics for Sociologists," *American Sociologist* (November, 1968) 316–18; "Ethical Problems of Academic Political Scientists," *P.S.* 1 (Summer, 1968): 3–28; "Statement on Problems of Anthropological Research and Ethics," *American Anthropologist* 69 (July–August, 1967): 381–2; "Statement of Ethics of the Society for Applied Anthropology," *Human Organization* 22 (1963–1964): 237; "Code of Professional Ethics and Practices," *Public Opinion Quarterly* 24 (Fall, 1960): 529–30; "Standards for Reporting Public Opinion Polls," American Association of Public Opinion Research, reported in Harold Mendelsohn and Irving Crespi, *Polls, Television, and the New Politics* (Scranton: Chandler, 1970), 134–35; and "AAUP Statement on Professional Ethics," *American Association of University Professors Bulletin* (September, 1966).
3. Herbert Kelman, "Human Use of Human Subjects: The Problem of Deception in Social Psychological Experiments," *Psychological Bulletin* 67 (January, 1967): 1–11.
4. L. Festinger, H. Riecken, and S. Schacter, *When Prophecy Fails* (Minneapolis: University of Minnesota Press, 1956).
5. Scott McNall, "The Career of the Radical Rightest," in Scott McNall, ed., *The Sociological Perspective* (Boston: Little, Brown and Company, 1974), pp. 392–406.

6. Laud Humphreys, *Tearoom Trade: Impersonal Sex in Public Places* (Chicago: Aldine, 1970).

7. Laud Humphreys, "Tearoom Trade," *Transaction* 7 (January, 1970): 15.

8. Kelman, "Human Use of Human Subjects," 2.

9. Stanley Milgram, "Behavioral Study of Obedience," *Journal of Abnormal and Social Psychology* 67 (1963): 371–78.

10. Earl Babbie, *Survey Research Methods* (Belmont: Wadsworth, 1973), pp. 352–53.

11. "Committee on Professional Ethics and Academic Freedom," *P.S.* (Summer, 1974): 317.

12. "Toward A Code of Ethics for Sociologists," 318.

13. "Ethical Problems of Academic Political Scientists," 19.

14. Kelman, "Human Use of Human Subjects," 6–9.

15. Donald Campbell, "Reforms as Experiments," *American Psychologist* 24 (April, 1969): 419.

16. From Associated Press, July 26, 1972.

17. Diana Baumrind, "Some Thoughts on Ethics of Research: After Reading Milgram's 'Behavioral Study of Obedience,'" *American Psychologist* 19 (1964): 421 23.

18. Stanley Milgram, "Issues in the Study of Obedience: A reply to Baumrind," *American Psychologist* 19 (1964): 848–52.

19. "Ethical Standards of Psychologists," 59–60.

20. Babbie, *Survey Research Methods*, 350–51.

21. We rely heavily on Carroll's account. James Carroll, "Confidentiality of Social Science Research Sources and Data," *P.S.* 6 (Summer, 1973): 268–80.

22. Ibid., 276.

23. "Committee on Professional Ethics and Academic Freedom," *P.S.* (Fall, 1973): 451.

24. "Toward A Code of Ethics for Sociologists," 318.

25. Oscar Fuebhausen and Orville Brim, "Privacy and Behavioral Research," *Columbia Law Review* 65 (1965): 1184–1211.

26. Ted Vaughan, "Governmental Intervention in Social Research: Political and Ethical Dimensions in the Wichita Jury Recordings," in Gideon Sjoberg, ed., *Ethics, Politics, and Social Research* (Cambridge: Schenkman, 1967), 50–77.

27. Particularly useful sources are Irving Louis Horowitz, "The Life and Death of Project Camelot," *Transaction* 3 (November–December, 1965), 3–7, 44–47; Gideon Sjoberg, "Project Camelot: Selected Reactions and Personal Reflections," in Sjoberg, *Ethics, Politics, and Social Research,* 141–61.

28. Jessie Bernard, "Letter to the Editor," *American Sociologist* 1 (November, 1965): 24–25.

29. Horowitz, "Life and Death of Project Camelot," 47.

30. "Statement on Problems of Anthropological Research and Ethics," 382.

31. "Ethical Problems of Academic Political Scientists," 18.

32. "Toward A Code of Ethics for Scoiologists," 316.

33. "Ethical Standard of Psychologists," 60.
34. "Ethical Problems of Academic Political Scientists," 19.
35. Ibid., 11.
36. "Standards for Reporting Public Opinion Polls," 134.
37. "Ethical Standards of Psychologists," 57.
38. "Ethical Problems of Academic Political Scientists," 13.
39. "AAUP Statement on Professional Ethics," *AAUP Bulletin* 55 (Spring, 1969): 86–87.

# APPENDIX a
# The Multitrait-
# Multimethod Matrix

Perhaps the most significant development in the use of convergent and discriminant construct validity is the multitrait–multimethod matrix technique developed by Donald Campbell and Donald Fiske.[1] In addition to supporting the need for both convergent and discriminant construct validity, they recommend the multiple measurement of a concept with different data collection techniques. They define *validity* as the amount of agreement between two attempts to measure the same trait (concept) through maximally *different* methods. Self-esteem, for example, is validated to the extent of the correlation between two maximally different measurements of it (such as measurement by survey research and measurement by content analysis). They define *reliability* as the amount of agreement between two attempts to measure the same trait (concept) through maximally *similar* methods. Self-esteem, for example, is deemed reliable to the extent that a measurement of self-esteem by survey research at one point in time correlates with itself when measured at a second point in time (test–retest) or to the extent that a measurement of one half of the test correlates with the other half (split-half) or to the extent that one form of the measurement correlates with a different, but equivalent form of the measurement (equivalent forms).

By taking different measurements ("multimethod") of different concepts ("multitrait"), Campbell and Fiske develop a multitrait–multimethod matrix. Using the hypothetico-deductive form, they are able to generate predictions or rules of what the correlation matrix should look like if the measures are both valid and reliable. Table A–1 shows the form of the multitrait–multimethod matrix. This table presents the correlations for three traits (political efficacy = A, self-esteem = B, and alienation = C, and two methods (survey research = Method 1 and content analysis = Method 2). $A_1$ refers to a measurement of political efficacy using Method 1, survey research; $A_2$ refers to a measurement of political efficacy using Method 2, content analysis; and $C_2$ refers to a measurement of alienation using Method 2, content analysis.

The multitrait–multimethod matrix presents three kinds of coefficients (numbers). The first type is called a *reliability coefficient* (RC). It correlates the scores on a trait using the test–retest, split-half, or equivalent forms techniques. The sets of reliability coefficients make up the reliability diagonal. The second type of coefficient is the *discriminant validity coefficient* (DV).[2] It measures the correlation between different traits. There are two types of discriminant validity coefficients: (1) the type in the *heterotrait–monomethod triangle,* which involves correlations between different traits using the same method ("hetero" means different; "mono" means single or one). This triangle is represented by a closed line triangle. (2) the *heterotrait–heteromethod triangle,* which involves correlations between different traits using different methods. This triangle is represented by a dashed line triangle. The third type of coefficient shown in the

### Table A-1   MULTITRAIT–MULTIMETHOD MATRIX

|  |  | Traits | Method 1 (Survey Research) | | | Method 2 (Content Analysis) | | |
|---|---|---|---|---|---|---|---|---|
|  |  |  | $A_1$ (PE) | $B_1$ (SE) | $C_1$ (A) | $A_2$ (PE) | $B_2$ (SE) | $C_2$ (A) |
| Method 1 | (PE) | $A_1$ | RC |  |  |  |  |  |
| (Survey | (SE) | $B_1$ | DV | RC |  |  |  |  |
| Research) | (A) | $C_1$ | DV | DV | RC |  |  |  |
| Method 2 | (PE) | $A_2$ | CV | DV | DV | RC |  |  |
| (Content | (SE) | $B_2$ | DV | CV | DV | DV | RC |  |
| Analysis) | (A) | $C_2$ | DV | DV | CV | DV | DV | RC |

RC = reliability coefficient; CV = convergent validity coefficient; DV = discriminant validity coefficient; ◺ = heterotrait–monomethod triangle; ⌐◺ = heterotrait–heteromethod triangle

table is the *convergent validity coefficient* (CV), which measures the correlation between different measures of the same trait. The set of convergent validity coefficients makes up the convergent validity diagonal.

Table A-2 shows hypothetical correlation coefficients. The student will learn more about correlation coefficients in Unit 12, Descriptive Data Analysis. For now it will suffice to say that a correlation coefficient is a measure of association between two variables varying from a perfect positive association of +1.0 to a perfect negative association of −1.0. The strength of an association increases as the coefficient approaches +1.0 or −1.0. Thus, −0.8 is equally strong as +.8; −.8 is stronger than +.6; and +.8 is stronger than −.6.

Campbell and Fiske provide four general rules concerning the interpretation of the matrix with respect to validity.

1. *The convergent validity coefficients (CV) should be high.* Measurement of the same trait by different methods should produce high correlations. If high correlations are not produced, then the researcher may doubt whether the same property is being measured with each method. The student will notice in Table A-2 that the CV's (.85, .80, and .83) are quite high.

2. *The convergent validity coefficient (CV) should be higher than the discriminant validity coefficients (DV) occupying the same row or column as the CV coefficient.* In other words, measuring the same trait using different

methods (CV) should produce a higher correlation than measuring different traits using different methods (DV). Accordingly, in Table A–2 the correlation $A_1A_2$ (.85) between political efficacy measured by survey research and political efficacy measured by content analysis should be higher than the correlation $A_1B_2$ (.50) between political efficacy measured by survey research and self-esteem measured by content analysis. Similarly, the CV of .85 should be higher than the correlations $A_1C_2$ (−.45), $A_2B_1$ (.51), and $A_2C_1$ (−.47).

3. *CV coefficients should be higher than the DV coefficients in the heterotrait–monomethod triangles.* In other words, measuring the same trait using different methods (CV) should produce a higher correlation than measuring different traits using the same method. Thus, in Table A–2 the CV coefficients in the validity diagonal (.85, .80, and .83) should be higher than the DV coefficients in the top heterotrait–monomethod triangle (.62, −.47, and −.65) and the right hand heterotrait–monomethod triangle (.68, −.56, and −.71).

4. *The same ordering of relationships should appear in each of the triangles.* That is, if $A_1A_2$ (.85) is greater than $A_1B_2$ (.50), which is greater than $A_1C_2$ (−.45), then $A_1A_2$ (.85) should be greater than $A_1B_1$ (.62), which should be greater than $A_1C_1$ (−.47). Similarly, if $A_1C_2$ (−.45) is less than $B_1C_2$ (−.52), then $A_1C_1$ (−.47) should be less than $B_1C_1$ (−.65). Thus, the pattern of relationships within a triangle should be replicated in other triangles.

The multitriat–multimethod matrix is a comprehensive approach to the evaluation of measurements. Reliability is assessed by the magnitude of the coefficients on the reliability diagonal. Convergent construct validity is assessed

**Table A–2**  HYPOTHETICAL CORRELATIONS

| | | Traits | Method 1 (Survey Research) | | | Method 2 (Content Analysis) | | |
|---|---|---|---|---|---|---|---|---|
| | | | $A_1$ (PE) | $B_1$ (SE) | $C_1$ (A) | $A_2$ (PE) | $B_2$ (SE) | $C_2$ (A) |
| Method 1 | (PE) | $A_1$ | (.92) | | | | | |
| (Survey | (SE) | $B_1$ | .62 | (.90) | | | | |
| Research) | (A) | $C_1$ | −.47 | −.65 | (.85) | | | |
| Method | (PE) | $A_2$ | .85 | .51 | −.47 | (.87) | | |
| 2 | (SE) | $B_2$ | .50 | .80 | −.53 | .68 | (.93) | |
| (Content Analysis) | (A) | $C_2$ | −.45 | −.52 | .83 | −.56 | −.71 | (.89) |

by the magnitude of the CV diagonal and of the predicted strong relationships (such as between political efficacy and self-esteem). Discriminant construct validity is tested by the magnitude of predicted zero or weak relations (such as between political efficacy and alienation) and by the application of rules 2 to 4. Through such a multimethod approach to measurement and operationalization, social scientists can better test and evaluate the validity of their indicators.

## LEARNING AID

**1.** Be able to state and explain the four rules for testing validity in the multitrait–multimethod matrix.
**2.** Be able to evaluate the reliability and validity of measurements by interpreting correlations in a multitrait–multimethod matrix.

## FOOTNOTES

1. Donald Campbell and Donald Fiske, "Convergent and Discriminant Validation by the Multitrait–Multimethod Matrix," *Psychological Bulletin* 56 (March 1959): 81–105.
2. The use of the labels *discriminant validity coefficient* and *convergent validity coefficient* is not employed by Campbell and Fiske. Our interpretation of these coefficients is that they provide a basis for testing discriminant and convergent validity.

# APPENDIX b
# Some Measures of Association and Their Characteristics

| Name of Measure | Level of Measurement | Interpretation: Percentage of variation explained? | Symmetry |
|---|---|---|---|
| Lambda | classificatory | yes | symmetrical or asymmetrical |
| Tau (Goodman & Kruskal) | classificatory | yes | symmetrical or asymmetrical |
| Cramer's $V$ | classificatory | yes ($V^2$) | symmetrical |
| Phi | 2 dichotomies | yes ($\phi^2$) | symmetrical |
| Q | 2 dichotomies | no | symmetrical |
| Percentage difference | 2 dichotomies | no | asymmetrical |
| Spearman's rho | comparative | yes ($\rho^2$) | symmetrical |
| Kendall's tau | comparative | yes ($\tau^2$) | symmetrical |
| Gamma | comparative | no | symmetrical |
| Somer's $D$ | comparative | yes | symmetrical or asymmetrical |
| Pearson's $r$ | quantitative | yes ($r^2$) | symmetrical |

The table above presents some common measures of association. The second column of the table indicates the level of measurement requirements for each of the measures. In all these measures, both variables are required to have the same level of measurement. Other measures are available whenever the variables have different levels of measurement. The third column indicates whether the association coefficient may be interpreted in terms of the proportion or percentage of original variation accounted for, as discussed in Unit 12. Some coefficients must be squared for such an interpretation to apply (*e.g.,* Pearson's r). The final column notes whether the association is a symmetrical or asymmetrical one (see page 269). Certain measures, such as lambda, have the flexibility to be calculated both ways.

Gamma and Q are two measures that deserve special mention, because they are found often in research but they do not possess the variation explanation interpretation discussed in Unit 12. The two measures are equivalent. Q is simply a gamma computed on two dichotomous variables. Gamma uses only the explained variation for its computation. The explained variation consists of all pairs of observations with dissimilar classifications on each of the two variables. This explained variation is separated into the positive ordered pairs and the negative ordered pairs. Positive ordered pairs are ones in which one member of the pair ranks above the other pair member on both variables. In negative ordered pairs, one member of the pair ranks higher than the other pair member on one of the variables, but lower on the other variable. The formula for gamma is

*Gamma*

$$G = \frac{p_+}{p_+ + p_-} - \frac{p_-}{p_+ + p_-}$$

where $p_+$ = proportion of positive ordered pairs of observations
$p_-$ = proportion of negative ordered pairs of observations

*Gamma* is the difference between the proportion of positive ordered pairs of observations and negative ordered pairs. A positive gamma denotes a predominance of positive ordered pairs of observations; a negative gamma denotes a predominance of negative ordered pairs. A predominance of positive ordered pairs means that observations with higher scores on one variable are likely to have higher scores on the other variable. The numeric coefficient is a measure of how likely this is. Thus, a gamma of −.45 indicates that the difference between the proportion of positive ordered pairs and the proportion of negative ordered pairs is .45, with a predominance of negative ordered pairs.

# APPENDIX C
# Multivariate Analysis—
# An Elaboration

The material in this appendix is designed to elaborate more fully the brief sketch of multivariate analysis provided in Unit 12. Multivariate analysis goes beyond the descriptive orientation of univariate analysis and the single-factor explanations and predictions of bivariate analysis. Multivariate techniques facilitate a more elaborate testing of a hypothesis and alternative hypotheses, the comparison of competing hypotheses, and the creation of more sophisticated explanations and predictions.

The introduction of additional variables to the original bivariate relationship permits an analysis of three types of effects:

1. *Control effects.* The additional variables serve to test the validity of the bivariate relationship and to specify conditions under which the relationship between two variables is strengthened or weakened.

2. *Relative effects.* The additional variables serve to assess the relative impact of each independent variable, while controlling the effects of the other independent variables.

3. *Conjoint effects.* The additional variables serve to determine the combined effect of the independent variables on the dependent variable.


## CONTROL EFFECTS

The use of additional variables as controls or test factors focuses the data analysis on the original bivariate relationship. The multivariate analysis is directed at examining the nature of the bivariate relationship and at specifying any conditions under which the relationship is altered. The analysis of control effects for the purpose of explanation and hypothesis testing may be accomplished by use of the partial association measures mentioned in Unit 12 or by the analysis of cross-classification tables. The latter approach offers a more visual image of the control effects. Recall that the bivariate table was created by subdividing the dependent variable distribution among the categories of the independent variable. The dependent variable distribution can then be compared among the independent variable categories. A multivariate table is formed by subdividing the original bivariate distribution among the categories of the third variable. In this way, the bivariate relationship may be compared among the control variable categories.

In general, the introduction of a control variable can affect the initial bivariate relationship in five different ways:[1]

1. A *replicating effect.* The control may exhibit no effect at all, in which case the initial relationship is replicated.

2. A *reducing effect.* The initial bivariate relationship may be diminished or even may vanish.

3.  A *revealing effect*. The relationship may be strengthened or enhanced.

4.  A *reversal effect*. The direction of an initial relationship may be reversed.

5.  A *refining effect*. Some combination of the first four effects may refine the nature of the relationship.

Each of these effects will be demonstrated and discussed in turn.

THE REPLICATING EFFECT

The replicating effect occurs whenever the original bivariate relationship remains substantially unaltered by the control variable(s). The theoretical significance of the replicating effect is its confirmation of the initial bivariate relationship. Additional replication effects with other relevant controls affirms the explanation of the dependent variable provided by the initial independent variable.

In a table, if the dependent and independent variables are dichotomies, one measure of the association between the two variables is the percentage difference between the two independent variable categories on one of the dependent variable categories. In the hypothetical example presented in Table C–1A, the percentage difference (d) between men and women drinkers is −17% (d = 22% − 39% = −17%). This difference remains the same within each category of the control variable (Table C–1B). Clearly, the relationship remains substantially the same and the control variable has no effect. The original relationship is replicated.

THE REDUCING EFFECT

The reducing effect designates situations in which the initial bivariate relationship is diminished or even vanishes upon application of the control variable.

The reducing effect is an empirical phenomenon that can result from three very different kinds of causal relationships among the three variables.

**Table C–1A**  ORIGINAL BIVARIATE RELATIONSHIP OF ALCOHOL USAGE BY SEX

|  | Men | | Women |
|---|---|---|---|
| Nondrinkers | 22% | | 39% |
| Drinkers | 78 | | 61 |
| (*N*) | (250) | | (200) |
| | | $d = -17$ | |

**Table C–1B** MULTIVARIATE RELATIONSHIP OF ALCOHOL
USAGE BY SEX AND EDUCATION

|  | High School or Less | | More than High School | |
|---|---|---|---|---|
|  | Men | Women | Men | Women |
| Nondrinkers | 23% | 40% | 21% | 38% |
| Drinkers | 77 | 60 | 79 | 62 |
| (N) | (125) | (100) | (125) | (100) |
|  | $d = -17$ | | $d = -17$ | |

Moreover, the determination of which interpretation is appropriate is a theoretical and conceptual problem, not a statistical one.

One interpretation is that the initial bivariate relationship may be spurious. The original independent and dependent variables vary conjointly, not because one is the cause and the other the effect, but because both are effects of the control variable. Temporally, the control variable precedes the other two variables, and it accounts for or explains away the initial spurious relationship. The example in Tables C–2A and C–2B illustrate this interpretation. The party of the judge appears to be related to the ideological classification of the decisions (Table C–2A). However, the appointing president explains the initial conjoint variation (Table C–2B). President Johnson appointed primarily liberal judges and mostly Democrats; President Nixon did the opposite. This interpretation may be diagramed in the following fashion:

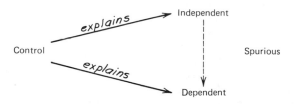

A second situation that can be reflected in a reducing effect is one in which the initial relationship is real, but the control variable intervenes temporally and causally between the independent and dependent variables. Variation in the dependent variable is accounted for by the control variable. Variation in the control variable is accounted for by the independent variable. To the extent that the initial relationship is reduced, the impact of the independent variable on the dependent is less direct. In such a causal sequence, the control variable

**Table C–2A** ORIGINAL BIVARIATE RELATIONSHIP OF
CLASSIFICATION OF JUDGES' DECISIONS BY POLITICAL
PARTY OF JUDGES

|  |  | Party of Judge | |
|---|---|---|---|
|  |  | Repub. | Democ. |
| Judges' Decisions Predominantly | Liberal | 29% | 63% |
|  | Conservative | 71 | 37 |
|  | (*N*) | (70) | (100) |
|  |  | $d = -34\%$ | |

is often called an intervening variable, as demonstrated in the following
diagram:

Independent —— *explains* ——▶ Control —— *explains* ——▶ Dependent

Whereas the first two possibilities involve theoretical distinctions in the
causal sequence, the final type of reducing effect involves a conceptual distinction. The initial relationship is a result of the close conceptual relationship of
the independent variable to the control variable. The control variable
constitutes either a more specific *component* of the independent variable or a
more *expansive concept* of which the independent variable is a component. For
example, social status is an expansive concept generally considered to consist of
components such as income, education, and occupation. An association between
social status and civic participation may dissipate with a control for income. In

**Table C–2B** MULTIVARIATE RELATIONSHIP OF
CLASSIFICATION OF JUDGES' DECISIONS BY POLITICAL
PARTY OF JUDGES AND APPOINTING PRESIDENT

|  | Johnson | | Nixon | |
|---|---|---|---|---|
|  | Repub. | Democ. | Repub. | Democ. |
| Liberal | 80% | 80% | 8% | 12% |
| Conservative | 20 | 20 | 92 | 88 |
| (*N*) | (20) | (75) | (50) | (25) |
|  | $d = 0$ | | $d = 4$ | |

such a case, the income component of social status will be the major element in explaining the initial relationship. The situation could be reversed. A reducing effect might be noted when the control variable is an expansive concept, encompassing the independent variable as a component. In this case, the expansive concept explains the reduced relationship. In diagram form,

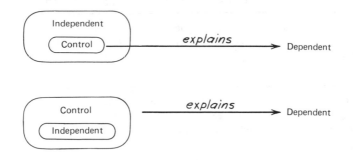

THE REVEALING EFFECT

The revealing effect describes situations in which the initial bivariate relationship increases in intensity. In the extreme, two variables may appear to be unrelated (Table C–3A), when, in fact, the appropriate control reveals the existence of a relationship (Table C–3B). Because of the possibility of this effect, it certainly is advisable to consider theoretically relevant factors that might suppress the emergence of a relationship between two apparently unrelated variables.

THE REVERSAL EFFECT

One of the most startling control effects is the reversal. This effect is one in which the direction of the initial relationship is reversed. This occurrence is

**Table C–3A** ORIGINAL BIVARIATE RELATIONSHIP OF ATTITUDE TOWARD CONFLICT BY SOCIAL CLASS[a]

|  |  | Middle Class | Working Class |
|---|---|---|---|
| "War and conflict are inevitable." | Agree | 59.7% | 58.7% |
|  | Disagree | 40.3 | 41.3 |
|  | (N) | (124) | (138) |
|  |  | $d = 1.0$ |  |

**Table C–3B** MULTIVARIATE RELATIONSHIP OF ATTITUDE TOWARD CONFLICT BY SOCIAL CLASS AND EDUCATION[a]

| | 0–8 Years | | 9–12 Years | | 12+ Years | |
|---|---|---|---|---|---|---|
| | Middle Class | Working Class | Middle Class | Working Class | Middle Class | Working Class |
| Agree | 71.4% | 59.7% | 68.8% | 62.2% | 48.2% | 38.4% |
| Disagree | 28.6 | 40.3 | 31.2 | 37.8 | 51.8 | 61.6 |
| (N) | (21) | (72) | (45) | (53) | (58) | (13) |
| | $d = 11.7$ | | $d = 6.6$ | | $d = 9.8$ | |

[a] Tables C–A and C–B are adapted from Lewis Lipsitz, "Working Class Authoritarianism: A Re-evaluation," *American Sociological Review,* Vol. 30, (Feb., 1965), Table 1, p. 108. Reprinted by permission of the American Sociological Association.

especially important since the interpretation of the initial relationship is reversed. In Table C–4A working class status appears to be more conducive to civil rights support than does middle class status. However, the control of a relevant variable, race, reverses the interpretation. Among both races, middle class respondents are more likely to be classified as "high" on civil rights support.

THE REFINING EFFECT

The refining effect discloses a mixed, conditional effect by the control variable on the initial bivariate relationship. The control variable serves to specify conditions under which the original relationship is intensified or weakened, thereby refining the interpretation of the initial relationship. Categories of the control variable interact with categories of the independent variable to produce varied effects on the dependent variable. Although refining effects are easily de-

**Table C–4A** ORIGINAL BIVARIATE RELATIONSHIP OF CIVIL RIGHTS SUPPORT BY SOCIAL CLASS[a]

| | | Middle Class | Working Class |
|---|---|---|---|
| Civil Rights Support | High | 37% | 45% |
| | Low | 63 | 55 |
| | (N) | (120) | (120) |
| | | $d = -8$ | |

**Table C–4B**   MULTIVARIATE RELATIONSHIP OF CIVIL
RIGHTS SUPPORT BY SOCIAL CLASS AND RACE[a]

| | | Nonwhites | | Whites | |
| --- | --- | --- | --- | --- | --- |
| | | Middle Class | Working Class | Middle Class | Working Class |
| Civil Rights Support | High | 70% | 50% | 30% | 20% |
| | Low | 30 | 50 | 70 | 80 |
| | (N) | (20) | (100) | (100) | (20) |
| | | | $d = +20$ | | $d = +10$ |

[a] Reprinted from Tables 4–7 and 4–8 from *The Logic of Survey Analysis,* by Morris Rosenberg, (©) 1968 by Basic Books, Inc. Publishers, New York.

tectable in cross-classification tables, the use of partial measures of association to assess control effects is likely to obscure the presence of a refining effect. The partial measure of association will tend to average out the separate effects within each category of the control.

Table C–5A reveals very little difference in anomia levels between urban and rural dwellers. However, a control for race alters the initial relationship (Table C–5B). Moreover, the change is not consistent within the two control variable categories. Among blacks, there is either a very slight reversal effect or a replicating effect, depending on how much reliance one wishes to place on the difference between −2% and +3%. Among whites in the sample, a clear revealing effect emerges.

The interpretation of the relationship between anomia and urbanism is refined. Among whites, urban dwellers are considerably more likely than rural dwellers to exhibit high anomia. Among blacks, there is little difference, although a slight tendency is evident for high anomia to be exhibited more frequently among rural blacks than urban blacks.

**Table C–5A**   ORIGINAL BIVARIATE RELATIONSHIP OF
ANOMIA BY URBANISM[a]

| | Rural | | Urban |
| --- | --- | --- | --- |
| High Anomia | 39% | | 41% |
| Low Anomia | 61 | | 59 |
| (N) | (300) | | (626) |
| | | $d = -2$ | |

**Table C-5B** MULTIVARIATE RELATIONSHIP OF ANOMIA BY URBANISM AND RACE[a]

|  | Blacks | | Whites | |
|---|---|---|---|---|
|  | Rural | Urban | Rural | Urban |
| High Anomia | 46% | 43% | 21% | 37% |
| Low Anomia | 54 | 57 | 79 | 63 |
| (N) | (211) | (436) | (89) | (190) |
|  | | $d = +3$ | | $d = -16$ |

[a] Adapted from Lewis M. Killian and Charles M. Grigg, "Urbanism, Race, and Anomia," *American Journal of Sociology,* Vol. 67 (May, 1962): p. 662. By permission of University of Chicago Press.

## RELATIVE EFFECTS

Explanations of social and psychological phenomena require the use of several concepts. Voting behavior, drug abuse, learning effectiveness, personality traits, and other social–psychological phenomena cannot be explained in terms of a single independent variable. Multivariate analysis enhances explanation by specifying the relative separate effects of several independent variables, while systematically controlling the effects of the other independent variables.

In assessing relative effects, the focus is no longer on how the original bivariate relationship is altered by the control variable.[2] Rather, each nondependent variable takes a turn as the independent variable and otherwise serves as a control variable. Attention is directed to the effect of each independent variable on the dependent variable, controlling for the effects of the other independent variables.

Examine the data presented previously in Table C–3B of this Appendix. The percentage differences between the middle class and working class for each level of education are 11.7, 6.6, and 9.8, respectively. If we sum these numbers and divide by 3, we have an average difference of 9.4 (a weighted average is not required here). This average difference represents one measure of the effect of social class on attitude toward conflict, controlling for education. The effect of education on the attitude, controlling for social class, may be similarly assessed. Simply average the percentage differences between the low and high education categories for each social class. Thus, for middle class respondents, the impact of education is the difference between 71.4% and 48.2%, which is 23.2%. For working class respondents the difference is 59.7% − 38.4% = 21.3%. The average effect of education, measured in this way, is about 22.2%. Comparing the education effect of 22.2 with the social class effect of 9.4 prompts the conclusion that education has a greater relative effect on attitude toward conflict than does social class.

Relative effects may be seen more clearly if the data are presented in a somewhat simplified table. For example, whenever the dependent variable is a dichotomy, there is no need to report percentages for both categories. If 71.4% of the low education middle class respondents "agree" with the attitude statement, then it is superfluous to report that 28.6% are in the only other category. Often, multivariate distributions are presented in which the percentages in the table represent the percentage who are classified by a particular dependent variable category. A careful reading of the table title will reveal when this is so. In such a table, the independent variables will form both the rows and columns.

**Table C-6**  THE PERCENTAGE WHO AGREE THAT "WAR AND CONFLICT ARE INEVITABLE" BY SOCIAL CLASS AND EDUCATION[a]

|  |  | Social Class | |
|---|---|---|---|
|  |  | Middle Class | Working Class |
|  | 0–8 | 71.4% (21) | 59.7% (72) |
| Education | 9–11 | 68.8% (45) | 62.2% (53) |
|  | 12+ | 48.2% (58) | 38.4% (13) |

[a] The number in parentheses represents the base on which the percentage was calculated.

In Table C-6, any percentage represents the percentage of observations from among the two independent variable classifications represented by that table cell who agree with the attitude statement. Thus, 71.4% of the low education middle class respondents agree that "war and conflict are inevitable." The number in parentheses indicates the number of cases classified by the two independent variable categories. It corresponds with the column total for those two categories in Table C–3B.

Comparison of Table C–6 with Table C–3B reveals a greater compactness and efficiency in Table C–6. Yet, Table C–6 either presents or implies the same information as presented in Table C–3B.

A major deficiency of multivariate table analysis is that the number of observations in each combination of variable categories diminishes as the number of categories proliferates from the addition of more variables. Statistical analysis becomes more unreliable as the number of observations in a variable category decreases. For quantitative data, this problem is relieved by certain statistical techniques that permit the computation of certain partial measures of association that mathematically control the effects of other variables. For example, *partial correlation* permits Pearson's *r*, a quantitative measure of association, to be computed between a dependent variable and each of a series of independent variables in turn while mathematically controlling the effects of the other independent variables in the analysis. *Multiple regression* exercises the same control power while establishing the predictive relationships between the variable to be predicted and each of the predictor variables.

Table C-7 presents a multivariate analysis of the age at which persons first acquire a political party identification. The partial correlation coefficients (partial *r*) reveal that the "family influence" variable is associated most strongly with the dependent variable. Its association coefficient is the highest.

The "partial *b*" column supplies the partial regression coefficients. Note that the partial *b* for "*N* Active Parents" is −1.30. This is interpreted to mean that controlling for the effects of the other three independent variables, a one unit increase in "*N* Active Parents" results in a 1.30 earlier (decrease in) age at initial party identification. The "se *b*" stands for the standard error of the regression coefficient, a measure of variation. If the size of the "se *b*" exceeds half the size of the partial *b*, then predictions with the partial *b* are considered unreliable.

**Table C-7** A MULTIVARIATE ANALYSIS OF AGE AT INITIAL PARTY IDENTIFICATION USING SELECTED INDEPENDENT VARIABLES

| Dependent Variable—Age at Initial Party Identification | | | |
|---|---|---|---|
| Independent Variables | partial *r* | partial *b* | se *b* |
| 1. Family Influence | −0.42 | −4.18 | 0.365 |
| 2. *N* Partisan Agents | −0.36 | −1.45 | 0.203 |
| 3. *N* Active Parents | −0.12 | −1.30 | 0.359 |
| 4. Parental Power | −0.14 | −1.42 | 0.384 |
| $R = 0.564$ | | | |

## CONJOINT EFFECTS

In addition to partialing out the relative effects on the dependent variable of competing independent variables, a goal of data analysis is to explain the greatest proportion of variation in the dependent variable as possible. It is possible to measure the conjoint or combined effect of independent variables on the dependent variable.[3]

Table C-8 presents the same data given earlier for the reversal effect (Table C-4B), except that only the percentages of "high" scores on the civil rights support variable are presented. The conjoint effects of social class and race are assessed by examining the diagonal categories of the two independent variables that maximize the difference in the dependent variable category reported. Thus, the combination of being middle class and nonwhite maximizes high scores on the civil rights support variable. High scores are minimized among working class whites. The difference between the two groups is 50%. This difference can serve as a measure of conjoint influence.

**Table C-8** THE PERCENTAGE WHO SCORE "HIGH" ON CIVIL RIGHTS SUPPORT BY SOCIAL CLASS AND RACE[a]

|  | Middle Class | Working Class |
|---|---|---|
| Nonwhites | 70% | 50% |
|  | (20) | (100) |
| Whites | 30% | 20% |
|  | (100) | (20) |

[a] The number in parentheses represents the base on which the percentage was calculated.

A statistical technique, called *multiple correlation,* computes a Pearson's $r$ (now labeled $R$) for the combined impact of quantitative independent variables on a dependent variable. In Table C-7, the multiple correlation coefficient is 0.564. $R^2$ is a measure of the proportion of variation in the dependent variable accounted for by the independent variables. In Table C-7, that proportion is about 32%.

## LEARNING AID

1. The five different kinds of control effects are:
2. The revealing effect may be described as:
3. Some researchers discovered a fairly strong relationship between education

and voting turnout. However, the relationship virtually disappeared when the degree of political interest was introduced as a control variable. What type of effect occurred? Describe the causal relationship pattern that is likely to exist among the three variables.

**4.** What are the conjoint effects in Table C–6?

**5.** What are the relative effects in Table C–8?

. . . . . . . . . . . . . . . . . . . . . . . . . . . . . . . . . . . . . . . . . . . . . . . . . . . . . . . . . . . . . .

**1.** replicating effect; reducing effect; revealing effect; reversal effect; refining effect.

**2.** situations in which the effect of the control is to increase the intensity of the initial bivariate relationship.

**3.** A reducing effect occurred; the initial relationship vanished. We suspect that the initial relationship is real and the control variable intervenes.

**4.** The combined effect of the two variables is a difference of 71.4% and 38.4%, which is 33%. The combination of low education and middle class maximizes agreement with the attitude statement (71.4%). The combination of working class and high education minimizes agreement with the attitude statement (38.4%).

**5.** The social class difference among nonwhites is 20%. Among whites the difference is 10%. The average effect of social class, controlling for race is 15%. The racial difference among middle class respondents is 40%. Among the working class, the difference is 30%, for an average of 35%. Comparison of the social class effect (15%) with the racial effect (35%) reveals that race has the greater impact.

## FOOTNOTES

1. More comprehensive treatments of control effects can be found in Herbert H. Hyman, *Survey Design and Analysis* (Princeton, N.J.: Princeton University Press, 1955) and Morris Rosenberg, *The Logic of Survey Analysis* (New York: Basic Books, 1968).

2. This explanation relies heavily on the presentation of Rosenberg, *Logic of Survey Analysis,* pp. 169–78.

3. Rosenberg, *Logic of Survey Analysis,* pp. 179–82.

# APPENDIX d[*]
# Blue Collar Anger: Reactions to Student and Black Protest[†]

H. EDWARD RANSFORD[‡]

*University of Southern California*

[*] We are including two research articles published in professional journals to illustrate principles and concepts presented in the text. The principles and concepts that we particularly want the student to notice are identified by boldface type enclosed in brackets.

[†] An earlier version of this paper (in which Vincent Jeffries was junior author) was presented at the 1971 meeting of the American Sociological Association in Denver, Colorado, September, 1971. Professor Jeffries participated as co-investigator in all phases of a larger research project from which these data were taken. I am especially indebted to Vincent Jeffries for helpful suggestions and criticisms of earlier drafts of this paper. I also gratefully acknowledge the comments of Joseph Gusfield and Thomas Lasswell. This investigation was supported by Biomedical Sciences Support grant FR–07012–03 from the General Research Support Branch, Division of Research Resources, Bureau of Health Professions Education and Manpower Training, National Institutes of Health.

[‡] From *American Sociological Review* 37 (June 1972): 333–346. Reprinted by permission of author and publisher.

## [Abstract]

*The hypothesis that working class respondents are especially antagonistic toward the black and student movements is tested with a sample of white Los Angeles residents (N = 477). In support of the hypothesis, working class persons and those with less than a high school education (in contrast to those higher in the occupational and educational hierarchies) are more likely to:*

*(a)   express punitive attitudes toward student demonstrators,*

*(b)   oppose granting students more power, and*

*(c)   feel blacks are pushing too hard for things they don't deserve.*

*To locate rationales that would explain these relationships, intervening and specification variables were introduced in the analysis. These variables are: respect for authority, belief in the American Dream, belief that the needs of the working man are neglected, and perceived powerlessness. Substantial support for these explanations of blue collar anger is found.*

## [Problem]

Little is known about the reactions of the white majority to campus protest and black demands. It seems obvious that a great many majority group Americans are angry, even outraged, by such incidents as student takeovers of buildings or by black power demands for reparations or preferential hiring in industry. The major question of this paper is whether this anger is randomly distributed in the socioeconomic structure, or is far more likely to be found in the working class environment. Are blue collar people uniquely antagonistic toward the goals and methods of student and black demonstrators?

A number of recent themes in the race and stratification literature suggest that working class people should be more antagonistic toward black protestors than those higher in the socioeconomic structure. Van den Berghe observes that race relations in the United States have shifted from total subordination of blacks in power, privilege, and prestige ("paternalistic" race relations) to a kind of competitive relationship found in advanced industrial societies.

> In such a dynamic industrial society with its great geographical mobility and its stress on impersonal market mechanisms and universalistic and achieved criteria of occupational selection, race relations are quite different from what they are under agrarian conditions. The master-servant model with its elaborate caste etiquette and its mechanisms of subservience and social distance breaks down to be replaced by acute competition between the subordinate caste and the working class within the dominant group. (van den Berghe, 1967:29, 30)

In industrialized, multiracial societies when the caste-paternalistic lid is lifted, the white working class is most likely to feel threatened by black upward mobility. Working class people have small, but hard earned, amounts of power, privilege and prestige that they are anxious to protect. (Skolnick, 1969:210–240)

In addition to van den Berghe's description of the macro processes, a number of more specific rationales link blue collar position with anger toward protest activity. It is these more middle range and measurable rationales that form the core of this paper.

## THEORETICAL EXPLANATIONS AND HYPOTHESES

### [Hypothesis]

At least three somewhat distinct (though partly overlapping) explanations can be advanced for the hypothesis that working class people will be more antagonistic toward student and black demands than people higher in the class structure. All three indicate that the protest methods and demands of students and blacks grate especially hard on the values, outlooks, and economic fears of the working class person.

### [Alternative explanations, theories]

1. *The Conformity-Idealization of Authority Explanation.* A number of studies indicate that the blue collar environment stresses the value of respect for authority. In the socialization of children, for example, a recent study (Kohn, 1969) shows that blue collar parents are more likely to emphasize obedience and neatness in contrast to middle class parents who emphasize internal dynamics such as curiosity and self realization. The stress on conformity and obedience is due in part to occupational environments. Blue collar persons typically are in occupations which demand repetition, conformity and adherence to rules. Thus Kohn and Schooler (1969) find that men's opportunities to exercise occupational self direction—that is, to use initiative, thought and independent judgment in work—interpret much of the relationship between class and authoritarian orientations. Other studies indicate that working class persons are less sophisticated in cognitive thinking. Being less well read and educated, as well as isolated from people with different views from their own, their thinking is concrete, simple and stereotyped (Lipset, 1960:87–126). Lane and Lerner (1970:105) make the same point when they note that blue collar men emphasize attributes of individuals rather than attributes of abstract systems. They hold to simple moral and ethical perceptions of the world rather than perceptions involving relativity of judgment or competing values. The lesser degree of cognitive or abstract thinking feeds into the same point, that working class people are more likely to conform to basic institutions than to question the existing system.

From this perspective, it follows that working class persons will be more outraged by campus protest and black demands than those higher in the class structure. Student protest and black protest symbolize a classic flaunting of authority and downgrading of institutions. The four letter words, the styles of dress, and the direct confrontation methods all suggest disrespect for authority.

2. *Belief in the American Dream—Neglect of Workingman's Needs.* This revised class conflict model, as opposed to a Marxian model in which the white working class is a revolutionary force for change, sees the blue collar worker as reaffirming traditional beliefs in the openness of the American system. Hostility is directed toward the black lower class as undeserving of special opportunity as well as toward white liberal persons in power who seek to remake traditional America at the workingman's expense. Working class people have made modest economic gains through union victories and through their own hard work and sacrifice. They are far from economically secure, however. They believe poor people and black people are at the bottom of the class structure because of their own laziness, not because of racism or other institutional barriers (Lane and Lerner, 1970). Given their beliefs in hard work and the openness of the American structure, working class persons are hostile toward ghetto rioters and black demands for quotas and preferential job treatment. It is not simply that they feel blacks do not deserve special opportunity. They are angry because it seems to them that they are being asked to pay the biggest price for "social justice" (See Schneider, 1970). If they yield to demands for special opportunities and super-seniority for black workers, they, not the secure upper-middle-class people, face the greatest threat of being laid off.

From the workingman's point of view, far too much attention is being paid to the poor, and especially the black poor. In a recent survey (Newsweek, 1969), sixty-five % of white middle Americans felt that blacks have a better chance than whites to get financial help from the government when they're out of work. Increasingly, white workers perceive that it is easier for an unemployed black to get aid and sympathy than a hard working white. Further, working class people are angry because they perceive that they are taxed heavily to support welfare budgets for the poor, and they have fewer mechanisms like business expense accounts, to escape taxation. In short, they feel they are paying for the special opportunities given minority persons—compensations they believe to be unnecessary in a free and open society.

Although this second explanation for blue collar anger (the American Dream and neglect of the working man's needs) is more clearly related to antagonism toward black militance, it also ties in with antagonism toward campus activism. A perception of the American system as open and just is antithetical to the student activist view that the American system is racist, elitist, exploitative, and excessively authoritarian. Further, the quintessence of the American Dream is sending one's children to college so they can advance in the social structure and have a better life. It is only with great sacrifice, however, that the working class family can send their children to college. The shouting of affluent youth, "On Strike—Shut It Down!" is a multiple outrage to blue collar people. Activist students are not only attacking American values, but threatening to close an only recently opened channel of mobility for working class children.

3. *The Powerlessness Explanation.* From this point of view, a critical dimension of the disaffection of white working class people is their sense of powerlessness over "radical" changes occurring in the country, and over political decisions directly affecting their lives. Working class people may perceive that they have few means to affect political change. Their occupational roles do not evoke respect and power in the larger society. Even in their own union the rank and file often have no real voice in making policy.

Recent student and black protest has, no doubt, heightened these feelings of political powerlessness. The worker may perceive that black and student militants have reached power centers and are forcing institutional changes that seem to him a distributive injustice or direct threat (for example, preferential hiring for blacks, relaxed extrance requirements and special aid for minority college students, and plans for increased school and residential integration that may affect him especially as an inner city resident living close to the ghetto). Of the "power structure's" various components, blue collar workers may view the government as especially hard to move and preoccupied with the problems of blacks.

The powerlessness explanation would predict that white working class people who feel politically powerless i.e., who expect public officials to be unresponsive to their needs, will be especially antagonistic toward student and black activists. Each gain in power for militant students or blacks may be perceived as a reciprocal loss in power, status, or a way of life for the working class person.

Note that the concept of powerlessness used in this study denotes a perception of the social system and does not necessarily refer to personal apathy or fatalism. Indeed, the more militant white action responses to black and student protest (such as "hard hat" demonstrations or the Tony Imperiale Armed Citizens Committee) suggest a high degree of personal confidence and efficacy combined with a low expectancy of being able to move a large impersonal system through normative action.[1]

---

[1] The several definitions and measures used for the concept powerlessness have caused confusion in recent studies. For example, the consistently used interpretation for the correlation between powerlessness and violence in my Watts research (Ransford, 1968) was powerlessness as *a low expectancy of gaining redress through institutional channels* (voting, the courts, civil rights movement etc.). However, a few recent reports on riot participation and riot attitudes have cast my findings into the category of apathy and fatalism (Forward and Williams, 1970; Paige, 1971). For a comment and rejoinder on the relationship between powerlessness and black militancy, see Ransford (1971) and Forward and Williams (1971).

Another conceptual distinction relevant to this study distinguishes political efficacy from political

There is a distinct difference in the logic of the first two explanations and this third powerless explanation. The first two view class position as the source of certain outlooks and values (respect for authority, belief in American Dream, and belief that needs of working class persons are neglected); and these in turn prompt antagonism toward student and black rebels. That is, we are dealing with "interpretation" logic or variables that intervene between X and Y.[2] In the powerlessness explanation we are specifying which segments of the white working class will be most antagonistic toward student and black activites, i.e., using a "specification" logic. Stated differently powerlessness per se does not clearly lead to antagonism toward student and black activists (many supporters of student and black demands may feel alienated from establishment politics); but rather, it is the combination of the blue collar perception of distributive injustice and feelings of powerlessness that should prompt antagonism toward students and blacks.

## HYPOTHESES

From the above discussion, we hypothesize that working class respondents compared to those higher in the socioeconomic structure will be more likely to report: (a) hostility toward student demonstrators, (b) opposition to the student demand for increased power in running the university, and (c) a feeling that blacks are pushing too hard and too fast for things they don't deserve. In each

[2] When one treats a psychological variable (e.g., "respect for authority") as intervening between a social structural variable (e.g., occupational status) and another psychological variable (e.g., attitudes toward black demands), it is possible that the intervening variable is not historically or even logically prior but merely part of the same psychological outlook—in this case, a specific example of a more general orientation. However, in this analysis a more plausible interpretation is that the intervening attitudes result logically from the working class situation, have developed over a period of time, and logically precede current attitudes toward student and black protest. Note in addition, there is no direct contamination between the intervening and dependent variables, that is, no mention of students, blacks, or protest in the intervening variable items.

---

trust (Paige, 1971). The study suggests that self reported rioters in the Newark disorder were high on political efficacy but low on political trust. Paige notes that most measures on political efficacy blur these two dimensions. Applied to this study, it is possible that working class whites scoring high on political powerlessness feel equally a distrust of government as well as an inability to influence it. Although the distinction between efficacy and trust is important, the problem is to develop a measure of efficacy/powerlessness that is not contaminated by distrust. Thus in Paige's study, to avoid the distrust element, political efficacy was operationally defined as "political information" and finally measured by the (black) respondent's ability to identify the race of nine black and white officials. Obviously, there is a great gap between the nominal definition of efficacy and the final measure of racial information. The problems of developing a measure of system powerlessness free of system distrust are so great that one seems required to choose between a certain amount of distrust "mixed in" or an index with a serious problem in internal validity. Although some distrust may be built into our measure of powerlessness, the items seem most directly concerned with a low expectancy of effecting government through normative action.

hypothesis we predict a negative linear relationship between socioeconomic status and antagonism toward student and black militants.

### [Partial correlation]

Using a partial correlation technique, we develop refinements of these basic hypotheses to test for the importance of the three above theoretical explanations.

### [Problem]

In addition to the test of main hypotheses, two supplementary questions will be explored: will class position continue to predict hostility toward student and black demonstrators with (1) age held constant and (2) sex held constant? For example, have recent developments in generation consciousness and youth culture become so important that young adults will be more sympathetic to student and black protest regardless of socioeconomic position?

## SAMPLE AND MEASUREMENT OF VARIABLES

### [Sample]

Data for this study consist of the responses of a probability sample of 477 Caucasian adults (twenty-one years or older) to a personal interview schedule. The sample was drawn from white areas of Los Angeles, primarily in the San Fernando Valley during the latter part of 1969 and the first few months in 1970. Not only was this a period of extreme campus unrest nationally, but on two campuses in or near the sample area, student demonstrators took control briefly of campus offices. The valley section of the Los Angeles Metropolitan Area contains a population of approximately one million. Although the sample is undoubtedly typical of some suburban areas across the country, a somewhat special characteristic of this territory should be noted. The San Fernando Valley is a large sprawling suburban region without the white, ethnic communities one finds in Newark, Chicago, Wisconsin, or New York. For example, there is no Italian or Polish neighborhood in the valley. Some evidence suggests that blue collar hostility toward demonstrators is apt to be especially acute when working class position is mixed with ethnic identification (Greeley, 1969). In such working class ethnic communities, common frustrations and interpretations of a demonstration may be easily shared and developed. Accordingly, any relationship that we find between socioeconomic position and hostility may exist even more so in working class ethnic communities elsewhere in the country.[3]

---

[3] Another possible sample bias is that only those who voted in the 1969 Yorty-Bradley mayoral election were included. This selection procedure could have produced a bias toward the best informed and most politically active residents. However, due to the extremely emotional issues in this election, (a take-over of city hall by black power extremists and a drastic decline in law and order)

## [Disproportionally stratified]

Though subjects were selected by a probability model (involving random areas, blocks, and block corners as interviewer starting points) the sample should be classified as "disproportional stratified" since blue collar areas were oversampled to provide sufficient cases for testing the hypotheses.[4] We controlled carefully for the respondent's sex. Approximately equal numbers of males and females (one respondent per household) were interviewed.[5] Finally, it should be emphasized that the working class respondents in our sample are employed and in predominantly semi-skilled or highly skilled positions. That is, we are testing hypotheses dealing with the "organized" working class vs. strata above this group. There were too few lower blue collar respondents in our sample to view separately (80% craftsmen, foremen, and operatives vs. 20% unskilled).

*Independent Variable.* Socioeconomic status, the study's independent variable is indexed by occupation and education taken as separate measures. Though occupation and education are commonly combined into an index of SES, it seemed important in this paper to view their effects separately since they tap slightly different aspects of the working class anger thesis. For example, education seems more likely to be associated with intellectual flexibility and breadth of perspective. Occupation, at least in Marxian theory, would seem more likely to be associated with work-related hostilities and peer group communication. For example, blue collar workers may develop common interpretations of radical demonstrations because of their occupations, quite apart from their educational experiences.

## [Ordinal scale]

The occupations were coded into an ordinal scale with blue collar lowest, business white collar (clerical, sales and managerial) intermediate, and

---

[4] The decision to sample primarily from the San Fernando Valley was based on the need for a predominantly white area with widely differing socioeconomic levels within the Los Angeles city limits (city residents were needed to study the Yorty-Bradley mayoral election, another aspect of the project). As a result, integrated racial areas such as Crenshaw-Baldwin Hills district as well as areas of white concentration outside the city limits were excluded from the sample design. The San Fernando Valley was divided into 115 units of equal geographical size. Twenty areas from the Eagle Rock section of Los Angeles (not a part of the Valley) were also included. Random areas were selected as well as random blocks within these areas. Approximately eleven interviews were conducted in each selected area (fifteen to twenty interviews in blue collar areas).

[5] Since ninety percent of the females did not have full-time occupations outside the home, most were classified by their husband's occupation. Their education level, however, is their own.

---

in my judgment the sample is not highly biased toward either the best informed or the most politically active. Unusually high voter turnout indicated that many normally politically apathetic persons did vote in this election.

professional white collar high. Professionals were ranked above "business white collar" because so few high ranking executives and major business owners are in the sample compared to the more uniformly high status for the professionals. For example, using the Bogue scale (Bogue, 1963) which ranks occupations in status from 44 to 180, the mean score for the blue collar group was 92.5, for business white collar 116.1 and for professionals 137.1.

*Dependent Variables.* Hostility toward student demonstrators is measured by the following three items (marginal percentages in parenthesis):

1. Even if they don't break the law, college students who are involved in demonstrations should be expelled (Agree 36%, Disagree 64%).
2. College students who break the law during campus demonstrations should be given the strongest punishment possible by law (Agree 70%, Disagree 30%).
3. College students who engage in illegal demonstrations deserve to be beaten by the police (Agree 13%, Disagree 81%, DK 6%).

### [Index]

On finding a fairly high association among the items (Gammas ranging from .60 to .93) a trichotomized index was constructed. Those agreeing with two or three of the items were called "high" in hostility toward student demonstrators; those agreeing with one were called "medium" and those disagreeing with all were called "low."

### [Indicator]

The following single item was used to measure feelings toward the issue of student power:

Students should be given more say in running the colleges (Agree 47%, Disagree 53%).

### [Index]

Antagonism toward black protest was measured by the following items:

1. Negroes deserve the things they are asking for (Agree 60%, Disagree 40%).
2. Negroes are asking for special treatment from whites to which they are not entitled (Agree 67%, Disagree 33%).
3. Negroes are pushing harder and faster than they have a right to (Agree 48%, Disagree 52%).

With high association among the items (Gammas ranging from .51 to .79) a trichotomized index was formed with the same cutting points as the student hostility score.

*Intervening and Specification Variables.* Respect for authority was measured by four F scale items that seemed most directly related to obedience to authority and conformity. An example is the item: "The most important thing to teach children is absolute obedience to their parents" (Agree 63%, Disagree 37%).

Belief in the American Dream and neglect of working man's needs required two separate measures. "Belief in the American Dream" was measured by a two item index[6] (example: "If anyone is poor in this country today he has only himself to blame." Agree 32%, Disagree 68%); while "neglect of workingman's needs" was captured by a single item ("There's more concern today for the 'welfare bum' who doesn't want to work than for the hard working person struggling to make a living." Agree 74%, Disagree 26%).

## [Forced-choice items]

Political powerlessness was measured by a score consisting of three forced choice items.[7] Two of the items were taken from a scale developed by Neal and Seeman (1964), the third from a scale developed by Olsen (1969). Two examples are: "I don't think public officials care much what people like me think." (25%) versus "People like me can have an influence on what the government does." (75%); and "The average citizen can have an influence on government decisions." (69%) versus "This world is run by the few people in power and there's not much the little guy can do about it." (31%).

Note that these are somewhat rough indices of attitude variables with few items per index and a minimum demonstration of unidimensionality. As a result, the findings must be regarded as less than conclusive.

## FINDINGS

Is the working class person more hostile toward student and black demands than those higher in the socioeconomic structure?

## [Relative effects]

Table 1 shows that this is indeed the case, with occupation moderately correlated with each dependent variable and education showing a stronger relationship. For example, 50% of the blue collar workers score high on student hostility, compared to only 25% of professionals. Education is an even more powerful independent variable, ranging from 50 to 18%. About half the blue collar workers and persons with a high school education or less agree with at least two of the very punitive student hostility items. The most striking relationship in Table 1 is the association between education and the belief that black demands are unjustified. Seventy-seven percent of those with less than high school feel blacks are pushing too hard as opposed to 31% of the college graduates.

[6] Gamma = .63 for the two items.
[7] Gamma intercorrelation = .76, .71, and .52.

## [Controlling for third variable]

**Table 1.**  INDEPENDENT VARIABLES (OCCUPATION AND EDUCATION) BY STUDENT DEMONSTRATOR HOSTILITY, STUDENT POWER, AND BLACK DEMANDS UNJUSTIFIED.

| | Student Demonstrator Hostility % | | | | Opposition to Student Power % | | | Black Demands Unjustified % | | | |
|---|---|---|---|---|---|---|---|---|---|---|---|
| Occupation | Low | Medium | High | N | Low | High | N | Low | Medium | High | N |
| Blue collar | 12 | 37 | 50 | (163) | 34 | 66 | (164) | 12 | 18 | 70 | (164) |
| Business white collar* | 26 | 44 | 30 | (159) | 52 | 48 | (162) | 21 | 33 | 46 | (155) |
| Professional white collar | 34 | 41 | 25 | (137) | 50 | 50 | (139) | 29 | 31 | 40 | (131) |
| | Gamma = −.32 | | | | Gamma = −.21 | | | Gamma = −.34 | | | |
| | p < .001 | | | | p < .01 | | | p < .001 | | | |
| Education | | | | | | | | | | | |
| Less than high school | 3 | 47 | 50 | (60) | 27 | 73 | (63) | 8 | 15 | 77 | (60) |
| High school graduate | 15 | 40 | 45 | (149) | 42 | 58 | (149) | 17 | 24 | 59 | (150) |
| Some college | 35 | 36 | 29 | (152) | 49 | 51 | (153) | 22 | 31 | 47 | (146) |
| College graduate | 36 | 46 | 18 | (104) | 60 | 40 | (106) | 37 | 32 | 31 | (99) |
| | Gamma = −.37 | | | | Gamma = −.30 | | | Gamma = −.37 | | | |
| | p < .001 | | | | p < .001 | | | p < .001 | | | |

\* refers to clerical, managerial and sales.
Note:  Statistical significance determined by chi square.

Though it was considered essential to differentiate between occupational and educational status in this analysis, it also seemed important to assess the impact of each with the other held constant. Overall, partial correlation analysis (linearity is assumed in each relationship) reveals that education more strongly determines antagonism toward student and black militants than does occupation.[8] However, these general correlations may be masking important subgroup

**[Pearsonian r]**    [8] The Pearsonian r between occupation and education is .49 in these data. The r between occupation and "student demonstrator hostility" is −.20 p < .01; with education controlled r = −.08 N.S. In contrast, the r between education and "student demonstrator hostility" is −.31 p < .01; with occupation controlled r = −.24 p < .01. The r between occupation and "opposition to student power" is −.14 p < .01; with education controlled r = −.04 N.S. In contrast, the r between education and "opposition to student power" is −.24 p < .01; with occupation controlled, r = −.19 p < .01. The r between occupation and "black demands unjustified" is − .25 p< .01; with education controlled r = −.12 p < .05. In comparison, the r between education and "black demands unjustified" is −.30 p < .01; with occupation controlled r = −.19 p < .01. This analysis (showing education to be the more powerful independent variable) must be viewed as suggestive rather than conclusive. For a discussion of the problems in assessing the independent effects of correlated variables, see Blalock (1964).

comparisons. Accordingly, Table 2 presents the joint effects of occupation and education on antagonism in cross tabular form. For ease of presentation, only the "high antagonism" end of the dependent variables are shown (the total linear relationships are captured by the gammas). Unfortunately, it was not possible to have the entire educational range for each occupation. Understandably, there were too few blue collar-college graduates and white collar-less-than-high-school persons to compute percentages for these subgroups. Nevertheless, within each occupaional group are three meaningful education levels that allow for important comparisons. On the issue of "student demonstrator hostility," Table 2 shows that about half the blue collar persons are highly antagonistic regardless of educational achievement. However, for the white collar groups (business, professional) education has much more impact on hostility toward student demonstrators. One possible interpretation is that

### [Controlling for occupation]

Table 2. PERCENT SCORING "HIGH" ON STUDENT DEMONSTRATOR HOSTILITY, OPPOSITION TO STUDENT POWER, AND BLACK DEMANDS UNJUSTIFIED, BY EDUCATION WITH OCCUPATION CONTROLLED.

| Education | % High Student Hostility | N | % High Opposition to Student Power | N | % High Black Demands Unjustified | N |
|---|---|---|---|---|---|---|
| | | | Blue Collar | | | |
| Less than high school | 54 | (48) | 74 | (50) | 81 | (48) |
| High school graduate | 48 | (62) | 61 | (61) | 66 | (65) |
| Some college | 51 | (37) | 62 | (37) | 61 | (36) |
| College graduate | — | — | — | — | — | — |
| [Gamma] | Gamma = −.15 | | −.17 | | −.25 | |
| | N.S. | | N.S. | | p < .20 | |
| | | | Business White Collar | | | |
| Less than high school | — | — | — | — | — | — |
| High school graduate | 48 | (56) | 51 | (57) | 54 | (56) |
| Some college | 19 | (62) | 50 | (62) | 46 | (59) |
| College graduate | 16 | (32) | 33 | (33) | 29 | (31) |
| | Gamma = −.38 | | −.23 | | −.20 | |
| | p < .02 | | p < .15 | | p < .15 | |
| | | | Professional White Collar | | | |
| Less than high school | — | — | — | — | — | — |
| High school graduate | 35 | (31) | 65 | (29) | 59 | (27) |
| Some college | 27 | (41) | 50 | (42) | 40 | (40) |
| College graduate | 18 | (65) | 41 | (66) | 31 | (62) |
| | Gamma = −.30 | | −.33 | | −.38 | |
| | p < .06 | | p < .05 | | p < .02 | |

[Chi Square]   Note: Statistical significance determined by chi square.

the "blue collar situation," explicated in the three theoretical statements, overrides any effects of education. Conversely, many white collar workers are somewhat more removed from this situation (of perceived powerlessness, distributive injustice, neglect of workingman etc.) so that an individual's education may have far greater effects. A less pronounced but similar pattern—homogeneity of outlook in the blue collar category versus large differences in the white collar group—can be seen with "opposition to student power" and "black demands unjustified." The one exception is the uniquely antagonistic response toward black demands of blue collar-less-than-high-school persons. Table 2 also reveals that hostile attitudes toward students and blacks are not unique to the blue collar group. They are shared by less well educated business and professional persons, in particular high school graduates. For example, professional persons with a high school degree show approximately the same proportion opposed to student power as blue collar workers. Similarly business white collar persons with a high school degree have the same proportion antagonistic toward student demonstrators as blue collar persons.

Our next task is to find if these relationships between socioeconomic status and antagonism operate for both the males and the females in the sample. The three theories for working class anger (conformity, American Dream-worker neglect, powerlessness) seem to apply most directly to the blue collar male. However, as co-managers of the household, blue collar wives would probably share some of the same frustrations as their husbands. Though the overwhelming percentage of women sampled were not employed outside the home, it seems logical to expect that they would resemble their husbands in outlook toward students and blacks. Table 3's data suggest that the association between occupation and student-black antagonism operates for both males and females, but is consistently stronger for males. This is especially true for the correlation between occupation and "black demands unjustified." The relationship is twice as strong for males as for females, with blue collar males being the most antagonistic toward black demands. We can speculate that blue collar males are unusually hostile because they are hit most directly by the work world frustrations defined in the three theories. However, when education is the independent variable, the relationships are more nearly equal in strength for males and females. Education probably reflects slightly different personal characteristics than does occupation, such as intellectual breadth and flexibility. Perhaps this dimension is more uniform for males and females regardless of employment status.

People in blue collar jobs and those with less than high school graduation are clearly more antagonistic. But are the theoretical reasons we have advanced for blue collar anger correct? To what extent do respect for authority, belief in the American Dream, and belief that worker needs are neglected, interpret the relationship between SES and student-black antagonism? One may first note (Table 4) that occupation and education correlate with each of the three in-

**Table 3.** PERCENT SCORING "HIGH" ON STUDENT DEMONSTRATOR HOSTILITY, OPPOSITION TO STUDENT POWER, AND BLACK DEMANDS UNJUSTIFIED, BY THE INDEPENDENT VARIABLES (OCCUPATION, EDUCATION), WITH SEX CONTROLLED.

| | % High Student Hostility | N | % High Opposition to Student Power | N | % High Black Demands Unjustified | N |
|---|---|---|---|---|---|---|
| Occupation | | | Males | | | |
| Blue collar | 57 | (70) | 67 | (70) | 81 | (70) |
| Business white collar | 30 | (79) | 54 | (81) | 52 | (79) |
| Professional white collar | 23 | (61) | 48 | (62) | 37 | (59) |
| | Gamma = −.40 | | Gamma = −.24 | | Gamma = −.49 | |
| | p < .001 | | p < .20 | | p < .001 | |
| Education | | | | | | |
| Less than high school | 57 | (28) | 79 | (29) | 82 | (27) |
| High school graduate | 50 | (52) | 52 | (50) | 69 | (52) |
| Some college | 34 | (70) | 57 | (70) | 56 | (69) |
| College graduate | 19 | (69) | 45 | (71) | 35 | (68) |
| | Gamma = −.39 | | Gamma = −.25 | | Gamma = −.44 | |
| | p < .001 | | p < .02 | | p < .001 | |
| Occupation | | | Females | | | |
| Blue collar | 43.5 | (85) | 64 | (88) | 61 | (87) |
| Business white collar | 29 | (80) | 42 | (81) | 40 | (76) |
| Professional white collar | 20 | (76) | 51 | (77) | 42 | (72) |
| | Gamma = −.25 | | Gamma = −.18 | | Gamma = −.23 | |
| | p < .05 | | p < .02 | | p < .05 | |
| Education | | | | | | |
| Less than high school | 44 | (32) | 67 | (34) | 73 | (33) |
| High school graduate | 42 | (97) | 61 | (99) | 54 | (98) |
| Some college | 24 | (82) | 46 | (83) | 39 | (77) |
| College graduate | 17 | (35) | 29 | (35) | 23 | (31) |
| | Gamma = −.35 | | Gamma = −.37 | | Gamma = −.38 | |
| | p < .001 | | p < .001 | | p < .001 | |

Note: Statistical significance determined by chi square.

tervening variables, and they in turn, correlate with antagonism toward students and blacks.[9] However, our theory states that blue collar anger results from the combination of respect for authority, worker neglect and belief in the American Dream. Accordingly, we need a statistical design that will handle the

[9] In the relationships between occupation and the intervening variables there is, again, a definite sex pattern with occupation having a stronger effect for males than females. For example, the r between occupation and authoritarianism is −.35 p < .001 for the males and −.18 p < .01 for the females. For "Belief in the American Dream" the comparable r's are −.27 p < .001 vs. −.10 p < .06. For "Neglect workingman's needs" the r for males is −.35 p < .001 vs. −.09 p < .10 for females.

**Table 4.** CORRELATION COEFFICIENTS (PEARSONIAN) BETWEEN INDEPENDENT VARIABLES AND INTERVENING VARIABLES AND BETWEEN INTERVENING VARIABLES AND DEPENDENT VARIABLES.

| | Intervening Variables | | |
|---|---|---|---|
| A.  Independent Variables | Respect for Authority | Belief in American Dream | Neglect Workingman's Needs |
| [Pearsonian r] | | | |
| Occupation | −.26* | −.18* | −.21* |
| Education | −.37* | −.23* | −.22* |

| | Dependent Variables | | |
|---|---|---|---|
| B.  Intervening Variables | Student Demonstrator Hostility | Opposed to Student Power | Black Demands Unjustified |
| Respect for authority | .48* | .35* | .36* |
| Belief in American dream | .36* | .28* | .37* |
| Neglect workingman's needs | .44* | .33* | .47* |

\* = p < .01
[One-tailed test]   Note: Statistical significant determined by student's T (one-tailed) test.

combined effect of all three intervening variables. Table 5 presents partial correlations (Pearsonian) between socioeconomic status and the student-black antagonism variables with the intervening variables held constant singly and in combination.[10]

## [Reducing effect]

Our expectation is that the strength of the relationship between SES and antagonism will diminish considerably with these intervening variables held constant. In all instances, the original zero order relationship drops appreciably with all three variables controlled. For example, the original r between education and student demonstrator hostility is a moderate −.31, but drops to −.12 with the three intervening variables simultaneously controlled. Table 5 also reveals that the control for respect for authority reduces the zero order correlation slightly more than the other intervening variables. However, since the intervening variable indices did not have the same number of items, one cannot conclude that respect for authority is a more important intervening link than

[10] For the correlation and partial correlation analysis (Tables 4 and 5) all attitude variables were "opened" to include four ranks. For example, the one item measure of "worker needs neglected" contained all four Likert levels (strongly agree, agree, disagree, strongly disagree) instead of the two rank (agree, disagree) version used in the cross-tabulation tables. For a discussion of the use of the product moment correlation coefficient with ordinal data, see Labovitz (1967).

the belief in the openness of the American system or the belief that work-ingman's needs are neglected. The only surviving relationships are those between education and black antagonism (partial r = −.16 p < .01) and occu-pation and black antagonism (partial r = −.16 p < .01). Apparently, there are other reasons for hostility that we have not fully measured, for example, a perceived threat from black economic progress.

## [Refining effect]

*Specification: Control for Powerlessness.*
Table 6 largely supports the hypothesis that working class persons who feel politically powerless will be especially antagonistic toward the student and black movements. Consistently, SES is more strongly associated with antago-nism toward rebels for the "highs" in powerlessness than for the "lows" in powerlessness (though some differences are small). Further, the blue collar group and the less-than-high-school group scoring high in powerlessness are more antagonistic toward students and blacks than anyone else in the sample.

## [Partial correlations]

Table 5. PARTIAL CORRELATIONS BETWEEN INDEPENDENT VARIABLES (OCCUPATION AND EDUCATION) AND THE DEPENDENT VARIABLES WITH RESPECT FOR AUTHORITY, BELIEF IN AMERICAN DREAM, AND NEGLECT OF WORKINGMAN, CONTROLLED SINGLY AND JOINTLY.

| Correlation Between Occupation and: | Zero Order | (1) Respect for Authority Controlled | (2) American Dream Controlled | (3) Worker Neglected Controlled | Simultaneous Control 1, 2, and 3 |
|---|---|---|---|---|---|
| Student demonstrator hostility | −.20* | −.09 | −.17* | −.14* | −.07 |
| Opposed to student power | −.14* | −.06 | −.12* | −.09 | −.04 |
| Black demands unjustified | −.25* | −.18* | −.23* | −.19* | −.16* |
| Correlation Between Education and: | | | | | |
| Student demonstrator hostility | −.31* | −.16* | −.25* | −.25* | −.12* |
| Opposed to student power | −.24* | −.12* | −.18* | −.18* | −.09 |
| Black demands unjustified | −.32* | −.20* | −.24* | −.23* | −.16* |

* = p < .01
Note: Statistical significance determined by student's T (one-tailed test).

## [Controlling for powerlessness]

**Table 6.** PERCENT SCORING "HIGH" ON STUDENT DEMONSTRATOR HOSTILITY, OPPOSITION TO STUDENT POWER, AND BLACK DEMANDS UNJUSTIFIED, BY THE INDEPENDENT VARIABLES (OCCUPATION, EDUCATION), WITH POWERLESSNESS CONTROLLED.

| | % High Student Hostility | N | % High Opposition to Student Power | N | % High Black Demands Unjustified | N |
|---|---|---|---|---|---|---|
| Occupation | | | Low Powerlessness | | | |
| Blue collar | 43 | (79) | 60 | (80) | 65 | (79) |
| Business white collar | 30 | (101) | 44 | (104) | 42 | (101) |
| Professional white collar | 23 | (101) | 53 | (102) | 36 | (94) |
| | Gamma = −.29 | | Gamma = −.07 | | Gamma = −.29 | |
| | p < .01 | | N.S. | | p < .01 | |
| Education | | | | | | |
| Less than high school | 36 | (25) | 67 | (27) | 75 | (24) |
| High school graduate | 41 | (92) | 55 | (94) | 56 | (93) |
| Some college | 30 | (98) | 50 | (99) | 43 | (94) |
| College graduate | 18 | (77) | 43 | (77) | 32 | (72) |
| | Gamma = −.32 | | Gamma = −.20 | | Gamma = −.32 | |
| | p < .001 | | N.S. | | p < .01 | |
| Occupation | | | High Powerlessness | | | |
| Blue collar | 60 | (71) | 72 | (71) | 75 | (73) |
| Business white collar | 28 | (57) | 54 | (57) | 54 | (54) |
| Professional white collar | 30 | (36) | 40 | (37) | 43 | (37) |
| | Gamma = −.36 | | Gamma = −.41 | | Gamma = −.38 | |
| | p < .01 | | p < .01 | | p < .01 | |
| Education | | | | | | |
| Less than high school | 59 | (34) | 77 | (35) | 77 | (35) |
| High school graduate | 50 | (56) | 61 | (54) | 66 | (56) |
| Some college | 28 | (53) | 55 | (53) | 57 | (51) |
| College graduate | 19 | (26) | 32 | (28) | 30 | (27) |
| | Gamma = −.42 | | Gamma = −.40 | | Gamma = −.40 | |
| | p < .001 | | p < .01 | | p < .01 | |

**Note: Statistical significance determined by chi square.**

The relationship least affected by this control is one between education and black demands unjustified. Perhaps the least skilled perceive themselves threatened directly by black economic advancement, and this holds whatever their feelings of political powerlessness.

*Control for Age.* Are younger working class respondents more sympathetic with black and student demands? Has the youth movement invaded the socioeconomic structure to the extent that the outlooks of younger "working class" respondents will be similar to the outlooks of younger "middle class" respondents? For brevity, the data will be described rather than shown in table form. Occupation and education persist in predicting student power and black demands unjustified with three age groups held constant (21–30, 31–45, and over 45). **[Reducing effect]** But among the young (21–30) occupation is only weakly associated with student hostility (Gamma = −.23 p = N.S.) and education washes out completely as a predictor of student hostility (Gamma = −.05, p = N.S.). In other words, younger "working class" respondents feel much the same as younger "middle class" respondents on the question of punitive treatment toward student protestors: both groups tend to be non-punitive. But on the question of student power and black demands, the younger blue collar workers are just as antagonistic as older blue collar workers. In fact, the greatest polarization by class occurs within the younger group. For example, 76% of young blue collar workers feel black demands are unjustified vs. only 29% of young white collar professionals (Gamma = 50, p < .02). On the issues of student power and black demands, young blue collar workers and young well educated professionals are worlds apart in outlook.

## DISCUSSION AND CONCLUSIONS

The thesis that white working class people are highly antagonistic toward students and blacks demanding massive changes receives moderate support from this analysis. We stress the term "moderate support." Though there is a definite socioeconomic differential (especially for males and those scoring high in political powerlessness), fairly sizeable segments of all educational and occupation strata have reacted with anger to protest of the 1960's. Still, blue collar workers are found to be more uniformly high in antagonism toward student and black protest regardless of educational level; whereas, white collar workers display more heterogeneity of outlook according to educational achievement. This suggests that merely acquiring education will not substantially reduce the blue collar worker's level of hostility toward militants.

### [Confirmation]

Not only are the major relationships between SES and antagonism supported but, given the limitations of indices with only a few items, we find some confirmation for each of the three theoretical explanations (respect for authority, American Dream-worker needs neglected, and political powerlessness.) However, the partial correlation table indicates that the explanations do not fully interpret the correlations between SES and "black demands unjustified." **[Relative effects]** Further research is needed to locate other rationales for blue collar anger and to test for their relative effects.

An especially interesting finding is that for two dependent variables (student power and black demands unjustified) the greatest class polarization was found among young adults. **[Cohorts]** This finding supports Lipset's contention that the generation gap is grossly overstated and that the greatest differences in political outlook and behavior are within the youth group rather than between age cohorts (Lipset, 1970:370–372).

The mass media have probably tended to overstereotype the white working man as a narrow-minded, intolerant bigot. His angry responses to students and blacks are often viewed as the effect of a prejudiced personality. In contrast, our model shows blue collar anger to be rooted in the actual or perceived social situation. From this perspective, much of the workingman's anger is a rational response to tangible strains, independent of personal bigotry. A lack of decision making power on the job, the fact of hard earned dollars going for tax programs to aid blacks with no comparable programs for working class whites, a power structure unresponsive to the needs of the workingman—these stresses probably effect working class anger as much as personal prejudice.

In addition, white working class people who feel politically powerless are especially antagonistic toward student and black protestors. Research in the black community conducted shortly after the Watts riot (Ransford 1968) suggests a parallel finding: blacks who scored high in social powerlessness (low expectancy of gaining redress through institutional channels) were more willing to use violence to get their rights. Similarly, a violence commission report (Skolnick, 1969) notes that militant white reactions to protest (armed citizens groups) are found especially among those who are angered by excessive concern for minorities and who feel ignored by the polity. Apparently the potential exists for black as well as white militant action when individuals perceive a distributive injustice and, in addition, feel blocked in gaining redress through institutional channels.

This situation is clearly described by what Lipset (1970:510) has termed the "New American Dilemma," viz., how to square the American promise with lower class ghetto life for blacks, and at the same time not withdraw the promise from the white working class. A recent statement by Pete Hamill summarizes this dilemma well.

> The working class white man is actually in revolt against taxes, joyless work, the double standards and short memories of professional politicians, hypocrisy, and what he considers the debasement of the American Dream. . . . Any politician who leaves the white man out of his political equation does so at very large risk. The next round of race riots might not be between people and property but between people and people. And that could be the end of us (Hamill, 1969).

### REFERENCES

Blalock, H. M.
1963 "Correlated independent variables: The problem of multicollinearity." Social Forces 42 (December):233–237.

# "Blue Collar Anger: Reactions to Student and Black Protest" 469

Bogue, Donald
1963 Skid Row in American Cities. Chicago: University of Chicago Press.
Forward, John R. and Jay R. Williams
1970 "Internal-external control and black militancy." Journal of Social Issues 26 (Winter): 75–92.
Forward, John R. and Jay R. Williams
1971 "Rejoinder" Journal of Social Issues 27:233–236.
Greely, A. M.
1969 "America's not so silent minority." Los Angeles Times, Opinion. (Dec. 7):1–2.
Hamill, Pete
1969 "The revolt of the white lower middle class." New York Times (April 14).
Kohn, Melvin
1969 Class and Conformity. Illinois: Dorsey.
Kohn, Melvin and C. Schooler
1969 "Class, occupation and orientation." American Sociological Review 34 (October): 659–678.
Labovitz, Sanford
1967 "Some observations on measurement and statistics." Social Forces 46 (December): 151–160.
Lane, Robert E. and Michael Lerner
1970 "Why hard hats hate hairs." Psychology Today 4 (November):45.
Lipset, Seymour M.
1960 Political Man. New York: Doubleday:87–126.
Lipset, Seymour M. and E. Raab
1970 The Politics of Unreason. New York: Harper.
Neal, Arthur G. and Melvin Seeman
1964 "Organizations and powerlessness: A test of the mediation hypothesis." American Sociological Review 20 (April):216–226.
Newsweek
1969 "The troubled American: A special report on the white majority." 71 (October 6):28–73.
Olsen, M.
1969 "Two categories of political alienation." Social Forces 47:288–299.
Paige, Jeffery M.
1971 "Political orientation and riot participation." American Sociological Review 36 (October):810–820.
Ransford, H. Edward
1968 "Isolation, powerlessness and violence: A study of attitudes and participation in the Watts riot." American Journal of Sociology 73 (March):581–591.
Ransford, H. Edward
1971 "Comment on: Internal-external control and black militancy." Journal of Social Issues 27:227–232.
Schneider, Michael M.
1970 "Middle America." The Center Magazine (Nov./Dec.):2–9.
Skolnick, Jerome H.
1969 The Politics of Protest: Report to the National Commission on the Causes and Prevention of Violence. New York: Ballantine Books.
van den Berghe, Pierre L.
1967 Race and Racism. New York: John Wiley and Sons.

# APPENDIX e*

# Social and Political Participation of Blacks[†]

MARVIN E. OLSEN[‡]

*Indiana University*

* We are including two research articles published in professional journals to illustrate the principles and concepts presented in the text. The principles and concepts we particularly want the student to notice are identified by boldface type in brackets.

† Part of the research on which this paper is based was supported by National Science Foundation grant number GS–1951. I am indebted to Virginia Fisher for much of the computational work reported in the paper. Copies of the interview schedule and data not reported in this paper are available from the author on request.

‡ From *American Sociological Review* 35 (August, 1970):682–97. Reprinted by permission of author and publisher.

## [Abstract]

*Recent research has suggested that although blacks often participate less actively than whites in voluntary associations and voting, when socioeconomic status is controlled this relationship is reversed, with blacks becoming more active than whites. The present study expands this line of research into a wide variety of social and political activities, and also adds age as a second control variable. The general tencency for blacks to be more active than whites under these controlled conditions is found to occur in every type of activity investigated. Comparison of data collected in 1957 and 1968 indicates that the tendency has become more pronounced in recent years. Myrdal's "compensation" interpretation of this trend, which has been accepted by all previous writers on this topic, is challenged as inadequate, since it does not explain black participation in such realms as mass media exposure, community activities, partisan political activities, and contacts with the government. An alternative "ethnic community" thesis is proposed, and is partially substantiated by the finding that blacks who identify as members of an ethnic minority tend to be more active than nonidentifiers.*

## [Previous research]

Several studies of participation rates in various types of social and political activities have concluded that in the United States blacks generally tend to be less active than whites. For instance, Wright and Hyman (1958) reported that blacks in their national sample belonged to fewer voluntary associations than did whites;[1] the voting studies conducted by Campbell, *et al.* (1954:191–192; 1960:316) and by Janowitz and Marvick (1956:26) all found lower rates of voting among blacks than whites; and there is evidence from research by Woodward and Roper 1950) that blacks are less active than whites in most forms of political involvement. Only in the area of church participation do blacks appear to be somewhat more active than whites Lenski, 1961:40).[2]

These racial differences in social and political participation are usually at-

---

[1] A notable exception to this generalization is provided by Babchuk and Thompson (1962), who found that the percentage of persons belonging to one or more voluntary associations was higher in their all-black sample of Lincoln, Nebraska, than in previous studies with predominantly white samples. However, their conclusion that blacks actually belong to more organizations than whites is questionable on at least two counts: (a) they were comparing blacks in a university community, where one would expect to find higher rates of participation, with whites in other communities and in national samples; and (b) they apparently did not take into account the total number of associations to which a respondent belonged, but only whether or not he belonged to any. For these reasons, their conclusion must be at least partially discounted. Dahl (1961:294–295) also found higher rates of political activity among blacks than whites in New Haven, Connecticut, but again, the fact that this is a university community may have affected his data.

[2] This differential occurred only among Protestants; white Catholics were more active than blacks in Lenski's study.

471

tributed to the tendency of white persons to have on the average considerably higher socioeconomic statuses than do blacks. Socioeconomic status, as indicated by occupation, education, and income, is known to correlate positively and fairly strongly with almost all forms of social and political participation. Hence the argument is made that many blacks are prevented or inhibited from becoming active participants by their low levels of occupational, educational, and income achievement. Implicit in this reasoning is the supposition that if blacks were to rise on these status dimensions until their average levels equalled those of whites', all racial differences in social and political participation should eventually disappear.

## [Controlling for SES]

Although we cannot actually manipulate large numbers of blacks in this manner, we can approximate the same situation by controlling for the effects of socioeconomic status, and then comparing blacks with whites on various measures of participation. Orum (1966) recently carried out such an analysis, using a combination of national and community data, for voluntary association participation and voting. Without controls, his data showed the expected tendency for blacks to be less active than whites in both these realms. When socioeconomic status was controlled, however, he found a slight tendency for this relationship to be reversed—especially in regard to active participation (as opposed to nominal membership) in voluntary associations, membership in political organizations, and voting outside the South. On these measures, blacks at any given socioeconomic status level tended to be somewhat *more* active than whites with similar statuses. His finding suggests that in this society there may in fact be differences in social and political participation between blacks and whites that are not caused by socioeconomic status—differences that are opposite from what one might assume.

## [Controlling for age]

A second, less common "explanation" for lower levels of participation by blacks in these activities at the present time is the differential age distribution between the races. Because blacks generally have higher birth and death rates than whites, their age distribution tends to have a broader base. That is, a greater proportion of blacks than whites normally fall in the "young adult" age category. Since persons under 40 years (and especially those under 30) are known to have lower rates of participation in many social and political activities than do older persons (except for those over 70), this age factor could ᴜe another underlying cause of the observed tendency for blacks to participate less than whites. Controlling for age together with socioeconomic status should therefore further clarify the "real" differences (if any) between whites and blacks in rates of social and political participation.

The research reported in this paper is essentially an extension of Orum's earlier work, in that it examines differences between blacks and whites in participation rates with socioeconomic status controlled. However, it differs from Orum's study in at least four respects. (1) It measures participation in a variety of realms in addition to voluntary associations and voting, including mass media exposure, community activities, cultural events, church activities, informal interaction with friends and relatives, political discussion, partisan political activities, and interaction with governmental officials. (2) In addition to controlling socioeconomic status, it also adds age as a control variable. (3) It utilizes a computer program (MCA—Multiple Classification Analysis) which applies controls statistically (in a manner analogous to partial regression) so that the resulting "adjusted" mean participation rates are based on the total sample rather than only small subsamples.[3] (4) It separates black respondents into those who do and those who do not identify as members of an ethnic minority, and examines participation rates in both these categories. This research is not an exact replication of Orum's study, but rather expands his work in several directions and thus provides an independent and more rigorous test of his empirical generalizations.

## THEORETICAL ARGUMENTS

### [Problem]

If it is true, as suggested by Orum's work, that blacks actually tend to participate more actively than whites in a wide range of social and political activities, once the limiting effects of socioeconomic status (and possibly also age) have been removed, what theoretical interpretation can be given to this empirical generalization?

### [Compensation theory]

One line of reasoning, first suggested by Myrdal (1944) and reinterated by both Babchuck and Thompson (1962) and Orum (1966), might be termed the

---

[3] The MCA program enables one to examine the effects on a designated dependent variable of any nominally or ordinally scaled "predictor" or independent variable, while statistically controlling other related predictor variables. For each category of every predictor variable, the program gives both the "unadjusted" mean score of the dependent variable and an "adjusted" mean which takes into account the effects of all other predictor variables (i.e., partials out their effects.) The program also determines for each predictor variable a zero-order (eta), partial (beta), and multiple (R) correlation coefficient. These coefficients are roughly analogous to Pearsonian r's, in that they indicate, when squared, the proportion of total variance in the dependent variable being explained. They do not, however, assume a linear model or designate the direction of the relationship. In this paper, signs indicating direction have been affixed to the coefficients on the basis of visual inspection of the mean scores for blacks and whites. For further information about the MCA program, see Andrews et al. (1967).

"compensation" thesis. Their argument is that blacks attempt to compensate for the racial discrimination they encounter in many realms of social life by forming relationships and organizations among themselves, in which they can at least partially escape white racism. In Orum's (1966) words: "Since Negroes are deprived of the usual social and psychological satisfactions of everyday life, they are compelled to seek such satisfactions collectively through other means. Opportunities for association are restricted by explicit or tacit observance of segregation in public places of entertainment. The oppressive atmosphere of slum dwellings also does not offer a congenial environment for social activity. Quite naturally, then, clubs and associations become focuses for Negroes' social life."

This explanation may very likely have considerable validity in regard to voluntary associations of all kinds, and also in the areas of church participation and interpersonal relationships with friends and relatives. But the compensation argument does not seem relevant to more "public" kinds of activities such as mass media exposure, community activities, cultural events, voting, partisan political participation, and contacts with the government. In one way or another, all of these activities bring blacks into closer contact with the white community. If black activism represented only an attempt to escape from or compensate for white racism, blacks should avoid these kinds of assimilating activities, regardless of socioeconomic status or age. To the extent that black activism extends into these areas also, the compensation argument proves inadequate.

### [Ethnic community theory]

An alternative explanation, which might be termed the "ethnic community" thesis, has been suggested by Lane (1959:Chap. 17), although its roots lie in the Marxian notion of class consciousness. Lane was concerned only with political activities, but his argument is perhaps equally applicable to all types of participation. In essence, this thesis suggests that members of ethnic minorities—whether based on race, religion, or nationality—may become active in social and political affairs because of social pressures exerted upon them within their ethnic community to conform to the norms of that community. Members of such an ethnic community are often more aware of their common bonds, and hence are more socially cohesive, than are white Anglo-Saxon Protestants—largely because of discrimination by WASP's. As a consequence, their ethnic community serves as a salient reference group for them. If the norms of this community stress social and political activism, these people will tend to exert pressures (both informal and formal) upon one another to conform to these norms by taking part in a variety of activities aimed at improving their common conditions. This process is perhaps most clearly visible in politics, and Lane discusses a number of contributing factors, including special concerns that are particularly salient to the ethnic community, close identification with ethnic leaders, reliance on collective rather than individual solutions to common problems, and the actions of political machines. But it could just as well operate in the nonpolitical realms of media exposure community activities, and cultural events.

## [Test implication]

To provide at least a partial test of this ethnic community thesis, we shall in this study compare participation rates among ethnic identifiers and nonidentifiers. If ethnic identifiers tend to be more active than nonidentifiers, this would suggest that these people perceive the existence of an ethnic community which presumably serves as a reference group for them and thus influences their actions.

## RESEARCH DESIGN

### [Survey research]

The principal set of data for this research was taken from the 1967–68 Indianapolis Area Project of the Institute of Social Research at Indiana University. (A secondary set of data used for comparative purposes is described later in the paper.) **[Sample]** The population for this study was the entire "urbanized area" (i.e., central city and surrounding suburbs) of Indianapolis, from which a sample was drawn using probability sampling with quotas.[4] A total of 750 adults were interviewed by trained graduate students and professional interviewers during January–March 1968. To minimize subjective interviewer biases, most of the questions on the schedule were of a "closed" nature with predetermined response categories.

### [Operational definitions]

The independent variable of race was dichotomized as Caucasian or "white" (N = 592) and Negro or "black" (N = 154). The one Oriental who fell into the sample, as well as three whites with extensive missing data, were excluded from this analysis.

[4] This procedure, developed by the National Opinion Research Center, uses probability sampling down through the selection of blocks (or clusters of blocks), but chooses individual respondents by quotas within five different categories defined in terms of age for men and employment status for women (which are the factors that have been found to affect availability for interviewing most directly). Quotas for each category in each block are determined by the composition of the population living in that census tract. In addition, strict controls are imposed on the interviewers to insure that no dwelling units with potential respondents are skipped. Although this procedure adds a small amount of sampling error (estimated to be less than 10% in most cases), it provides considerable savings in time and costs. For additional details of this sampling technique, see Sudman (1966).

The control variable of socioeconomic status was measured with occupation of the head of the household (coded by Duncan Socioeconomic Index numbers), education of the respondent (total number of years of all kinds of education completed), and total family income (in 1967 before taxes). In addition to being combined into a single eight-category SES Index, each of these factors was also analyzed separately. The variable of respondent's age was coded into six ten-year categories.

A total of 15 different dependent variables were utilized, all but the first of which were indexes constructed from two or more separate questions. These measures and their component items were as follows: (1) Voluntary Association Memberships (total number of associations to which the person belonged, including unions but excluding churches); (2) Voluntary Association Participation Index (which also took into account frequency of attending meetings and serving on committees or holding offices);[5] (3) Political Organization Participation Index (activities in organizations other than political parties that were primarily oriented toward politics);[6] (4) Mass Media Exposure Index (listening to informational or public affairs programs on television and radio, reading newspapers, and reading "serious" magazines);[7] (5) Political News Exposure Index (listening to news programs on television and radio, reading national and international news and editorials in newspapers, and reading political articles in magazines); (6) Community Activities Index (attendance at all kinds of community affairs and participation in various community service programs); (7) Cultural Events Index (attendance at plays, lectures, concerts, operas, and similar events);[8] (8) Church Participation Index (based on church membership, frequency of attendance, and participation in other church activities); (9) Friends Interaction Index (number of close personal friends, frequency of visiting them, and membership and participation in informal friendship groups); (10) Relatives Interaction Index (number of relatives in the community and frequency of visiting them); (11) Political Discussion Index (discussing politics with neighbors, friends, relatives, and co-workers); (12) Registration and Voting Index (current registration, voting in the last local election, voting in the 1966 Congressional election, and voting in the 1964 and 1960 Presidential elec-

[5] For each voluntary association to which a person belonged, he received one point for mere membership, two points if he attended at least half the meetings, and three points if he had ever held office or served on a committee in the organization. A respondent's points from all of his voluntary associations were then summed to determine his index score.

[6] Points on this index were again based on membership, attendance, and office/committee activity.

[7] Points were awarded for number of hours per week spent listening to all such informational programs on radio and television, for number of daily newspapers read regularly, and for number of serious magazines read regularly. All of these were then summed to determine a person's index score. Unless otherwise noted, this same type of procedure was followed in constructing all the other participation indexes.

[8] In this case, a single score was determined for frequency of attendance at any of the events mentioned above.

tions);[9] (13) Partisan Political Activities Index (wearing a campaign button or displaying a political poster or bumper sticker, contributing money to a campaign, and attending a party meeting, rally, or dinner); (14) Partisan Political Involvement Index (doing volunteer work for a political party or candidate, and serving on a committee or holding office in a political party); and (15) Governmental Contacts Index (writing a letter to a state or federal legislator, contacting a public official in some manner, and attending a meeting of a public committee, board, commission, or council). All of these measures were coded into six-category scales, from low to high.

## RESULTS AND ANALYSIS

*Race and Participation Without Controls.* Zero-order relationships between race and each of the fifteen dependent participation variables are shown in the first column of Table 1. None of the mean differences between blacks and whites are very large, but there is a general tendency for the coefficients to be negative (that is, for blacks to be less active than whites) or else essentially zero. More specifically, blacks score lower than whites in seven areas, including such crucial ones as Voluntary Association Participation, Political News Exposure, Political Discussion, and Governmental Contacts. On the other hand, blacks do score higher than whites on seven other indexes, but most of these differences are quite minimal (the coefficients for Community Activities, Registration and Voting, Partisan Activities, and Partisan Involvement are all .03 or less). It is perhaps surprising that these black respondents scored as high as they did on the above four indexes, but these findings are in fact consistent with results from several other recent studies that have found marked increases in political activity among blacks in recent years.[10] Only in the areas of Church Participation and Friends Interaction do blacks participate to a noticeably greater extent than whites, but both of these findings were also to be expected. Many of these relationships—both positive and negative—are not statistically significant by themselves, but our concern here is with overall trends, not separate relationships, and particularly with changes in these zero-order correlations when controls are introduced.[11]

[9] A respondent received two points if he was currently registered to vote. For each of the three elections, he received two points if he voted, or one point if he did not vote but either (a) was registered, or (b) was ineligible to register because he did not meet age or residency requirements.

[10] This literature is reviewed by Orum (1966) in considerable detail and therefore is not repeated here.

[11] Because of this emphasis on trends across numerous variables, rather than with separate relationships, tests of statistical significance are not reported in this paper. Even though a number of relationships may not be statistically significant by themselves, if they are consistently in the same direction it is statistically valid to assume that the overall tendency they represent does exist in the total publication. The probability of obtaining numerous consistent relationships (no matter how small) without the existence of an overall general tendency in the population is usually quite low.

**Table 1.** RACE AND 15 INDICATORS OF SOCIAL AND POLITICAL PARTICIPATION: WITHOUT CONTROLS, WITH SOCIOECONOMIC STATUS STATISTICALLY CONTROLLED, AND WITH BOTH SOCIOECONOMIC STATUS AND AGE STATISTICALLY CONTROLLED

| | Without Controls | | SES Index Controlled | | SES Index and Age Controlled | |
|---|---|---|---|---|---|---|
| | Whites | Blacks | Whites | Blacks | Whites | Blacks |
| Voluntary Association Memberships | | | | | | |
| $\bar{x}$ | 1.40 | 1.11 | 1.29 | 1.55 | 1.27 | 1.60 |
| Eta[a]/Beta[b] | | −.07 | | .06 | | .08 |
| Voluntary Association Participation | | | | | | |
| $\bar{x}$ | 2.01 | 1.76 | 1.86 | 2.34 | 1.82 | 2.43 |
| Eta/Beta | | −.05 | | .09 | | .12 |
| Political Organization Participation | | | | | | |
| $\bar{x}$ | 0.07 | 0.07 | 0.06 | 0.10 | 0.03 | 0.05 |
| Eta/Beta | | 0 | | .04 | | .04 |
| Mass Media Exposure | | | | | | |
| $\bar{x}$ | 2.24 | 2.19 | 2.15 | 2.55 | 2.12 | 2.66 |
| Eta/Beta | | −.02 | | .11 | | .15 |
| Political News Exposure | | | | | | |
| $\bar{x}$ | 2.77 | 2.40 | 2.68 | 2.79 | 2.63 | 2.94 |
| Eta/Beta | | −.10 | | .03 | | .08 |
| Community Activities | | | | | | |
| $\bar{x}$ | 1.84 | 1.95 | 1.75 | 2.23 | 1.74 | 2.34 |
| Eta/Beta | | .03 | | .13 | | .15 |
| Cultural Events | | | | | | |
| $\bar{x}$ | 0.40 | 0.25 | 0.36 | 0.41 | 0.36 | 0.42 |
| Eta/Beta | | −.07 | | .02 | | .03 |

*Race and Participation with SES Controlled.* On all three indicators of socioeconomic status, blacks scored on the average much lower than whites in this sample. As a result, 51% of the whites but only 18% of the blacks fell in the upper four categories of the SES Index (tau C for the SES Index with race = −.28). Hence controlling for socioeconomic status should affect most or all of the above zero-order correlations, raising the mean scores for blacks and lowering those for whites.[12]

[12] The tendency of mean scores to increase for blacks, and decrease for whites, is a statistical consequence of the adjusted procedure which standardizes all scores to an average socioeconomic level.

Table 1. (*Continued*)

| | Without Controls | | SES Index Controlled | | SES Index and Age Controlled | |
|---|---|---|---|---|---|---|
| | Whites | Blacks | Whites | Blacks | Whites | Blacks |
| Church Participation | | | | | | |
| x̄ | 2.56 | 3.00 | 2.49 | 3.27 | 2.45 | 3.42 |
| Eta/Beta | | .10 | | .18 | | .22 |
| Friends Interaction | | | | | | |
| x̄ | 2.72 | 2.99 | 2.71 | 3.06 | 2.69 | 3.12 |
| Eta/Beta | | .06 | | .08 | | .10 |
| Relatives Interaction | | | | | | |
| x̄ | 2.37 | 2.40 | 2.36 | 2.47 | 2.38 | 3.36 |
| Eta/Beta | | .01 | | .03 | | −.01 |
| Political Discussion | | | | | | |
| x̄ | 1.37 | 1.17 | 1.30 | 1.44 | 1.31 | 1.41 |
| Eta/Beta | | −.06 | | .04 | | .03 |
| Registration and Voting | | | | | | |
| x̄ | 3.23 | .3.33 | 3.16 | 3.61 | 3.09 | 3.86 |
| Eta/Beta | | .02 | | .10 | | .17 |
| Partisan Political Activities | | | | | | |
| x̄ | 1.34 | 1.47 | 1.30 | 1.65 | 1.27 | 1.76 |
| Eta/Beta | | .03 | | .08 | | .11 |
| Partisan Political Involvement | | | | | | |
| x̄ | 0.51 | 0.57 | 0.36 | 0.66 | 0.46 | 0.77 |
| Eta/Beta | | .02 | | .06 | | .10 |
| Governmental Contacts | | | | | | |
| x̄ | 0.99 | 0.79 | 0.91 | 1.09 | 0.90 | 1.16 |
| Eta/Beta | | −.05 | | .05 | | .07 |

[a] Eta is a measure of total zero-order association, which when squared indicates the total amount of variance in the dependent variable explained by the independent variable.
[b] Beta is a measure of partial association, which indicates the strength of the relationship between the independent and dependent variables with the effects of the control variable(s) held constant.

The second column of Table 1 reports the adjusted mean scores for blacks and whites and the resulting beta coefficients with the SES Index controlled, using the Multiple Classification Analysis computer program. Note that in every instance the mean score for whites has decreased and that for blacks has increased, so that all the coefficients have risen in magnitude and all are now positive. This holds true regardless of whether blacks initially scored lower or higher than whites. In other words, on every measure of social and political participation investigated here, controlling for socioeconomic status increases the level of participation of blacks above that of whites, which in many cases reverses the direction of the initial relationship. Some of these changes are only very slight, especially in the cases of Friends Interaction and Relatives Interaction. Nevertheless, the fact that all 15 variables shifted in the same direction under these controlled conditions suggests that the overall trend is real, even if some of the relationships do not reach statistical significance.[13]

. . . To ensure that this trend was the result of controlling for socioeconomic status as a whole, and was not being produced by just one or two of its components measures, the entire analysis was repeated with occupation, education, and then income as separate control variables, using both statistical and physical control procedures. Although the resulting data are not given here, all three status measures had essentially equal effects on each of the 15 participation variables. Moreover, in all cases controlling a single status measure produced less change in the dependent variables than that produced by the composite SES Index—that is, their effects are additive. The overall tendency observed here thus appears to be a consequence of controlling for socioeconomic status as a unitary phenomenon, and is not a unique effect of occupation, education, or income taken separately.

*Race and Participation with SES and Age Controlled.* As previously mentioned, young adults are frequently much less active in many realms of social and political activities than are older persons. Blacks in this sample tended on the average to be considerably younger than whites; 57% of the blacks but only 43% of the whites were under age 40. Hence controlling for age, in addition to socioeconomic status, should further accentuate the previously noted trends for participation rates among blacks to exceed those for whites in all areas. The results of this analysis are given in the third column of Table 1. On 11 of the 15 participation variables, this double control has the effect of increasing the mean differences between whites and blacks above those obtained with just the SES Index controlled. That is, the adjusted mean participation rates for whites are lowered still further, whereas those for blacks are raised even higher, with resulting increases in the positive beta coefficients. The figures for three of the remaining participation indexes—Political Organization Participation,

[13] Although the only specific type of voluntary association listed in Table 1 is political organizations, separate analyses were also conducted for several other categories of associations: labor unions; fraternal, veterans, and patriotic organizations; business, civic, and professional organizations; educational, youth-serving, cultural, and charitable organizations; and social, recreational, and sports organizations. The general tendency for participation rates for blacks to shift above those for whites with socioeconomic status controlled was observed in all these categories except labor unions. (In that case the zero-order relationship was slightly positive in favor of blacks (.05), and remained essentially unchanged when the SES Index was controlled.) The eta and beta coefficients for the other categories were as follows: (a) fraternal, etc., organizations changed from −.06 to .01; (b) business, etc., organizations changed from −.06 to .03; (c) educational, etc., organizations changed from 0 to .09; and (d) social, etc., organizations changed from −.09 to .02.

Cultural Events, and Political Discussion—remain essentially unchanged, while the relationship for Relatives Interaction is reversed (with whites scoring slightly higher than blacks). Overall, controlling for age does not appear to produce as noticeable shifts in black-white participation rates as does controlling for socioeconomic status, but the two controls taken together do tend in most cases to strengthen further the general tendency for blacks to score above whites.

*Ethnic identification among blacks.* As mentioned previously, one means of testing the validity of the ethnic community explanation of social and political participation among blacks is to separate black respondents who identify as members of an ethnic minority (N = 82) from those who do not (N = 44). (Twenty-eight blacks could not or would not respond to this question, and are omitted from the following analysis.) [Test implication] The ethnic community thesis would predict that ethnic identifiers should score higher than nonidentifiers on all measures of participation.

Table 3 lists the means for these two categories of blacks on all the participation variables; in the first column no controls are applied, while in the second column the SES Index is controlled. With both sets of data, ethnic identifiers score higher than nonidentifiers on 13 of the 15 participation variables. Many of these differences of means are not large, but the trend is consistent. In general, the differences become greater when socioeconomic status is controlled. Only on Voluntary Association Memberships and Relatives Interaction do nonidentifiers score higher than identifiers, and the significance of these deviant cases is blunted by the fact that Voluntary Association Participation (which includes attendance and personal involvement as well as membership) and Friends Interaction both conform to the dominant pattern.

*Time Trends.* Is the observed tendency for blacks to be more active socially and politically than whites of comparable socioeconomic statuses a fairly recent phenomenon, or has it been occurring for some time? The compensation explanation would argue that it has probably been happening for a long period of time, whereas the ethnic community thesis would suggest that it may have been a more recent outgrowth of the civil rights movement of the past decade [Crucial test].

With the Indianapolis data we can trace the trend back to 1960 by examining voting rates in the earliest two elections included in the Registration and Voting Index: the 1964 and 1960 Presidential elections. A greater percentage of eligible blacks than whites voted in both elections: for 1964 the figures are 86% of the blacks versus 79% of the whites, while the comparable figures in 1960 are 89% and 82%. When the SES Index was controlled by subclassification, this higher voting rate among blacks was found to hold at all socioeconomic levels except the very highest category in the 1964 election (with an N of

**Table 3.** MEAN PARTICIPATION RATES FOR BLACK ETHNIC IDENTIFIERS AND NON-IDENTIFIERS: WITHOUT CONTROLS AND WITH SOCIOECONOMIC STATUS CONTROLLED

|  | Without Controls | | SES Index Controlled | |
|---|---|---|---|---|
|  | Identifiers | Nonidentifiers | Identifiers | Nonidentifiers |
| Voluntary Association Memberships | 1.11 | 1.20 | 1.58 | 1.62 |
| Voluntary Association Participation | 1.87 | 1.70 | 2.51 | 2.26 |
| Political Organization Participation | 0.17 | 0.14 | 0.25 | 0.21 |
| Mass Media Exposure | 2.21 | 2.20 | 2.56 | 2.50 |
| Political News Exposure | 2.56 | 2.30 | 2.95 | 2.59 |
| Community Activities | 2.06 | 2.05 | 2.42 | 2.34 |
| Cultural Events | 0.30 | 0.23 | 0.46 | 0.38 |
| Church Participation | 3.22 | 2.70 | 3.47 | 2.92 |
| Friends Interaction | 3.01 | 2.95 | 3.10 | 3.01 |
| Relatives Interaction | 2.23 | 2.84 | 2.31 | 2.87 |
| Political Discussion | 1.18 | 1.11 | 1.56 | 1.34 |
| Registration and Voting | 3.63 | 2.86 | 3.86 | 3.08 |
| Partisan Political Activities | 1.63 | 1.32 | 1.80 | 1.48 |
| Partisan Political Involvement | 0.68 | 0.48 | 0.78 | 0.55 |
| Governmental Contacts | 0.87 | 0.82 | 1.15 | 1.08 |

only 7). The MCA program was then used to control both the SES Index and age simultaneously. The resulting data are as follows: (1) For the 1964 election, the unadjusted means (without controls) are 0.87 for blacks and 0.79 for whites, whereas the adjusted means (with controls applied) are 0.97 for blacks and 0.77 for whites. (2) For the 1960 election, the unadjusted means are 0.89 for blacks and 0.82 for whites, whereas the adjusted means are 1.00 for blacks and 0.80 for whites. The same trend found in all previous analyses is evident here; when controls are applied, mean figures for blacks increase while those for whites decrease, thus widening the differences in participation rates between the races. Apparently, then, this phenomenon has been occurring in Indianapolis in the area of voting since at least 1960.

## [External validity]

To go back further in time than 1960, we must turn briefly to a second set of data drawn from the 1957 Detroit Area Study conducted by the Institute for Social Research at The University of Michigan.[14] This study also dealt with social and political participation and provided many of the ideas on which the Indianapolis research was based. Since the schedule used in the Detroit study differed in many ways from that employed in Indianapolis, and since the social and political structure of the two cities are quite diverse, these two sets of data are not strictly comparable. Nevertheless, by examining the results of the Detroit study we can obtain some indication as to whether or not the trend observed in Indianapolis in the 1960's also occurred in another city during the previous decade.

Nine social and political participation variables can be measured with the Detroit data, all of which are similar or identical to those used with the Indianapolis study: Voluntary Association Participation,[15] Political Organization Participation, Political News Exposure,[16] Church Participation,[17] Friends Interaction,[18] Political Discussion,[19] Voting,[20] Partisan Political Activities,[21] and Partisan Political Involvement.[22] The Socioeconomic Staatus Index constructed with the Detroit data, using the variables of occupation, education, and income, was almost identical to the Indianapolis index.[23]

Table 4, which gives the results of the Detroit analysis, is similar in format

[14] The Detroit sample, drawn entirely from Wayne County, was selected using a stratified multi-stage area-probability design in which the primary sampling units were political precincts stratified according to dominant political preference and ethnic homogeneity of the residents. Random procedures were then used within precincts, blocks, and dwelling units. For a more detailed description of this design, see Eldersveld (1964:24–34). Interviews were conducted (again by graduate students and professional interviewers) with 596 persons during January–February 1957, but because of missing data the working N is reduced to 579.

[15] This index and the following one for participation in political organizations are both identical to the comparable indexes for Indianapolis.

[16] With the Detroit data, this index is based on watching the 1956 convention and other political programs on television, reading political articles in magazines, and number of newspapers read regularly.

[17] This index is based only on church membership and attendance and does not take into account other church-related activities.

[18] This index is based only on frequency of visiting friends, neighbors, and co-workers.

[19] This index is identical to the comparable one for Indianapolis.

[20] This index is based on voting in the 1956, 1952, and 1948 Presidential elections, plus the average frequency of voting in all local elections. It does not take into account registration.

[21] This is a single item asking whether or not the respondent had ever contributed money to a political campaign.

[22] This is also a single item, asking whether or not the respondent had ever done any volunteer partisan work.

[23] Occupation was coded using the standard Census Bureau categories; the education question was similar to that for Indianapolis; and income data are for 1956.

**Table 4.** RACE AND NINE INDICATORS OF SOCIAL AND POLITICAL PARTICIPATION IN DETROIT: WITHOUT CONTROLS AND WITH SOCIOECONOMIC STATUS STATISTICALLY CONTROLLED

| | Without Controls | | SES Index Controlled | |
|---|---|---|---|---|
| | Whites | Blacks | Whites | Blacks |
| **Voluntary Association Participation** | | | | |
| x̄ | 1.96 | 1.42 | 1.86 | 1.84 |
| Eta/Beta | −.10 | | −.01 | |
| **Political Organization Participation** | | | | |
| x̄ | 0.03 | 0.00 | 0.02 | 0.01 |
| Eta/Beta | −.07 | | −.03 | |
| **Political News Exposure** | | | | |
| x̄ | 4.66 | 4.05 | 4.58 | 4.40 |
| Eta/Beta | −.11 | | −.03 | |
| **Church Participation** | | | | |
| x̄ | 3.29 | 3.25 | 3.23 | 3.49 |
| Eta/Beta | −.01 | | .06 | |
| **Friends Interaction** | | | | |
| x̄ | 1.26 | 1.65 | 1.21 | 1.86 |
| Eta/Beta | .09 | | .14 | |
| **Political Discussion** | | | | |
| x̄ | 1.67 | 1.36 | 1.62 | 1.61 |
| Eta/Beta | −.09 | | −.01 | |
| **Voting** | | | | |
| x̄ | 2.51 | 2.14 | 2.45 | 2.40 |
| Eta/Beta | −.10 | | −.01 | |
| **Partisan Political Activities** | | | | |
| x̄ | 0.10 | 0.00 | 0.09 | 0.03 |
| Eta/Beta | −.12 | | −.08 | |
| **Partisan Political Involvement** | | | | |
| x̄ | 0.14 | 0.10 | 0.13 | 0.13 |
| Eta/Beta | −.05 | | 0 | |

to Table 1 except that socioeconomic status is the only control variable reported.[24] (The Detroit data were analyzed with socioeconomic status and age simultaneously controlled, but these results were virtually identical to those for SES alone, and hence are omitted here.)[25]

The overall pattern observed in Detroit in 1957 is virtually the same as the one in Indianapolis in 1968. Without controls, blacks score lower than whites on all these participation measures except Friends Interaction; the slight positive zero-order relationships obtained in Indianapolis for Community Activities, Church Participation, Relatives Interaction, Registration and Voting, Partisan Political Activities, and Partisan Political Involvement do not appear in the Detroit data. When the SES Index is controlled, however, the adjusted mean figures for whites decrease and those for blacks increase in every case. Again, the low socioeconomic statuses of many blacks limit their rates of social and political participation, but these racial differences in participation are largely reduced or eliminated when SES is controlled.

There is, nevertheless, a crucial difference between the results of the Detroit and Indianapolis analyses. In Indianapolis, all of the relationships became positive when SES was controlled, with the adjusted means for blacks being higher than those for whites on all participation measures. In Detroit, in contrast, only one relationship—for Church Participation—is reversed with SES controlled, although four others—for Voluntary Association Participation, Political Discussion, Voting, and Partisan Political Involvement—almost reach this point. In other words, although the same basic trend is evident in both cities, it was apparently not as strong in Detroit in 1957 as in Indianapolis in 1968.

## SUMMARY AND DISCUSSION

Orum (1966) summarized the findings of his study of social and political participation among Negroes with the statement that "in terms of over-all organizational participation—membership and activity—Negroes are not any more apathetic than whites. In fact, we found that Negroes are more likely to be active in organizations. Voting trends, moreover, indicate that Negroes are less indifferent now to civic affairs than they were ten years ago." The main conclusion emerging from this present research is that Orum's generalization can be broadened to include a much wider variety of social and political

[24] Blacks in the Detroit sample were even more disadvantaged in terms of socioeconomic status than were Indianapolis blacks; only 13% (compared to 18%) of them scored in the upper half of the SES Index. However, this difference may be due largely to the time difference between the two studies.
[25] The apparent reason for the failure of the age variable to affect participation rates in Detroit is that in this sample the age distribution for blacks is slightly higher (rather than lower) than that for whites; 21% of the whites but only 11% of the blacks were under age 30. Nevertheless, the slightly older average age of blacks did not decrease their participation rates.

activities—once racial differences in socioeconomic status (and also age) are taken into account.

In many of these areas blacks as a whole still participate somewhat less extensively than do whites, although in other areas (at least in Indianapolis in 1968) blacks participate as actively or slightly more actively than whites. More significant, however, is the consistent finding that with socioeconomic status controlled (as described in Footnote 3), participation rates for whites decline while those for blacks increase in every activity investigated in both Indianapolis and Detroit. This tendency was strong enough in Indianapolis in 1968 to produce positive relationships for all 15 measures of social and political participation; with the effects of socioeconomic status held constant, adjusted participation rates for blacks were higher than for whites in every instance. Moreover, simultaneously controlling for age strengthened most of these positive relationships even further. Although present in Detroit in 1957, the trend was weaker and produced only two positive relationships among the nine participation measures examined. Controlling for age did not significantly alter any of these Detroit relationships.

What light do these findings throw on the competing compensation and ethnic community theoretical explanations of black participation in social and political activities? The compensation argument is supported by the general tendency for black-white participation differences to decline when socioeconomic status is controlled that occurred at least as early as the mid-1950's—before the militant civil rights struggle and "black power" movement began. (In this context, it might also be noted that some of Orum's data were collected as early as 1955.)

On the other side of the ledger, however, three findings of this research can be interpreted as tending to verify the ethnic community thesis. First, blacks appear to be participating quite actively not only in voluntary associations—which was the original basis for Myrdal's (1944) compensation arguments—but also in such areas as the mass media, community activities, cultural events, voting, partisan political events, and contacts with the government. If their activities represented primarily an attempt to escape from white racism through participation in all-black voluntary associations, they presumably would not be entering these additional areas, all of which bring them into direct interaction with the dominant white community. Hence additional factors beyond escaping from racial discrimination must be operating.

Second, when the recent data from Indianapolis are compared with the earlier data from Detroit, a clear time trend emerges. In most of the social and political areas examined in Detroit, blacks still participated less actively than whites after socioeconomic status was held constant. In contrast, in all 14 areas investigated in Indianapolis, blacks generally tended to participate more actively than whites of comparable socioeconomic levels. To the extent that we can draw inferences from this comparison of two different cities, this time trend would suggest that the civil rights efforts of the 1960's may have given blacks increased impetus to take part in all kinds of social and political activities.

Third, the finding that blacks who identify as members of an ethnic community tend to participate more actively in most areas than do nonidentifiers (both without and with socioeconomic status controlled) also supports the ethnic community explanation. If we are correct in assuming that ethnic identifiers look to the black community as a reference group more than do nonidentifiers, and that the currently prevailing norms of the black community stress activism, then the higher rates of activity among identifiers suggest that membership in a cohesive ethnic community does propel many individuals toward participation in a variety of social and political arenas.

Perhaps the fairest assessment we can make at this time concerning the relative merits of the compensation and ethnic community theses is that both are at least partially valid in respect to blacks in the contemporary United States. It is undoubtedly true that many black people have been for a long time seeking to escape racial discrimination by forming and participating in their own voluntary associations. But it also seems almost self-evident that the recent emphasis on "black pride" and "black power" must certainly have stimulated many black persons to extend and intensify their participation in numerous realms of social and political life. In short, the compensation and ethnic community theses undoubtedly offer complementary, not contradictory, explanations of the tendency for blacks to participate more actively than whites of comparable socioeconomic and age levels in many social and political activities. Both processes could well be operating together on many blacks in this society, and both would tend to heighten their participation rates.

Moreover, assuming that the civil rights movement will continue in the future, it would seem fairly safe to predict that the tendency for blacks to become increasingly active can only expand. Indeed, to the extent that blacks succeed in raising their socioeconomic levels, the statistically adjusted participation figures obtained in this research could well become actual rates—with blacks as a whole being noticeably more active than whites in all forms of social and political participation.

To assess more adequately the validity of the compensation and ethnic community arguments, further research must go beyond measurement of participation rates to probe in depth the social forces that push blacks toward active participation, their individual reasons for becoming involved in all kinds of social and political activities, and the resulting outcomes of these actions.

Finally, beyond the concern of this paper with the *quantity* of black social and political participation lies the crucial question of the *nature* of these activities. Will blacks increasingly turn their attention and efforts inward toward the black community, creating their own social and political systems that are largely independent of the larger society, or will they seek fuller participation in the systems that whites have created and dominated for so long? And regardless of the direction of this expanding black activity, what will be its goals and its consequences for the total society? Will blacks attempt to isolate themselves from white society, merely accommodate themselves to it, gradually alter it, or radically change it? These last questions clearly extend beyond social science into the formulation of public policy, but they are burning issues in our society today which social scientists can study and possibly help to resolve.

## REFERENCES

Andrews, Frank, James Morgan and John Sonquist
   1967   Multiple Classification Analysis. Ann Arbor: University of Michigan Institute for Social Research.
Babchuck, Nicholas and Ralph V. Thompson
   1962   "Voluntary associations of Negroes." American Sociological Review 27 (October): 647–655.
Campbell, Angus, Phillip E. Converse, Warren E. Miller and Donald E. Stokes
   1960   The American Voter. New York: Wiley.
Campbell, Angus, Gerald Gurin and Warren E. Miller
   1954   The Voter Decides. Evanston, Ill.: Row, Peterson.
Dahl, Robert A.
   1961   Who Governs? New Haven, Conn.: Yale University Press.
Eldersveld, Samuel J.
   1964   Political Parties: A Behavioral Analysis. Chicago: Rand McNally.
Janowitz, Morris and Dwaine Marvick
   1956   Competitive Pressures and Democratic Consent. Ann Arbor: University of Michigan Press, Michigan Governmental Studies No. 32.
Lane, Robert E.
   1959   Political Life: Why and How People Get Involved in Politics. New York: The Free Press.
Lenski, Gerhard
   1961   The Religious Factor: A Sociological Inquiry. New York: Doubleday and Co.
Myrdal, Gunnar, Richard Sterner and Arnold Rose
   1944   An American Dilemma. New York: Harper and Brothers.
Orum, Anthony M.
   1966   A Reappraisal of the Social and Political Participation of Negroes. American Journal of Sociology 72 (July):32–46.
Sudman, Seymour
   1966   "Probability sampling with quotas." Journal of the American Statistical Association 61 (September):749–771.
Woodward, Julian L. and Elmo Roper
   1950   "Political activity of American citizens." American Political Science Review 44 (December):872–875.
Wright, Charles R. and Herbert H. Hyman
   1958   "Voluntary association memberships of American adults: Evidence from national sample surveys." American Sociological Review 23 (June):284–294.

# Index